AFTER TRUMP

AFTER TRUMP

RECONSTRUCTING THE PRESIDENCY

BOB BAUER AND JACK GOLDSMITH

Lawfare Press / Washington, DC

ISBN: 978–1–7354806–1–9 (paperback)
ISBN: 978–1–7354806–0–2 (ebook)

Lawfare Press
Lawfare Institute
P.O. Box 33226
Washington, DC 20033–3226
www.lawfareblog.com
@lawfareblog

Manufactured in the United States of America

Originally published in paperback and ebook by Lawfare Press in September 2020

Editorial production by Amy Marks

Cover design by Quenby Moone

Cover photograph by Abbie Rowe, National Park Service, courtesy Harry S. Truman Library & Museum

Interior design: 1106 Design

For Anita and Leslie

Contents

PREFACE

It is Inauguration Day and the last day of the presidency of Donald Trump. Prompted by the chief justice of the United States, the president-elect—left hand on the Bible, right hand raised—takes the presidential oath prescribed by Article II of the U.S. Constitution: "I do solemnly swear . . . that I will faithfully execute the Office of President of the United States, and will to the best of my Ability, preserve, protect and defend the Constitution of the United States."

If it is January 20, 2021, the country will likely still be struggling with a global pandemic, vast economic dislocation caused by this public health crisis, searing national debates about racial injustice, and a deeply polarized political culture. If it is 2025, it is too far into the future to predict the course and effects of a second Trump term, or the then-prevailing political, social, and economic issues topping the national agenda.

But no matter when it happens, or who Trump's successor is, or what other issues demand attention, some of the most momentous and difficult questions the next president of the United States will face concern how to reconstruct the battered and much-changed presidency that Trump will have left behind.

Trump operated the presidency in ways that defied widely held assumptions about how a president might use and abuse the powers of the office. His mercurial personality, pathological mendacity, shamelessness, open disrespect for law and norms, vicious attacks on officials and institutions, intermingling of public and private interest, and indifference to facts did enormous damage to the great office that he assumed on January 20, 2017. And his words and actions exposed the presidency's vulnerability to dangerous excesses of authority and dangerous weaknesses in accountability. Trump was not the first president to raise these dangers, obviously, but he did so unlike any of his predecessors.

One of the most important things that the new president can do to "faithfully execute the Office of President of the United States" is to affirm and commit to the basic norms and institutional restraints that guided the presidency before Trump. This will likely be an extraordinarily challenging task, since the nation faces massive problems that demand vigorous government but might still be saddled with a Congress that in recent decades has proved feckless. The imperative for bold executive leadership will be strong. But as Arthur Schlesinger, Jr., taught, a "constitutional Presidency [can] be a very strong Presidency" as long as the president demonstrates that he has "checks and balances incorporated within his own breast" and "understand[s] the legitimacy of challenges to his own judgment and authority."[1] It will also be vital that the next president selects senior officials—especially an attorney general and White House counsel—who share these commitments.

But reconstructing the presidency will require much more than the right attitude by the president and senior executive branch officials. It will also require a comprehensive examination of the many fissures in the structure of the office that a future president might choose to exploit in a fashion similar to Trump—yet more skillfully and to greater effect. That examination, and proposals for the needed reconstruction of the presidency, are the aims of this book. These are admittedly immodest aims. Yet in the fourteen chapters that follow, we explain why broad reform is needed and propose more than fifty concrete changes to the laws, regulations, and norms that govern the presidency in what is the first attempt to think comprehensively about the proper shape of the post-Trump executive branch.

We begin in Part I by focusing on better protections against abuses of presidential power for personal and political gain. Part I proposes ways to counter the growing foreign state intervention in presidential campaigns, eliminate financial conflicts of interest, formalize tax disclosure requirements, prevent the executive branch from using its law enforcement tools to intimidate and retaliate against the press, and constrain misuse of the pardon power.

Part II focuses on the complex relationship between the White House and the Justice Department that is central to the rule of law in the United States. The problems here range from the danger of politicized prosecution, to deficiencies in the special counsel regulations, to inadequate guidance for FBI investigations of presidential campaigns and presidents, to the problem of a too-powerful White House counsel's office.

Finally, Part III focuses on two issues where power has shifted significantly, and in our view excessively, from Congress to the president in recent decades: presidential discretion to use military force (including presidential control over nuclear weapons), and presidential control over vacancies in senior executive branch positions. It also briefly discusses other reforms that Congress and the new president should consider, including reining in some presidential emergency powers and adjusting the laws that govern the enforcement of congressional subpoenas against the executive branch.

These reforms have no chance of being implemented while Trump is president. He won't embrace them, and it is doubtful that we will see a Congress capable of overriding his vetoes. This book is thus primarily about how to think about reform after Trump leaves the scene, whether that is in 2021 or 2025. Our primary aim is to spark informed debate about whether and how reform should proceed. We hope that the historical and legal background we provide in each chapter, the concise recounting of relevant events that transpired during the Trump administration, and our analysis of various reform approaches can be useful in the coming debates even if the reader is not convinced by our particular proposals or arguments.

We both served at high levels of government in the executive branch in two very different presidential administrations. Bauer was Barack Obama's White House counsel. Goldsmith served as George W. Bush's assistant attorney general in the Office of Legal Counsel. We have both written extensively on the presidency. We have both been supportive of presidential power in some contexts and critical of it in others. We are worried about the institution of the presidency, we believe reform is necessary, and we worry about the wrong types of reform. This book is our effort to frame the debate and strike the right balance.

★

RECONSTRUCTING THE PRESIDENCY

In this chapter, we explain the need to reform the post-Trump presidency, anticipate objections and concerns, and outline the principles that should guide reform.

THE NEED FOR REFORM

Trump is not the first president to spark questions about the legitimacy of presidential power. But his characteristic excesses have not been those of his predecessors. The George W. Bush administration often invoked Article II powers to disregard congressional statutes in important contexts. Trump has not done so to the same degree. The Obama administration engaged in presidential action that often rested on aggressive interpretations of congressional statutory delegations. Trump has done some of that, especially during the conflict with Congress over pandemic relief, but not as much. Despite his targeted killing of Iranian Gen. Qassem Soleimani, Trump has not been as aggressive as his two predecessors in expanding available unilateral presidential war powers. Nor did Trump follow through on his campaign pronouncements that indicated a readiness to break the law by, for example, reinstating waterboarding, censoring the internet, using the military for indiscriminate attacks on civilians, throwing his opponents in jail, and the like.

Trump did proudly claim a "right to do whatever I want as president,"[1] and he has shown little patience for the idea that law meaningfully constrains his freedom of action. But the argument for reform of the presidency does not rest primarily on Trump's defiance of the law. Trump's law-breaking bark—though undoubtedly corrosive, as we explain below—has often been worse than his bite. And many of his efforts to break the law have been checked by courts and executive branch officials. The case for reform rests less on Trump's law-breaking tendencies and more on how his conception of the office of the presidency and his actions in it have exposed gaps and ambiguities in the law and norms governing the office, and broader weaknesses in presidential accountability. These concerns flow from four related elements of Trump's conduct of the presidency.

First, as has been noted widely, Trump is indifferent to the nonlegal norms of presidential behavior that have been established since Watergate to constrain presidential power and ensure presidential accountability. The examples are too legion to list but include his refusal to release his tax returns; his frequent public comment on and threats to intervene in law enforcement actions; his abandonment of routine White House press briefings and presidential press conferences; and his vicious personal attacks on judges, governors, executive branch officials, and even private citizens.

Second, Trump has merged the institution of the presidency with his personal interests and has used the former to serve the latter like no previous occupant of the office.[2] To give just a few examples, many of which are norms violations as well: He repeatedly sought to intervene in the special counsel's investigation of himself and his associates, and declined to cooperate with the special counsel where his own conduct was at issue. He has often publicly urged the Justice Department to investigate and prosecute his political opponents. He has used the presidency to make money off his businesses. He has used his control over diplomacy to seek the assistance of foreign powers to win an election. He has used the bully pulpit at the height of the coronavirus public health crisis to glorify his television ratings and attack his political opponents. He has tried to direct law enforcement to protect friends, family, and himself, and he has threatened to use the pardon power to do the same.

Third, Trump has aggressively and often mendaciously attacked core institutions of American democracy—especially the press, the judiciary, Congress, state and local governments, and many elements of his own executive branch, including the Justice Department and the intelligence agencies. Trump's institution-bashing usually goes hand in hand with his brand of populist anti-elitism and his resistance to limits on the assertion of his personal will. "The populist tends to believe that institutions are inherently corrupt because they are so easily captured by 'elites,'" notes Eric Posner.[3] Trump routinely makes these claims, and he clearly sees in institutions and institutional process impediments to the achievement of his purposes. Trump's attacks on institutions differ dramatically from the truth-shading and institution-criticizing that occurs in ordinary politics. Trump frequently tells big, verifiable lies in the course of condemning these institutions and persons in harsh, vicious, and demeaning ways. And he does so with the apparent intent and clear effect of weakening public confidence in these institutions. These institutions and related norms have often held up well to Trump's onslaught. But Trump has done a lot of damage, and he has paved the way for worse.

Fourth, Trump deploys authoritarian rhetoric and threatens authoritarian action, often before large crowds, even if he typically does not follow through. He has implied that he is not bound by law, or that he wants to break free of it, even though in the end he usually stops just shy of what would, by general agreement, be clear violations of the law. He threatens to crack down on the press with lawsuits but does not actually do so. He incites citizens to law-defiant behavior—for example, in his tweets urging citizens to disregard stay-at-home orders in some of the states during the coronavirus pandemic. He is harshly critical of leaders of democratic allies and allied institutions like NATO, and he expresses admiration for foreign authoritarian leaders like Vladimir Putin, though his administration has maintained traditional NATO policies and relationships and has heavily sanctioned Putin's Russia. In all of these contexts, and more, Trump's rhetoric matters even when it does not result in action or policy change. Especially when combined with Trump's indifference to norms, this rhetoric understandably disturbs many people, including many in the institutions under attack. And, of course, it weakens confidence in those institutions.

Taken together, the cluster of Trump's behaviors—the disregard for norms and attacks on institutions, the elevation of the personal over the public, the ceaseless lies, the vilification of and all-out assault on his opposition, and his authoritarian and law-defiant impulses and rhetoric—constitute classic *demagogic* behavior. Posner has defined a "demagogue" as "a charismatic, amoral person who obtains the support of the people through dishonesty, emotional manipulation, and the exploitation of social divisions; who targets the political elites, blaming them for everything that has gone wrong; and who tries to destroy institutions—legal, political, religious, social—and other sources of power that stand in their way."[4] This fits Trump to a T.

Against this background, the case for reform of the presidency is straightforward. Trump has shown that the current array of laws and norms governing the presidency is inadequate to protect institutions vital to the American constitutional democracy and to ensure that the president is, and appears to be, constrained by law. Not every reform proposed in this book is a response to Trump's demagogic political and governing style. Some of Trump's excesses, and some flaws in presidential regulation, had been emerging in prior presidencies. But Trump's particular brand of executive action has added significantly to past problems in ways that now demand comprehensive treatment.

It is possible that the threats posed by Trump to the presidency and other American institutions will end when he leaves the scene, and that the next president will attend more closely to the norms, institutional practices, and rhetorical constraints of Trump's predecessors. On this view, the problems presented by Trump are personal to him and are not structural or pervasive ones that demand reform.

We do not share this view, for four reasons.

First, the experience with Trump has made clear that many of the laws and norms governing the presidency are defective. Some norms—such as the ones concerning release of public information about taxes, wealth, and business operations—proved ineffective and should not be left to the happenstance of who is president or a presidential candidate. As we explain in Chapters Two and Four, these norms should be embodied in binding statutes rather than in norms that the president and candidates can ignore should they wish to incur the political costs (or should they decide that trashing the norms is politically advantageous). Other norms should be fortified for any future presidency. As we explain in Chapter Eight, Robert Mueller's investigation was the nation's first significant experience with the 1999 special counsel regulations, and many problems emerged from their use. For constitutional and practical reasons, Congress cannot comprehensively legislate on this topic, which must remain subject to a large degree to norms and executive branch regulation, albeit more powerful ones.

Second, while this book is limited to reforms of the presidency, it is not limited to reforms of only the president and the White House. The experience with Trump has revealed that other elements of the executive branch suffer from inadequate guidance and accountability, and sometimes excessive zeal or poor judgment, in important contexts. Consider three controversies over the past several years about FBI investigations of the president or presidential campaigns: the Hillary Clinton email investigation, the Trump campaign investigation, and the counterintelligence and obstruction of justice investigations of President Trump that began in 2017. One of the reasons that these investigations were so controversial is that the law and other guidance on how to handle such investigations were underdeveloped or unclear. Another reason is that officials conducting these investigations sometimes did not adhere to relevant norms. These types of investigations will always be politically controversial, but better, clearer, and firmer rules can help a lot going forward.

Third, even before Trump became president, our deeply polarized politics were leading presidents and their congressional allies to sweep past or give less weight to institutional practices that stood in the way of achieving short-term political aims. The bitter battles over nominations to the judiciary are one example. But they reflect a wider collapse of comity within Congress concerning the basic ground rules for partisan contestation that has undermined its capacity to enact major legislation or even to reach timely agreements on funding government operations. On the issues that most divide the parties, the norms that have guided and checked their interactions have been under pressure for a while and have become characterized by a downward spiraling tit-for-tat of norm-busting actions. Trump's norm-busting is a part of this pattern, and indeed, many people think that Trump is as much an effect of these larger pressures as a cause. But whatever the cause and effect may be (an issue to which we return later in this chapter), norms regulating government institutions are under threat everywhere and must be attended to.

Fourth, and relatedly, while presidents after Trump might be more respectful of norms, the American people also may continue to elect presidents who distrust elites or profess to do so, who reject expertise and create "alternative facts," who attack and circumvent formal governing institutions, and who disrespect traditional principles of governance. The presidential selection process is now thoroughly democratized and lacks its traditional "vetting" function that, to some extent, the parties once performed. The two political parties, and the polity, are deeply polarized. And the perceived failures of elite institutions along a number of dimensions may continue to fuel populist sentiment on both the right and the left, especially in presidential elections. These presidencies may not be predictably Trumpist in their policies. A populist demagogue in the Oval Office purporting to embody the true will of the people against the elites can be a Democrat or a Republican, on the left or well to the right. And that future president might have a better command of the governance tools of the presidency than Trump, and be defter in circumventing legal and norms-based limits. In many ways, Trump, despite his destructiveness, has often been incompetent at operating the levers of the presidency to achieve his ends; a future president might not be so incompetent.

OBJECTIONS AND CONCERNS

We anticipate a cluster of related objections to, or concerns about, our arguments that the presidency demands reform.

Rhetoric and "Manners"

One objection is that Trump's harsh rhetoric and bad manners don't matter. On this view, he is a democratically elected president who ran and won on a platform that claimed that establishment institutions were corrupt, and he pledged to change those institutions dramatically. His defiance of norms in order to weaken the press and governmental institutions, and his other behaviors described earlier, amount to nothing more in substance than executing the wishes of the electorate. This view accepts that Trump is rude, brash, shameless, and ill-mannered in executing this mandate. And it maintains that the institutions Trump was elected to change—especially the press and the executive branch bureaucracy—have made clear in their reactions to Trump that they hold precisely the biased establishment views that Trump was elected to redress. According to this view, the reforms we suggest to buck up the norms and institutions governing presidential behavior are undemocratic.

We take this concern seriously, as far as it goes. In particular, we accept that the American people have the prerogative to elect a rude, norm-breaking president who is contemptuous of institutions. Indeed, the possibility is one premise for our analysis of the need for reform.

We nonetheless conclude that reforms in the areas covered by this book are warranted. The principles defended in this book are that the presidency is a public trust, that presidents should not be permitted to abuse the powers of the office to advance their private interests or to politicize law enforcement but should instead be accountable to Congress and the people through rigorous transparency and other mechanisms. These general principles, which we derive from the arc of constitutional history and practice, are rarely contested and should not be up for grabs. Moreover, for the reasons laid out in detail throughout this book, we reject the notion that Trump's authoritarian and institution-attacking rhetoric, and his brash behavior, are irrelevant to the proper functioning of the presidency.

Wrong Institution

A related objection is that we are focusing on the wrong institution. As noted earlier, Trump is not the only agent of norm-breaking behavior, and he and his presidency may be more of an effect of a larger breakdown in governing norms than a cause. Other institutions—including Congress, political parties, the electoral system, and the press—are dysfunctional in ways that have contributed to the nation's difficulties, and to problems in the presidency.

We accept these points. Throughout this book, we explain how pathologies in the presidency are exacerbated by pathologies in other institutions, and we are often quite critical of those institutions. We might have written a book on how to reform these other institutions.

But we have not written that book. Our expertise concerns executive power, and we believe that reform of the presidency is more likely, and more likely to have immediate efficacy, than reform of the other institutions. For purposes of our analysis, therefore, we will largely accept the other institutions as we find them and offer proposals to reform the presidency in that light.

For similar reasons, we do not propose a novel role for courts in policing the presidency. Courts have always played an important but limited role in checking presidential excesses. They are important because they occasionally resolve separation of powers disputes that lay down principles that govern presidential action. It is possible that a more robust judicial role would address some of the problems in the presidency that we identify. But a more robust role for courts is hard to manufacture and direct. And in any event, courts often face many hurdles to adjudicating the legality of presidential action, including standing, the political question doctrine, the absence of a cause of action, the secrecy of presidential action, and the like, especially in the context of foreign relations. This is why governing precedents in this area are few and far between and often not directly on point for contemporary problems. For purposes of the reforms proposed in this book, we assume and accept Supreme Court jurisprudence as we find it.

Is Reform Feasible?

A different concern about our project is whether reform of the presidency is feasible. We have acknowledged that the nation's political system has been moving in a norm-breaking direction for a while, and that the American people may continue to elect norm-breaking presidents in the future. One might think that reform cannot get off the ground, much less succeed, if its aims are persistently opposed by the American people in their choice of presidents and representatives. Moreover, the broader problem of political dysfunction that we have acknowledged makes it hard now to imagine a Congress that is motivated to engage with the robust reforms proposed here, let alone disciplined enough to do so.

Yet presidential reforms of the 1970s show that major scandals arising out of extreme presidential dysfunction and congressional acquiescence can quickly and unexpectedly be followed by landslide elections that produce large majorities in Congress determined and able to engage in meaningful reform. Something similar could happen as early as 2021, or it might not happen for a while. This book is a road map for when the eventuality occurs.

It is also a road map for when we have a president who is interested in reforming the presidency. Again, although we have acknowledged that future presidents might be less interested in legal and normative self-restraint than past ones, that assumption might be wrong. Many presidents after Richard Nixon, starting with his successor, Gerald Ford, imposed and recognized self-restraints that over the decades developed into important and efficacious norms. Ford's successor, Jimmy Carter, articulated a broad agenda for reform and signed into law key reform initiatives, such as new requirements for legislative and executive branch financial disclosures. We do not know who the next Ford or Carter might be in this respect, or when he or she might appear on the scene. Ultimately, the proper operation of the presidency depends on the character of the president who, at a deep level, values American institutions, including institutions with competing interests that are so vital to the proper functioning of our government.

This means that, when all is said and done, reform depends on the American people. They are not dysfunctional in the ways that Congress is, but they are deeply distrustful of federal governmental institutions and are splintered and distrustful of fellow citizens in some pretty dramatic ways. This is a problem far beyond our jurisdiction, but it affects our task. "Laws are always unstable unless they are founded upon the customs of a nation," Alexis de Tocqueville once said.[5] The laws and norms that govern the presidency work only if a wide swath of the population believes in them, and their legitimacy, and wants them to work. The right kinds of laws and norms can guide action in a proper direction and check many abuses. But ultimately, the efficacy of checks on the presidency depends on the identity of the man or woman whom the American people choose to elect, and the types of pressure that the American people place on members of Congress and other government actors to resist executive branch abuse.

We are mindful of the uncertain prospects for reform. But it is our view that the need for reform is urgent, and the debate over the content of those reforms, to which we hope this book contributes, should not be

delayed until the ripening of conditions for their successful enactment.
When the moment comes, it will be important to make the most of it,
and fast.

Ignorance About the Future

Jim Baker was a seasoned government attorney who served as FBI general counsel during the many difficult episodes that the bureau faced
from 2016 to 2018. When asked about the need for and efficacy of reform
within the FBI with respect to investigations of presidential campaigns
or candidates, he stated:

> The problem is that the next thing that is big and con-
> troversial will not fall into that category, which is why
> it will be big and controversial and hard to figure out.
> That was the hard part here. We went to the books that
> we had available to us, and there's some guidance that's
> available, and we applied the law. . . . But with respect to
> a lot of these questions, and how you handle them and
> how you approach it, it's just very difficult. Hindsight is
> 20–20. You are always trying to solve the last problem. . . .
> The future is always going to throw things at us that we
> haven't thought of before.[6]

This is all true. No reform of the presidency is ever perfect. There is
always a danger of under-regulation and over-regulation. There is also
an ever-present danger of focusing too much on the last problem and of
not adequately anticipating future problems.

Relatedly, every reform effort has unintended consequences. This
problem has haunted reform programs in the past and is a challenge to
current reform initiatives. Legislators make laws but not usually as they
please, and a legislative compromise might be worse than no legislation
at all. A reform may be misdirected or off-target because the problem it
is meant to address was analyzed inadequately: The data was misread or
flawed. What follows from the reform may be markedly different from
what its drafters intended. It is also possible for a reform to be cast too
broadly, failing to be sufficiently focused or tightly structured, with

the result that it does as much harm as good, or that the damage done exceeds the benefits realized. Or, relatedly, reform might create perverse incentives that produce self-defeating results.

The examples are legion. Following Watergate, the provision for the appointment of independent counsels to address allegations of senior executive branch wrongdoing was meant to ensure investigations free from political manipulation or taint. It was also expected to restore public confidence in the apolitical administration of justice. Instead, it became the focus of bitter partisan disputes in which the impartiality of independent counsels themselves was called into question. The law thrust the courts into a supervisory role, on the assumption that they would insulate the process from the reality or suspicion of political intervention; and yet even the judiciary did not escape unscathed from the politics of scandal. Moreover, the statute appeared in operation to supply incentives for long-running and expensive investigations, sometimes over complex or obscure issues of purported official misconduct. The effect was to thicken the clouds of scandal over Washington and reduce public confidence further.

We are sensitive to these challenges throughout this book, and especially to how reform initiatives can be "weaponized" by political opponents and exacerbate the original problem. One tool in this effort is to pay heed to the lessons of history, which we discuss later in this chapter.

FOUR PRINCIPLES TO GUIDE REFORM

A Strong Presidency

In proposing numerous reforms to the presidency, we begin from the assumption that a powerful, vigorous presidency is vital to the proper functioning of American democracy. Our aim is not to chop down legitimate presidential powers. It is rather, like Arthur Schlesinger Jr.'s in *The Imperial Presidency*, to devise "a strong presidency within an equally strong system of accountability."[7]

Article II of the Constitution vests the president with the "executive Power" and adds a handful of enumerated powers. The Constitution also checks these powers. It requires interbranch collaboration in the exercise of certain traditionally executive functions (such as appointing executive branch officers and making treaties). And it gives Congress some of the executive powers exercised by the English king (such as the power to declare war) as well as numerous powers to check the presidency, including the control over the purse, a veto-override authority, and impeachment.

Despite the paucity of enumerated powers and the many checks, the presidency has been the central engine of the federal government from the outset, and has grown massively in size and influence over the centuries. Congress over time proved unable to legislate with the efficiency and precision needed to manage society in the face of growing technological and social complexity. In the twentieth century, it delegated massive legislative authority on practically every important policy topic to the more nimble, discriminating, and forceful executive branch, often with minimal guidance. The Supreme Court's constitutional invalidation of the legislative veto in *INS v. Chadha* in 1983 eliminated Congress's major tool for controlling the presidential exercise of delegated power.[8]

Presidential control over foreign and military affairs followed a similar path. As the United States rose to a global superpower, and as the world grew more dangerous, the commander in chief assumed more and more responsibility for national security. And Congress, in turn, gave the president a massive intelligence and military bureaucracy, a fearsome arsenal of weapons, and few hard constraints. The federal courts have, for the most part, gone along with the program in both domestic and foreign affairs.

The central quality that makes the executive branch the appropriate locus for these tasks is its energy, which Hamilton in *Federalist* No. 70 described as "a leading character in the definition of good government."[9] Energy in the executive is a counterpoint to the separation of powers, which by design "has an inherent tendency toward stalemate and inertia," as Schlesinger has explained. "One of the three branches of government must take the initiative if the system is to move," Schlesinger notes. "The executive branch alone is structurally capable of taking that initiative."[10] This is why most of the federal government's greatest achievements over the centuries—from Washington's masterful stewardship at the birth of the nation, to union victory in the Civil War, to Franklin D. Roosevelt's management of the Great Depression and World War II, to many of the most important victories of racial justice (with help from the Supreme

Court, to be sure), to almost all major legislative initiatives (conservative and liberal), to the successful confrontation with the Soviet Union—came through energetic presidential leadership.

The importance of a powerful presidency became apparent with Trump's weak response to the coronavirus pandemic. The problem was not just Trump's failure to grasp the scale of the problem or to plan for it properly, his early efforts to minimize the danger, the steady diet of inaccurate or contradictory information he fed the nation, his open (and unsubtle) efforts to use the crisis to advance his political fortune rather than seek to achieve national unity, or his general miscarriages of leadership. The problem was also that Trump failed to use the legal tools of the presidency to meet the crisis. Unlike most situations in recent decades where presidents have invoked emergency powers, the coronavirus presented a genuine emergency that would have justified Trump's taking more forceful action than he did to meet the threat—for example, by invoking the Defense Production Act much earlier and more aggressively than he did in order to ensure that the nation had adequate and proper medical supplies. But Trump dawdled and acted tentatively when he did finally, if not consistently or decisively, take some action. And the nation suffered as a result.

The need for a powerful presidency is one of the reasons why we do not argue for major constitutional surgery on the presidency—for example, by making the attorney general more independent of the president, or by trying to slice off the president's power to interpret law for the executive branch (which is currently delegated presumptively to the attorney general and the Office of Legal Counsel) and place that authority in an independent body.

We do not endorse such changes to the nature of the presidency, for several reasons.

First, we are fully aware of the pathologies and dangers of executive branch auto-interpretation of the law by the Office of Legal Counsel and other executive branch personnel, but we doubt such changes can be implemented without a constitutional amendment that, in the present and foreseeable political environment, seems impossible. Even absent such an amendment, Congress can affect the president's control over law enforcement by outsourcing it a bit to actors within and outside the executive branch. In the chapters that follow, we propose ways to strengthen these mechanisms. But the Supreme Court has acknowledged that "there are some 'purely executive' officials who must be removable by the President at will if he is to be able to accomplish his constitutional role"—a description that surely applies to the attorney general and the Office of Legal Counsel.[11]

Second, although politicized law enforcement is an evil to be avoided, and one for which we propose reforms, executive branch interpretation and enforcement of the law are not, and should not be, devoid of political direction. Presidents are elected to devise and manage a governing program, and their success in this endeavor requires them to marshal all the authorities and resources available for this purpose. Every administration is necessarily "political" in this sense. As we explain in Chapter Seven, this nonobvious but important point is one reason why Congress rejected radical restructuring of the president's relationship to the Justice Department, even after Watergate.

Third, and relatedly, in a time of anxiety about the presidency, there is a tendency to try to take political considerations out of executive branch action by placing executive responsibility in nonaccountable actions or institutions. The basic problem with this strategy—and, we argue, a problem to be avoided—is that it places responsibility for politically divisive actions in an actor who is not politically accountable if the decisions he or she makes are wrong or controversial. Weakening the control of accountable actors over core executive decision-making was the strategy of the 1978 independent counsel statute. And in some sense it was FBI Director James Comey's strategy in taking the unusual step of announcing his conclusion that Hillary Clinton should not be indicted, rather than following the Department of Justice chain of command, which gave the attorney general authority and responsibility to make the call. One theme in our proposals is the importance of political accountability to the proper functioning of the executive branch. Another important and, to us, inextricable idea is the need for transparency of executive branch action so that executive branch actors can be held accountable for their actions—by the press; by judges; through congressional oversight, including impeachment; and ultimately in elections.

One should not mistake our inclination against constitutional surgery for the executive branch as an inclination against bold reforms. Some of our proposals are modest, but many are not modest, and some—for example, our proposal to winnow down the Office of White House Counsel and place many of its legal responsibilities in a Justice Department component—are ambitious to the point of radical. In short, we accept the basic constitutional contours of the presidency that currently prevail and offer reforms of various levels of ambition within those contours.

Law v. Norms

As we have already alluded to, law and norms are different things. Constitutional law is the supreme law of the land that presidents under Article II of the Constitution must faithfully enforce, including against themselves. Constitutional law legally empowers and constrains presidents in ways that cannot be changed absent a constitutional amendment. Statutes are laws enacted by Congress. They must conform to the Constitution (for example, the Constitution prohibits *ex post facto* laws), and they too bind presidents legally until the statutes are changed by Congress itself. And there are other laws that bind executive branch officials in various ways—regulations, executive orders, and the like.

Norms are different. They are *nonlegal* principles of appropriate or expected behavior that presidents and other officials tacitly accept and that typically structure their actions. Examples of presidential norms include holding regular press conferences, taking daily intelligence briefings, maintaining a distance from and certainly not directing the attorney general's prosecutorial decisions, disclosing income tax returns during a presidential campaign, and getting an annual medical checkup and announcing the results to the public. Norms are rarely noticed until they are violated, as the nation has experienced on a weekly and often daily basis during the Trump presidency.

Sometimes it is appropriate to change norms into laws. When FDR sought a third term in office, he violated the norm of a two-term presidency that traced back to George Washington. He did not act illegally in doing so, and the American people ratified his decision when they reelected him in 1940. But the American people had second thoughts after Roosevelt died. They converted the norm into constitutional law, the Twenty-Second Amendment, so that no president could again run for a third term.

One might wonder why so much regulation of the presidency takes place through norms rather than law. There are at least two reasons. First, the Constitution does not permit Congress to regulate some elements of presidential behavior. The president's power to communicate in good faith with the attorney general about a pending case is probably one example. This power is tied so closely to the president's Article II control over the prosecutorial power, and is so central to executive power, that Congress probably cannot regulate it in most instances. And yet there is a powerful norm that has developed inside the executive branch, in the shadow of congressional concern, that imposes a pretty rigid separation between the White House and the Justice Department on prosecution issues. As we explain in Chapter Seven, this norm worked pretty well, but not always, for forty years after Watergate and needs reinforcement after Trump's presidency.

The second reason to prefer norms over laws is flexibility. When norms work well, they have real bite. As a general matter, however, they are more flexible than laws in the sense that a deviation from norms in the exceptional case results only in political sanctions. Presidents have a constitutional obligation under Article II to comply with laws even in unusual or unforeseeable cases where many reasonable people might think an exception is appropriate. But presidents have no constitutional or even legal obligation to comply with norms, and so norms are easier to disregard in exceptional cases. Norms are much less effective in a case like Trump's, since a shameless president or one indifferent to political sanctions can simply disregard them. But the virtue of norms over laws is that sometimes a justifiable case for disregarding norms arises. And relatedly, norms are easier to change or update when they grow stale, since the executive branch can adopt and implement these types of reforms unilaterally without recourse to Congress or the amendment process.

In the pages that follow, we sometimes argue for changing norms to laws, and other times we argue for maintaining norms but changing their content. These choices are contextual. As we explain in the body of our analysis, the issues raised by Trump's finances and conflicts of interest resulted from the mistaken belief that norms rather than law would suffice to induce proper behavior. We argue for statutory reform in these and other cases. Some of the controversies posed by the institutions responding to Trump—for example, the special counsel mechanism, and the FBI's investigation of the Trump campaign and presidency—arose from what now seem like imprecisely crafted regulations (the special counsel) or the absence of regulatory guidance (the FBI's investigation). In these cases, we argue for strengthened norms and processes to be achieved by reforms internal to the executive branch.

But laws without the support of associated norms can fail to do all the work required for sound choices: Compliance with legal obligations is, of course, always necessary, but it may not be sufficient in novel circumstances or where there is good-faith disagreement about the law. Systematic processes that allow for legal and normative issues to be raised and considered is also essential. Indeed, as we explain later, process is a leading indicator of whether the legal and normative issues are being taken seriously. And, as we also explain, well-targeted transparency measures can hold the key actors accountable. Among other functions, transparency can help induce adherence to process.

The Golden Rule

In recent memory, critics of one party have tended to construe exercises of power by honorable presidents of another party in extreme, uncharitable terms. Such criticism of the presidency tends to be opportunistic and hypocritical.

Democrats tended to like a strong presidency when Barack Obama was in office pursuing progressive ends, and many tended not to imagine or acknowledge how their support for Obama squared with their criticisms of George W. Bush, especially in foreign and national security affairs, or how they might view Obama's exercises of power if a conservative president were using the same tools to pursue conservative ends. Republicans tended to do exactly the same thing in reverse: They were harshly critical of Obama's exercises of power even though they supported analogous exercises of power for quite different ends by Bush and Trump. Similarly, critics and defenders of the presidency tend to like or dislike the actions of the accountability institutions for the presidency—congressional oversight, the special counsel, and the like—depending on whose ox is being gored. We expect that Trump's supporters will find the proposals in this book more congenial once he has left the scene—especially if he is replaced by a Democrat as president.

This is not a new phenomenon. From the beginning of the nation, Schlesinger notes, "views of the proper distribution of power between the Congress and the President depended a good deal less on considerations of high principle than on preferences about the uses to which power was put."[12] The politicization of constitutional argument around the presidency might be inevitable, but it is a hurdle to intelligent reform and should be resisted. We will try to resist it by applying a variation of the golden rule in our analysis: Always imagine whether a constraint on the presidency would be legitimate if your preferred president were in office or, reciprocally, whether a conferral of presidential discretion would be legitimate if exercised by a president of another party. This thought experiment does not answer every question posed about presidential power. But it should help to screen somewhat for the confirmation biases and political NIMBY-ism that seem to have intensified in contemporary, polarized American politics.

The Lessons of History

The presidency is a 230-year old institution. The final principle that guides us is the need for sensitivity to the lessons that history has taught about how the presidency, and reforms of the presidency, operate. No period is richer in relative historical lessons than the 1970s, following Nixon's presidency.

Trump and Nixon differ in many ways, but they also share important traits: an indifference to law, a host of visible psychological difficulties, pathological anti-elitism, and a related hatred of vital government institutions and the press. These traits led both men to act in some extreme ways that exposed fundamental flaws in the presidency. After Nixon resigned, Congress and the executive branch engaged in a series of fundamental reforms—on war powers, ethics, financial disclosures, special prosecutors, campaign finance, presidential records, and much more—that guided the presidency for almost half a century. While those reforms were in some respects very successful, a number fell short of expectation, and Trump's presidency has made clear that in many ways they were not adequate to the task.

We have a lot to say in the chapters that follow about the so-called Watergate-era reforms, which present the essential backdrop to understanding the problems that bedevil the presidency today. But at the outset, we sound a cautionary note about oversimplifying the "Watergate analogy." The so-called Watergate reforms were based on multiple rationales and sprang from multiple sources and perspectives that were significant as much for their differences as for their similarities.

One aspect of the reform program was anchored in a long-standing Progressive reform tradition dating back to the turn of the twentieth century. This tradition was concerned with promoting "good government" through the promotion of expert, merit-based policymaking; transparency; and checks on undue political and interest group influence made possible by uncontrolled campaign spending and political patronage. An example is the enactment of the major 1974 amendments to the Federal Election Campaign Act, strengthening and establishing a range of controls and transparency requirements for money raised and spent to influence federal elections.

A second strand of reform was prompted by the perceived skew in the balance of constitutional power between the legislative and executive branches, especially but not only in the field of war powers and national security. For example, the War Powers Resolution was a Watergate-era reform but not a response to the scandal itself, just as the Foreign Intelligence Surveillance Act (FISA) of 1978 built on legislative and judicial reforms stretching back to the 1960s to establish a supervisory role for the courts in reviewing and approving executive branch applications for electronic surveillance of foreign agents on U.S. soil.

A third and distinctive reform program was concerned directly with the systematic presidential abuses of power revealed by the Watergate investigations. In the grip of deep resentments and distrust, Nixon disregarded the legal and normative limits on the misuse of executive branch departments and agencies to investigate and harass his political opponents. Among the reforms enacted in direct response to this episode, the Ethics in Government Act provided for a judicially appointed and supervised "independent counsel."

These three very different sources of reform make it misleading to speak of them collectively as a "response" to Watergate. The reforms were also varied in their staying power and effectiveness. The independent counsel statute was controversial in application, susceptible to partisan manipulation, and debilitating to a functioning presidency. The law died in 1999 with the blessing of both major parties and was replaced with the Justice Department regulations that governed Robert Mueller's investigation of the 2016 election but that have problems of their own. Over these same decades, the campaign finance laws crumbled as political actors excelled at evasive strategies and the Supreme Court greatly restricted Congress's authority to regulate in this area. As Trump's presidency showed, the era's personal financial disclosure requirements have failed to adequately check self-interested government service. And in the field of national security, the War Powers Resolution did not rebalance constitutional war powers, and the FISA process, which seemed to work for a while, is now widely seen as error filled and dysfunctional in practice.

There is one other aspect to the Watergate experience that is not captured fully by an exclusive focus on legal reforms and developments. This was the recognition and honoring of norms of executive branch conduct that were influenced in part by law, in part by executive order, and in part by example in the post-Nixon years. Prominent among these norms was the expectation of professional, independent law enforcement made possible by government lawyers who serve the public and not the president's personal and political interests. This expectation set a standard that both parties affirmed and that presidents publicly embraced in the years following a scandal in which the president appeared as an unindicted co-conspirator in a criminal case brought against, among others, his attorney general and White House counsel. Another norm born of Watergate was presidents' voluntary release of their tax returns. A beleaguered Nixon conceded that "[t]he confidentiality of my private finances is far less important to me than the confidence of the American people in the integrity of the President."[13]

By the time of Donald Trump's presidency, however, these and other norms were under assault, for reasons we have already explained. The proposals in the chapters that follow are informed by the Watergate experience and seek to define with precision the nature of the problems that have emerged and to target reform measures accordingly.

★

PART I

★

THE PRESIDENT

This part addresses conflicts of interest between a president's exercise of constitutional authorities for the general public welfare, and his or her personal (including financial) and political self-interest. Trump has raised this issue in multiple contexts in ways that have no precedent in American history. Prior to Trump, norms rather than legal commands did almost all the work of regulating and, for the most part, preventing these conflicts of interest from arising or appearing to arise. Trump has made clear that norms alone do not suffice.

The chapters in this part focus on reforms arising from five major problems in this vein that emerged or grew untenable during the Trump presidency:

- *Political Alliances with Foreign State Interests.* Of the many controversies in the Trump administration, none has rivaled in intensity and duration the allegations that he sought to build mutually advantageous political alliances with foreign states that would support first his election and then his reelection. One episode led to the Mueller investigation; another led to Trump's impeachment, trial, and subsequent acquittal. Other known episodes have not yet received official scrutiny.

- *Self-Enrichment in Office.* Presidents in the modern era have complied with norms that serve to protect against the conflict between ongoing personal financial interests and the exercise of the powers of the office. The accepted mechanisms for resolving these issues have been the establishment of independent "blind" trusts to manage a president's assets while in office and limiting investments to mutual funds or diversified investment vehicles that effectively eliminate the risk of conflicts. Trump pledged to follow this norm and isolate himself from his far-flung national and international business interests, but he defied the norm in practice for his entire term.

- *Transparency of Finances.* For decades, presidents and vice presidents also followed a norm of voluntarily releasing their tax returns to provide the public with additional sources of information about potential conflicts and for other purposes. Trump refused to abide by this norm during his candidacy and throughout his presidency. The result was a fierce political controversy, conflict with Congress, federal and state litigation, and most corrosively, the appearance and possible reality of corruption.

- *Attacks on a Free Press.* Trump is not the first president to have contentious relations with the press. No president has gone as far as Trump in his virulent, constant attacks on the role and credibility of the news media. His White House has attempted to revoke press passes of reporters who provoked his ire and for months at a time suspended daily press briefings. In addition, his administration has taken regulatory action affecting the interests of specific, disfavored news organizations, raising reasonable suspicions of harassment or retaliation.

- *Abuse of the Pardon Power.* Presidents before Trump have periodically engendered controversies over alleged personal or political motivation for the grant of pardons. Trump has exceeded them all in his enthusiasm for the political uses of this ostensibly "absolute" constitutional power. With rare exceptions, Trump has circumvented the traditional role of the Department of Justice in scrutinizing pardon applications and making recommendations to the attorney general and the president. Instead, Trump has made his decisions primarily on the basis of political points he wishes to make and connections of personal importance to him. He also announced that he could, if he wished, pardon himself for any alleged federal offenses.

FOREIGN STATE INFLUENCE

One of the more arresting charges against President Trump in former National Security Adviser John Bolton's memoir was that Trump asked the leader of the People's Republic of China, Xi Jinping, to "ensure he'd win" the 2020 election by mobilizing China's "economic capability" to buy more American agricultural products and help him secure the farm state vote.[1] Bolton also alleged that Trump "offered to reverse" criminal law enforcement prosecution against the Chinese telecommunications company Huawei if Xi reached a trade deal—an offer, Bolton claimed, that was "primarily about getting Trump re-elected in 2020."[2]

Bolton's charges raise the issue of a president's or presidential candidate's establishment of a mutually beneficial alliance with a foreign government to help win or hold office, in return for policy concessions to the government at the time of the deal or if electoral success is achieved. His allegations are hard to verify as we write these words, but they ring true because similar charges have been rife throughout Trump's presidency.

The Trump 2016 presidential campaign's various contacts with Russian officials and agents led to the appointment of a special counsel, whose investigation "did not establish that members of the Trump Campaign conspired or coordinated with the Russian government in its election interference activities" but did establish that "the Campaign expected it would benefit electorally from information stolen and released through Russian efforts."[3] Then, in 2019, an executive branch official, acting under whistleblower protection, alleged that the president had solicited the assistance of Ukraine in investigating a leading candidate for the Democratic Party's 2020 presidential nomination. This episode resulted in a House vote to impeach Trump and a Senate trial that ended in acquittal.

We are less interested in this chapter in relitigating these much-covered events than in understanding and redressing the major gaps that they revealed in U.S. law concerning foreign state influence on U.S. elections. Any such influence presents a special threat if the foreign power finds a willing partner in an American president or presidential candidate, since the partnership would help the foreign power target its resources to achieve maximum political impact. This was the new and dangerous threat that became salient and plausible during the Trump era, and it is the primary focus of our proposed reforms.

BACKGROUND

The controversies of 2016–2020 occurred against the background of long-standing American concern about foreign powers seeking illicit channels of influence over the U.S. government. James Madison was among those who believed that the "two great evils to be avoided" in conceiving the presidency were a "cabal at home and influence from abroad."[4] The Emoluments Clause is one expression of this anxiety. Another is the constitutional prohibition on the election of a president who is not a natural-born citizen.

At various times in American history, the fear of insidious foreign state political conspiracies fomented what could be fairly described as panics. The "red scare" of 1919–1920 prompted a frenzied search for anarchist and communist subversives outside the U.S. government who were dedicated to overthrowing it. McCarthyism in the 1950s shifted the concern to communist infiltration of the U.S. government that sought to surreptitiously sway American policy in favor of foreign state interests. Congress investigated and enacted laws that aimed to root out communist influence and conspiracies. In 1959, in a sign of the anxious times, Richard Condon published *The Manchurian Candidate*, a best-selling tale of a foreign power's plot to elevate to the presidency a politician under its control.[5]

Yet until the 1960s, American legal reforms did not specifically address the various ways that foreign powers could act to influence the electoral process. It certainly did not anticipate or seek to address the threat of the potential complicity of American presidents and presidential candidates in foreign electoral interventions. The threat was real. In 1968, the Soviet Union's ambassador to the United States, Anatoly Dobrynin, carried out instructions from Moscow to offer Democratic candidate for president Hubert Humphrey "any conceivable help in his election campaign—including financial aid."[6] Over breakfast with Dobrynin, Humphrey rebuffed the offer. The Soviet ambassador had made a similar offer to Adlai Stevenson in early 1960, which was also rebuffed.

There was at least one instance of an alliance between a presidential candidate and a foreign power—during the 1968 presidential election. Late in the campaign, Richard Nixon, through intermediaries, reached an agreement with the South Vietnamese government to resist an eleventh-hour initiative by President Lyndon Johnson to achieve peace between North and South Vietnam. We can never know whether this episode was a factor in Nixon's victory over Democratic nominee—and Johnson's vice president—Hubert Humphrey. When the episode came to public light long after the Nixon presidency, it was received as one more sordid exhibit in the record of a uniquely scandalous presidency.

In 1966, Congress took the first step toward regulating foreign state influence over the electoral process when it amended the Foreign Agents Registration Act of 1938 (FARA).[7] FARA was enacted in response to findings about the public relations and propaganda activities of German agents in the United States in the years preceding World War II. The law aimed to ensure that "the United States Government and the public know the source of certain information from foreign agents intended to influence American public opinion, policy, and laws."[8] The original act required agents of foreign governments who acted "within the United States" to register with the attorney general and disclose the foreign government's identity and their activities on its behalf.[9] It did not then impose limits on foreign national spending directly, or through U.S. agents, on federal, state, or local elections.

The 1966 FARA amendments brought direct electoral intervention within the scope of the statute by requiring covered agents to disclose campaign contributions. The Senate Foreign Relations Committee explained that the amended FARA aimed to address the problem of foreign agents "whose object is not to subvert or overthrow the U.S. Government, but to influence its policies to the [satisfaction] of his particular client."[10] The attention paid to political contributions in particular reflected congressional findings that there was "growing use" of this "means to influence Government policies."[11] But the law applied only to the activities of U.S. agents within the United States, not to initiatives undertaken directly by a foreign state, and it did not reach any political activity coordinated by a foreign power with an American political candidate.

The Watergate reforms of the 1970s imposed a new prohibition on foreign national political contributions to American political campaigns. The 1974 amendments to the Federal Election Campaign Act of 1971 (FECA) contained this core prohibition, which was retained in Congress's revision of the law in the wake of the Supreme Court's constitutional review in *Buckley v. Valeo*:[12]

> It shall be unlawful for a foreign national directly or through any other person to make any contribution of money or other thing of value, or to promise expressly or impliedly to make any such contribution, in connection with an election to any political office or in connection with any primary election, convention, or caucus held to select candidates for any political office; or for any person to solicit, accept, or receive any such contribution from a foreign national.[13]

The "contributions" subject to the prohibition were defined broadly to apply to anything of "value," which includes an "in-kind" contribution such as a good or service that a donor might buy for a candidate's use or benefit.[14] (As we explain later in this chapter, the reach of the term "thing of value" was of central importance in the special counsel investigation of contacts between the 2016 Trump presidential campaign and Russian nationals representing themselves to be acting on behalf of their government.)

The amended FECA structure, like the 1966 FARA amendments, did not aim to regulate a presidential campaign that actively colluded or coordinated with a foreign power. It was concerned narrowly with the growing temptations of the campaign money chase. In this sense, the law conceptualized foreign interests much like any special interest seeking favor with candidates by underwriting their campaign costs. It prohibited candidates from soliciting foreign contributions, and from accepting them. But in this and other material respects, the prohibition largely tracked with the ban on contributions to candidates and parties from U.S. corporations and labor unions. Congress did not focus on the possibility of a federal candidate engaging with a foreign power in a mutually rewarding political alliance.

Congress's actual focus was on display in the one pertinent investigation of a presidential election prior to the Trump administration. In 1996, the Republican-controlled Congress investigated allegations of foreign sources of financing of President Bill Clinton's reelection campaign. Republican leadership first lodged the sensational charge that the People's Republic of China had hatched a scheme to funnel foreign funds to the Clinton campaign to enhance its competitive advantage. The emphasis soon shifted to allegations that the Clinton campaign's thirst for resources had led it to loosen "vetting" and other fundraising disciplines that would have guarded against foreign-source contributions. Democrats responded with their own case against comparably lax fundraising practices on the Republican side, which had also opened the door to foreign support. The purported foreign state conspiracy faded from view, and the episode resulted in calls for a tightening of the campaign finance laws to close "loopholes" exploited by a range of interests, including but not limited to foreign state actors.[15]

In a partial (and delayed) response to this episode, Congress enacted the Bipartisan Campaign Reform Act of 2002, popularly known as the McCain-Feingold Act.[16] A relatively minor provision in the act clarified and tightened but did not substantially alter the then-existing ban on foreign national campaign contributions. It specified that the prohibition on foreign national spending in federal elections applied to "independent expenditures," such as the funding for advertising on behalf of (or in opposition to) candidates without coordination or prior agreement with their campaigns. It closed loopholes for the potential receipt of foreign money by parties and enhanced the criminal penalties for violations. Nothing in the reform tackled the question of a more complex, concerted foreign state alliance with a candidate, including the question of whether and when such an alliance would implicate the making or receipt of contributions in the form of a "thing of value."

This historical sketch of the American concern with foreign state electoral intervention would not be complete without noting the Supreme Court's 2010 decision in *Citizens United v. Federal Election Commission*.[17] The court struck down on First Amendment grounds the federal law prohibition on independent, uncoordinated spending by corporations and unions to support or oppose a candidate. The decision did not purport to affect the foreign national independent spending ban. Many observers worried, however, that the erosion of the corporate ban could create openings for foreign nationals to utilize wholly owned U.S. companies to move money under their direction into U.S. elections. In his January 2010 State of the Union address, President Obama famously (and controversially) made this point with members of the Supreme Court seated before him. *Citizens United*, he contended, "will open the floodgates for special interests—including foreign corporations—to spend without limit in our elections."[18]

In 2011, a three-judge district court for the District of Columbia considered a First Amendment challenge, premised on the implications of *Citizens United*, to the comprehensive prohibition on foreign national spending in U.S. elections. The case, *Bluman v. FEC,* involved two individual foreign nationals who wished to make direct contributions, publicly reportable and within dollar limits, to various candidates. In an opinion by then-Judge Brett Kavanaugh, the court rejected the First Amendment challenge and upheld the constitutionality of the law. It reasoned:

> It is fundamental to the definition of our national political community that foreign citizens do not have a constitutional right to participate in, and thus may be excluded from, activities of democratic self-government. It follows, therefore, that the United States has a compelling interest for purposes of First Amendment analysis in limiting the participation of foreign citizens in activities of American democratic self-government, and in thereby preventing foreign influence over the U.S. political process.[19]

The Supreme Court summarily and unanimously affirmed the opinion.[20]

With the exception of the later-discovered secret negotiations between Nixon's campaign and the South Vietnamese government, we know of no president or presidential campaign prior to Trump's that was accused of an active political alliance or collusion with foreign interests. The legal principles canvassed thus far leave a great deal of room for that possibility, however. A president or presidential campaign can provide such a foreign state with major advantages in interfering with presidential elections. A request, suggestion, or guidance from the candidate or his or her team may help enhance the efficiency and effectiveness of the foreign state intervention. Those suggestions could serve to guide the foreign state actor in their choice of political messages or the geographic targeting most consistent with the campaign's strategic objectives. By directing or materially influencing foreign state spending and other activity, the candidate could benefit substantially as much as he or she would if the money were provided to the campaign for its direct expenditure for the same purpose.

Any such collaboration between a foreign state and a president or presidential campaign might rise to an express or implicit "deal" in which the foreign state bargains for special policy consideration or treatment in return for the support it provided. But even a president or candidate who did not incur a formal debt or make a clear agreement to receive political support for services rendered may later come under the pressure of various forms of obligation. In the context of domestic campaign finance regulation, the Supreme Court has characterized the concern as a "subtle but equally dispiriting form[] of corruption," one "[j]ust as troubling to a functioning democracy as classic *quid pro quo* corruption."[21] If this is an issue in the sphere of campaign finance law as it applies to politicians unduly influenced by fellow citizens, then it is much more so where the obligation is incurred toward a foreign government.

The Federal Election Commission (FEC), the federal agency tasked to oversee elections, has been unable to devise a regulatory answer to these concerns, and we discuss its deficiencies in connection with the reforms we propose. Before doing so, we should say a brief word about why the bribery laws are also not currently structured to address this problem.

The primary bribery statute prohibits a public official from receiving or accepting, or agreeing to receive or accept, "anything of value personally … in return for … being influenced in the performance of any official act."[22] The 2020 articles of impeachment against President Trump did not include a count on bribery. But the House Judiciary Committee impeachment report concluded that Trump in the Ukraine matter violated the bribery statute because the "favor" he requested constituted a *personal* benefit of helping him win the 2020 presidential election.

A bribery analysis in this context would require difficult distinctions between deals for the personal benefit of a politician and arrangements more in the nature of political "logrolling." Politicians routinely make deals with an eye on the political return, and it is not easy to separate out those cases where the political bargain justifies the application of legal sanctions. A president might seek the cooperation of a foreign government in timing the announcement of a successfully negotiated executive agreement or treaty for maximum political effect. This cooperation could extend to choices in the wording of joint statements, or the planning for the setting for the announcement. And the foreign government might yield on all these "favors" in the interest of getting an agreement that may stand up well on the policy merits. The application of the bribery statute in this and related contexts would cut deeply into the conduct of "politics" in the commonly accepted sense and is far beyond our aims here.

Unlike the bribery statute, the Federal Election Campaign Act of 1971[23] targets a distinctive form of foreign national electioneering: spending to make campaign contributions or to finance direct contact with voters to influence an election. But it is similarly not structured to deal effectively with other more complex channels for foreign electoral influence. Its focus is on support that can be translated into *dollar values*, and the law exempts from prohibition various foreign national campaign activities that cannot be easily quantified, such as personal time that a foreign national may volunteer to a campaign. This exemption covers such a volunteer's use of the internet to communicate support for or opposition to a candidate, or assistance in the development of a political committee's website and other intellectual property.[24]

Even where more substantial, institutional foreign national interests are involved, the rules distinguish between money spent directly for campaign activity and other more subtle but still significant avenues of influence. Consider the case of a U.S. corporation wholly owned by a foreign parent. Under the FECA and implementing regulations, the U.S.

executives of the subsidiary may establish a political action committee, or PAC, to support candidates in federal elections. The U.S. executives may fund the U.S. subsidiary PAC with personal contributions; the PAC, in turn, may contribute to candidates. This PAC serves a corporate political purpose—and, potentially and perhaps invariably, the foreign parent's political purposes. A corporate official who is a foreign national may not fund or "directly or indirectly participate in" this PAC activity, but the PAC's activities are otherwise permissible, because the *money* that the PAC raises and spends comes out of American pockets. In this way, the law disregards the overall organizational context within which the establishment of the PAC occurs and foreign political purposes may be advanced. The executives of the U.S. subsidiary will typically need no explicit direction to understand the interests of the parent to whom they are ultimately accountable.

Another example concerns foreign nationals who participate in campaigns by volunteering their time to a candidate, party, or other political organization active in U.S. elections. The FEC's rules do not permit foreign nationals to control or determine the spending of funds raised for campaigns. But the agency does allow them to devote valuable time as uncompensated volunteers to the candidates or political committees of their choice. Because the campaign finance law exempts volunteer activity, the agency has applied the allowance to both foreign nationals and U.S. citizens.

The FECA's anchoring concern with money—a quantifiable relationship—becomes even more apparent when it is contrasted with FARA's focus on disclosure. The agent of a foreign principal for FARA purposes need not be compensated in order to be subject to that statute's reporting requirements. Nor does the statute require that an agency relationship be based on foreign "direction or control." A "request" that the U.S. citizen act as agent is sufficient to establish a regulated agency relationship. And, in serving the interests of the foreign principal, the agent need not make contacts with U.S. officials to bring his or her activities within reach of the statute. The mere provision of advice, as a "public relations counsel" or "political consultant," suffices to bring the relationship within the law's reporting requirements. In other words, FARA disclosure requirements sweep widely in addressing the potential for foreign influence over the U.S. governmental process.

The federal campaign finance law's limits in addressing foreign nationals are partly a function of the perceived constitutional barriers to more extensive regulation. The courts have always closely scrutinized the burdens on Americans' free speech and association posed by congressional regulation of campaign spending. These constitutional issues have become implicated even in the rules targeted at foreign nationals. Foreign nationals cannot assert First Amendment protections for campaign-related activity, but Americans retain those rights when drawing on advice or encouragement from foreign nationals or when amplifying their views. Rules that are either unclear or overbroad as applied to foreign nationals could unduly affect U.S. citizens in conducting First Amendment–protected activity. As we discuss later in this chapter, the special counsel's report on the Russia investigation expressed concern that the application of the campaign finance law to a June 2016 meeting between senior Trump campaign aides and representatives of the Russian government might present such constitutional issues.

These types of constitutional concerns add to the difficulties encountered in applying this statutory framework to the new, growing concern with foreign government intervention in the U.S. electoral process. There are other limits on direct regulation in this context. For example, it is difficult to conceive of a prohibition on a presidential candidate's publicly seeking foreign support, such as when Trump in 2016 exhorted the Russians to locate missing Clinton emails. Once WikiLeaks published emails that the Russians stole, Trump's campaign was constitutionally free—as were news organization and other U.S. citizens—to recirculate and draw attention to them. Nor, for that matter, were the Russians or any other foreign government prohibited from expressing opinions about issues with direct relevance to, and potential impact on, the presidential election. The Russian government cannot finance ads in the United States calling for a vote for Trump. But it can pay for politically charged "issue advertising" that dovetails with his campaign's messaging on major issues, such as the dangers of inadequately controlled immigration or the need for a less antagonistic relationship with Russia.

But, as the *Bluman* case that was affirmed by a unanimous Supreme Court makes clear, Congress has broad authority to implement effective prohibitions on foreign electoral interference. It may draw lines, even ones that may affect U.S. citizens, that more tightly circumscribe foreign national campaign-related activity than is possible within the traditional campaign finance law framework as it applies domestic political actors.

In our discussion of potential reforms, we suggest how the lines could be redrawn and note the potential contributions of specific legal reforms to the development or reinvigoration of norms. But, first, we review the ways in which President Trump and his campaign exposed the weakness of the norms and laws meant to prevent foreign national interference in U.S. elections.

THE TRUMP ERA

The 2016 presidential election, and President Trump's preparations for a 2020 reelection campaign, brought questions of "collusion" with foreign state interests to the forefront of American domestic and foreign affairs. Here, we briefly recap these well-known events.

Russia and the Special Counsel Investigation

The order appointing Robert Mueller as special counsel authorized him to conduct an investigation concerning "any links and/or coordination between the Russian government and individuals associated with the campaign of President Donald Trump."[25] Mueller's final report found and detailed "numerous" such links.[26]

Most notable among the many links was the meeting at Trump Tower in June 2016 between the campaign's senior management—Donald Trump, Jr.; campaign chairman Paul Manafort; and Trump's senior adviser and son-in-law, Jared Kushner—and a delegation from Moscow. Trump Jr. had arranged the meeting after an intermediary told him by email that the "'Crown prosecutor of Russia ... offered to provide the Trump Campaign with some official documents and information that would incriminate [Democratic presidential nominee] Hillary [Clinton] and her dealings with Russia'" as "'part of Russia and its government's support for Mr. Trump.'" Trump Jr. answered that "'if it's what you say I love it,'" and he arranged the meeting. The Trump team came to the meeting "expecting to receive derogatory information about Hillary Clinton from the Russian government."[27] At the meeting, the Russians made claims about information on the Clinton campaign but could not substantiate them.

In addition to these and other contacts between the Trump campaign and people with ties to the Russian government, the Mueller Report established that the campaign knew beginning in June 2016 that WikiLeaks would release information damaging to the Clinton campaign. It was around this time that Trump stated publicly that he hoped Russia would recover emails supposedly missing from Clinton's private server when she was secretary of state. The special counsel concluded that the Trump campaign "showed interest in WikiLeaks's releases of documents and welcomed their potential to damage candidate Clinton."[28]

Despite these contacts and expectations, the special counsel investigation "did not establish that the Trump Campaign coordinated with the Russian government in its election interference activities," and it concluded that there was insufficient evidence to support criminal charges of various kinds, including ones related to the core concern with any "assistance [Russia provided] to the [Trump] Campaign in exchange for any sort of favorable treatment in the future."[29] It was not enough that the Trump campaign was interested in the support and signaled its openness to it, or that the Russians might have responded to the signals. Mueller concluded that an actual agreement, supported by the evidence, was required to support criminal charges.

Mueller also concluded that constitutional and other unresolved ambiguities in the campaign finance laws—especially on the question of whether and when opposition research could constitute a "thing of value" for purposes of the foreign contribution ban—precluded a prosecution related to the Trump Tower meeting. Moreover, he did not find that the Russians delivered any such information directly to the Trump campaign. Rather, using WikiLeaks as the means of distribution, the Russian government hacked and released emails sent and received by the Clinton campaign chairman. Mueller did not uncover evidence that the Trump campaign had collaborated in the plan to hack this account.

In sum, Trump's engagement with Russia presented the special counsel with what appeared to him to be significant complications of fact and law. Russia had every reason to believe that Trump and his campaign welcomed its intervention, and it did intervene. What Mueller found to be missing, for purposes of the legal case that he evaluated, was the Trump campaign acting as co-conspirator rather than cheerleader.

Ukraine and Impeachment

On July 25, 2019, President Trump had a telephone conversation with Ukraine President Volodymyr Zelensky. After Zelensky had thanked Trump "for your great support in the area of defense," Trump asked Zelensky for several favors, including this one concerning former Vice President Joe Biden, a leading candidate for the Democratic nomination for president:

> The other thing, There's a lot of talk about Biden's son, that Biden stopped the prosecution and a lot of people want to find out about that so whatever you can do with the Attorney General would be great. Biden went around bragging that he stopped the prosecution so if you can look into it …. It sounds horrible to me.

Zelensky responded by pledging to cooperate.[30]

The call became public with news reports of a whistleblower complaint alleging that Trump in this conversation, and in subsequent actions, sought to condition the release of military aid appropriated for Ukraine on its government's compliance with the requested "favor" of an investigation into Trump's political rival.[31] The White House responded with the release of a summary transcript of the call. The president pronounced the call exculpatory. House Democrats disagreed, and, on September 9, 2019, the speaker of the House tasked the House Permanent Select Committee on Intelligence (the House Intelligence Committee) with the initiation of an inquiry into whether the president's actions constituted an impeachable offense. Two days later, the Trump administration released the aid to Ukraine—after a delay the Government Accountability Office later concluded was a violation of the Impoundment Control Act of 1974.[32] Even after his actions were discovered, Trump continued to urge foreign governments (including Ukraine and China) to investigate Biden.

After conducting hearings, the House Intelligence Committee found that Trump had solicited foreign interference in the 2020 election and sought to procure it with official acts, namely, a head of state meeting at the White House and the release of $391 million of vital military aid, on the announcement of these investigations.[33] The committee concluded that the withholding of military aid lacked "any legitimate foreign policy, national security, or anti-corruption justification" and "by withholding vital military assistance and diplomatic support ... President Trump compromised national security to advance his personal political interests."[34] The committee split entirely along party lines in reaching this decision.

The House Intelligence Committee then referred the findings to the House Judiciary Committee, which heard testimony on the applicable constitutional standard and then, again along strict party lines, voted on the articles of impeachment. The full House voted to impeach President Trump on December 18, 2019. Article I, charging the president with "abuse of power," cited his solicitation of Ukraine's intervention in the 2020 election through that government agreement to publicly announce investigations "that would benefit his reelection, harm the election prospects of a political opponent, and influence the 2020 United States Presidential election to his advantage."[35] The Russian matter appeared by indirect reference: "These actions were consistent with President Trump's previous invitations of foreign interference in United States elections."[36] The Senate tried this charge, and another finding that the president had obstructed the House's inquiry, and acquitted him.

REFORM

A "Joint Statement" on 2020 election security issued by key federal government departments and agencies stressed the intention of "[o]ur adversaries ... to undermine our democratic institutions, influence public sentiment and affect government policies." It added that "Russia, China, Iran, and other foreign malicious actors all will seek to interfere in the voting process or influence voter perceptions."[37] Potential "collusion" with a president or presidential campaign in such foreign state influence operations will likely continue to be a facet of these increasingly sophisticated foreign government interventions in the American electoral process. The Trump-era investigations and public controversies have exposed many uncertainties and deficiencies in the laws governing how presidents and campaigns can interact with foreign governments. We propose three major reforms to meet these concerns.

Campaign Reporting of Foreign Government Political Contacts

Special Counsel Mueller found that "Russian-government-connected individuals and media entities began showing interest in Trump's campaign in the months after he announced his candidacy in June 2015."[38] As described, the Russians' intense interest included communication between the candidate's son and a correspondent who professed to speak for the Russian government in conveying its support of Trump and desire to help his campaign. The Trump campaign, however, never brought these contacts and communications to the attention of the Federal Bureau of Investigation (FBI). Indeed, candidate Trump publicly denied any special connection with or relationship to Russia.

A requirement that candidates or campaigns report contacts with foreign governments and their agents must be central to any reform program responding to the events of 2016. In 2019, Senator Mark Warner, the ranking Democrat on the Senate Select Committee on Intelligence, introduced a bill with one version of this requirement.[39] A candidate, "official, employee, or agent" of a federal political campaign would have to disclose to the campaign committee treasurer each "reportable foreign contact" with a foreign national or someone believed to be a foreign national, along with a "summary of the circumstances" of any such contact. Contacts subject to this reporting would include the making of a contribution or donation, or the "coordination or collaboration with, an offer or provision of information or services to or from, or persistent and repeated contact with a government of a foreign country or an agent thereof."

Under the Warner proposal, the campaign treasurer would have to notify the FEC, which within one week would make a report to the FBI. Each campaign committee would also have a *public* quarterly reporting obligation. The campaign would have to adopt, and the candidate would have to certify, establishment of a compliance policy that would be provided to campaign employees who, in turn, would have to certify receipt. The bill also contains "rules of construction" that state that the proposed legislation does not impose any "additional limitation" on the right of foreign nationals "to express political views or to participate in political discourse."

In concept, a reform of this kind serves key purposes. At a basic level, it strengthens the channels of information available to the government in tracking potential foreign electoral interventions like Russia's in 2016. It is good policy to deter candidates who may be open to and encourage foreign government support. The bill would not prohibit foreign contacts but would generate normative pressure and caution by requiring disclosure. Had there been such a law in 2016, Russians could have scheduled a meeting with the Trump campaign at Trump Tower and presented their views on Russia-America policy or their preference for the election of Donald Trump. The campaign could have "taken the meeting" but would have been required to disclose it.

The clear norm-reinforcing component is an important element of this approach. A campaign subject to this reporting requirement will pause to consider its policies on these contacts. It can be certain that any such contact will prompt press inquiries with demands for more detail than even the law requires about how the contact came about and whether substantive discussions ensued between the campaign and the foreign government. Opposing candidates will be quick to take up this line of questioning. A campaign will be under pressure to report contacts but not follow up on them, which would discourage a foreign government from further attempts (or from making them in the first place). Or in the event that the contact is benign—for example, the Belgian ambassador wishes to brief the campaign on European Union issues—a campaign might be more comfortable accepting the invitation and worry less about the political effects of disclosure.

The Warner bill is one of a number of conceivable reforms built around a notification structure. We believe that this is the right structure to respond to the core problem of a campaign's contact and potential collaboration with a supportive foreign power. But we would urge amendments to this structure in three significant ways.

First, the reform should clearly distinguish permissible policy communications with foreign governments from impermissible campaign interference. Foreign governments have an interest in the positions of anyone who may become president; they welcome the chance for introductions or meetings that afford opportunities to "get to know" the candidates or present concerns and interests of their government. They may well make an offer of information as they urge the candidate to fashion policy stances with due regard for all material facts about their soundness and consequences. Should these types of exchanges qualify as "reportable foreign contacts," campaigns may well be reluctant to engage in them for fear of damaging headlines and opposition attacks. It also does not seem an especially prudent or efficient use of law enforcement resources to report to the FBI a foreign government's communication with a campaign about its interest in the candidate's trade policy.

Moreover, American candidates burnish their own credentials in the national and foreign policy fields by inviting those discussions. It is not uncommon for major-party nominees to take trips overseas to meet with, and to be seen in serious discussion with, foreign policy leaders. Barack Obama did this in 2008, as did Mitt Romney in 2012. The law should protect this activity while subjecting to notification meetings or discussions for the purposes of sharing views on what the candidate would need to do to win—and how the foreign government could assist in that campaign objective.

The risk that should command attention is a foreign government's offer of campaign assistance—a direct intervention in the electoral process. In this chapter's last section, we note the importance of clarifying the application of the law barring foreign national electoral spending to the offer or provision of opposition research. In offering assistance of any kind in harming an opponent's prospects, the foreign government has engaged in what should be a prohibited electoral intervention.

Second, the Warner bill designates the FEC as the agency to be charged with enforcing the reporting requirement. By and large, its responsibilities would be ministerial, presenting relatively little risk that the partisan make-up of the commission, its membership split by statute between the two major parties, will affect the integrity of its enforcement responsibilities, as it has on other major issues. Nonetheless, there is some risk of politicized enforcement. This is another reason, as discussed previously, why we have proposed that the Justice Department handle this and other aspects of enforcement of reforms guarding against undue foreign state interference in elections.

The Justice Department possesses authority for the criminal enforcement of the campaign finance laws while the FEC possesses jurisdiction over civil enforcement. In 1977, the FEC and the Justice Department entered into a memorandum of understanding (MOU) to govern the management of their shared responsibilities. But the department has indicated that the MOU is no longer controlling and is overdue for reconsideration. There is considerable uncertainty, including major disagreement within the FEC, about how the concurrent authority should be exercised.[40] We propose that this issue be resolved, at least in part, by having the foreign national prohibitions revised and the Justice Department given primary authority for their interpretation and enforcement.

Apart from the poor match between the structure of the campaign finance laws and the objectives of reform in this area, the FEC has been unable to do much with even the tools at its disposal. Its enforcement of the federal campaign finance laws has come under severe and sustained criticism for ineffectiveness. To be fair, the Justice Department has been criticized in its own right for laxity in the administration of FARA, especially for failure to track and curb the development of loopholes through which organizations have engaged in activities that fall outside the reach of the statute. But the indictments filed in the Mueller investigation, coupled with other issues raised about the effectiveness of Justice Department enforcement, have apparently refocused the department on more vigorous enforcement of FARA's controls on foreign national initiatives to influence government policy and public opinion.[41] The growing problem of direct electoral interference is related, and the regulatory response is a natural one for the department to assume primary responsibility for.

The Justice Department would always have the authority to refer to the FEC matters more suitable for civil disposition. Given the high likelihood that foreign national–presidential campaign discussions of campaign activity will raise threshold questions of criminal liability more so than in routine campaign finance cases, we would see the department conducting the review of potential illegal activity in the first instance and determining whether civil or criminal process is more appropriate.

The department would also be the better choice for issuing advisory opinions on the application of the reforms to specific factual circumstances. In the case of all the reforms we propose, these questions will arise and U.S. citizens and organizations should be able to seek guidance. The FEC is now charged with issuing this guidance in the form of advisory opinions, but as a six-member agency whose appointees are split evenly between the two major political parties and often deadlock on major issues, it is not the most credible or reliable source of this guidance.

Conferring this enforcement responsibility on the Justice Department may serve a norm-reinforcing function. The FEC's reputation for partisan division and ineffectiveness too much precedes it. The agency's woes have been associated with the steady deterioration in the effectiveness of campaign finance laws and with aggressive legal risk-taking by political actors who wager that they can outmaneuver this civil enforcement authority or depend on commissioners affiliated with the same party to block or hinder enforcement. Lodging the lead authority in the Justice Department underscores the heightened commitment to compliance with this part of campaign finance law. It will give pause to affected political actors accustomed to lax regulation. Over time, this reformed enforcement regime may encourage more care in engaging in activities that raise these kinds of questions.

Third, we question the public reporting requirement. The disclosure to the FBI seems in tension with the public report. The agency's counter-intelligence function stands to be impaired by alerting the foreign interest to the U.S. government's investigative interest. Should it appear that the contacts indicate a foreign intervention, as in the case of Russia in 2016, the government should be the source of that disclosure after an assessment of the national security threat and the determination of whether specific action should be taken. The surfacing of a "foreign reportable contact" is highly prejudicial in the course of a presidential campaign, and it does not seem necessary or appropriate that the campaign make a public disclosure if the campaign has met its law enforcement reporting obligation and is assisting the law enforcement inquiry. The public reporting requirement sets in motion political currents and pressures that do not advance the public policy purposes of reform along these lines.

Finally, we note that as of June 2020, efforts to pass the Warner bill in the Senate had stalled. In that month, the sponsors sought to include it in a National Defense Authorization Act, but Republican opposition forced its removal as a condition of passage of the broader measure. One Republican senator had previously denounced it as a "blatant political stunt,"[42] earning her a Twitter commendation from President Trump, who dismissed the proposed bill as a "do-over on the Mueller Report."[43]

Prohibition of Campaign–Foreign State Political Alliances

The special counsel also considered whether any of the Trump campaign–Russia discussions or activities implicated the registration and reporting requirements of FARA.[44] Recall that FARA applies to the campaign or campaign-affiliated individuals who function as "agents" of a "foreign principal," such as the Russian government, if they engage in "political activities" within the United States. For purposes of this statute, political activities include:

> any activity that the person engaging in believes will, or that the person intends to, in any way influence any agency or official of the Government of the United States or any section of the public within the United States with reference to formulating, adopting, or changing the domestic or foreign policies of the United States or with reference to the political or public interests, policies, or relations of a government of a foreign country or a foreign political party.[45]

FARA has never been applied to a political alliance between a political candidate and a foreign power. Its definition of "political activities" does not expressly include any such collaboration or aim at activities intended to influence voters rather than the public more broadly, and the Justice Department has never interpreted it otherwise. FARA does include a requirement that a registered foreign agent include in the mandated public disclosures "any contributions of money or other things of value made by him during the preceding sixty days ... in connection with an election to any political office or in connection with any primary election, convention, or caucus held to select candidates for any political office."[46] Beyond this, the statute is not specifically concerned with campaign activity, and the engagement in such activity on behalf of the foreign principal is not a trigger for registration under the statute.

Moreover, a *reporting* requirement is an entirely inadequate answer to the danger of the relationship at issue in a president's or presidential candidate's solicitation and acceptance of electoral support from a foreign government. This danger calls for stronger medicine: a prohibition rather than mere disclosure.

The federal campaign finance law prohibition does not cover the kind of political alliance with which we are concerned here. As noted, it is concerned with direct, quantifiable foreign national spending to influence elections. As the Mueller Report demonstrated, it does not clearly, or without constitutional difficulties, reach problematic relationships between a candidate and a foreign national except where "a thing of value," judged with reference to the commercial market, passes between them. A different approach is required—one better tailored than either FARA or the FECA—to address the risks that became apparent in the 2016 election.

We propose amending and extending the scope of Section 219 of the U.S. criminal code, which currently prohibits, on pain of fine or jail, "public officials" from entering into a FARA reportable relationship.[47] This law as originally enacted in 1966 applied to an "officer or employee of the United States in the executive, legislative, or judicial branch of the Government."[48] In 1984, Congress amended the law to specify that it applied to "public officials" of the United States. The amendment defined "public officials" to include members of Congress as well as "an officer or employee or person acting on behalf of the United States ... in any official function." No legislative history explained the nature of the change, and the amendment did not on its face bring within the prohibition's scope the president, or a major-party candidate or nominee for president. In an opinion issued in 1987, the Justice Department's Office of Legal Counsel opined that the purpose of the law was to "bring Members of Congress within [Section 219's] prohibition" and to subject covered public officials to criminal penalties "[e]ssentially ... for conduct that would usually constitute a violation of the Emoluments Clause."[49] It suggested in this way that the statute was aimed at compensated agency relationships, prohibiting them altogether.

The Office of Legal Counsel provided no citation or analysis for its claim that Section 219 is an aid to enforcement of the Emoluments Clause,

and indeed, it acknowledged that Section 219 "is both broader and narrower than the Emoluments Clause itself."[50] By its terms, Section 219 goes
further than the Emoluments Clause and constitutes a prohibition on a
public official entering into an agency relationship that would otherwise
give rise, for all other U.S. citizens, to a FARA reporting obligation. As
such, it serves as a strong foundation on which to address, with appropriate revision, contacts between a candidate, or his or her campaign, and
a foreign national to collaborate in campaign-related conduct.

We propose to amend Section 219 to create a new tier of regulation
of agency relationships between U.S. persons, citizens, or organizations
and foreign nationals. Under FARA, a foreign principal's advancement
of its public policy or public relations goals through an agency relationship with a U.S. citizen or organization is permissible, but reportable,
except in the case of such a relationship with a public official, which is
prohibited. Section 219 as amended under our proposal would prohibit
any such relationship with public officials and presidential candidates
for the purpose of influencing an election. The aim is to ban any case
where a presidential campaign and foreign nationals communicate in
the service of their mutual goal of seeing the candidate elected.

The amendments we propose would include in principal part:

- Presidents would be specifically identified as "public officials"
  subject to the statute, and the category of persons covered by
  the law would be expanded beyond "public officials" to include
  presidential candidates, including independent candidates for
  the office in the general election, and the campaign organizations
  acting on their behalf.

- For purposes of Section 219 as it applies to "public officials" and
  (with the amendment we propose) presidential candidates, the
  FARA definitions of "agent," a foreign principal's "request" for
  political activity, and "political activity" would each be revised
  as follows:

  - A candidate or the candidate's campaign organization becomes
    an "agent" of the foreign principal upon agreeing to a foreign
    national's specific and unambiguous request for collaboration

in political activities. We take the view that the foreign national offering to support a candidate is aiding the campaign but also promoting its own interest. By collaborating with the foreign national, the campaign is serving its own and the foreign national's purposes. So, in this context, the candidate would be deemed under the reformed law to be an "agent" of the foreign principal.

- A "request" of a "foreign principal" subject to the reformed statute would include any such offer of support or proposal for cooperation or action in concert to conduct political activities.

- An agent's "political activities" would be defined to reach "communications, actions or agreements with a foreign principal for the purpose of influencing any election to federal, state, or local office."

- The public official, candidate, or candidate's campaign organization would be barred from soliciting these "political activities" from the foreign national.

The application of this reform to the Trump Tower case illustrates how this reform would work. The Russians informed the Trump campaign that the Russian government supported Trump's election and would come to the United States with an offer of opposition research to use against Hillary Clinton. Under a revised Section 219, this would have constituted a specific and unambiguous "request" for cooperation or action in concert to conduct election-related "political activities." Once the Trump campaign had acceded to the request, it would have entered into a prohibited agency relationship subject to criminal penalties. The statute as reformed would also apply in this situation if the Trump campaign had in the first instance solicited this support. Whether the candidate would share personally in the liability would depend on evidence of his or her knowing involvement.

Our proposal would make illegal not just the Trump Tower episode. It would ban and criminalize *any* relationship between foreign states and their agents, on the one hand, and public officials (including the president) and presidential candidates, on the other, for the purpose of

influencing an election. For example, Section 219 would make criminal
the Nixon campaign's 1968 engagement with the government of South
Vietnam, discussed earlier. It would prohibit a candidate or his or her
campaign from engaging with a foreign government in a discussion of
how it could encourage U.S. communities with strong heritage identifi-
cation with the foreign country to turn out to vote for that candidate. It
would similarly bar a candidate's or campaign's planning with a foreign
national to organize a program of public communications through the
internet from overseas, anonymized accounts to distribute messages
consistent with the campaign's themes and issue priorities.

FECA contains reasonable exceptions to the foreign national electioneering prohibition that could be preserved under our proposal. Individual
foreign nationals may now personally volunteer time to a campaign, so
long as they do not raise money for the campaign or participate in determining how the campaign's funds are spent. For example, an exchange
student from France could participate in a neighborhood canvass, helping
to distribute campaign literature. Moreover, a campaign may purchase
campaign-related materials from foreign commercial firms, subject to
the requirement that it pay "the usual and normal charge" for the good
and service, which is defined as the prevailing "commercially reasonable
rate."[51] These and similarly limited foreign national involvement in U.S.
political campaigns would be allowed to continue under our proposed
reforms, which are focused on prohibiting agreements between campaigns
and foreign actors, such as foreign states, to collaborate in their mutual
interest to influence an election.

"Things of Value" Provided by a
Foreign Power to a Campaign

Special Counsel Mueller determined that the federal campaign finance
laws did not clearly capture information, such as opposition research,
that a foreign government might offer to a presidential campaign. He
acknowledged the breadth of the definition of contribution—"a thing of
value"—and of the basis in FEC rulings for treating opposition research
as such a contribution "in-kind." At the same time, he noted that there
was no judicial precedent on this issue, which he seemed to relate to
the unresolved constitutional questions about when an exchange of

information was a regulable contribution rather than First Amendment protected. Mueller expressed concern that an expansive reading of the law on this issue could bleed into a constitutionally troubling criminalization of information-sharing between a U.S. campaign and a U.S. citizen.[52]

The issue requires attention because there is no reason to believe that a foreign government embarking on interference in a U.S. election would not resort in the future to the same means of supporting its favored U.S. campaign. Most conventional opposition research is not of the kind that a foreign government possesses special advantages in producing. But, as documented at length in the Mueller Report and related indictments, a foreign government is in a position to do what the Russians did—deploy its intelligence or diplomatic services to extract information through hacking or other programs that a U.S. campaign would not have a legal means of obtaining on its own. Therein lies the foreign power's comparative advantage in the opposition research market. Moreover, as Mueller noted, "A foreign entity that engaged in [opposition] research and provided resulting information to a campaign could exert a greater effect on an election, and a greater tendency to ingratiate the donor to the candidate, than a gift of money or tangible things of value."[53]

We propose a reform that addresses the problem without risking the spillover effect on U.S. citizens and purely domestic politics that concerned Mueller. This could be accomplished by amending only that portion of FECA that bans contributions from foreign nationals,[54] and clarifying that a "thing of value" extends to services and materials that may not have a clearly identified market value but that a campaign deems useful. The law could define a foreign national contribution of a "thing of value" to include any "information, whether provided orally or in writing, that a foreign government or political party (or any person acting on their behalf) provides to a candidate or authorized committee, or to the officers, employees, or agents of such a committee, for the express purpose and intended use of promoting the election or defeat of any clearly identified candidate." The reformed law would prohibit a candidate, a campaign, or the campaign's agents, from soliciting such a prohibited contribution from a foreign national.

★

FINANCIAL CONFLICTS
OF INTEREST

During Donald Trump's 2016 presidential campaign, he had much to say about the success of his private business and the wealth he earned from it. On the night of the Michigan and Mississippi primaries, March 9, he famously used his prime-time cable coverage to lay out for the audience samples of various Trump products. "I built a great, great company," he proclaimed. "You have the water. You have the steaks. You have the wines and all of that."[1] As unorthodox as this primary-night product promotion was, Trump was then just a candidate who held no office. Upon his election, he pledged to separate from his business and put his Trump Organization assets into an independently administered trust.

By the fourth year of his term, however, Trump "accomplished something no president before him has done: fusing his private business interests with America's highest office."[2] Up to that point, "he has spent one out of every three days as president visiting one of his luxury resorts, hotels or golf courses. He has leveraged his powerful international platform to promote his developments dozens of times. And he has directed millions of dollars from U.S. taxpayers to his businesses around the globe." Trump also continued to promote his properties, as he did when he tweeted in March 2019 that he was "[v]ery proud of perhaps the greatest golf course anywhere in the world": the Trump International Golf Links in Aberdeen, Scotland.[3] "Also, furthers the U.K. relationship!"

he added, highlighting how openly he connected this business interest to this presidency.

In this chapter, we focus on Trump's extraordinary mingling of presidential duties with his personal business interests. This practice has highlighted a range of inadequacies in the regulation of and accountability for presidential conflicts of interest, and it has demonstrated the need for comprehensive reform to achieve the complete separation of a president from his or her private business.

BACKGROUND

Congress in 1989 clarified that presidents and vice presidents are exempt from the core financial conflict-of-interest statutes, which set out divestiture and blind trust requirements for senior executive branch appointees.[4] The exemption was justified on the theory that, because presidents and vice presidents must discharge their constitutional responsibilities, they cannot be held to remedial measures such as "recusals" that are appropriate for appointed officials. The Department of Justice had embraced this theory fifteen years earlier in suggesting that any presidential or vice presidential conflict-of-interest requirements might constitute an impermissible addition to the qualifications to hold office specified in the Constitution.[5]

This regime left it to the public and the political process to monitor whether a president carried out his or her duties with an ethical focus on the public interest. Over a number of presidencies, these forces shaped what appeared to be a durable norm. As Daphna Renan has noted, presidents "long complied with a structural norm pursuant to which the President conducts himself as if bound by those statutory [conflict of interest] restrictions."[6] The power of the norm was evident in advice that presidents received from within the executive branch. In an opinion issued by the Office of Legal Counsel in the Ford administration, then–Assistant Attorney General Antonin Scalia affirmed that the president was not subject to executive orders and regulations governing financial conflicts. He noted, however, that "it would obviously be undesirable as a matter of policy for the President or Vice President to engage in conduct" proscribed by the rules, "where no special reason for exemption from the generally applicable standards exists."[7]

Until Barack Obama, every president since Dwight Eisenhower had established a blind trust for financial holdings to prevent a risk of conflict.[8] Obama did not set up one because he maintained his relatively uncomplicated financial interests exclusively in mutual funds and bank accounts. There was, to be sure, variation in the stringency of the trust arrangements that presidents established. Lyndon Johnson appointed "two business associates and family friends" as trustees for the purportedly independent management of radio and television facilities. One of the trustees was the executive director of the broadcasting stations, which meant that "Johnson must have had some degree of comfort that the trustees would not sell his interests."[9] Jimmy Carter specified in his trust that the trustees could not sell his share of a family farm.

In the wake of Watergate, Congress passed the Ethics in Government Act of 1978, which subjected the president to a statutory transparency requirement as a check on conflicts of interest.[10] Along with other senior executive branch officials and members of Congress, the president would be required to comply with annual public reporting of financial holdings. These "personal financial disclosure" reports make public, within broad ranges, sources of income, assets, and liabilities. This reporting is limited in scope and detail and does not require information about closely or privately held entities in which the president would have a significant financial interest. A law enacted in 2012 required the financial disclosures of the highest officials in the executive branch, including the president, to be posted on the internet for public viewing.[11]

These financial reporting requirements are not associated with any more substantive obligations. If a president's report reflects holdings or transactions that may pose conflict-of-interest questions, the president answers for them to the public, and perhaps to Congress in response to oversight or investigative inquiries. But there are no further legal requirements, or consequences. Presidents thus set their own conflict-of-interest standards. What they choose to do depends on their understanding of and sensitivity to long-standing norms, and to the political pressures of the moment.

The Domestic and Foreign Emoluments Clauses place constitutional prohibitions on the president's or other federal officials' receipt of compensation, gifts, or other financial benefits. The Domestic Emoluments Clause, found in Article II, Section 1, of the U.S. Constitution, states that the president "shall not receive" emoluments from "the United States or any of them."[12] The Foreign Emoluments Clause, found in Article I, Section 9, is written in the passive voice and does not specifically reference the president. Instead, it provides that "no Person holding any Office of Profit or Trust under them, shall, without the Consent of the Congress, accept of any present, Emolument, Office, or Title, of any kind whatever, from any King, Prince, or foreign State."[13] There is disagreement, as yet unresolved by the Supreme Court, whether this provision applies to elected federal officials, including the president.

However, Congress assumed that the Foreign Emoluments Clause applies to the president when it exercised its power to "consent" to foreign "emoluments" in the Foreign Gifts and Decorations Act of 1966. That statute specifically applies to the president and supplies congressional consent for gifts of "minimal value" that might be received in the course of hospitality provided by a foreign government or official.[14] Congress has also provided this consent to allow retired members of the uniformed services to accept compensation for employment by foreign states, subject to the further condition that any such employment is approved by the secretary of the relevant branch of the armed forces and the secretary of state.[15] In each case, Congress implicitly found that the gifts or compensation may or do constitute "emoluments," but by express "consent" it has removed the receipt of these benefits from the strictures of the clause.

THE TRUMP TRUST

A few weeks after he became president, Trump pledged to abide by conflict-of-interest norms. "While I am not mandated to do this under the law, I feel it is visually important, as President, to in no way have a conflict of interest with my various businesses," he tweeted. Trump added that "legal documents are being crafted which take me completely out of business operations."[16]

Yet Trump would take "visual" appearances only so far. A little over a week before Trump became president, his lawyer, Sheri Dillon, explained the legal structure that Trump would use to address the matter. Dillon insisted that Trump embraced the spirit of the norm that had prevailed for decades. "President-elect Trump wants the American public to rest

assured that all of his efforts are directed to pursuing the people's business and not his own," she said.[17] But Trump did not divest any of his
assets. And unlike every other president since the 1950s who had complex
business arrangements, he declined to establish a blind trust. Rather, he
simply rolled his interests into a trust managed by his son Eric and the
chief financial officer of the Trump Organization.

Dillon argued that a more stringent blind trust or divestiture strategy,
which was not legally required, would present costly complexities and
subject the president's "massive" business "empire" to unjustified and
draconian financial losses. But she pledged that the structure Trump
established would "completely isolate" him from the management of
his company with "sharply limited … rights" to information only in the
aggregate about how his business was faring.

Dillon also addressed the restrictions applicable to Trump under the
Foreign and Domestic Emoluments Clauses of the U.S. Constitution. She
maintained that only the receipt of income from services provided as a
consequence of his officeholding would run afoul of the constitutional
provisions. Trump was free, Dillon argued, to benefit from "fair value
exchanges that have absolutely nothing to do with an officeholder."
But Dillon announced that to address any issue of appearances, the
president-elect would commit to the voluntary donation to the U.S.
Treasury of profits to his business interests from foreign government
sources. Presumably on this basis, Trump would not seek Congress's
consent to their acceptance in the first instance.

Dillon also announced that in addition to Trump's "complete isolation"
from management, he would build into the trust structure procedures for
screening conflict-of-interest problems. The Trump Organization would
establish the position of "chief compliance counsel" charged with assisting the firm to prevent "any actions that could be perceived as exploiting
the office of the presidency." In addition, an independent ethics adviser
would review all new proposed transactions for any conflict issues.

The ethics adviser subsequently appointed to the position, Bobby
Burchfield, described four vetting standards that he would apply:

- The transaction would have to be "in the regular course of business and/or at fair value."

- Any party to a transaction with the Trump Organization would have to be an "entity of repute" scrutinized as a "real party in interest" with legitimate sources of funding.

- There could be no indication that the parties, or the Trump business, were seeking to enter into a "sweetheart deal" influenced by the president's official position. This would require "looking beyond just the value of the deal" for any suggestion of an intent to exploit the power of the presidency for commercial gain.

- There could be no prospect that the transaction would "embarrass or diminish the President or the Presidency."

Through the application of these standards, the ethics adviser would either disapprove transactions or identify issues that, as a condition of entering into a deal, the Trump Organization would have to address and resolve.[18]

The president's supposedly complete isolation from management did not mean he would eschew business income to meet his daily and other expenses. During the 2016 campaign, Trump announced that he would not accept the compensation provided by statute for the president: "The first thing I'm going to do is tell you that if I'm elected president, I'm accepting no salary, OK? That's no big deal for me."[19] He repeated the pledge after he was elected and stated that he would return his salary to the United States and target the repayments to different agencies that would then have the benefit of the funds. To meet his expenses, the president decided to call on personal resources held in trust. A revision of the trust in February 2019 provided Trump a right of withdrawal on request and bound the trust to supply him with support for "maintenance, support or uninsured medical expenses."[20] The law governing trusts generally treats "maintenance expenses" as those required to keep up an "accustomed manner of living"—that is, the normal costs of living typically incurred by the particular trust beneficiary.[21]

In short, Trump switched his government-paid salary for access to trust funds to meet his living expenses. He was making what he evidently believed to be the political point that he was a successful, wealthy businessman who did not need taxpayer support and could magnanimously return to the American people the money he did not take. But this rearrangement of his finances while in office raised again the question of how much attention the president would pay to private business interests now tied directly to the payment of his day-to-day living expenses.

On a formal level, Trump and his advisers had laid claim to a "limited right" to information about the performance of his businesses that would consist of a quarterly briefing from his son Eric, who would serve as the co-chair of the trust advisory committee.[22] But there have always been indications that Trump would remain apprised more closely of the state of his business in other, informal ways. In 2017, the director of revenue management for the Trump International Hotel in Washington, D.C., wrote an email, later leaked, in which he noted that the president had asked him for an assessment of the business. "DJT is supposed to be out of his business and passed on to his sons, but he's definitely still involved …. I had a brief meeting with him a few weeks ago, and he was asking about banquet revenues and demographics."[23] The hotel denied that the conversation ever took place and insisted that the email reflected nothing more than the employee's wish to inflate his own importance.

But by 2020, the *Wall Street Journal* would report that the president did in fact keep a "close" watch on the operation of his business.[24] The president was involved in "regularly" questioning employees on how the business was running, wishing to keep his son Eric "on his toes." Trump was also reportedly critical of Eric's "handling of scrutiny from federal and state investigators, who have probed matters at the Trump Organization and the Trump Foundation"—but any such judgment of his son's performance would be possible only if the president had access to information about how his son was managing this legal scrutiny.

Though the public has little additional detail about the quarterly briefings and whether Trump was pursuing other channels of information about his business, the president was open about his desire to stay publicly associated with his properties. He made regular visits to his golf properties in the United States and in Scotland. Organizations tracked the visits and reported that, as of May 15, 2020, Trump visited his golf properties at least 245 times.[25] The president kept up this practice in the face of criticism that he appeared to be promoting his business. Meanwhile, Trump properties, especially the hotel down the street from the White House, attracted customers from foreign governments and interests, and from domestic groups with interests in government policy. It also attracted Attorney General William Barr, who personally paid $30,000 to have a 200-person holiday party at the hotel in December 2019.

The president has answered concerns about these arrangements by denying that his incumbency was a boon to his business interests. His hotel probably drew clientele seeking to find favor, or to avoid giving offense, by staying there on business affairs that involve the administration. But the Trump brand name could also have driven away customers unwilling to associate with his controversial policies and statements. Trump has made just this claim as proof of the significant sacrifice he made in giving up his business career for public office. "This thing [the presidency] is costing me a fortune," he has claimed.[26]

In one respect, Trump's properties did benefit from a specific clientele whose business payments for bookings and services could be tracked. The Secret Service released records showing that, as of March 2020, the Trump organization had charged the Secret Service more than $628,000. The Mar-a-Lago resort property in Palm Beach, Florida, charged a nightly rate of $396.15. At the Trump National Golf Club in Bedminster, New Jersey, the Secret Service rented a cottage on site for its operations for $17,000 a month for the summer of 2018 and part of the following summer as well. The *Washington Post* reported that this rental charge was "unusually high for homes in the area."[27] Eric Trump, now managing the Trump Organization along with his brother Donald, Jr., had previously told the press that the company would charge the Secret Service only the "cost of housekeeping," which he cited as being on the order of "50 bucks."

Of course, the Secret Service payments did not represent a major windfall for the Trump Organization, even if the aggregate payments over the first three and a half years of Trump's presidency were not negligible. But the net financial effect of the presidency on Trump's personal fortune is immaterial. An assessment of the risk of serious conflicts of interest does not rest on an accounting of profits and losses. That there is even an argument about the personal profitability of Trump's presidency is a problem. A president should not be in the position of arguing the point one way or the other. The involvement of a president with an ongoing business, thriving or faltering, always raises the question of whether public power has advanced—or is available as required to advance—personal interests.

The questions raised by Trump's business interests are not limited to how much he stands to gain, but also how much those interests might subject him to other pressures. Trump had long boasted that he was a master of high leverage: "the king of debt."[28] In 2020, the significance of this indebtedness drew particular scrutiny when the press reported that one of the New York commercial real estate properties in which the Trump Organization held a 30 percent interest owed $211 million on loans from the Bank of China. The bank disputed the report, claiming that it had sold off its interest in the loan shortly after it was made. However, records on file with the state of New York indicate that, in 2017, the bank still retained a secured creditor's interest in the property's fixtures. Once again, the bank insisted that the list was a "technical error."[29] Whatever the facts of this particular property and its creditors, the episode illustrated another facet of the conflict-of-interest questions presented by Trump's active business interests.

When the president's trust arrangement was first announced, it attracted opposition within the executive branch. The Office of Government Ethics (OGE) pushed Trump to follow the norm of abiding by the same standards as his executive branch subordinates. In January 2017, the OGE director, Walter Shaub, stated that "it's been the consistent policy of the executive branch that the President should act as though the financial conflict of interest law applied."[30] Trump's lawyers would later question the historical basis for this claim. They pointed out, for example, that President Carter arranged for a close personal associate to be appointed as trustee, not someone who would have met the standard for a trustee's independence under federal statutory conflict law. But Shaub believed that Trump's revocable trust arrangement lacked any of the material features of a blind trust. "It's not even close," he said. The president's quarterly briefings were among the reasons that the trust lacked meaningful protective features. "There's not supposed to be any information at all," Shaub noted. Shaub also disagreed that divestiture was unworkable and noted that prior presidents had made financial sacrifices. Trump stood his ground, and Shaub left the government.

Congress could have intervened with oversight and by exercising its authority to explicitly withhold "consent" for income from any foreign state sources received into the Trump trust. When controlling both chambers until January 2019, Republicans were not receptive to inquiries into the president's business arrangements. Democrats attempted to take matters into their own hands. In 2018, 200 Democratic members of the House and the Senate sought judicial intervention to require the president to seek congressional consent. The U.S. District Court for the District of Columbia ruled that the members had standing to bring the suit. The court also agreed with them that an "emolument" was on the broadest construction any "profit," "gain," "benefit," or "advantage," and not, as the president's lawyers argued, only "profit arising from an official's services rendered pursuant to an office or employ."[31] In February 2020, however, the U.S. Court of Appeals for the D.C. Circuit ruled that the members of Congress "lack standing to assert the institutional interests of a legislature" and dismissed the case.[32]

After the Democrats won the House majority in the 2018 midterm elections, they did not investigate the Trump trust structure or assert that the Trump trust's receipt of income from foreign state sources required advance congressional "consent." They focused instead on alleged violations in the operation of the trust. Several House committees investigated whether groups, "including at least one foreign government," attempted to curry favor with Trump by booking rooms at his hotels but never staying in them.[33] They also looked into alleged irregularities in the Trump Organization's leasing arrangement with the General Services Administration for the Trump International Hotel in Washington, D.C. The House Oversight and Judiciary committees announced an investigation into military stays at a Trump-owned property in Turnberry, Scotland, and substantial increases in military refueling at a nearby airport after Trump won the election.

Some members of Congress called for the House to take action more broadly based on its "consent" authority under the Foreign Emoluments Clause. They argued for a resolution declaring that that payments to Trump businesses from foreign governments are "emoluments" and that the House does not consent to their receipt. Congress did not pass any such resolution, and the House Judiciary Committee did not include an emoluments charge in the articles of impeachment that the House subsequently approved on December 18, 2019. It was reported that the House leadership was concerned that any specific action on the Emoluments Clause issue would undermine the pending lawsuit filed by individual lawmakers.

President Trump appeared unfazed by these events. On October 17, 2019, he announced that the next G-7 summit would be hosted at the Trump National Doral Miami resort. However, two days later, Trump reversed course. He claimed in a tweet that he did so because "the Hostile Media & their Democrat Partners went CRAZY!"[34] But news reports suggested that Trump's decision was driven by Republican lawmakers critical of the move and the notable absence in Fox News coverage of a vigorous defense of his position.

Trump did not express legal concerns about the arrangement. Yet had the president proceeded, the substantial government contract with his company would have raised issues under both Emoluments Clauses even if, as he proclaimed, the rooms were provided "at cost." Commentators noted that the hosting of a major international event at Doral would have generated an abundance of publicity helpful to the attraction of business and profits in the future. Moreover, providing the rooms and accommodations at cost did not mean that guests would not make other profitable purchases, such as for food and drink. And the "at cost" expenditures during the Florida off-season could have reduced aggregate overhead costs. The term "at cost" is also ambiguous because it likely would not include separate allocations for the additional personnel required to work during that time or for any renovations or other spending to prepare for the event.

And yet Trump and those Republicans urging him to retreat from the plans for the Doral summit seemed moved more by the worry bluntly described by Acting White House Chief of Staff Mick Mulvaney: "people think it looks lousy."[35] It seems that the norm rather than constitutional law threw the president on the defensive and forced him to reconsider and reverse his decision. For all of Donald Trump's brazen norm-busting, this norm turned out to have bite, at least in this one context. And yet it is hard to assess the broader significance of the episode, since without the impeachment that was pending at the time, congressional Republicans might have reacted less strongly to the proposed Doral summit. But whatever might have happened in different circumstances, it is clear that the president's own party concluded that in this instance he had gone too far.

By spring 2020, Trump continued to fend off political and legal challenges to his retention of active private business interests—interests that he was to some extent overseeing and promoting—while in office. He might have lost the Doral battle, but he seemed to be winning the war over his unique "trust" arrangement. The norms in effect for the modern presidency for more than a half-century proved generally ineffective in preventing both the appearance and the reality of a president mixing interests of personal profit with public duties.

Then came the coronavirus pandemic, which led Congress to address Trump business–related conflict-of-interest issues unique to the extraordinary circumstances. In providing emergency relief to businesses devastated by the national lockdown, it barred the president's commercial enterprises from participating in the benefits made available through "stimulus" legislation. The CARES Act, passed in March 2020, excluded them from the class of businesses eligible for loans, loan guarantees, or other investments. This disqualification applied to any business in which the president and his children held, "directly or indirectly[,] … a controlling interest.[36] The law also applied to the vice president, heads of executive departments, and members of Congress, but it was clear that congressional Democrats had pressed for the provision to close off access to emergency public funding for Trump businesses. "Democrats and other critics of the president were concerned that Trump's businesses would receive bailout money because the tourism industry is one of the hardest hit by the coronavirus."[37]

The coronavirus emergency highlighted the conflicts issues in other ways. Under the catastrophic conditions facing the hospitality industry, the Trump Organization sought to renegotiate the terms of its lease with the General Services Administration for the property occupied by the Trump International Hotel in Washington, D.C. Eric Trump stressed that the relief sought was only temporary and that he and his brother wished only to have the federal government "treat us the same" as other federal tenants.[38] Of course, these requests for relief were being directed to agencies that answer, ultimately, to the president. The Trump Organization also sought to alleviate the economic stresses generated by the pandemic by seeking the postponement of payments on loans owed to Deutsche Bank—which was reportedly under an ongoing federal investigation.

It was possible that, in this situation, Trump's interests would be addressed on fair, arms-length terms, no different from others. But it was more reasonable to assume that those on the other side of the negotiating table would *not*, in Eric Trump's words, "treat us the same." An official of Palm Beach County pithily noted the problem when expressing anxiety about the Trump Organization's request for relief from the lease payment schedule for the Trump International Golf Club. If the county failed to grant the Trump interests the desired terms, it "could anger the president and lose out on federal assistance" in the coronavirus emergency.

REFORM

However inadequate in the judgment of critics, Trump's revocable trust arrangement demonstrates that even he was unwilling to declare himself free of all ethically grounded conflict-of-interest limits in the pursuit of private business interests. Like the Doral episode, this suggests a norm with at least enough bite that Trump was prepared to pay it lip service.

The norm has two components that each require attention in thinking about reform. First, the presidency is a full-time job that is not compatible with other professional or business commitments. Presidents are expected to live in government-supplied housing and to receive support by government-supplied staff, and they may not decline round-the-clock Secret Service protection. They owe all of their energies to the conduct of the presidency. Second, this full-time commitment guards against the threat that other commitments or interests could interfere with or conflict with presidents' discharge of their responsibilities solely in the public interest. Both components operate together to limit presidents to the business of the nation, not their own. Enforcement of the norm requires attention to passive as well as actively pursued investments or other financial interests that could undermine public confidence in the president's integrity and impartiality.

Trump's discretionary trust arrangement insufficiently protects this interest in a full-time president with appropriate checks on potential financial conflicts of interest. The inadequacies fall into two categories: the failure of the structure to "completely isolate" the president from active involvement with his business, and a lack of transparency about its operation.

The ethics screening process the president and his advisers devised contemplates prior approvals of any "new deals," while allowing the adviser to work with company management to resolve identified issues and permit those deals to progress. The president's lawyer claimed that the trust provides for appointment of the adviser to the senior management team; but neither Trump nor his legal advisers have provided details about how this arrangement works in practice. The outside ethics adviser has spoken about the standards that he claimed to apply, which are sweeping in scope. But, citing the attorney-client privilege, he has declined to be more specific about transactions that may have posed issues he was required to address. The result is an entirely privatized arrangement that purports to address important public concerns without any formal public accountability.

Congress could request information on a voluntary basis or seek it through compulsory process, on a case-by-case basis or on a set schedule, such as annually. In other words, it could subject the more or less privatized arrangement to public monitoring. A president could resist it, however, by arguing that if the president is exempt from statutory conflict-of-interest requirements, Congress has only the most limited legitimate need for the information and must demonstrate this need with each request. In this and related contexts, including tax disclosure, which we discuss in Chapter Four, Trump has tried to carve out a broad zone of immunity against congressional inquiry. There is no reason to assume that he will be the last president to adopt this position.

The net effect of this state of affairs is to drive Congress toward inquiries into reported instances of specific wrongdoing. A hint of scandal becomes the opening for the demand for presidential accountability and strengthens Congress's hand in conducting oversight or the basis for impeachment. But this means that presidential conflicts of interest are investigated, not regulated. The result is a scattershot rather than systematic treatment of conflict issues. And the partisan setting in which these issues are often raised and investigated can distort the congressional debate and weaken the prospects for a bipartisan resolution. Moreover, the presidency itself is hobbled by the onset of scandal and associated investigations. More comprehensive and effective regulation of financial conflicts would limit the incidence and costs of these controversies.

Relatedly, and especially in the polarized politics of our time, the extent to which Congress is motivated to inquire likely depends on which of the parties commands the majority at any one time. A president's party is not a reliable inquisitor. The reluctance of parties to police their own is a feature of hard-core contemporary partisanship: Neither party wants to open up lines of attack for the opposition. Such viral partisanship also typically means that the president's accusers will claim that the other party's presidential conflict-of-interest charges are motivated by partisanship. The more evident that motivation, the more certain it is that the president's allies will resist.

Absent more detailed legal regulation to achieve transparency, it cannot be expected that self-regulation, which is essentially what Trump has offered, will be open for adequate public review. The president's lawyers setting up the discretionary trust arrangement claimed that it would protect against actual or apparent conflicts, but as operated it simply does not accomplish even the minimal requirement of preventing apparent conflicts. The president meets regularly with his son Eric, who is one of the co-trustees, to discuss the business and to receive reports on how it is faring, and the press reports that he also seeks out information from company employees. In this respect he is not in fact "completely isolated" from the management of the business, and he certainly does not appear to be. Any regular briefing that he receives is an opportunity for him to express an opinion about some aspect of his business's operation.

The president's regular presence at his commercial properties also presents obvious appearances of conflicts of interest. A president has the widest choice of venues for any meeting or public appearance. Trump's regular visits to his golfing and resort properties may be consistent with or further the commercial interests of those properties. And since the president, who styles himself a savvy businessman, must be aware of the potential promotional impact of his appearances, he is vulnerable to the entirely reasonable suspicion that this is his intent.

In light of these deficiencies in the Trump trust arrangement, and the failure of norms to do adequate work, we propose the following reforms.

A Ban on Presidential Participation in a Business Interest

The president should not be able to maintain an active or supervisory role in the oversight of any businesses in which he or she has an interest on the day he or she takes the oath of office. The president should be barred from serving as an officer or director of any such business, and should not have a direct or indirect, formal or informal, consultative or advisory role, including any right or arrangement by which he or she has access to information about the business interests not available to the general public. The restriction would apply to the president's solicitation of third-party support for a business interest, such as a meeting with a potential investor. We propose that the president be required to certify annually, subject to criminal penalties for false statements, that he or she has met these requirements. The certification could be made in connection with the filing of his or her personal financial disclosure reporting under the Ethics in Government Act.

A reform structured with these features would prevent a president, like Trump, from skirting the "complete isolation" standard that he articulated but did not satisfy. Under this rule, Trump would not have been able to meet with his son, or any other trust personnel, for private briefings. He could not have communicated formally or informally, as news reports indicate that he did, with employees or staff involved in his business interests. The president would have to rely on public data only. In sum, the president could draw on income held in a trust. He or she could not, however, manage or oversee directly or indirectly the management of his or her assets. The key to enforcing this set of restrictions is the certification the president would be required to make.

Because the president would have no advisory or consultative role, he or she could not be required to report in detail on the assets, liabilities, and identities of those holding interests in the businesses in which he or she has a significant or substantial financial stake. He or he should have no access to the information necessary to meet a reporting requirement. However, once the president had identified his or her business interests, *the businesses* should have this disclosure requirement, which would be satisfied through a filing with the OGE and posted publicly to its website.

A Ban on Presidential "Blind Trusts"

The House of Representatives passed a reform bill in 2019, H.R. 1, that would have amended the Ethics in Government Act to require that the president make a choice.[39] He could either (1) divest himself of assets, transferring them to cash or to investments that pose only a remote or inconsequential threat of a conflict; (2) place business and personal assets in a diversified or blind trust; or (3) report more extensively on his financial interests. We do not favor this approach.

First, this bill is a step too far in the direction of Congress ordering the president's finances. The first option, divestiture, is really no option at all for many potential presidents. Divestiture would harshly penalize presidents with wealth from serving (and thus deter them from running in the first place) and is a step that, once taken, sets a precedent that could lead to abuse. Congress has no legitimate interest in the president's wealth or far-flung business interests per se. The issue of concern, rather, is the president's pursuit of business interests while in office, and his dependence on private funding for personal expenses, that generates the greatest risks of conflicts of interest that Congress should appropriately act to prevent.

Second, to achieve the satisfaction of core transparency interests in relation to a president's ongoing business interests, the president should *not* have the option of using a "blind trust" arrangement. Congress and the public should have visibility into the financial affairs and business associates of any firm, partnership, LLC, or other entity in which the president has a significant financial interest. We favor this full transparency in addition to strong controls, subject to severe penalties for their violation, on a president's involvement in the direction of his financial affairs.

A blind trust separates the president from the management of assets while affording privacy. But it also means that the public is denied access to information about how investment and other financial decisions are made. The trust is obligated to report only total value, not underlying assets. A blind trust strategy also depends on the president's scrupulous avoidance of informal channels of information about his financial interests. By definition, the corrupt (or corruptible) president is not reliably scrupulous.

In our view, the businesses in which the president has such an interest should have to report publicly those interests, including the name of persons with interests in the firm or other entity, and the value of assets and liabilities. This transparency invites scrutiny of any apparent tie between official policy and personal gain by the public, by press and watchdog groups, and by Congress. It allows for the detection of suspicious patterns in the trust's investment strategies and for questions to be asked that the president or trust representatives would be under pressure to answer.

This public checking function also limits the potential for abuse of office even if the president has not directed an investment decision. A president has the option of liquidating investments and holdings and reinvesting the proceeds in noncontroversial diversified mutual funds. By choosing instead to maintain his investments in a trust, a president can potentially benefit from a wide range of possible investments directly or indirectly affected by government actions. A trustee without any direction could choose to steer assets to investments that have become more attractive as a result of an administration's regulatory or legislative actions or proposals. Imagine, for example, a president who advocates defense buildup and whose trust then invests heavily in defense contractors, or an environment-friendly president whose trust invests in clean energy firms. In myriad ways, the president's actions and initiatives shape or influence the market and, therefore, the choices open to the trustee to maximize the president's wealth.

A president's financial representatives are free to pursue an active, even aggressive, wealth management strategy, but it is best that the public has the information necessary to detect or evaluate any connection between his official duties and personal business interests. While a president may direct a blind trust to avoid investments of certain kinds—for example, in munitions or tobacco—he cannot so restrict the scope of the trust's activities that it can avoid all questions about the relationship between official actions and financial returns. Having decided to remain active in the market and to run that risk, a president is fairly held to the strictest standard of transparency. Coupled with a stringent prohibition on any consultative or advisory role in the management of the trust, this transparency seems indispensable in addressing the risks of evasion and enhancing public confidence.

Prohibition of a President's "Rejection" of a Government Salary

A more straightforward but modest reform to shore up the expectation that the president works only for the public is a prohibition on a president's ability to "decline" his or her statutory government salary. This salary is meant to compensate for a full-time position as president, and the president's acceptance of the salary is one important way he or she expresses recognition of this commitment. Of course, the president, like any other taxpayer, may choose to donate his or her salary to charity. But the law should be changed to deter any personal or political advantage from doing so. It should be amended to deny him or her any deduction. And the president should be further prohibited from donating portions of his or her salary, as Trump has done, to federal agencies.

At present a president's rejection of his or her salary is political showmanship. He or she accomplishes nothing for the operation of the government, such as reducing the deficit. But it is not a harmless political move. The replacement of a public with a private salary misrepresents the president's true obligation, which is to attend to a full-time presidency. Just as the president is required to accept security and to live during his or her terms of office in the White House, his or her payment for doing the job is an additional way that service to the public is defined and expressed. By refusing this pay, a president unilaterally redefines the terms of his or her tenure.

An analogous restriction under federal law is the provision of Secret Service protection. Congress by statute prohibits the president (and vice president) from declining this protection. The prohibition, which no president has challenged, further illuminates the problem of privatizing the terms of the president's "employment." If free to reject this security, a president might take intolerable risks, to the detriment of the nation. The prohibition thus expresses the view that the president must accept the job on the condition that he or she submit to a publicly funded, government-operated security regime. Similarly, a prohibition on foregoing the presidential salary expresses the view that the presidency is a full-time job, not just one activity among others, such as private business pursuits, that then presents the potential for conflicts of interest.

Even if the president refuses to spend or donates to charity his or her government salary, a statutory prohibition on declining it clarifies expectations and may help establish, over time, a norm. The presidency is a full-time position, for which the incumbent is compensated with taxpayer dollars, and there should be no alternative of seeking out—and relying exclusively on—other forms of income while in office that inevitably raise conflict-of-interest issues.

Congressional Assertion of Its Authority to "Consent" to Emoluments

Even with basic conflict-of-interest controls such as those we propose, a foreign government could invest in a president's legacy business, or support it, through patronage of commercial facilities and in other ways, for the benefit of the president, family members, and associates. To the extent that the president retains a direct financial interest in these businesses, he could benefit personally while in office or know that he will do so in the future when he returns to private life and business affairs. Even if the president complies with the prohibition on an advisory or consultative role, which would restrict him only to the information also available to the public, he could still learn from public sources about foreign state investments in his businesses or, as in the case of commercial properties, leases or patronage.

Congress has not responded to Donald Trump's challenge to conflict-of-interest norms by exercising its constitutional consent authority to police the enforcement of the Foreign Emoluments Clause. As noted, the Foreign Gifts and Decorations Act, one of a handful of statutory exercises of congressional consent authority under the Foreign Emoluments Clause, is directed only at gifts of "minimal value" that a foreign government might bestow on a president.

In light of the issues raised during the Trump presidency, Congress should amend this law to provide that the president or the business in which he holds a financial interest would report to the House and Senate Foreign Relations committees, and to the OGE, interests in, and income reasonably anticipated or received from, foreign state investment vehicles or foreign-state-controlled businesses. The committees would then make these disclosures public.

The disclosures would not be limited, as Trump's lawyers have argued in ongoing litigation, to compensation received for the performance of official duties. Instead, the reform would adopt the broad definition of reportable "financial interests" in the Ethics in Government Act. Those interests include property interests and assets, investment and noninvestment income, and rents and royalties. As an example of the sweep of the disclosure requirements, the OGE defines a property interest, whether held in a trade or business or for investment or the production of income, to encompass "stocks, bonds, pension interests and annuities, futures contracts, mutual funds, IRA assets, tax shelters, beneficial interests in trusts, personal savings or other bank accounts, real estate, commercial crops, livestock, accounts or other funds receivable, and collectible items held for resale or investment."[40] Reportable investment income includes dividends, annuities, or contract payments.

In designing a reform that focuses on foreign state sources, Congress could include exceptions, subject to implementation by the OGE, for interests "too remote or too inconsequential" to constitute "emoluments" for which congressional consent is required. This standard of excepted interests applies under current OGE rules to executive branch officials who would otherwise be disqualified by those interests from participating in particular matters within the scope of their professional responsibilities. The OGE exemptions are grounded in a recognition that "in certain cases, the nature and size of the financial interest and the nature of the matter in which the employee would act are unlikely to affect an employee's official actions."[41]

On the basis of these reportable, nonexcepted foreign state financial interests, Congress could determine whether to provide "consent" to the president's receipt of this benefit. The provision for public reporting would serve a basic transparency purpose but also the goal of holding Congress accountable for the decision to exercise, or not, its consent authority. A president-elect would be required to file the first report within 30 days from the date of the election. Should Congress fail within 60 days thereafter to provide affirmative consent, the statute would require that the president sell off the interest.

Thereafter, under our proposal, the president would have no further supervisory or other involvement in his business or businesses, and all subsequent reporting requirements would fall on the businesses in which he held an interest. Should the president over the course of the term come to acquire foreign government–sourced interests, the business in which he held the interests would be required to file supplemental reports, and Congress would again have to act within 60 days to consent. If it failed to do so in the case of interests acquired during the term, the business would have to sell off the interest *and* pay the proceeds to the U.S. Treasury. This additional requirement during the term is necessary to ensure that, absent congressional consent, the president has not obtained any financial benefit from these sources while in office.

This reform structure may present numerous questions of application, especially if a president, like Trump, has wide-ranging and complex global business interests. Congress will necessarily have to craft the law to supply the OGE with sufficient authority, subject to ongoing oversight, to address technical issues that are certain to arise. We have laid out here the basic principles that should guide reform design.

We acknowledge that it is an open question whether the Foreign Emoluments Clause applies to the president and thus whether Congress can regulate the president pursuant to its consent power in that clause. We agree with the weight of lower court and scholarly analysis that concludes that the Foreign Emoluments Clause applies to the president, but the matter is not open and shut. Only the Supreme Court can definitively resolve this issue. But we expect that most if not all future presidents would not challenge the constitutionality of our reform proposal. And the statute could in the interim go a long way in establishing the right norms even if there were eventually litigation over the matter. And in any event, the Supreme Court cannot resolve the issue unless it is presented to it in a challenge to the statute, assuming that one can be crafted.

Elevated Congressional Role in Enforcement

Oversight of executive branch ethics requirements rests with the Office of Government Ethics, an independent agency. But the OGE currently lacks enforcement authority—it cannot compel testimony nor levy penalties, for example. Proposals for addressing presidential conflicts have included mechanisms to equip it with these powers. The House bill would provide the OGE director, who serves for a five-year term on nomination by the president and confirmation by the Senate, with enhanced protection from political pressure. Under current law, the president may fire the director for cause. H.R. 1 would substitute more specific grounds for dismissal: "inefficiency, neglect of duty, or malfeasance in office."[42]

We have reservations about the OGE's role in enforcing safeguards against presidential conflicts of interest. Even with limitations on presidential firing authority, the history of Trump's clashes with the OGE exposes the problems inherent in an enforcement structure that empowers an agency head to investigate and seek civil penalties against the president. It is a standing invitation to a president's political opposition to pressure the OGE to investigate. Presidents would have reason, in turn, to staff the OGE with "our people."

We would see a role for the OGE in advising and assisting the president with compliance, but we would propose checks and avenues for formal enforcement for which Congress would be primarily responsible. The Government Accountability Office should be charged with annually auditing and publicly reporting to Congress on compliance with the presidential conflict-of-interest rules. The Government Accountability Office would review the president's annual certifications that he or she did not engage on a consultative or advisory basis with businesses in which he or she had a financial interest, and the office would audit reports filed by those businesses pursuant to the requirement we propose.

Congress would use the annual audits to determine whether additional oversight is required. Should the reports reveal evidence of willful disregard of the conflict-of-interest requirements, Congress would refer the matter to the attorney general for review and potential investigation.

★

TAX DISCLOSURE

After Watergate, a norm of voluntary disclosure of presidential and presidential-candidate tax returns emerged. Presidents since Jimmy Carter have voluntarily released tax returns to the public on a year-by-year basis. And from 1980 until 2016, all major-party presidential nominees did the same, as did many major-party candidates seeking their parties' nomination. Donald Trump refused to comply with this norm on the ostensible ground that his taxes were constantly under audit. His actions have revealed the continued relevance of the tax disclosure norm and the need to translate it into enforceable law.

BACKGROUND

The tax disclosure norm originated in controversies over Richard Nixon's compliance with the Tax Reform Act of 1969. That law had closed a loophole for certain charitable contributions of papers by public figures for any such contributions after July 25, 1969. Testimony during the Watergate hearings led the *Washington Post* in 1973 to look into the substantial tax deduction that Nixon had taken for the donation of his vice presidential papers to the National Archives. It turned out that lawyers for the president and the appraiser of the papers had backdated a deed of gift to support the deduction well after the July 25, 1969, cutoff date. It also emerged that the president's advisers lobbied both Congress and the Treasury Department to preserve the deduction. They had planned to take it for the 1969 tax year and energetically sought to preserve it in the president's personal interest.

A White House lawyer and the gift appraiser were eventually convicted for the fraud, and one of Nixon's private lawyers was indicted but not convicted. To contain the controversy, the president voluntarily released his tax returns, requested a congressional investigative report on his compliance, and agreed to pay back taxes determined to be owed in the amount of $476,000, with interest. The furor over Nixon's tax problems led to his famous (or infamous) declaration: "People have got to know whether or not their president is a crook." He added, by way of reassurance, "Well, I am not a crook."[1]

Events in the aftermath of Watergate showed how tax compliance transparency, as a protection against presidential and vice presidential conflict of interest, grew into an expectation. After Spiro Agnew resigned as vice president, Nixon nominated Gerald Ford to replace him pursuant to the Twenty-Fifth Amendment. When Ford became president, he nominated Nelson Rockefeller to be vice president. The confirmation processes specified by Section 2 of the Twenty-Fifth Amendment included a review of both Ford's and Rockefeller's tax returns. In both cases, Congress's request for this information, together with the agreement by both nominees to provide it, indicated both branches' understanding that such a review was appropriately part of the confirmation inquiry into qualification and fitness.

In Rockefeller's case, the tax issues dominated the inquiry. Conflict-of-interest considerations, not those of tax compliance, were the reason. Rockefeller came from one of the most famous monied families in America, and his returns were complex. There had been questions in the past about his use of this wealth, such as his donation of significant gifts to public officials and members of his staff. When, after a protracted review, the Senate Judiciary Committee reported favorably on his nomination, the committee highlighted its conflict-of-interest concerns. These were, it stated, possibly unavoidable in the light of the volume and complexity of the family's financial and business holdings. But it took comfort in the absence of any indication of major improprieties over the course of his public career—and, notably, in Rockefeller's *public disclosures* of his holdings.[2]

In 1977, early in the Carter administration, the Internal Revenue Service (IRS) amended its Internal Revenue Manual, which sets out agency policy and procedures, to subject a president's tax returns for special administrative treatment. It provided that "[t]he individual tax returns for the President and the Vice President are subject to mandatory review[.]"[3] This policy was intended in part to remove from any IRS official's or employee's judgment the sensitive issue of whether to recommend or undertake an audit of a president's or vice president's return. Because the audits are mandatory, there is no choice to be made. The policy remains in effect today.

The Carter administration set out an additional ground for supporting this procedure. It "helps to allay any concerns in the public about the President's payment of taxes," noted White House Press Secretary Jody Powell at the time.[4] The theory is simple and powerful: As head of the executive branch that oversees the enforcement of the tax laws, the president must be above any suspicion that he or she is not meeting the compliance obligations imposed on all other citizens. Moreover, as the Nixon controversy illustrated, presidents have the power to influence the administration of the tax laws in their own favor. The fullest possible understanding of the president's financial position serves to limit the prospect of this form of abuse of power or to assist in exposing any abuse when it occurs.

From the Carter administration until Trump's presidency, presidents released their returns.[5] With the exception of Gerald Ford, who released tax information for nine years but only in summary form, so did the major parties' presidential nominees. In time, even those candidates bidding for their party's nominations began to release their taxes, though the practice was not uniform. By 2016, when pressing her Democratic primary opponent Senator Bernie Sanders to release his returns, Hillary Clinton declared that "there is a long-standing expectation that everybody running release their tax returns."[6] In the 2020 Democratic primary, a late entry into the nominations contest, Michael Bloomberg, drew intense questioning about when he would release his returns. He insisted that he had observed this norm when he was mayor of New York City (though he had made redacted versions available only for press inspection, with no copying allowed). He committed to adopt an expansive practice as a candidate for president. "We will put out [the returns], it tells everyone everything they need to know about every investment that I make and where the money goes," he said.[7] Bloomberg acknowledged that this was information "everybody ... need[s] to know."

While the release of returns has depended on presidential and presidential-candidate compliance with the norm, Congress has legislated other transparency measures to provide the public with information about a presidential candidate's or president's income and assets. Under the Ethics in Government Act of 1978 (EIGA), presidential (and other federal) candidates must file a financial report within 30 days of becoming a candidate, or on May 15, whichever is later. The report must contain a statement of assets and liabilities, and must include other information such as positions held with any organization. The candidates report only within broad dollar ranges, but they must list specific assets by type and name. Presidential candidates file these reports with the Office of Government Ethics, which is charged with reviewing them for completeness and making them available to the public. Federal elected officials, including presidents and vice presidents, are required to file such reports annually.

When President Carter signed the legislation into law, he stated its purposes broadly: The "public [would have available] an assessment of whether or not [a] candidate or ... public official is honest."[8] The EIGA took its place alongside the Federal Election Campaign Act (FECA) amendments of 1974 as an additional post-Watergate transparency measure to better inform the electorate about the sources of potential conflicts of interest affecting official conduct. The FECA amendments had addressed that question of "actual corruption and avoid[ing] the appearance of corruption" as it was raised by political contributions.[9] The EIGA provided a check on those conflicts arising from personal finances. When a group of federal judges challenged the application to the judiciary of the act's personal financial disclosure requirements, a unanimous appellate court in *Duplantier v. United States* upheld the law on this "accountability" rationale.[10]

The EIGA and tax disclosures are not, however, co-extensive: The report required by the EIGA is missing information relevant to a candidate's personal finances that only tax returns supply. Tax returns reveal all sources of income, deductions taken, charitable contributions made (or not), and the existence of off-shore accounts. Tax returns may also reveal details about foreign business dealings through disclosures about the payment of foreign taxes, foreign partnerships and corporations, and foreign gifts. Additionally, tax returns are far more precise than required ethics disclosures: Under the EIGA, candidates need only report assets and income according to categories of value. Candidates with incomes between $5 and 25 million, for example, all check the same box. Tax returns, by contrast, include specific figures. Nixon's legally suspect tax deductions based on the donation of his presidential papers—a controversy that eventually led to the voluntary disclosure of his tax returns—is a telling example of the type of information that only tax returns can reveal.

The disclosure of returns in all their detail also represents a substantial surrender of privacy, going well beyond the summary required by the EIGA. And yet candidates, including very wealthy ones, have for years complied with the norm of tax return disclosure, and the press and public have come to expect that they would. This history reshaped the expectation of privacy among candidates in favor of disclosure.

THE TRUMP ERA

Even Donald Trump did not assert a privacy interest when he made clear, as candidate and president, that he would not release his returns. Nor did he contend that the publication norm was misconceived or that he was abandoning the practice on principle. Instead he claimed that his returns were currently under audit and that "no lawyer would tell you to release your tax returns while you're under audit."[11]

There is no public information to confirm that Trump is in fact under audit, and so it has been natural for critics to dismiss his claim as an obvious ploy—especially because Trump has stated that his returns are *always* under audit. "I get audited every single year," he said in February 2016.[12] Also unhelpful to his cause is the absence of any legal obligation to treat as confidential returns under audit. Trump could release his returns as he chooses. He could identify the specific issues that may have surfaced during the audit.

Trump's claim is that his private rights as taxpayer transcend any obligations he may have as president. Most taxpayers, or their lawyers, would believe it imprudent to release returns under audit. One might, for example, fear that crowdsourced public commentary on taxes could move the IRS unfavorably on some audit issues. Experts reviewing the returns might spot issues that the IRS overlooked, or suggest in public

commentary an argument on particular issues that move internal deliberations within the agency against the president. Irrespective of the merits,
the agency decision-making process could be distorted by public pressures.

But, of course, the president is not a private citizen, and his appeal
to the rights of ordinary taxpayers is of no avail. He is, while president,
always under audit—because he is president. Both the IRS policy mandat-
ing the audit of presidential returns and the norm of voluntary disclosure
underscore that a president's tax returns are a matter of public concern.
The interest in privacy afforded and expected by all other taxpayers is
outweighed in the case of presidents and vice presidents by the public
interest in both the content of the returns and the impartiality of the
IRS procedures for review. Moreover, the appeal to the disadvantages of
release when a president's returns are under audit is disingenuous: Under
the standing IRS policy, each year of *every* president's returns is subject
to audit. Yet all presidents since Carter have released returns without
regard to the audit process, acknowledging the transcendent public
interest reasons to reject a defense such as the one Trump has adopted.

Trump did, however, try to minimize the importance of his refusal
to release his returns. He insisted that "you don't learn much in a tax
return," and that EIGA reporting covers all the disclosures that may be
necessary in the public interest.[13] It turned out, however, that there might
be a great deal to learn. In May 2019, the *New York Times* reported that
Trump had reported to the IRS more than a billion dollars in losses over
a ten-year period, offsetting nearly all of his tax liability for that period.
This was the result of massive deductions taken on real estate development projects. The losses and deductions were not reflected—and were
not required to be disclosed—in Trump's financial disclosures under
the EIGA. While tax returns show both income and losses, financial
disclosures include only the former. In his defense, Trump tweeted that
"almost all real estate developers" reported these kinds of losses, and then
negotiated or renegotiated loans with banks: "it was sport."[14] While the
practice of loss carry-forwards is legal, it is impossible to know without
more information whether Trump's claimed losses were legitimate. The
New York Times's reporting, and Trump's assertion that his real estate
activities enabled him to avoid income tax, underscored the importance
of the returns and the significance of the information they add to the
data reflected in EIGA reports.

As a predictable result of Trump's refusal to release his returns, he has faced questions about the motivations behind major tax law changes he actively and successfully advocated that contained provisions favorably affecting real estate development interests like his own. A provision repealing favorable tax treatment of "like-kind" asset exchanges exempted commercial real estate, and real estate developers also enjoyed special relief from a limit imposed on deductions of interest by large businesses.

Trump has stood his ground in the face of sustained press attention and criticism to reverse course, honor the norm, and release his returns. Congress then sought to employ legal remedies, and the arguments moved to the courtroom. The House Ways and Means Committee requested that the secretary of the Treasury provide the president's returns. It did so in reliance on a statute that authorizes congressional access under specified confidentiality procedures to "any return or return information."[15] The president's lawyers objected that the committee had no legitimate legislative purpose, only a baldly political one, in making this demand. When the secretary declined on those same grounds, the committee issued a subpoena for the materials on May 10, 2019.

A month later, the administration also released an opinion from the Office of Legal Counsel that supported the secretary's position on the absence of a legitimate legislative purpose. The opinion began with the proposition that "Congress could not constitutionally confer upon itself the right to compel a disclosure by the Executive Branch of confidential information that does not serve a legitimate legislative purpose."[16] It then questioned the "real reason" for the committee's interest in the president's tax filings. After arguing that Congress's oversight authority did not encompass "congressional power to expose for the sake of exposure,"[17] the Office of Legal Counsel noted the partisan context in which Democrats had been pressing for the public release that the president had refused to make voluntarily. It found that the committee's formal assertion of a legislative interest in the oversight of the IRS's presidential audit program was "pretextual" and concluded that the Treasury Department need not comply with the subpoena.

The Ways and Means Committee then sought to enforce its subpoena.[18] Other congressional committees also became locked in legal struggles for access to information about the president's finances, including his tax returns. In the course of other investigations of the president's financial affairs, the House Oversight and Reform Committee, Permanent Select Committee on Intelligence, and Financial Services Committee subpoenaed extensive information about the president, members of his family, and affiliated businesses from the president's accounting firm and banks with which he has done business. The president sued to enjoin enforcement. These cases presented the question of whether Congress could obtain access to tax returns on the basis of its constitutional authority to investigate potential presidential wrongdoing and to consider potential legislation to counter money-laundering and foreign state influence over U.S. government policy and the political process.

The president dispatched lawyers to another legal proceeding to defend against the surrender of his tax returns. In New York, the district attorney of the County of New York, acting on behalf of a grand jury, subpoenaed Trump's personal financial records, along with records of the Trump Organization and affiliated businesses, in connection with a criminal investigation of a variety of matters, mostly unknown to the public, but one of which involved alleged "hush money" payments by Trump to conceal extramarital affairs. The subpoenas were served on third-party custodians of these records: a financial institution and an accounting firm. The subpoena for the accounting firm records included "any tax returns and related schedules, in draft, as-filed, and amended form." The president challenged the enforceability of the subpoena on the ground that he possessed "temporary absolute presidential immunity" from criminal investigation while in office. The solicitor general did not join Trump on this point but did argue for a heightened standard that state prosecutors would have to satisfy to obtain personal financial information.

The United States Supreme Court decided both the state criminal and congressional committee cases in July 2020. In the criminal case, the court ruled that the president had no immunity from the grand jury subpoena and that a heightened standard was unwarranted, but added that the president could rely on standard principles to challenge misuse of a subpoena and could also challenge prosecutions that threatened his capacity to discharge his constitutional duties.[19] With regard to the House of Representative subpoenas, the court noted that they raised "significant separation of powers issues" even for the president's private information and remanded to the lower courts with guidance about how to accommodate both "the significant legislative interests of Congress and the unique position of the President."[20] The bottom line was that the Supreme Court decisions invited more litigation and made it doubtful that Trump's tax returns would be released before the election.

Two "blue states," New York and California, devised additional potential avenues for acquiring access to the returns. California enacted a statute conditioning major-party candidate access to the primary election ballot on making available their last five years of tax returns. The state would then release the returns to the public. It presented the law as serving the purpose of better informing voter choice. The California Supreme Court struck down the ballot access requirement as inconsistent with a state constitutional provision that candidates qualify for the primary election ballot if "found by the Secretary of State to be recognized candidates throughout the nation or throughout California...."[21] New York took a different tack, enacting a law that authorized the state to release a president's *state tax* returns upon request of one of the three congressional committees authorized to request returns under federal law. Trump filed suit in the U.S. District Court for the District of Columbia, but the court held that it lacked jurisdiction.[22] Trump did not carry this fight to New York, nor did Ways and Means or other authorized committees make the request of New York that most likely would have triggered a suit by the president to prevent release.

In summing up the experience with Trump and his tax returns, it is important to emphasize the ways in which the norm in favor of disclosure has continued to have force. Trump has suggested that he has met basic obligations with his financial reporting under the EIGA. And his stated reasons for not providing the returns have been personal to him—the "audit"—and imply that once the audit is behind him, he will make the returns publicly available. Once the battle with Congress and New York was joined, Trump added the claim that the investigative pursuit of his returns was motivated by partisanship and disruptive to the conduct of his office. Thus Trump has not challenged the norm but, rather, has pleaded extenuating circumstances. This is markedly different from many of Trump's frontal attacks on norms, such as his persistent intervention in federal law enforcement decisions that affect his interests, or his attacks on the judiciary.

REFORM

The Trump presidency has demonstrated that the norm of voluntary disclosure does not suffice to serve the important policy of presidential and presidential-candidate tax return disclosure. Trump is the first post-Watergate president to refuse any part of a voluntary release of tax return information, much less the full release that other presidential candidates and presidents have made. But he may not be the last, especially if his stonewalling goes unaddressed. The Trump experience shows that absent a legal disclosure requirement applicable to all presidents and presidential candidates, the public cannot easily or expeditiously get access to a president's records even if, in the words of the Supreme Court, they are "of intense political interest for all involved."[23]

The time has come to enact a federal requirement for the production of tax returns. The alternatives offered to date are unsatisfactory. The congressional demand for this particular president's returns has required for its enforcement litigation with uncertain prospects, and this struggle is inevitably caught up in partisan acrimony over legislative motive. A turn to the states to condition ballot access on this disclosure has proved similarly flawed. The appropriate response to Trump's norm evasion is federal legislation. Such legislation must address at least four issues, which we discuss in turn here.

Who Reports?

We propose that the federal tax disclosure law applies to major-party nominees and third-party and independent candidates who have qualified for the ballot in the general election in a sufficient number of states to secure an Electoral College majority.

Our proposal applies the reporting obligation to a narrower class than the one the EIGA established for purposes of the general personal financial disclosures. The EIGA reporting threshold is keyed to the level of campaign spending that triggers a presidential "candidacy" under the federal campaign finance laws. This spending threshold is set very low: $5,000 in contributions received or funds spent in a calendar year to establish and advance the candidacy. As a practical matter, presidential candidates who may never be regarded as "serious" are subject to this reporting requirement.

But, as noted, this reporting is very general, organized into broad ranges of assets, income, and liabilities. It does not involve a surrender of privacy comparable to the compelled release of tax returns.

The more exacting and intrusive tax-reporting requirement seems most appropriate for candidates within the class of major-party nominees and independent and third-party candidates possessing a realistic chance of becoming president. The leading congressional proposal, the For the People Act of 2019, as passed by the House, limits candidate reporting to major-party presidential and vice presidential nominees in the general election, but it does not apply to independent and third-party general election candidates.[24]

In our view, the significance of tax information militates strongly in favor of mandated disclosure by *all* those candidates in a general election within potential reach of the White House. A serious independent or third-party candidacy is not purely hypothetical. Ross Perot mounted one in 1992, qualifying for the ballot in all fifty states and possessing the personal financial resources to run a competitive national campaign. Yet while Perot's campaign suggested he might release his returns, he never did. He did not win any state's electoral votes but received just shy of 20 percent of the popular vote.

We would subject one more category of tax filers to this mandatory requirement: any of the president's or vice president's family members who have senior executive branch positions within the executive offices of the president or vice president, or at the departments or agencies. Independent adult family members would typically be off-limits and able to pursue independent private lives and order their financial affairs as they see fit. However, once again, the Trump experience revealed how a president may choose immediate family members to take on major public responsibilities. In those cases, the same conflict-of-interest concerns that shape the disclosure requirements for the president would seem appropriate for immediate family members in senior government positions whose financial affairs could influence, or appear to influence, the president's official conduct. This requirement should apply without regard to whether the family members serving in these official roles are compensated or receive only nominal compensation.

A president might challenge in court such financial disclosure requirements on the ground that, unlike the requirements of the EIGA, the new requirements apply to the president but not Congress. Nixon unsuccessfully brought a claim of this kind in a suit to protect his privacy interests after Congress enacted the Presidential Recordings and Materials Preservation Act of 1974, which asserted public control over, and access to, presidential recordings and a broad range of other records from his administration.[25] Nixon alleged violations of separation of powers principles and personal privacy rights. In rejecting these claims, the Supreme Court found that the separation of powers claim lacked force where the law in no way "prevents the Executive Branch from accomplishing its constitutionally assigned functions." It similarly found no merit in the alleged infringement of the privacy right where the public has a clear interest in the information and the president could not show that it was "unrelated to any acts done by [presidents] in their public capacity."[26]

This conclusion is consistent with presidential practice. Presidents for years have released their returns without any evidence that the disclosure adversely affected the performance of their duties. None resisted on the grounds that it would, and even Trump has not suggested any such impediment, resting his opposition to disclosure on its effects on an ongoing audit and, after the struggle with Congress and New York commenced, on the illicit motives behind the legislative and criminal subpoenas. All presidents in the post-Watergate period appeared to acknowledge the public's legitimate interest in the disclosure. Again, Trump, while broadly and incorrectly asserting that there is little to be learned in a return, has never denied the public interest in this information or argued that his privacy interests outweighed whatever value it might have.

Vehicle for Reform: Amendment to the Ethics in Government Act

Congress can amend the EIGA to require the annual release of a president's (and vice president's) tax returns, and thereby strengthen the provisions that address presidential accountability for conflicts of interest. The reformed statute would specify the date of release on the date that all citizens must file their tax returns: April 15. And the president would not be entitled to an extension because, given the clarity and importance of the law, he or she has adequate notice to do what is necessary to get the returns in publishable shape on time. The proposed law is simply a codification of generally consistent presidential practice pursuant to norms since Watergate and until Trump. During this period, presidents always voluntarily released their forms on April 15 and never required extensions.

The amended law would provide for the president to file returns with the Office of Government Ethics, which also receives and reviews for compliance with statutory requirements the annual personal financial disclosure reports required under the EIGA from the president, vice president, and other senior executive branch officials. The Office of Government Ethics would ensure that the returns are complete, and it would be authorized for this purpose to consult as required with the IRS. It would then make the returns public.

Finally, the law should provide for the public release of the mandatory IRS audit of the president's and vice president's returns. The audit could be subject to release when completed without regard to the results: The law could provide for the disclosure of even a "clean" audit. Alternatively, the audit results could be released in the event that the IRS determined that the president owed additional taxes, interest, and penalties and the president either accepted and paid the amounts owed or successfully contested the finding in whole or in part.

Role for Congress

In the event the president failed to file the return with the Office of Government Ethics, or did not do so by the statutory deadline, Congress, through the Joint Committee on Taxation, could require the secretary of the Treasury to produce it and could file suit as necessary to ensure the secretary's compliance. The committee's involvement also serves as a check on the performance of the Office of Government Ethics.

An alternative approach to ours would dispense with a requirement that the president and vice president (and candidates for the offices) disclose their returns and instead impose the obligation on the IRS to release them. However, the reform we propose aims to uphold one norm—that high officials and candidates disclose their taxes—without undermining another norm, namely, that the IRS should hold taxpayer tax filings confidential. Until Donald Trump declined to provide his returns, the norm of voluntary release operated successfully over many decades. The aim of putting enforcement teeth into a voluntary disclosure regime that failed can and should be achieved without creating an exception to the norm against IRS publication of returns. This latter norm is consistent with our proposed requirement that the mandatory IRS audit of the president's filings be released. The audit is the IRS's *own* work product, and by the time the audit is made public, the personal tax information it reflects will have been disclosed.

Presidential and Vice Presidential Candidates

The House reform bill would assign enforcement responsibility to the Federal Election Commission for presidential and vice presidential candidates as well as incumbents, all of whom would file their returns with the FEC. The agency would then make them publicly available. In the event that a candidate or incumbent does not meet the filing requirement, the FEC would be authorized to require the production of returns from the secretary of the Treasury.

This enforcement structure may seem suitable for candidates because the FEC administers the campaign finance laws and the associated disclosure requirements. But the FEC is also an agency whose membership appointments are subject to a partisan selection process, and it has developed, perhaps inevitably, a reputation for political conflicts that impede its ability to perform its statutory responsibilities. The FEC is not well positioned to perform the role here of ensuring that incumbents and candidates provide this information—which is personal financial, not campaign finance information—for public review. We would propose, then, that the enforcement responsibility for both incumbents and candidates reside with the Office of Government Ethics, subject to the same congressional enforcement authority in the event of noncompliance.

★

THE PRESS

The importance of the press to governmental accountability in our constitutional democracy is reflected in the First Amendment to the Constitution, which protects "freedom ... of the press." The Constitution protects the press "so that it could bare the secrets of government and inform the people," Justice Hugo Black wrote in the *Pentagon Papers* case in 1971. "Only a free and unrestrained press can effectively expose deception in government," he added.[1] The structure of the press has changed radically since 1789 and even since 1971, as we shall see. But the press continues to serve this vital role in the U.S. constitutional scheme.

All politicians are exquisitely attuned to public opinion and have no choice but to worry about their press. That is why they court reporters, do what they can to "manage" or shape news stories and commentaries, and often complain about the results. The higher the office, the greater the resources available for these purposes, and the more time and money is spent on the problem. With the rise of new media and the twenty-four-hour news cycle, the pressure to monitor and control for this variable in the competition for public favor has grown much more intense.

The president is in the most challenging position. The press presents more than an obstacle, or asset, to be shaped in the service of reelection. It also impacts the president's capacity to manage public opinion in support of a governing program. What Jeffrey Tulis has termed the "rhetorical presidency" makes it incumbent on the president "to promote policy initiatives nationwide, and to inspirit the population."[2] Presidents appreciate that at this stage in the institutional evolution of the office, a president must provide "active and continuous presidential leadership of popular opinion."[3] The press, "as an autonomous institution" devoted to scrutinizing and critiquing what presidents say, is "as much a rival and impediment to as facilitator of presidential initiatives."[4] Good press aids the governing objectives of a president. Bad press undermines them.

Tension in the relationship between the president and the press is a durable feature of American politics. Trump is not the first president to see the press as more "enemy" than rival: out to get him, refusing to cover him (or his opposition) fairly, and committed to his political destruction. But in both his rhetoric and the centrality of press animus to his political program, Trump exceeds all predecessors in ways that invite reconsideration of the law and norms that govern White House relations with the many and varied institutions that seek to cover it.

BACKGROUND

For approximately the first two-thirds of the last century, presidents sought to sway the press in their favor, or temper critical coverage, by capitalizing on journalistic rules of the road that are very different from those that apply today.[5] To the extent that the White House press corps in particular defined its relationship with a president, it was not, at heart, adversarial. Reporters did not generally view it as their mission to keep their distance from the president and White House officials, or to cast a sharply critical eye on public postures by looking behind them for inconsistencies or undisclosed motives. Reporters enjoyed generally clubby relationships with politicians as "insiders." What a congressional reporter observed in 1956 was also true of the White House press corps: The job was "a little like being a war correspondent; you really become a part of the outfit you are covering."[6]

In this milieu, journalists tended to organize stories around what a president professed that he was intending or doing. A statement that the president made, or a press release through the White House, received attention as "news." The president maintained significant control of his message. And some facts about politicians' conduct, such as their personal life, were off-limits for public reporting.

The 1960s and early 1970s brought shocks to the nation that awakened the press to its too-trusting posture toward the White House. The awakening began with the Eisenhower administration's many lies to the press about the May 1960 downing of the U-2 spy plane over the Soviet Union, and John F. Kennedy's acknowledgment to a *New York Times* editor that if the paper had not caved to Kennedy's pressure to tone down its pre-Bay of Pigs reporting, the country might have been "saved ... from a colossal mistake."[7]

And then it became clear that the course of the war in Vietnam did not comport with several administrations' claims about it. In 1971, the *New York Times* and the *Washington Post* published the Pentagon Papers, a classified Defense Department study that suggested that the Kennedy and Johnson administrations had concealed from the public material facts about the origins of the conflict, the policy justification for it, and the failure of U.S. military strategy. The narrative of disingenuous presidential advocacy was bolstered by the Nixon administration's failed lawsuit to enjoin the publication of the Pentagon Papers. This was the first executive action to seek by judicial decree a "prior restraint" on news organizations since President John Adams's enforcement in 1798 of the Alien and Sedition Acts.[8] The Supreme Court sided with the press, and the lawsuit quickly came to be seen as an attempted cover-up of the cover-up.

As one of us has written previously, American journalists emerged from the episode "with a permanently skeptical attitude about whether the government was telling the truth, a realization of its power to defy the government even on matters of war, and a romantic self-conception of its role in American democracy."[9] All of these beliefs were strengthened after a raft of criminal lies—by the president, the attorney general, and many other senior officials—were uncovered during the Watergate scandal. Aggressive and even heroic reporting on Watergate, especially by Carl Bernstein and Bob Woodward, was widely seen to have been the catalyst for other government actors—especially Congress and the courts—to perform their constitutional functions.

These events occurred against a background of other structural forces that had since the turn of the century been moving the national press to reconceive its mission. For much of American history, journalists did not draw sharp lines between fact and opinion, or between news and entertainment. Newspapers pitched to readerships interested in perspectives on politics fully compatible with their own. Papers tended to align reliably with political parties and partisan outlooks.[10] This changed steadily throughout the twentieth century. By the 1970s, the national press had adopted a professional standard that aimed to penetrate the fog of government claims and provide readers with analysis of the reality behind them. This standard in part reflected the economic opportunities open to the profession. Attracting a national customer base required appealing to various viewpoints, and "objectivity" allowed news organizations to break out from the limitations that a one-sided stance imposed on potential growth. Consistent with this model, journalists began to self-identify as independent craftsmen and craftswomen schooled in the discipline of a distinctive occupational pursuit that included obtaining and relaying the "facts."

By the early 1970s, this professional self-conception had dovetailed with the awakening driven by manifold government misrepresentations to transform the press into an institution with a sharply adversarial stance toward the presidency. The trend in the 1960s was well summed up by George Reedy, Lyndon Johnson's White House press secretary, who declared that "it is inevitable that newspapermen eventually become the 'enemy.'"[11] In just fifteen years, journalists had gone from "war correspondents" who were part of the administration "outfit" into the enemy itself.

The growing antagonism between the press and the presidency was accompanied by a generally leftward drift in elite journalism during this period.[12] The sociologist Daniel Patrick Moynihan, an aide to President Nixon, had this in mind when he wrote in 1971 that "the national press ... very much reflects the judgment of owners and editors and reporters as to what is good and bad about the country and what can be done to make things better."[13] Almost fifty years later, the deputy general counsel of the *New York Times*, David McCraw, could write in similar terms about the outlook of the reporting corps at the nation's flagship news entity:

> They believe, all other things being equal, that the little guy is getting screwed, economically, politically, and in every other way. The reportorial default is to think that most regulations are good, the rich and connected don't need more money or more power, and most social policies in the long run hurt the poor, the sick, and the disadvantaged[.][14]

McCraw describes these as "the most basic prejudices of the profession."[15] He did not mean reporters holding these "prejudices" consider themselves partisans. At the same time, the perspective he attributes to journalists as a class clearly maps more onto "liberal" rather than "conservative" viewpoints. As Daniel Okrent, formerly the public editor or ombudsman of the *Times*, wrote as the answer to the question "Is the New York Times a Liberal Newspaper?": "Of course it is."[16]

While every president since at least the 1960s has felt the sharp pinch of adversarial journalism, and while all have had difficult relationships with the press, the leftward tilt in the values of elite journalism has meant that Republicans have long been less trustful of the media than Democrats. Unsurprisingly, this asymmetry has meant that the Republican Party more than the Democratic Party has programmatically aimed to discredit the media, including at the presidential level. Before Trump, of no president was this more true than Richard Nixon.

When Nixon became president in 1969, his conflicts with the press were already notorious. Nixon understood the press animus against him to have both a political and a personal element. The press held "an ideological bias against nonliberals combined with a personal bias against him," according to Nixon's close aide William Safire.[17] And Nixon, in turn, possessed a pure "hatred of the press" that "carried him beyond the bounds of good sense."[18] Nixon's open contempt for the press can obscure the institutional dimension of the conflict.

The Nixon White House perceived the newly adversarial press as competing for the attention of the American public and attempting to shape their judgments of administration policies and priorities. It also believed, as senior aide Patrick Buchanan argued, that the president had "the right of untrammeled communication with the American people."[19] Or as Vice President Spiro Agnew declared:

> [T]he President of the United States has a right to communicate directly with the people who elected him, and the people of this country have the right to make up their own minds and form their own opinions about a Presidential address without having a President's words and thoughts characterized through the prejudices of hostile critics before they can even be digested.[20]

According to historian David Greenberg, "Getting a fair hearing from the public, Nixon believed, required discrediting the media."[21]

This attitude led Nixon to downgrade and reconceptualize the press secretary's role and subsume it under a major new communications apparatus run by a director of communications who was charged with managing the dissemination of the president's message. Prior administrations had tended to draw on the ranks of former reporters for press secretaries. Veterans of the trade knew how it was practiced and understood what "care and feeding" journalists might require for a productive relationship. Ronald Ziegler, the president's choice for the job, came to the White House with a very different experience—as a "corporate public relations man," recruited from the world of commercial advertising.[22] His job was to control tightly the administration's projection of program and image. "Look, I know about the way the media work," he declared. "I bought advertising space for years."[23]

By the end of Nixon's first term, the institutional press had concluded that the president had begun a profoundly unhealthy change in the relations of his government and the news media. The National Press Club in Washington, D.C., commissioned a study, published in 1973, which concluded that the president had instituted a "policy of massive official hostility" to the press.[24] The administration did not merely work for the best, most favorable coverage it could get. It aimed to "diminish whatever impact [journalists'] reporting might have on the public's insight" into this presidency and to "undermine the integrity of the national press corps in the public's eye." It combined "this startling directness and persistence" of attack with a steadily more severe restriction of interaction with the press. Press conferences dwindled in number to the fewest since the Hoover presidency. It was "the most 'closed' Administration in memory," and the result was a "deep estrangement" of government and media.

The press also complained that the administration had embarked on a campaign of intimidation. Vice President Agnew extended his critique of bias to raise the question of "the trend toward the monopolization of the great public information vehicles and the concentration of more and more power in fewer and fewer hands."[25] Buchanan publicly raised the possibility that the media faced antitrust action. And acting at White House direction, Nixon's chairman of the Federal Communications

Commission (FCC), the agency empowered to grant broadcast licenses, called the heads of networks to ask for transcripts of on-air press commentary that followed a presidential address. It appeared that he was trying to send a message about the "instant analysis" that so infuriated the president and his aides, and that the vice president had argued interfered with Nixon's right to communicate directly with the American people.[26] The director of communications directed his staff to contact local stations in advance of those speeches to inquire into their plans for its coverage and post-address commentary.

The administration also began to plot more insidious acts of intimidation. In an internal memorandum, senior aide Jeb Magruder recommended a range of actions to subdue the antagonistic media, including monitoring through the FCC and the use of the Internal Revenue Service (IRS) to "look into the various organizations that we are most concerned about."[27] Later events suggested that these steps were not merely notional. The administration wiretapped and tailed reporters, and brought an antitrust suit targeted at the networks' lucrative entertainment programming practices. Allies of the president organized challenges to licenses held by local stations owned by the *Washington Post*.

And then there was Nixon's enraged reaction to CBS reporter Daniel Schorr's critical news coverage. Schorr was placed on Nixon's "Enemies' List," and Nixon demanded "an FBI check on that bastard. And no stalling this time."[28] The FBI interviewed Schorr's friends and colleagues widely, which ensured that their activities came to light. The administration denied any impropriety. It claimed improbably—and falsely—that Schorr was under consideration for a senior-level administration appointment within the field of environmental policy. Senator Sam Ervin of North Carolina, later the chairman of the Senate Watergate investigation, denounced the administration for its "efforts of wholesale intimidation of the press and broadcast media."[29]

These strategies did not turn out well for Nixon. The press did not let up on him, and its role in the Watergate scandal, resulting in the only presidential resignation in U.S. history, became the stuff of legend. But the fundamental transformation of the White House–press relationship did not reverse itself after Nixon departed from the scene. Under subsequent administrations, the relationship between the White House and the press remained tense and competitive, and, under the stress of scandal and events, passed through periods of outright hostility and deep mutual distrust. Subsequent administrations also built up ever-more sophisticated operations to seek to manipulate or circumvent the institutional press in order to get the desired message out to the American people.

The conflict as it has raged in recent times has taken an even darker turn as the technology and economics of the industry have changed dramatically. The age of digital media has taken a dramatic toll on the traditional newsroom. Newspapers in markets across the country have shut their doors, and journalists by the thousands have lost their jobs, as the once well-established, dominant news organizations lose customers to a plethora of new sources of information on the internet.

In addition, social media now determine how much of an audience new media can hope to attract, which means that with today's polarized politics, "most people prefer news that reinforces their existing ideological views."[30] As Ezra Klein has observed, "[T]he strategy of the digital business model is to be the most appealing thing to some people."[31] Because modern media offer a plethora of choices, those who are less interested, or uninterested, in politics can avoid political coverage or commentary, with the result that news media in search of an audience are "biased toward and dependent on the fraction of the country with the most intense political identities" and interests. The "opinionated press," as Klein calls it, tends to be less concerned with sharp distinctions between fact and opinion. It responds to the more segmented market in which consumers pick the news product that caters to their ideological or political preferences. And it measures success largely by the metrics of social media: the "clicks" their stories generate and the circulation of reported material on Twitter.

The sharply fragmented and increasingly political news media, on the left and the right, exacerbate the problem of White House–press relations with the "opposite-party" strand of the media. A polarized politics means that some media outlets are trusted and others dismissed, if not loathed. Prominent politicians may accuse the media organizations of pure partisan political bias, or of reflecting the "corruption of corporate elites" that own cable and print press outlets.[32]

Presidents contending with this press environment have built on Nixon's innovations and now routinely build huge communications operations designed to push their messages through the cyber-clutter and to work around press narratives that might frustrate the achievement of their policy and political objectives. To this end, the White Houses since 2001 have themselves made intensive use of the internet and social media to communicate directly, daily, with the public. During the Bush administration, the White House began to livestream coverage of presidential events, established "Ask the White House" live web chats with White House and Cabinet officials, and began to use nascent social media. It was also the first administration to grant a mainstream blogger press credentials. The Obama administration built on these trends and widely deployed YouTube, Facebook, Twitter, and Flickr to gets its message out. By 2015, the *Washington Post* characterized the Obama White House as "its own media production company, one that can sometimes look like a state-run news distribution service."[33] The administration sought to "dazzle[] and draw[]" citizens to Obama's message by using familiar social media technologies,[34] and used "micro-targeting" to reach its intended audience "without the filter of the traditional media."[35]

THE TRUMP ERA

President Trump has never concealed his disdain for the press, and his public rhetoric tends by and large to be of the kind that Nixon avoided except in private conversations that, unhappily for him, were often captured by the White House taping system. No president has ever unleashed anything like Trump's stream of invective against the press. Through his favorite medium of Twitter, often paired with Facebook posts, Trump has expressed his views of the media in terms like "scum," "slime," and "garbage," and when he chose to build out the point, he also referred to journalists as "among the most dishonest human beings on earth" and the "enemy of the people." He has tweeted crude, digitally manufactured images of himself administering a physical beating to particular targets, like CNN. He has pushed the moniker of "fake news" so that it appears almost uniquely his own.

Like Nixon, and to a lesser degree several other presidents, Trump believes that he is the victim of coverage crafted by reporters at major news organizations—the "mainstream media"—who oppose his policies and who have dug in from the day of his election to portray him and his administration in the worst possible light. He associates this opposition with a broader and unprecedented establishment assault on his candidacy and his presidency. The press is an accomplice in this sinister series of machinations. The "deep state," the Democrats, "liberals," and "fake news" are arrayed against him in close collaboration. More recently, Trump has characterized even Fox News and the Drudge Report in similar terms.

The establishment or mainstream press for its part determined early on that the Trump administration could not be covered like any other. This president, many news organizations concluded, is a serial liar. Refusing a reportage of "equivalency," in which reporters straightforwardly report both a Trump claim and an opposition or expert response, these media outlets have adopted a policy of calling him out explicitly for falsehoods. There developed within the elite media an "overwhelming consensus … that the press should not normalize Trump—that the conventions of journalism must be altered."[36] Beginning in the first year of his presidency, Trump received unprecedentedly negative coverage.

It is hard to sort out in an objective way when the mainstream press's strong reaction to Trump was appropriate and when, provoked by a tweet or an action, the coverage broke with standards for impartial or "objective" coverage. But some journalists undoubtedly feed Trump's attacks on media bias when they announce their personal political views in regular appearances on Twitter and cable shows. This practice—by journalists on the left and the right—tends to blur the lines between personal and professional norms, especially since journalists often criticize or praise presidents and administrations in sharper ways through these outlets than in their reporting. The practice invariably raises a legitimate question of perverse personal incentives. As noted earlier, influence is often measured in the number of Twitter followers, and cable news appearances do not often reward measured analysis. In the Trump era, the practice has intensified, no doubt in part a response to Trump's prods and provocations.

Whatever the reasons, these practices tend to undermine journalists' credibility before oppositional audiences, and when engaged in by journalists on the left they tend to confirm some of the president's attacks on the press's bias. The overall effect is to further fragment journalistic outlets into sharp and opinionated right and left publications.

The conflict between Trump and the press is also exacerbated by Trump's populist tendencies. Trump portrays himself as the "voice" of the people in opposition to a rigged system that includes the mainstream media. The press that frustrated a populist president's quest for seamless, unobstructed messaging to the public is not only, as in all presidencies, an institutional rival. It is also a publicly avowed political enemy and target, a pillar of the system Trump had been elected to tear down.

And of course the conflict has been exacerbated by technological changes. Trump used social media, especially Twitter, like none of his predecessors. It is his prime instrument for creating and managing his press and for attacking news organizations and journalists. Trump is open about Twitter's and other social media platforms' unique functions in circumventing the established media organizations. At a White House "summit" on social media, before assembled conservative bloggers and tweeters, Trump championed the cause of "challenging the media gatekeepers and the corporate censors to bring the facts straight to the American people. ... [Y]ou communicate directly with our citizens without having to go through the fake-news filter." And he was frank about his admiration for the kind of material that could be successfully routed around the filter: "The crap you think of is unbelievable."[37]

Trump has also adopted the position, in litigation supported by the Department of Justice, that his Twitter account, @realDonaldTrump, is personal, not official. Twitter as a presidential weapon in the war against the press is very much in the foreground of the case. In a stipulation the administration filed in that case, the president acknowledged that his Twitter account enables him to "challenge media organizations whose coverage of his Administration he believes to be unfair." On this view, because his Twitter account is not a public forum, Trump is entitled to block access to the account. In addition to having the capacity to reach millions of Americans with a tweet whenever, and on whatever topic he chooses, Trump is arguing for the right to police the space and keep out unwanted responses.

Trump has so far lost that fight in court. A panel of the U.S. Court of Appeals for the Second Circuit found that "the First Amendment does not permit a public official who utilizes a social media account for all manner of official purposes to exclude persons from an otherwise-open online dialogue because they expressed views with which the official disagrees."[38] Trump strikingly deemed the issue one of "exceptional importance" in a rehearing petition that was ultimately denied.[39]

The significance of Trump's ardent commitment to social media as a primary medium of direct communication with the public cannot be understood apart from his attacks on the credibility of professional news organizations and the steps he has taken to block their channels of more traditional reporting. He is not only putting out his positions in the form, and with the timing, he prefers. All presidents have strived to do that. But Trump has coupled attempted press circumvention with sharply reduced White House briefings and presidential news conferences, and with systematic attacks on the credibility of the mainstream news media.

Like Nixon, Trump has taken a dim view of regular White House–press interactions in the West Wing briefing room. By tweet he informed his press secretary at the time, Sarah Huckabee Sanders, that she should not "bother" with briefings because the "press covers her so rudely & inaccurately."[40] The White House response was to cut down the number of these events. It had only one briefing in each of the months of September, November, and December 2018. And it did not have a traditional press briefing by the White House press secretary between March 2019 and April 2020, when Kayleigh McEnany became press secretary. McEnany held regular press conferences but adopted an unprecedentedly hostile posture toward her press audience.

The Trump White House adopted other strategies to limit press access. In May 2019, it established new rules for the issuance of press passes, arguing that the changes were justified by security concerns. The objective was to cut down on the number of "hard passes" issued to reporters to authorize ongoing access to the White House press space. It announced that these passes were subject to renewal only if reporters had entered White House grounds for at least 50 percent of the time in the preceding 180 days. Reporters would otherwise be required to apply for passes on a daily, weekly, or six-month basis. Exceptions would be made in "special circumstances," such as maternity leave.[41] These changes may seem to be of modest significance in light of the Trump administration's sharp reduction in daily briefings and news conferences. But they served the White House's apparent purpose in signaling the distance it wished to keep from the press and the tighter control it was prepared to exercise over access in the name of tighter "security."

The fight with the press corps en masse played out in confrontations with individual reporters as well and led to controversy over the circumstances in which the White House would revoke the credentials of reporters deemed too relentlessly critical. Trump has expressed his fury over the coverage of CNN, and one of its White House correspondents, Jim Acosta, has jousted combatively with the president in press conferences. In one such instance, the president, assailing Acosta as a "rude, terrible person," demanded that he "put down the mic" and yield the floor.[42] Acosta refused and seemed to brush away an aide who sought his microphone. The White House subsequently revoked his pass, contending that his actions threatened the conduct of an "orderly and fair press conference."[43]

CNN sued, and a court ordered the restoration of the credentials on the ground that the applicable regulations for the issuance of passes required notice to CNN, an opportunity for a response, and a written decision before they could be revoked. Acosta got his pass back. But the court noted that under the governing precedent, the White House could restrict access to the public, affording some or none at all, and the press had no greater right than anyone else. On what it termed a "highly, highly unusual set of facts," the court ruled only that with access *having been granted*, the administration was subject to procedural requirements in revoking a pass.[44] This access supported a "First Amendment liberty interest protected by a due process right [under the Fifth Amendment]."[45] The White House then revised its press pass rules to meet the requirement for rule-based transparency. Reporters could ask one question; the president had the discretion to allow for a follow-up. If he declined to invite or allow one, the reporter would be required to surrender the microphone or face the suspension of his or her pass.

Trump also dislikes his coverage in the *Washington Post*, owned by Amazon founder and chief executive Jeff Bezos. Trump took up a line of attack focused on the rates the U.S. Postal Service charged Amazon for the delivery of the company's orders—rates that Trump alleged to be disgracefully low. It then emerged that the president put pressure on the Postal Service to double the rates, and by executive order he established a task force to examine this and other strains on the Postal Service's finances. In spring 2018, the president's public campaign against Amazon caused a 10 percent drop in the company's stock price in less than forty-eight hours. (It later recovered.)

When the president and his administration opposed the proposed merger of AT&T and Time Warner, CNN's parent company, the *Financial Times* cited sources claiming that the opposition was "all about CNN."[46] This did not seem to be wild speculation. As AT&T advised the court in antitrust litigation with the government, the Trump presidential campaign had issued a release in 2016 with the specific announcement that "AT&T … is now trying to buy Time Warner and thus the wildly anti-Trump CNN. Donald Trump would never approve such a deal."[47]

Trump's aggressive behavior toward the press appears to have influenced members of his Cabinet, or given them free rein to express themselves in the same way. In January 2020, Secretary of State Mike Pompeo berated an NPR journalist, Mary Louise Kelly, after she included in an interview questions about Pompeo's treatment of Marie Yovanovitch, the former U.S. ambassador to Ukraine. Kelly reported that, after the interview, Pompeo continued to curse her and challenged her to locate Ukraine on a blank map. Pompeo released a statement the next day accusing Kelly of lying about the episode—and the following week, the State Department denied an NPR reporter the press credentials necessary to travel with Pompeo on a trip to Europe. The State Department Correspondents' Association protested the decision and charged that the removal of the reporter indicated that "the State Department [was] retaliating against National Public Radio."[48] Trump lauded Pompeo for his contentious interview with Kelly, telling him that he "did a good job on her, actually."[49]

In this war against the press, Trump could count on allies outside the administration as well. A number of news organizations reported in 2017 and 2019 that supporters of the president had begun to assemble "dossiers" to collect from social media accounts and elsewhere information derogatory to journalists covering the administration. The *New York Times* responded in 2019 with an extraordinary memorandum from its publisher to staff decrying this apparent escalation in the program of intimidation directed against the press by the "right wing." A.G. Sulzberger denounced it as an attack on the press that was "designed to harass and embarrass anyone affiliated with independent news organizations that have asked tough questions and brought uncomfortable truths to light."[50]

In sum, on every level—through rhetoric, restricted access, retaliation, and the apparent launching of smear campaigns by the president's political supporters—the Trump administration matched and, in some ways, exceeded the Nixon administration in the intensity of its efforts to subdue or work around an "enemy" press.

REFORM

The American press today is burdened with a number of severe challenges and pathologies that could alleviate some of the many problems that characterize White House—press relations if rederessed. Consistent with our general approach in this book, however, we take the press as we find it and propose reforms only for the executive branch.

A reform program to counter anti-press initiatives by administrations like Trump's faces several limitations. Presidents and indeed all executive branch officials are free to deal with some reporters and not others. They have the power to exclude critical press voices from opportunities to interview administration officials or even to attend selective, nonpublic press briefings. Presidents can decline to hold any press briefings. They can shut down the White House press briefing room altogether and bar only the reporters they dislike from access to the White House grounds. As one federal court stressed, when ruling on a state governor's directive that his administration discontinue any contact with two named reporters, it is a "pervasive feature … of journalists' interaction with government" that public officials favor some reporters and disfavor others.[51] Nor is there a legal route to tempering presidential rhetoric that is calculated to discredit the press in the eyes of the public. Presidents can denigrate the press with the same lack of restraint they exhibit when attacking any of their perceived "enemies."

There are, to be sure, legal limits on extreme presidential initiatives against the press. Imagine that a president directed the White House staff to harass and intimidate reporters by, for example, coordinating with the IRS to review tax returns and to initiate audits, and with the Justice Department to scour the public record for material it could use to open harassing "investigations." Such initiatives would implicate various laws, including, possibly, bans on the use of appropriated funds for other than their appropriated purposes, and the general conspiracy statute.[52] There are challenges to enforcing these laws against the president himself, which we discuss in Chapters Six and Eight, and impeachment always remains a remedy. The important point for now is that while extant laws might impact the most extreme and coordinated retaliatory behavior by a White House against elements in the press, they do not begin to address many forms of extreme abuse, refined by Trump, toward the press.

So supplemental approaches to reform are needed to address the problems that have arisen in the past four years, as well as worse problems that might arise in the future. In what follows, we focus on measures to (1) strengthen the mechanism for policing White House conduct toward the press and (2) shore up norms to keep the White House–press tensions from, in the words of a Justice Department report discussed later in this chapter, undermining "the essential role of a free press in fostering government accountability and an open society."[53] Trump may take pleasure in and seek political profit from casting aside norms. But that is all the more reason to consider ways to reaffirm and strengthen the norms for other executive branch officials, and to try to discourage other presidents from modeling their approach to the press on Trump's.

Defending Against Retaliation or Reprisal

Without the aid of executive branch agencies, the president has limited ways, beyond the restriction of access, to "punish" his or her press critics. A plan of active intimidation would typically require coordination with those agencies that enforce laws of importance to the day-to-day operations and long-term health of the news industry. Examples would be the Justice Department, in its enforcement of the antitrust laws, or the FCC. Harassment can also in theory be accomplished through the IRS. Measures to protect against presidential intimidation must forcefully defend these links in the chain from presidential direction to retaliatory action.

One such measure we propose is statutorily mandated inspector general review in the agencies that might carry out the intimidation. The Inspector General Act of 1978 authorizes inspectors general in various agencies to conduct audits and investigations relating to "programs and operations," and to focus in doing so on preventing and detecting "fraud and abuse."[54] If any actions are taken with official funds, in any program or operation, for other than official purposes—with "improper motive"—those actions may constitute such fraud or abuse.[55] Inspectors general have the authority to investigate directly by subpoena and interviews, and they can report directly to Congress. An action taken on the authority and with the resources of an official position to punish or harass critics in the press is an abuse that any agency inspector general should be empowered to investigate.

Current regulations provide protections against harassment of news media organizations through the abuse or misuse of the federal law enforcement investigatory process. Most notably, Justice Department regulations set out a policy "intended to provide protection to members of the news media from certain law enforcement tools, whether criminal or civil, that might unreasonably impair newsgathering activities."[56] In balancing law enforcement imperatives and the need to safeguard "the essential role of the free press in fostering government accountability and an open society,"[57] the policy mandates, among other requirements, that the attorney general should treat requests for subpoenas "with care … to avoid claims of harassment."[58]

We propose that the Inspector General Act be amended to define "abuse" to include official acts—whether or not under the direction of the White House or other senior agency officials—that constitute "reprisal against or an attempt to harass or intimidate" news media organizations or individual journalists in their employ. The amendment would encompass only "official acts," leaving to the political process the accountability of officials for speech critical of news organizations. The scope of official acts could be drawn from the definition in the criminal law and would include "any decision or action on any question, matter, cause, suit, proceeding or controversy, which may at any time be pending, or which may by law be brought before any public official, in such official's official capacity, or in such official's place of trust or profit."[59]

As in the case of every reform effectuated through investigative process, this one is subject to partisan abuse, or "weaponization." The proposed new inspector general authority could draw demands for investigations that, contrary to the purpose of this reform, sweep up and adversely affect the very news organizations it is intended to protect. For that reason, we would limit the inspector general's use of compulsory process to the investigation of official acts only. News organizations would participate in and support the investigatory process solely on a voluntary basis.

Just as the press's legitimate function requires protection, the Justice Department should not be prevented from conducting lawful investigations that involve obtaining needed evidence from reporters and news media organizations. There are a number of regulatory restrictions on the department's ability to seek to obtain such evidence, but the department should be able to do so consistent with these rules. The proposed inspector general reforms could generate "weaponization" by inviting claims of abuse that are intended solely or substantially to disrupt a lawful inquiry. We propose to address this potential problem in two ways.

First, the inspector general should have the authority to initiate an investigation only on a "look-back" basis, after the investigative steps affecting the media have been completed, or in the event of conflict, after they are resolved through negotiation and judicial process. This limitation on timing would not significantly weaken the effects of the reform. The known potential impact of an inspector general investigation, even if after-the-fact, should heighten the department's attention to these types of issues in the course of an investigation involving the press.

Second, the inspector general should not proceed with any such investigation if the attorney general certifies that the use of investigative tools directed at the media complied with procedures and limits set forth in current department rules for obtaining information from or questioning members of the news media (or, in the case of other agencies, with substantially similar rules). The requirement of a certification from the attorney general raises the stakes for the department in ensuring that the representation is accurate and in good faith. Moreover, this requirement could serve to heighten department attention to those rules and make it less likely that it would weaken, much less repeal, them.

For purposes of this reform, the rules subject to this compliance certification would have to include the following core elements, as reflected in current rules: First, the use of these law enforcement tools in seeking evidence from the media must, as a matter of department policy, be an extraordinary measure. Second, these tools could be used (1) only when essential to a successful investigation and after reasonable attempts have been made to obtain the information from alternative sources and (2) only after notice to and negotiation with affected news media members or organizations, unless the attorney general has determined that notice or negotiation would pose a clear and substantial threat to the integrity of the investigation, risk grave harm to national security, or present an imminent risk of death or serious bodily harm.

Under our proposal, the inspector general's findings and conclusions would be reported to Congress. The inspector general statute now mandates that the agencies transmit inspector general activities and findings to Congress, and these reports are both semiannual, to include summaries of "significant" problems or abuses, and "immediately," within seven calendar days, when those abuses or problems are "particularly serious or flagrant."[60] We would propose that the statute provide separately for inspector general reports on this look-back basis of press reprisal and harassment cases, and that all such reports must be transmitted to Congress within thirty days of completion. In the event that the inspector general did not investigate because the attorney general provided a certification of compliance with departmental procedures and limits, Congress would be so notified.

The main aim of an amendment to the Inspector General Act is to enhance and reinforce the fundamental norm that the federal government may not devote its investigatory and related resources to undermining the fundamental role of the press in our democracy.[61] By expressly identifying retaliatory actions against these organizations as a form of waste, abuse, or fraud, Congress would be sending a clear message to inspectors general that they should prioritize—and will be accountable for failing to investigate—any evidence of such improper conduct. The specifically mandated reporting requirements, including for investigations not pursued when the attorney general certifies compliance with department process, would enable Congress (and the press) to monitor performance and exercise oversight authority. Inspectors general could also be required to refer evidence of this retaliatory conduct to the Justice Department for examination of potential criminal offenses. A dual-track requirement, with one report to the department and the other to Congress, may ensure that the latter can keep the former honest.

Social Media and Other Public Communication Platforms

President Trump continues to litigate for the control he would like to exercise over his Twitter account. The controversy may seem limited in significance, and relative to other concerns in White House press relations, it is. Yet it retains no small amount of importance in a critical respect.

Nothing other than presidential self-restraint or regulation by social media platforms can be done to temper a president's uses of them to conduct unfiltered dialogue with the American public. However, Trump has gone further, declaring that his platform of choice, Twitter, is personal, not public, and that he can freely exclude other voices from access as he wishes. The online dialogue he seeks is one he can conduct with an audience he can screen and shape as he chooses. In that sense, Trump's treatment of his Twitter account is at one with the other restrictions on access that he is imposing on the press. The problem it creates is not so much that day-to-day it makes a practical difference, but the long-term implications for the presidency's relationship with the press are deeply troubling.

So far, the president has been unsuccessful in vindicating the legal principle. But Congress can and should resolve this issue decisively by amending the Presidential Records Act of 1978 (PRA) to specifically require the president to treat as a presidential record any tweets, including those deleted or altered, and any messaging through other social media or similar public communication platforms. It is widely, but mistakenly, believed that the National Archives has already taken this position. Not so. In fact, it advised Congress that it "does not make 'determinations' with respect to whether something is or is not a Presidential record. Rather, [it] provides advice and guidance concerning the PRA upon the request of the White House."[62]

The court ruling against Trump in the first round of litigation appears to have been based on the belief that the PRA had made such a binding determination and rested its decision that the account was official and not personal in part on that factor.[63] By amending the PRA to make this point explicit, Congress would shore up decisively the public claim on the personal accounts that a president has established on Twitter and other social media and public communication platforms, and end any efforts like Trump's to preserve these accounts as somehow personal property over which the president maintains complete control.

We propose that the president's personal accounts be specifically identified as "documentary material" under the PRA. This would bring the accounts under the statute's definition of "Presidential records" so long as the president uses these accounts to communicate "in the course of conducting activities which relate to or have an effect upon the carrying out of the constitutional, statutory, or other official or ceremonial duties of the President."[64] While the statutory preservation requirements cover "documentary materials ... in digital or electronic form,"[65] Trump has staked out a claim for a "personal communications" channel, usable for official commentaries and announcements, that the PRA would not reach. To ensure that no change in the leadership of the National Archives could result in a reversal of its current interpretation of the records requirements, an amendment to the PRA could provide that the exception in the statute for "personal records"[66] does not include any "accounts a President may create on social media or other public communication platforms prior to or during his or her term in office, if such accounts are used at any time, and to any extent, as a channel for communicating and interacting with the public about his or her administration, policies, or views on public policy or political matters."

This reform makes clear that the president can never claim a "personal" account for the conduct of official business that falls outside the Presidential Records Act and thus cannot block critics from access as they choose. It also signals the limits on presidents' use of social media to circumvent the press—to take down completely the "filter"—and build a media environment entirely to their liking and political advantage.

Press Passes

Federal regulations include the rules governing the granting of security clearances needed for White House press passes.[67] The precedent on which the court in the Acosta case relied, *Sherill v. Knight*,[68] involved the disputed denial of a clearance. The court that resolved Acosta's case used the same due process requirements: notice, an opportunity for reply, and a written decision. But the Acosta case was not concerned with security. The president and his aides revoked the pass because Acosta, in their judgment, had behaved obnoxiously, disrupting a "fair and orderly" press conference. It was widely understood to be the latest round in a running battle with CNN in which the president's primary objection was to its critical coverage.

Reform inevitably confronts the reality that the president controls press access to the White House. Presidents can display due regard for press preferences, such as those set out in the White House Correspondents' Association's published *Practices and Principles of Coverage Access for Independent White House Press*, or disregard them altogether. At present, the process by which the White House grants access is entirely informal. The press organization seeking a pass applies for one by letter, the White House Press Office responds affirmatively or negatively, and it does not have a published procedure for this process. The standards for granting or denying the application are also discretionary, published as and when the White House Press Office sees fit. The more formal process involves only the Secret Service's review of any such application for security purposes.

We propose the institution of a more formal set of procedures and practices for the next White House. If the next president sets a reformed standard for White House–press relations after Trump, it could have some effect on future White Houses. A similar standard-setting exercise that presidents have generally followed is the issuance on the first day in office of an "ethics" policy by executive order. Jimmy Carter led the way after Watergate, and presidents from both parties have met the expectation that they would do the same. Given the fraught state of relations between the press and the president, it would behoove the next president to establish in similar fashion a clear press policy, including the rules of access. Even if not bound by these access rules, future presidents would know that any changes they instituted would be evaluated against the baseline reform. Presidents like Trump might not care, but the departures they ordered would be clear, and it would be more difficult for them to simply publish new restrictions on the pretext of improving "security."

The regulation now in effect to govern security review of White House press applications provides a foundation for the next president to specify a new policy in clear terms.[69] We propose restructuring the rule so that it reflects all the qualification criteria for White House correspondent status. In effect, the rule would become a two-pronged test: First, the Secret Service would review for security clearances only applicants for a press pass who had otherwise met the qualification requirements established by the White House for access as a correspondent and *those qualifications would be specified in the regulation.* Second, the Secret Service would issue security clearances to qualified applicants who met those standards except—and only—where "the applicant presents a potential source of physical danger to the President and/or the family of the President so serious as to justify his or her exclusion from White House press privileges." If there is no basis for exclusion of the applicant as a serious security concern, he or she would be approved for the pass.

Much like the now-established practice that new presidents follow in promulgating ethical standards, a new White House would direct the re-publication of the rule with whatever requirements it proposes to apply for the granting of press passes and would be subject to the expectation that it would re-publish if it amended those qualifications in the course of the four-year term.

We propose that the White House qualifications conform as much as possible to the standards used by the other branches to grant news media access to their space and proceedings. The White House Press Office would follow the Supreme Court, the Senate, and the House in setting out criteria on issues such as what constitutes a news media organization and whether a journalist's regular reporting responsibilities require the applied-for access. Aligning the branches as much as feasible on these issues allays the concern that the White House might be tailoring its own standards to grant preferential access to certain news organizations.

The regulation would also be amended so that the due process requirements apply both to the initial clearance and to any revocation. This change would conform the rule to the relief ordered by the court in the CNN-Acosta case.

The White House that issues such a more comprehensive regulation can also, of course, revoke it, keeping in place only the due process requirements imposed by the court order that required the promulgation of the rule in the first instance. There is, however, value in calling on the next president to set expectations for the process and to establish transparency for subsequent departures. Proceeding in this fashion would mitigate the problems created when the White House makes up rules on the fly to address specific controversies like the Acosta matter. It also answers the concern expressed by the court in the CNN case that "whatever process occurred within the government is still so shrouded in mystery that the Government could not tell me at oral argument who made the initial decision to revoke Mr. Acosta's press pass."[70] A future administration guards against arbitrariness by adopting a clear rule. It makes a strong statement about the role of the press in the conduct of the presidency.

Congress

Congress can play an indispensable role in the protection of the press. In recent years it has taken action to protect news organizations from judgments rendered overseas in courts applying very different libel standards from our own. Yet it does not generally involve itself in domestic disputes over press access to the White House or struggles to overcome presidential resistance to critical coverage. It could and should. We noted previously that Congress did intervene once, in the Schorr episode, to put on record its concerns about the administration's vendetta against the press.

We have already recommended amendment of the inspector general statute to bring additional resources to the protections against press intimidation. The separate requirements we propose for reporting to Congress—including notifications when the attorney general certifies compliance with department procedures and limits—should serve to engage Congress and enhance the likelihood that these issues will stimulate oversight activity. Oversight could be conducted through the House and Senate Judiciary subcommittees concerned with protection of civil liberties and constitutional rights. Or the Senate and the House could create separate subcommitees dedicated to the issue of press freedom. Once again, the elevation of this issue clarifies, strengthens, and sets up an apparatus for the enforcement of norms.

THE PARDON POWER

*"I will **never** roll on Donald Trump,"* declared Roger Stone, Trump's friend, four months before he was indicted in connection with Special Counsel Robert Mueller's investigation of Russian interference in the 2016 presidential campaign. A jury convicted Stone in 2019 for obstructing a congressional investigation, making false statements to Congress, and witness tampering. The court sentenced him to forty months in prison.

When Trump commuted Stone's sentence in July 2020, many observers believed it was a reward for Stone's refusal to give Mueller evidence that Trump had lied when he told investigators that he recalled no conversation with Stone about WikiLeaks and Hillary Clinton's emails. Stone never did implicate his friend. And he lent credibility to the quid pro quo theory when, just before Trump's commutation, he told a journalist that Trump "knows I was under enormous pressure to turn on him." Stone added: "It would have eased my situation considerably. But I didn't."[1] After the commutation, Stone denied that he implied any quid pro quo: "I would not lie against my friend of 40 years so they could use it for impeachment …. They had nothing."[2]

Trump is not the first president to be accused of pardoning someone to avoid personal legal jeopardy, though the evidence of a quid pro quo is stronger in Trump's case than in prior ones. Many presidents have on occasion used the pardon power in controversial ways, or in ways that seem politically or personally self-serving. But no other president has, like Trump, used pardons systematically to serve political and personal goals. And no other president has threatened to pardon himself. There is every reason to think that Trump's controversial approach to pardons will continue after this book is published—either because Trump loses the 2020 election and thus cannot suffer politically from pardons during his remaining two and a half months in office, or because he wins the 2020 election and faces no electoral penalty from controversial pardons.

Many of the pardon abuses that Trump has committed and that he and future presidents may yet commit cannot be redressed through reforms short of a constitutional amendment. But the pardon power is far from absolute. It can be reformed to check some of its most extreme potential abuses, especially when pardons are part of a corrupt bargain.

BACKGROUND

Article II, Section 2, of the Constitution confers on the president the "Power to grant Reprieves and Pardons for Offences against the United States, except in Cases of Impeachment." This power extends to all forms of clemency, including pardons (which forgive the crime) and commutations (which eliminate or reduce the sentence for the crime). This power has only two express textual limitations: It is available only to excuse or mitigate the punishment of federal offenses, and it does not extend to impeachment.

Within its proper scope, the pardon power is broad and consequential. If granted before conviction, it "prevents any of the penalties and disabilities consequent upon conviction from attaching." If granted after conviction, it requires release from prison and "removes the penalties and disabilities, and restores him to all his civil rights."[3] The pardon power is not all or nothing. It authorizes the president to "'forgive' the convicted person in part or entirely, to reduce a penalty in terms of a specified number of years, or to alter it with conditions which are in themselves constitutionally unobjectionable."[4] Presidents need not give reasons for pardons (though by operation of norms discussed in the next section, they typically do so).

Many commentators go further and claim that the pardon power is "absolute."[5] Much of this rhetoric derives from stray comments in Supreme Court case law. *Ex parte Garland* (1866), for example, stated that the pardon power was (but for its express exceptions) "unlimited" and "not subject to legislative control."[6] The court there held unconstitutional a post–Civil War statutory requirement that attorneys seeking to practice in federal courts swear that they had not given "aid, countenance, counsel, or encouragement" to the Confederacy."[7] The primary grounds for the ruling were that the oath was an unconstitutional bill of attainder and ex post facto law. One of the plaintiffs had received a presidential pardon from punishment for his activities in the Confederacy and claimed the oath was inconsistent with the pardon. The court ruled that its view of the oath's unconstitutionality was "strengthened by ... the effect of the pardon ... and the nature of the pardoning power of the President."[8] In context, the pardon ruling in *Garland* was unnecessary to resolve the case, and the court's absolutist rhetoric went far beyond what was needed to resolve the issue before it.

A reader of this case, and of cases that describe the pardon power as "plenary,"[9] could be forgiven for concluding that "the Supreme Court [had] given the ... pardon power a broader scope than that enjoyed by the British king."[10] Not surprisingly, the executive branch has given full-throated support to this theory of "absolute power." A declaration from Woodrow Wilson's attorney general is typical: "[T]he President, in his action on pardon cases, is not subject to the control or supervision of anyone, nor is he accountable in any way to any branch of the government for his action."[11]

The story is, in fact, more complex. The exclusive, "unlimited" nature of the pardon power has been routinely overstated. The Supreme Court has suggested that Congress can enact general amnesties, though the executive branch has contested the point.[12] The court has also said that Congress can authorize executive branch authorities other than the president to rescind or mitigate fines.[13] While a well-specified pardon relieves the individual pardoned from the punishment for the crime committed and restores basic civil rights, a pardon does not necessarily restore the person pardoned to his or her original position.[14] Also, a president cannot force a pardon on the unwilling.[15] And there may be individual rights constraints on the pardon power. One lower court in a prominent case reviewed the conditions of a commutation to ensure that they were "directly related to the public interest" and did "not unreasonably infringe on the individual commutee's constitutional freedoms."[16]

There are surely other limitations on the pardon power that have never been made clear because the issue has never been pushed by

Congress or resolved by courts. For example, four justices noted that judicial intervention would be appropriate if "a state official flipped a coin to determine whether to grant clemency, or in a case where the State arbitrarily denied a prisoner any access to its clemency process."[17] A similar idea might apply to the president's federal pardon power. Another example is a presidential self-pardon. No president has ever granted one, and the issue has divided commentators. Finally, it is likely that Congress in a well-crafted statute can make it a crime for the president to use the pardon power corruptly—for example, for issuing a pardon in response to a monetary bribe. We discuss these latter two issues—self-pardons and criminalizing corrupt presidential pardons—in the "Reform" section of this chapter.

The history of presidents' use of the pardon power is long and complex. Here we recount the highlights relevant to assessing the Trump administration's pardon practice and our proposed reform.

Historical Overview

The Pardon Clause in Article II is silent about the proper bases for a presidential pardon. The dominant general understanding at the Founding, expressed by Hamilton in *Federalist* No. 74, was that pardons were appropriate to "mitigat[e] ... the rigor of the law" so that justice does not "wear a countenance too sanguinary and cruel" and to help "restore the tranquility of the commonwealth" following periods of upheaval.[18]

Presidents are not required to give reasons for pardons. But in practice they typically have, and those reasons have basically corresponded to the two purposes identified by Hamilton. First, presidents have sought to mitigate injustices in individual cases: to correct an apparent severity of sentences; to take into account trying personal circumstances, such as family illness; or to recognize that apart from the offense committed, the individual under consideration for a pardon had contributed distinguished public service over the course of a career.

Second, presidents have used pardons to serve the public policy aim of "restoring tranquility." This has occurred most notably when presidents granted general amnesties related to war or domestic upheaval. George Washington granted amnesty to those who participated in the Whiskey Rebellion, Thomas Jefferson pardoned those convicted under the Alien and Sedition Acts, Abraham Lincoln and Andrew Johnson issued broad pardons to further reconciliation of the Union and the Confederacy, and Jimmy Carter granted amnesty to hundreds of thousands of young Americans who had evaded the military draft during the divisive Vietnam War. The decision to pardon large numbers has not been limited to healing postwar social wounds. Pursuant to an initiative to reduce the sentences of individuals convicted of nonviolent crimes, Barack Obama's administration invited qualified federal inmates to apply for commutation, and Obama during his time in office commuted 1,715 sentences.

The number of pardons or commutations issued by presidents has varied over different periods in American history. "For most of our nation's history, the president's constitutional pardon power has been used with generosity and regularity to correct systemic injustices and to advance the executive's policy goals," including legal reform.[19] While precise numbers for the first hundred years of the Constitution are elusive, during this period "low-level pardoning took place largely out of the public eye, but with some regularity."[20] Individual pardons and commutations diminished over the course of the twentieth century. Presidents from McKinley through Carter granted about 30 percent of individual clemency petitions on average, but the average after Carter is well under 6 percent.[21] The absolute numbers of pardons and commutations per year dropped pretty steadily as well, especially during the presidencies from Reagan through George W. Bush, until Obama's clemency initiative.

Over the course of American history, the pardon process also grew more formalized and bureaucratized. By the mid-nineteenth century, presidents began to delegate to the attorney general the responsibility to screen and review pardon applications and make recommendations. Eventually the position of pardon clerk, later retitled pardon attorney, was established as part of an "administrative system ... [that's] made the unruly power part of the more general transformation of the justice system to an administrative state."[22]

The Department of Justice's formal role in this process remains in place today. Department regulations provide for the filing of a petition for clemency in the first instance with the pardon attorney. It is the function of this official to investigate fully the grounds for a potential pardon and for this purpose, he or she may draw upon the resources of the federal government, including the FBI. The pardon attorney's recommendations are submitted to the deputy attorney general, who coordinates a further review by the attorney general and a final recommendation, in writing, to the president. Consistent with the core rationales for the granting of clemency, the regulations identify a range of grounds for a favorable pardon recommendation, such as the severity of the sentence, illness, cooperation with law enforcement and other investigations, or other "equitable factors."

The role of the Justice Department has had the effect of "steering most clemency suitors away from the president's door."[23] The general agreement on the basis for pardons, and this system within the Justice Department for administering them, significantly reduced the potential for controversy about how the president exercises this constitutional authority. Presidents are, of course, free to adjust the priorities and standards that the department should follow in considering pardon recommendations. But it has well served presidents and their staffs to be able to direct petitioners to a process outside the White House and to affirm the application of a uniform set of standards for the consideration of pardons. If the reliance on the Office of the Pardon Attorney does not quite rise to the level of a "norm," it is at least a general expectation. Presidents who have circumvented this process have been certain to face questions.

Recent Pardon Controversies

In the decades before the Reagan administration, and with the dramatic exception of Gerald Ford's pardon of Richard Nixon, pardons and commutations had become a "routine and relatively low-key activity of the presidency that took place largely unnoticed."[24] Since the 1990s, three administrations prior to the Trump administration have been rocked by charges that presidents used the pardon power to serve predominantly political and personal self-interest.

Iran-Contra

The Iran-Contra scandal involved a secret arms deal with Iran in 1985, the proceeds of which were used to fund arms for the contras in Nicaragua in contravention of a congressional ban. As George H.W.

Bush was leaving office, he pardoned former Secretary of Defense Caspar Weinberger and five senior national security officials who had been convicted or indicted for perjury and obstruction of justice as a result of an investigation by an independent counsel.

Bush justified the pardons with typical reasons: the long periods of distinguished service of the defendants, family illness and old age that favored merciful consideration, and judgments by officials acting in good faith under the pressure of a Cold War. Bush also challenged the indictments and convictions on the ground that they represented a "criminalization of policy differences."[25] He contended that the independent counsel had injected himself and the criminal justice process into a dispute between Congress and the executive over their respective authorities in major matters of national security. But critics (including the independent counsel) charged that Bush's pardons shielded his administration, his aides, and possibly himself from accountability for what the independent counsel deemed to be criminal offenses. Bush left office the month following the pardons, and the controversy died down without congressional inquiry.

The Clinton Pardons

Pardon controversies from Bill Clinton's presidency also raised the specter of improper motives. One controversial pardon involved Clinton's 1999 grant of clemency to sixteen members of the FALN, a Puerto Rican nationalist organization, who had been convicted for involvement in bombings and other violence in pursuit of the goal of Puerto Rican independence. The clemency came with a condition that the pardoned FALN members must renounce acts of violence. Critics alleged that Clinton was motivated by politics, since his administration yielded to entreaties from Puerto Rican interest groups whose support would be useful to the looming Senate campaign of First Lady Hillary Clinton and the likely presidential quest of his vice president, Al Gore. Some evidence of political pressure surfaced when internal administration emails became public, but many distinguished figures supported clemency as well.

In a letter to Congress, Clinton claimed that "political considerations played no role in the process."[26] He explained that the clemencies served to mitigate "unduly severe" sentences since the individuals in question had not been convicted of doing bodily harm to anyone even though they were members of an organization that embraced violence in the pursuit of its goals. Clinton acknowledged that his White House counsel rather than the Justice Department had managed the "process," to the extent that there was one, and that the FBI and Justice Department officials had been opposed to clemency. Though Clinton made his case to Congress, he also asserted executive privilege in response to a congressional subpoena that sought information about his decision process. The White House argued that the pardon power was "not subject to legislative oversight."[27] Congress responded with extraordinary actions. Congress passed by overwhelming majorities—311 to 41 in the House, and 95 to 2 in the Senate—resolutions denouncing the pardons.

The second Clinton administration controversy occurred when the president issued 140 pardons and commuted thirty-six prison sentences on his last day in office. Many of those pardoned had not applied for pardons and were not vetted by the FBI. The pardons included one for Clinton's brother, who had been convicted of illegal drug use, and another for a witness who had refused to cooperate with the independent counsel investigation of the Clintons' involvement in certain land deals in Arkansas prior to Bill Clinton's presidency. The pardons that drew the most attention and criticism ended the criminal legal jeopardy of two fugitives from justice, Marc Rich and Pincus Green, who had fled prosecution for tax evasion. Press reports raised questions about whether the extraordinary pardons were rewards for financial support by the ex-wife of one of the two fugitives, who made large contributions to the Clinton presidential library and was a major Democratic Party donor.

One month after leaving office, Clinton answered critics with a written defense on the opinion page of the *New York Times*. Clinton noted that that the "exercise of executive clemency is inherently controversial" but acknowledged that "legitimate concerns have been raised" about the Rich and Green pardons.[28] He denied that the pardons were influenced by political contributions or contributions to the Clinton library. He expressed doubt that the law had been applied correctly in the Rich and Green prosecutions and noted that the "case for the pardons was reviewed and advocated" by his former White House counsel and three "distinguished" Republican attorneys. He also cited "foreign policy reasons" for his actions, which were the favorable views of "present and former high-ranking Israeli officials" who credited Rich with charitable work in Israel and contributions to the Palestinian-Israeli peace process. All in all, he concluded, his "pardon decision was in the best interests of justice," especially since he had conditioned them on the willingness of Rich and Green to waive defenses to any related civil charges the government might bring.

One striking feature of this episode is the investigation undertaken by the U.S. Attorney's Office for the Southern District of New York into illegal acts that may been committed in connection with the issuance of the pardons. According to press reports, the investigation centered on the possible "sale" of pardons, through the use of campaign contributions to induce the president to grant them, or any misrepresentations made on behalf the pardon seekers. The U.S. attorney at the time, James Comey, "did not find sufficient evidence to bring any charges and closed the case."[29] The political controversy did not end quickly. Congress held hearings. Senior Clinton administration officials, including the former deputy attorney general, Eric Holder, and two former White House counsels, testified about the advice they had given to the president on the eleventh-hour pardons. A number of these officials detailed their opposition to the pardons and described a White House—directed scramble to issue the pardons before the president's departure from office.

George W. Bush and the Libby Commutation

President George W. Bush commuted the sentence of Vice President Richard Cheney's former chief of staff, I. Lewis "Scooter" Libby. Libby had been convicted by Special Counsel Patrick Fitzgerald of lying to a grand jury and making false statements to the FBI in the course of Fitzgerald's investigation into the leak of the identity of a CIA officer. Bush's commutation meant that Libby's conviction stood and Libby had to serve a two-year probationary period and pay a $250,000 fine. But he served no jail time.

Bush explained his commutation as a response to a sentence that he viewed as "excessive."[30] Many commentators believed this was a plausible contention since before Libby's false statements to the grand jury or the FBI that had prompted his conviction, the prosecutor had determined that Libby was not the one who revealed the intelligence officer's identity. The lies for which Libby was convicted thus were not intended to protect him from discovery as the original source of the leak. And prosecutors did not conclude that Libby violated the federal law prohibiting disclosure of an intelligence officer's identity during his conversations with reporters on the subject.

But the Libby commutation also featured allegations of self-interested motive. The CIA officer whose name was leaked to the press was the wife of a former ambassador, Joseph Wilson. Wilson had alleged publicly that in making the case for the Iraq war, the Bush administration had fabricated a claim about that government's quest for the development of nuclear weapons. The administration responded with heated denials, but critics charged that Libby had arranged the leak on behalf of Cheney as an act of retribution against Wilson. Cheney pressed Bush hard for a full pardon on the reported ground that "[w]e don't want to leave anyone on the battlefield."[31] The commutation was thus seen by some as a political move in the large domestic "war" over the charges of lying about the Iraq invasion. Many also believed that the commutation was a reward for Libby bearing the full consequences of the prosecution and sparing the vice president. There was evidence in the accounts of other witnesses that prosecutors were keenly interested in Cheney's direct personal role in the matter.

More broadly, the Libby commutation occurred in an intensely political setting—a national debate about the Bush administration's rationale for going to war in Iraq. As in other arguably self-serving cases of this kind, the president kept within the White House the decision on whether and how to pardon Libby or commute his sentence. The vice president was Libby's chief advocate, the Justice Department's Office of the Pardon Attorney was not consulted, and the process set up by regulation for the review of pardons was not followed.

THE TRUMP ERA

A White House official reportedly stated that Trump was "obsessed" with his power to grant pardons.[32] It is, apparently, the president's "favorite thing" to talk about. He has turned to Twitter to announce pardons and once declared that he had the "absolute right to PARDON myself."[33]

Through July 15, 2020, Trump had issued thirty-six pardons or commutations that in the aggregate were a significant break from past presidential practice. First, of Trump's thirty-six pardons and commutations, an extraordinarily high 86 percent (31 out of 36) were self-serving in the sense of advancing a Trump political agenda item, or reflecting a personal connection to Trump, or involving someone Trump saw on television (usually on Fox), or concerning a celebrity he admired.[34] Prior presidents had issued self-serving pardons, some of which we described earlier. But none did so on anything approaching the systemic scale of Trump. Second, and relatedly, Trump rarely used the pardon attorney process in the Justice Department. Again, other presidents had sometimes skirted the pardon attorney. But Trump did so almost all the time. Based on public records, only five of the thirty-six cases—the five that lacked a personal or political connection to Trump—went through the Justice Department system. Unsurprisingly, those five people, but not the other thirty-one, appear to have been recommended for clemency by the pardon attorney.

A focus on some notable cases makes clear the political element in Trump's pardon practice. These are pardons or commutations that Trump had reason to believe would be consistent with his political messaging or lines of attack on political opponents, and those that are attractive to his "base." In August 2017, he pardoned the former sheriff of Maricopa County, Joe Arpaio, who was convicted of contempt of court for defying a federal court injunction against the profiling of Hispanics in an aggressive campaign to ferret out illegal immigration. Trump engaged in a singular act of showmanship in teasing out his intent to pardon Arpaio. He suggested the possibility during a Fox News interview and then again at one of his political rallies, in Phoenix, Arizona. He then announced the pardon on Twitter, applauding Arpaio for being a "patriot" and keeping Arizona "safe!"[35]

It was not only in the political stagecraft around the Arpaio pardon that Trump's approach to the pardon power is distinctive. Trump did not claim that Arpaio's conviction for contempt was a miscarriage of injustice, or that the injunction against his unconstitutional law enforcement strategies was legally defective. A critical assessment of the legal process, or an initiative for legal reform, played no part in his public justification. The White House stated that Arpaio was "worthy" of a pardon due to his life in public service. But Trump was attracted to Arpaio's ardor in pursuing a goal—an all-out attack on illegal immigration—that was

central to Trump's campaign and governing agenda. Trump was affirming in dramatic fashion his own bona fides on the issue. Nor could he
be viewed as falling back on a "public welfare" argument that a pardon
was required to suspend the normal operation of the legal system so that
political and social divisions could be healed in the larger public interest.
Trump was celebrating defiance of the law on a deeply divisive issue.

Trump's pardon of Arpaio was an intervention in an ongoing case,
but he also exercised the power in older cases that had become *causes
célèbres* in some Republican circles. He pardoned Scooter Libby with the
explanation that "I don't know Mr. Libby, but for years I have heard that
he has been treated unfairly."[36] Some critics were concerned that in the
middle of the Mueller investigation Trump was using the pardon to send
the message that those who were loyal, as some suspected Libby had been
to Vice President Cheney, could expect consideration of clemency. But
it is also possible that he was merely looking to redeem long-standing
conservative objections to Libby's conviction and frustration over Bush's
unwillingness to pardon him fully. Trump could demonstrate that, unlike
Bush, he was not prepared to leave Libby "on the battlefield."

A similar dynamic played out in Trump's pardon of conservative com-
mentator Dinesh D'Souza, who pleaded guilty in 2014 to making illegal
Senate campaign contributions. At the time of his pardon, D'Souza was
serving a five-year probationary period. In May 2018, Trump announced
by tweet his intention to issue the pardon that very day: "Will be giving
a Full Pardon to Dinesh D'Souza today. He was treated very unfairly by
our government."[37] The White House later stated that Trump believed
D'Souza was the "victim of selective prosecution for violations of campaign finance laws" and that he "accepted responsibility for his actions."[38]
And Trump explained further: "[D'Souza] should have [faced] a quick
minor fine, like everybody else with the election stuff .... What they
did to him was horrible."[39] In this case, as in other controversial ones,
Trump did not work through the Office of the Pardon Attorney. Justice
Department regulations would have excluded D'Souza from consideration
for a pardon because he had not completed his probation.

The D'Souza pardon was seen by many commentators to serve the
political aims of playing to the conservative base and tweaking political foes. Prior to prosecution, D'Souza had produced two films—*2016:
Obama's America* and *Hillary's America*—that were very critical of

Trump's predecessor and his 2016 presidential opponent. D'Souza and his supporters argued that his prosecution was itself political payback for the first film. D'Souza was prosecuted by the Office of the U.S. Attorney for the Southern District of New York, which at the time was headed by Preet Bharara. Trump had fired Bharara in 2017, and by the time of the pardon, Bharara was a vocal Trump critic. The pardon was widely praised in conservative circles. "Bravo! @realDonaldTrump," tweeted Sen. Ted Cruz. "Dinesh was the subject of a political prosecution, brazenly targeted by the Obama administration bc [sic] of his political views. ... This is Justice."[40] The pardon was widely decried as well. Trump has transformed the pardon power into an "everyday tool of culture war," said David Graham in *The Atlantic*. "As with so many of Trump's maneuvers, this is entirely within the legal bounds of his power but still largely outside the realm of propriety and precedent."[41]

When Trump pardoned Conrad Black, convicted of illegally diverting money from stockholders to himself, it did not escape notice that Black was a strong supporter who had authored a book entitled *Donald J. Trump: A President Like No Other.* Political motivations appeared to inform the pardon of a strong supporter and former Republican member of the California State Assembly, Pat Nolan. Nolan had been caught up in an FBI bribery sting and convicted of using his political office to solicit campaign contributions, and he had served his twenty-six-month sentence by the time the pardon came. The White House explained the pardon mainly on the basis of Nolan's post-prison work on criminal justice reform, victim's rights, and religious freedom.[42] But the pardon had come after a conservative magazine, *The American Spectator*, had urged Trump on, noting that Nolan "has advised Jared Kushner on crime, punishment, and reform," and linking what it described as the dishonest Justice Department investigation to a supposedly broken Justice Department pardon recommendation process and alleged FBI corruption related to Trump himself.[43]

Trump also used a pardon of former Illinois Gov. Rod Blagojevich to send a political message. Blagojevich, a Democrat, had been convicted of several crimes for extorting personal benefits, including campaign contributions, in return for an appointment to the Senate seat vacated by Barack Obama upon his election to the presidency. Trump became acquainted with Blagojevich's cause when the convicted governor, still pursuing an appeal, appeared on a program that Trump hosted, *Celebrity Apprentice,* where Trump praised him just before firing him. Once Trump became president, Blagojevich's wife took to the Fox News channel to hint that her husband was the victim of a political prosecution. Trump pardoned Blagojevich in February 2020, citing a "ridiculous sentence."[44] But Trump also made the political point that Blagojevich was prosecuted "by the same people—Comey, Fitzpatrick, the same group."[45] Trump was referring to James Comey, the former FBI director whom he fired and who subsequently successfully induced the appointment of a special counsel investigation into the Russia matter, and Patrick Fitzgerald (not Fitzpatrick), the special counsel in the Libby prosecution and Comey's attorney following his dismissal by Trump.

Trump's most corrosive exercise of the pardon power, however, was less about politics and more about personal legal interest. This was clearest in the commutation of the sentence of Roger Stone. Trump had told Mueller in writing that he did not recall discussing WikiLeaks with Stone, even though several witnesses told Mueller that he did. Had Stone testified to direct conversations with the president about WikiLeaks and its plan for leaking the stolen emails, it would have been devastating to Trump. In the two weeks after Trump gave his testimony, Trump publicly criticized "flipping," described Stone as "very brave" for not cooperating with Mueller, and praised Stone's "guts" in not cooperating with Mueller.[46] Mueller concluded that these and other statements by Trump "support the inference that the President intended to communicate a message that witnesses could be rewarded for refusing to provide testimony adverse to the President."[47] Once Stone was indicted, Trump more than once stated that he believed that Stone was treated unfairly. In a clear reference to clemency, he publicly signaled that he possessed "great powers" that he could exercise depending on how the process played out.[48] And then, of course, he commuted Stone's sentence rather than let him go to jail.

The president and his lawyers have clearly been considering pardons for others who were caught up in investigations of the president. Mueller discovered that the president's personal attorney, Michael Cohen, discussed with the president's personal counsel a possible pardon of crimes for which he was investigated and later convicted. Trump's private attorney, Rudy Giuliani, informed the *New York Daily News* in an interview that "[w]hen the whole thing is over, things might get cleaned up with some presidential pardons."[49] Trump has fallen out with Cohen and likely won't pardon him. But he has hinted publicly—in language like he used with reference to Stone—that he might provide convicted former campaign manager Paul Manafort with a pardon or commutation. Trump stated that he would not "take … off the table," and would decide when "ready" whether to issue, a pardon for Manafort.[50]

REFORM

The pardon power is a broad one, and no reform short of a constitutional amendment to chop down the power significantly can stop a president from using the power, as Trump has, to score political points, meet demands from a political constituency, or routinely make clemency decisions on the basis of personal relationships, likes and dislikes, and entreaties. Many constitutional amendments to the pardon power have been proposed over the years. An amendment would be a heavy lift but might be justified on a targeted basis to ban, for example, self-pardons—a topic, that, as we explain later in this chapter, can also be regulated by statute. But in general, we do not favor constitutional reform. The pardon power is an important one to preserve for purposes of mercy and rec- onciliation, even if it is subject to abuse. An amendment to restrict this avenue of relief from errors and excesses in the criminal justice system seems especially fraught, and ill timed, given the intense national attention focused on the system's serious failings, including the pervasive problem of racial bias and broad inequality in access to legal services. Yet beyond narrow and clearly defined limitations like the one on self-pardons, it is unclear what types of reform suitable for a constitutional amendment would preserve the just uses of this power while preventing its abuse.

Another reason we do not support constitutional reform is that statutory reform is capable of addressing the worst elements of abuse. The main concern that our proposals below address is that unbounded self-interestedness in the issuance of pardons can easily move into the territory of outright corruption. By prohibiting the most corrupt abuses, Congress can end doubt about the breadth of the "absolute" pardon power. It can also send a signal more generally that presidents would be unwise to regard the decision to pardon as a law-free zone that a president can occupy safely in consultation with only West Wing aides. This in turn can have a salutary impact on the operation of executive branch norms, especially with regard to officials subordinate to the president whom he needs to execute a pardon.

Bribery

A pardon or commutation is "absolute" for the beneficiary for the crime pardoned. But a pardon does not afford the president, as the grantor, immunity from commission of a crime in connection with granting a pardon. Nor does it cover any such separate crime committed by the grantee in seeking or accepting the pardon as part of a corrupt bargain.

Congress could, for example, make it a crime for the president and the grantee to engage in a bribery scheme in which the grantee makes a personal payment, a campaign contribution, or an offer of something else of value as part of an explicit quid pro quo arrangement. The president's subsequent pardon or commutation would remain fully in effect for the offense pardoned, in accordance with the Pardon Clause. But the anti-bribery law would apply to the independent criminal acts committed by the president and the grantee in the course of reaching an illegal agreement about the terms on which a pardon would be granted.

The current anti-bribery statute, 18 U.S.C. § 201, would clearly apply to someone who offered a bribe to a president in exchange for a pardon. There is a good argument that the anti-bribery statute also prohibits the president from offering or granting a pardon in exchange for a payment or something else "of value." The executive branch has for many statutes required a "plain statement" before the statute, especially a criminal one, is deemed to apply to the president. While the anti-bribery statute has no such plain statement, the Office of Legal Counsel has twice stated that the anti-bribery law is an exception to this plain statement rule in this context.[51] The plain statement rule is designed to protect the president from undue intrusion by Congress, the Office of Legal Counsel explained. But the bribery statute "raises no separation of powers questions were it to be applied to the President" because the Constitution "confers no power in the President to receive bribes."[52] As a result, "the Department of Justice has construed the federal bribery statute as applying to the President even though it does not expressly name the President."

That said, the application of the anti-bribery statute to the president is not certain, especially since it defines a covered "public official" as a "Member of Congress, Delegate, or Resident Commissioner, ... or an officer or employee or person acting for or on behalf of the United States, or any department, agency or branch of Government thereof."[53] In the absence of a plain statement, it is possible that a court might would rule that the president is not an "officer or employee" of the United States. There should be no doubt on this matter. We thus propose that Congress make clear that the president is a "public official" within the meaning of the bribery statute. Congress should also amend the statute's prohibition on a public official seeking or accepting a bribe "in return for being influenced in the performance of an official act" to make clear that "official act" includes a pardon.[54]

These changes are entirely consistent with the Justice Department's view of presidential prerogative and would clearly criminalize pardons as part of a bribery scheme. The amended bribery statute would not prohibit a president from pardoning a campaign supporter to reward his or her loyalty, without regard to the merits. Such a pardon may well be unworthy or controversial, but it would not be a crime for the president to use the pardon power in this fashion. Under the amended statute (and quite possibly under the current statute), the same pardon of a supporter would give rise to legal jeopardy if evidence surfaced that the president had entered into a corrupt agreement to grant the pardon in return for political contributions.

Obstruction of Justice

On the same principle that a pardon does not afford the president immunity from commission of an independent crime by granting a pardon, we also believe that Congress can and should expressly criminalize a pardon offered in exchange for the recipient's false or misleading testimony in a judicial or other official proceeding.

There is a good argument that an extant obstruction of justice statute, 18 U.S.C. § 1503, already prohibits a president from using a pardon in this way. Attorney General William Barr, who possesses a broad view of presidential prerogatives, stated during his confirmation hearing that "if a pardon was a quid pro quo to altering testimony, then that would definitely implicate an obstruction statute."[55] Earlier, in a June 2018 memorandum on obstruction of justice that Barr wrote prior to becoming attorney general, he emphasized that a president under current law "can commit obstruction in this classic sense of sabotaging a proceeding's truth-finding function" or "induc[ing] a witness to change testimony."[56] Enforcing an obstruction of justice statute against a president in this context did not impinge on the president's "complete" Article II authority over law enforcement, Barr explained, which does not extend to "commission of any of these inherently wrongful, subversive acts." The same logic would apply to the pardon power.

And yet just as in the case of bribery, the plain statement rule makes the prohibition on the use of pardons to obstruct justice needlessly uncertain. We thus propose that Congress clarify the issue by amending the bribery statute in two ways. First, consistent with the Barr analysis and as we propose in addressing bribery per se, Congress should make clear that the criminal prohibition of the bribery statute applies to the president and vice president. And, second, Congress should make clear that a pardon in exchange for false or misleading testimony would violate that statute. The statute at 18 U.S.C. § 201(b)(3) already makes it a crime to "corruptly give[], offer[], or promise[] *anything of value* to any person ... with intent to influence the testimony under oath or affirmation of such first-mentioned person as a witness upon a trial, hearing, or other proceeding" (emphasis added). The statute could achieve the purposes sketched above if Congress simply defined "anything of value" for these purposes to include a presidential pardon or commutation.

Such a statute would cover the possible case of Trump pardoning Stone in exchange for his refusal to cooperate with Mueller. There is little doubt that the bribery statute, especially as amended with the plain statement we propose, would be implicated if the president had dangled a monetary inducement of "value" for Stone to keep silent about the alleged conversations with WikiLeaks. Assume, for example that, in denouncing "flipping" and praising Stone for his "guts," the president had not implicitly referred to his "great [pardon] powers" but had stated instead: "I know Stone will be found innocent. He is a good friend and counselor, and I look forward to having him work with me in my GREAT businesses." On its face, this statement would justify the opening of a criminal investigation into whether this constituted a "corrupt ...

offer ... of anything of value" to influence specific testimony in an ongoing criminal proceeding. The reform we propose would establish that the outcome would be the same—exposure to criminal liability—if the "thing of value" offered was a pardon or commutation.

Proving this crime might, of course, be difficult, depending on the allegations and facts of the particular case. But even so, we believe this reform would have an impact. It is unlikely that Trump would have made public statements like those about Stone with reference to "anything of value" *other than* a pardon or commutation. The risk of criminal liability for influencing witness testimony would have been too great. His lawyers would certainly have so advised him. But Trump appears to believe that his "absolute" pardon power immunizes him. For this reason, a president with this view of the scope of the power could, as Trump did, regularly and openly reassure Stone that his "guts" would be rewarded and that, as Trump tweeted a month before the commutation, Stone "can sleep well at night."[57] A reform that brings the president and the exercise of the pardon power within the scope of the bribery statute would deter a president from pursuing any brazen scheme to use this power to induce a witness to lie, and would clearly authorize a criminal inquiry if he or she does.

There is a case to be made for an even broader prohibition. This would involve amending the obstruction of justice statute to criminalize pardons made in discrete contexts with the corrupt intent of influencing the due administration of law. Such a change would raise complex constitutional questions that we discuss fully in Chapter Eight in the context of special counsel investigations.

Self-Pardons

President Nixon reportedly considered pardoning himself but declined to do so. Trump is the first president to raise the possibility publicly, and it is easy to imagine him doing so before he leaves office.

The core worry about self-pardons is that a president can with the stroke of a pen avoid accountability under the law. A president who self-pardons remains subject to state laws, and the self-pardon would not relieve the president of other consequences, such as potential loss of a vocational license, including the license to practice law. Nonetheless it is no small matter, in a democracy committed to the proposition that no one is "above the law," that a president might engage in bribery and extortion, subvert the federal criminal justice system, and then immunize himself or herself from liability for federal criminal offenses committed while in office.

Despite these concerns, whether the pardon power includes a power to self-pardon is unsettled. Neither constitutional text nor judicial opinions speak overtly to the issue, and scholars are sharply divided.[58] The Constitution does contain hints, but they cut in many directions. The express limits on the pardon power (to federal crimes and excluding impeachment) might imply that there are no other limits, and the exception for impeachment might imply, as Andrew McCarthy noted, that "the Framers understood they were permitting the president to pardon himself" for crimes.[59] That said, Article I of the Constitution states that a person convicted after impeachment "shall nevertheless" be subject to a subsequent criminal trial; the Article II specification that the president has power to "grant [a] pardon" might imply a bilateral relationship that is absent from self-pardons; and the Take Care Clause might preclude the president from excluding himself or herself from the reach of law enforcement. This latter idea might have been what the Office of Legal Counsel meant when in 1974 it wrote without further explanation that self-pardons would "seem" to be disallowed "[u]nder the fundamental rule that no one may be a judge in his own case."[60]

In the face of this uncertainty, Congress's constitutional judgment can matter a lot, both in informing subsequent judicial review of a self-pardon and in giving a president pause about issuing one in the first place. For this reason, and for the reason stated by the Office of Legal Counsel in 1974, we propose that Congress make clear that a self-pardon is not authorized by Article II and has no force or effect.

As we explain fully in Appendix B, we would accomplish this in a statute with two parts. First, Congress would state its constitutional position in a preamble. The preamble would cite the Pardon Clause, the Take Care Clause, and the Impeachment Clause's express reservation of criminal liability for a president impeached and convicted who upon leaving office "shall ... be liable and subject to Indictment, Trial, Judgment and Punishment, according to Law." It would also take note of the Executive Branch's position against self-pardons, and express

Congress's independent constitutional judgment against them. Second, Congress would affirmatively prohibit the use of pardons in federal court as follows: "The President's grant of a pardon to himself or herself shall not be accepted by any federal court of the United States, nor deprive any such court of jurisdiction over any criminal or civil matter, nor operate to confer on the President any legal immunity from investigation or prosecution."[61]

PART II

★

PRESIDENT-JUSTICE DEPARTMENT RELATIONS

In this part we move from a focus on the president and the White House to the most consequential relationship in the executive branch that the president heads: the one between the president and the Department of Justice, headed by the attorney general.

Some of the most serious problems in American constitutional government arise when the president or the attorney general, or both together, use the formidable federal law enforcement power for corrupt ends—for example, by using a criminal investigation to harass or punish political opponents, or by countenancing lawbreaking by the president or senior executive branch officials. Watergate and related events implicated both problems and led to important reforms. The Trump presidency has revealed that in some respects these reforms were successful, and in others they were inadequate. It has also revealed serious gaps in guidance on how the Justice Department and the FBI should approach problems of possible presidential criminality or presidential action contrary to the national security interests of the United States.

This part focuses on five major problems that emerged or grew untenable during the Trump presidency:

- *Department of Justice Independence.* The tension between the president's constitutional control of law enforcement and the post-Watergate insistence on Justice Department independence reached a crisis point during the Trump administration. Topics here include the danger of politicized law enforcement and the efficacy of the norms of White House noninterference in the Justice Department's prosecutorial decisions.

- *The Special Counsel.* The independence of the Justice Department is most under pressure, and also most important, when the president or senior executive branch official is accused of a crime. Regulations adopted in 1999 aimed to address the obvious conflict of interest that arises in this situation. The Mueller investigation tested the adequacy of these regulations for the first time. In many respects, the regulations worked well. But in many other ways, they were wanting and need reform.

- *Investigation of the President.* The FBI process of opening a criminal or counterintelligence investigation of the president, which happened early in Trump's presidency, raises the risk of a politicized investigation of a president, or its appearance, most predictably as perceived by the president's party and supporters. It implicates tricky and underregulated questions of responsibility, accountability, and transparency that should be clarified. A related issue is election cycle investigations, which impacted both presidential campaigns in 2016.

- *Investigation of Past Administrations.* Attorney General William Barr's appointment of John Durham to investigate the investigation of the 2016 Trump campaign raises the question of when and how one administration should probe the counterintelligence or criminal investigations of a prior administration. The next administration will likely face this question in a few guises. But none will be more momentous than the questions of whether and how the new administration should investigate and possibly prosecute Trump for crimes in office, or pardon him if crimes were committed.

- *The White House Counsel.* The White House counsel, frequently called "the president's lawyer," runs a small legal shop in the White House whose power has been growing steadily for decades. This is a worrisome development since the White House counsel is heavily involved in practically all White House initiatives and may harbor the expectation more intensely than other government lawyers that he or she should see legal issues and advice through a political lens. The problems inherent in this political conception of the role reached new heights during the Trump administration.

JUSTICE DEPARTMENT INDEPENDENCE

Of the multitude of norms that Donald Trump has broken as president, perhaps none has caused more commentary and consternation than his efforts to defy Justice Department independence and politicize the department's enforcement of civil and criminal law. In this chapter, we examine these efforts and the damage they caused, and we propose reforms. In Chapter Eight, we discuss Trump's threats to Justice Department independence in his attacks on the special counsel.

BACKGROUND

The Constitution vests "the Executive power" in the president. This means, among other things, that it authorizes the president to enforce the law and makes him or her responsible for doing so. The Constitution also assigns the president the duty to "take Care that the Laws be faithfully executed."[1] This provision requires the president to comply with the law, but it is also a basis for the president's authority to interpret and enforce the law. What's more, the Constitution has long been interpreted to charge the president with conducting foreign affairs and protecting the national security. Congress can regulate these powers—to an uncertain degree— through enactment of substantive laws (such as anti-bribery laws and the prohibition on torture) and through direct regulation of the executive branch (such as through the Foreign Intelligence Surveillance Act).

The president is a busy person, and the bulk of his or her powers and duties are exercised in the first instance by the attorney general of the United States, who heads the 115,000-person Department of Justice. The attorney general presumptively controls the law enforcement function for the executive branch and also advises the president and other executive officials to ensure that they comply with the law. (The attorney general typically delegates the latter function to the Office of Legal Counsel.) The attorney general also has important responsibilities related to national security, including the control and supervision of the FBI.

The powers and responsibilities of the attorney general are supported by Article II of the Constitution and by congressional statute. The president remains in charge, however. "The Constitution requires that a President chosen by the entire Nation oversee the execution of the laws," the Supreme Court noted recently.[2] In making decisions about law enforcement and law compliance, presidents can seek and rely on legal advice from whomever they like, including the counsel to the president in the White House. The president has the formal authority to second-guess the attorney general's legal judgment, to direct the attorney general to enforce the law in a certain way, and to fire the attorney general if he or she refuses to comply with the order. In practice, as we shall see, matters are somewhat more complex.

The attorney general's powers, and especially the power to enforce the criminal law, are among the most important ones in the government. As chief prosecutor, the attorney general "has more control over life, liberty, and reputation than any other person in America," as Attorney General Robert Jackson once famously said. The attorney general or a prosecutor under his or her command can start a financially ruinous investigation and then can secure a grand jury indictment based on a "one-sided presentation of the facts," Jackson noted. The attorney general can also "pick people that he thinks he should get" and then order investigations and search the federal criminal code for a crime.[3]

For present purposes, the most serious worry about prosecutorial and law enforcement discretion is that it may be exercised to serve the political interests of the administration—either by investigating or prosecuting enemies, or by refusing to do so against allies who deserve scrutiny. This worry is exacerbated by the fact that the attorney general, who has presumptive control over that discretion, is a senior member of the president's Cabinet and often one of the president's friends or political advisers.

The problem is made yet more difficult by the fact that law enforcement is inevitably and properly "political" in the sense of reflecting the values and priorities of the elected president. As Watergate special prosecutor Archibald Cox, a man with credibility on this issue, put it in a 1974 hearing, "the treatment of the law and facts simply cannot be separated from ideas of economic, social, or political—in the higher sense of the word—philosophy."[4] Permitting political priorities to inform law enforcement is not the same thing as permitting partisanship to do so.[5] Prosecutions must always be based on "law and merit, and not on considerations of party affiliation, political image-making, or White House approval or influence," as John F. Kennedy's White House counsel, Ted Sorensen, noted in the same 1974 hearing.[6] And yet "politics is necessarily tied up with policy, with one's concept of the public interest and response to the public will," Sorensen acknowledged. "A president who campaigns on a 'law and order' issue, or a narcotics or civil rights or organized crime issue, must not be confronted with an Attorney General of sharply differing views appointed for a fixed term by his predecessor."

The line between properly political considerations and impermissibly partisan ones can be elusive and contested. Consider some examples. In November 1907, not long before the election of 1908, President Theodore Roosevelt determined that his administration would not sue U.S. Steel even though its acquisition of the Tennessee Coal & Iron Co. almost certainly violated the Sherman Antitrust Act. Roosevelt determined that such a lawsuit might hinder the economic recovery after the financial panic of 1907. This was a plausible judgment for Roosevelt to make, and a legitimate exercise of presidential discretion about relative priorities. But it was also controversial politically, in part because it had the consequence of benefiting Roosevelt's party in the presidential election that year.

The second example concerns Eric Holder's decision as Barack Obama's attorney general to reopen a preliminary investigation against some officials, including career officials, who were involved in the CIA enhanced interrogation program during the George W. Bush administration. Holder was acting in part on a recommendation by the Justice Department's Office of Professional Responsibility, and he made clear that his review would not target "anyone who acted in good faith and within the scope of the legal guidance given by the Office of Legal Counsel."[7] His action was nonetheless criticized for two reasons. First, career prosecutors, not political appointees, had previously reviewed all the cases in question and decided not to go forward with prosecution. Second, as former CIA General Counsel Jeffrey Smith noted, "the decision of one administration to prosecute career officers for acts committed under a policy of a previous administration" might "set the dangerous precedent that criminal law can be used to settle policy differences at the expense of career officers."[8] The reopened investigation lasted three years and resulted in no new prosecutions.

The dangers of interference may be clear enough if the president directs prosecutions of an opponent in a political campaign, a prominent supporter or funder of that campaign, or opposition political party organizations. Other cases may be murkier and less clearly "political." For example, a president might have committed to bring to justice certain "special interests" whom he or she has charged with ripping off consumers, engaging in deceptive and abusive lending practices, or putting dangerous drugs on the market. He or she campaigned on that commitment, pledging that his or her Department of Justice will not allow those misdeeds to go unpunished. Is a later directive to the attorney general to open investigations an improperly "political" one or the implementation of a defensible policy of redressing criminal corporate misconduct? Doubtless the president will realize the political benefits of redeeming a campaign promise—and of doing what he or she had said that he or she would do. Is this political, or, perhaps more to the point, improperly political?

Other complications have little to do with partisan politics but pit the independent law enforcement process against legitimate presidential policy objectives. A president may discover that the Justice Department is pursuing an investigation, and on the brink of bringing charges, against a foreign corporation based in a country with which the United States is engaged in sensitive trade or national security discussions. The head of that state raises concerns about the case and suggests that it is an impediment to good relations and the resolution of outstanding issues. Should the president agree to look into the matter and even ask the attorney general to determine whether the investigation could be slowed down or reconsidered?

From the beginning of the nation until the 1970s, these challenging problems of possible abuse of law enforcement powers—by the president, the attorney general, or U.S. attorneys—were regulated by congressional oversight, including the confirmation process; by journalists covering enforcement actions; by elections; and by the self-restraint bolstered by the weakest of norms.

This system did not survive Richard Nixon's administration. For decades prior to Nixon's presidency, FBI Director J. Edgar Hoover used the bureau's manifold and unregulated tools—electronic and other forms of surveillance, aggressive investigation, threats, and the like—to harass and discredit various political groups and individuals that Hoover deemed "subversive." Hoover often did so with the approval of attorneys general, and sometimes to aid the political agenda of presidential administrations. And then came Nixon. Hoover refused to play ball in most of Nixon's criminal machinations. But Nixon's corrupt attorneys general, John Mitchell and Richard Kleindienst, did. They and the president transformed the Justice Department into a lawbreaking arm to advance the president's political agenda. The administration's many well-known Watergate-related machinations are the famous example. But there are others, including Nixon's order to Kleindienst to drop a lawsuit against ITT, which had donated $400,000 to his reelection campaign.

Historical reforms to address these abuses came in the 1970s, both in the executive branch and in new laws enacted by Congress. Inside the executive branch, one important reform was the Attorney General Guidelines first promulgated during Gerald Ford's administration. These guidelines, and elaborate implementing guidance known as the Domestic Investigations and Operations Guide (DIOG), establish the rules that govern the bureau's investigative and intelligence collection activities. The guidelines and the DIOG address the problem of politicized investigations in guidance for "sensitive investigative matters." A sensitive investigative matter is one that is inherently politically sensitive or poses a danger of the appearance of politicization. These matters may concern investigations of domestic public officials, political candidates, religious or political organizations (or their members), or new media, or they may have an academic nexus.[9] The main prescription in the DIOG is that any official in the Justice Department who considers pursuing a sensitive investigative matter must first report up the FBI chain of command.

Another relevant executive branch reform is the White House–Justice Department "contacts policy" initiated by President Ford in 1974.[10] Every administration since then has issued its version of this policy. While each administration's policy differs in details, they all basically prohibit White House staff from contacting agencies, including the Justice Department, about investigations or enforcement actions. To simplify only a bit, all communications related to Justice Department prosecutions and investigations and other enforcement actions must take place between the Office of White House Counsel and the Office of the Attorney General. The policy has a number of standard exemptions—for policy issues, for matters important to the president's duties (especially involving national security), and for contacts "appropriate from a law enforcement perspective." Most notably, the contacts policy does not purport to apply to the president.

The guidelines, the DIOG, and the contacts policy might not seem like much. But as bolstered through decades of public affirmation and scrutiny, they were successful in fostering powerful norms of White House noninterference in, and nonpoliticization of, Justice Department criminal investigations.[11] In particular, it became generally accepted that partisan and personal considerations should play no role in investigating or prosecuting cases.[12]

A rare but notable violation of these norms occurred when the Justice Department under George W. Bush ordered the midterm firing of nine U.S. attorneys. Attorney General Alberto Gonzales testified that "nothing improper occurred" because "U.S. attorneys serve at the pleasure of the president," and because "[t]here is nothing improper in making a change for poor management, policy differences or questionable judgment, or simply to have another qualified individual serve."[13] Importantly, however, Gonzales acknowledged that "[i]t would be improper to remove a U.S. attorney to interfere with or influence a particular prosecution for partisan political gain."[14]

The Justice Department's Office of the Inspector General and Office of Professional Responsibility issued a report that "found significant evidence that political partisan considerations were an important factor" in the removals.[15] The "most troubling" removal concerned the U.S. attorney for the District of New Mexico, David Iglesias. The report concluded that Iglesias was removed due to complaints from "New Mexico Republican members of Congress and party activists about Iglesias's handling of voter fraud and public corruption" involving Democratic Party officials or interests and that the Justice Department removed Iglesias without any inquiry into his handling of the cases. The report noted that "Department leaders" had a "responsibility to ensure that prosecutorial decisions [are] based on the law, the evidence, and Department policy, not political pressure," and concluded that the leaders "abdicated their responsibility to safeguard the integrity and independence of the Department by failing to ensure that the removal of U.S. Attorneys was not based on improper political considerations." It also speculated that the pressure on Iglesias might have constituted obstruction of justice or criminal liability for "honest services" mail and wire fraud.[16]

One remarkable element of this episode was its vindication of the independence norm, since the president's undoubted constitutional power to fire U.S. attorneys did not prevent the norm violation from producing a scandal that forced Gonzales to resign in September 2007. The Justice Department clarified the legal context governing political interference in prosecutorial decisions after he resigned. The department offered its official views on the relevance of the law of obstruction of justice and mail and wire fraud in the conclusions of a special attorney, Nora R. Dannehy, who was appointed by Gonzales's successor, Michael Mukasey. In an analysis that the Obama Administration endorsed and relayed to Congress, Dannehy established that political intervention in the criminal justice system by Justice Department officials can in some instances violate relevant law and emphasized the sweep of the norms against politicized law enforcement beyond legal prohibitions.[17]

Section 1503 of Title 18 of the U.S. Code punishes anyone who "corruptly ... influences, obstructs, or impedes, or endeavors to influence, obstruct, or impede, the due administration of justice."[18] Dannehy interpreted the statute to penalize "only forward-looking conduct."[19] In the context of the Iglesias firing, she concluded that Section 1503 proscribed two types of conduct. First, it prohibited pressure on a U.S. attorney to "accelerate his charging decisions in [a particular case] or initiate voter fraud investigations to affect the election." And second, it prohibited an administration's action to "influence a judicial proceeding by removing" a U.S. attorney in order to replace him with one "who would act in a manner aimed at influencing the due administration of justice."

Dannehy further concluded that the evidence did not show that the New Mexico politicians who contacted Iglesias, or the Justice Department and White House officials involved in his firing, had violated the obstruction statute so construed. She acknowledged that New Mexico Sen. Pete Domenici was "in part politically motivated" to seek Iglesias's removal. But she concluded that "a public official does not violate the law [of obstruction] by seeking the removal of a United States Attorney for his failure either to pursue a particular case the official believes is legitimate or to pursue certain types of cases the official believes should be brought, even if the public official's motives are partisan and inconsistent with the values of [the Justice Department]."

The Dannehy letter is a summary of a presumably more fine-grained but unpublished legal analysis, and thus is not as clear or helpful as it could be. However, it appears to permit several conclusions.

First, an administration can lawfully bring political considerations to bear in determining the "types of cases" it wishes to bring. It could, for example, prioritize voter fraud prosecutions as a class and remove a U.S. attorney for failing to adopt this priority.

Second, the primary obstruction of justice statute, 18 U.S.C. § 1503, applies to the law enforcement actions of executive branch officials. This was an important general conclusion of the Dannehy letter, even though she fleshed out the meaning of obstruction only in the context of electoral interference. As Dannehy construed the statute, the firing of a U.S. attorney, or other pressure by a public official, can "influence, obstruct, or impede ... the due administration of justice" within the meaning of 18 U.S.C. § 1503 where its purpose is to accelerate a decision in a specific case affecting an election. She also stated an important limitation on this conclusion when the official has a good-faith belief that the prosecutorial decision in question is "legitimate." Dannehy is here addressing the problem of mixed motives. In the case of obstruction of justice by a private person, the general rule is that the mens rea element is satisfied in a mixed-motives case "if the offending action was prompted, at least in part, by a 'corrupt' motive."[20] Dannehy appears to conclude that the rule for "public officials" is the opposite: A belief in the legitimacy of the law enforcement action in question suffices to defeat obstruction of justice even if the motives are otherwise partisan.

Third, and importantly in light of this limitation on statutory obstruction of justice, Dannehy emphasizes that even if there is *legal* room for partisan motivation or considerations, Justice Department "principles"—specifically those of "fairness and justice"—weigh strongly against "undue sensitivity to politics." Dannehy criticized "[Justice Department] leadership" for its failure to uphold those principles, and for exhibiting "undue sensitivity to politics," because it "never determined whether the complaints about Mr. Iglesias were legitimate." Even though neither Domenici nor the Justice Department nor the White House broke the law by seeking Iglesias's removal, department officials should have examined the merits of Domenici's claims, and their failure to do so "bespeaks [their] undue sensitivity to politics." As a matter of department policy, they were required to "answer not to partisan politics but to principles of fairness and justice." The letter concluded with an affirmation of the attorney general's commitment to "ensuring that partisan political considerations play *no* role in law enforcement decisions of the Department" (emphasis added).

Fourth, Dannehy addressed the relevance of the statute at 18 U.S.C. § 1346, which provides that for purposes of mail and wire fraud, the term "scheme or artifice to defraud" includes "a scheme or artifice to deprive another of the intangible right of honest services." She interpreted its scope narrowly, concluding that there was no scheme to get Iglesias "to use his Office in return for anything of value, including his continued employment." She also concluded that "honest services fraud does not embrace allegations that purely political interests may have influenced a public official's performance of his duty." She did not elaborate on this finding but appeared to suggest that an official could not be charged with "honest services" fraud on the basis of a purely subjective intent to achieve a political goal. A prosecution on this theory would require the involvement of others, as in the case of an official acting for political purposes in return for "anything of value."[21] The Supreme Court subsequently narrowed the scope of the "honest services" statute to reach only bribes and kickbacks, but the Dannehy analysis highlights the challenges of drawing clear, practical lines against impermissible "politics" in law enforcement.[22]

None of the developments described in the last few pages—the Attorney General Guidelines, the DIOG, the White House contacts policy, and the Justice Department's legal conclusions about inappropriate department interference in ongoing prosecutions—purported to apply to or govern the president. Nonetheless, in the post-Watergate years, and despite Article II, a norm also developed to inhibit presidential involvement in, and comment on, pending investigations.

A rare violation of this norm prior to the Trump administration came when President Obama commented on the ongoing FBI investigation of Hillary Clinton's emails. "I don't think it posed a national security problem," he said. "This is not a situation in which America's national security was endangered."[23] The director of the FBI at the time, James Comey, later noted that Obama's comments "seemed to absolve [Clinton] before a final determination was made" and could lead an outside observer to reasonably wonder, "how on earth could his Department of Justice do anything other than follow his lead?"[24] Obama's comments were a contributing factor—there were, of course, many others—to the sharp contestation over the legitimacy of the Clinton case's resolution.

In addition to these executive branch rules, policies, and norms, Congress in the 1970s enacted numerous laws designed to tamp down on the political use of prosecutorial power. The 1978 enactment of the Foreign Intelligence Surveillance Act, on top of a 1968 law that required prior judicial approval for wiretaps and bugging, went a long way toward ending politically motivated surveillance in a criminal investigation.[25] (We discuss the contested case of the Carter Page Foreign Intelligence Surveillance Act application in Chapter Nine.) Statutory restrictions on Justice Department investigators' (and the president's) access to IRS tax records were designed to put an end to decades of politically motivated fishing expeditions for tax or other crimes.[26] Other reforms designed to end politically motivated investigations and prosecutions included the Privacy Act,[27] an improved Freedom of Information Act,[28] and statutory inspectors general in major departments with semi-independence and broadly defined authority to pursue "abuse."[29] Finally, Congress in 1976 made the FBI director a single-term, ten-year appointment in order to prevent too much power from amassing in one director (a la Hoover over the decades) and to give the director more political independence from the president and the attorney general.[30]

It is worth noting one sweeping reform that Congress declined to implement in the 1970s. In the wake of Watergate, Sen. Sam Ervin introduced a bill that would have made the Justice Department an independent agency headed by an attorney general appointed for a six-year term and removable by the president only for malfeasance. "I have become convinced of the utter necessity of removing the department, insofar that it is possible, from the play of partisan politics," Ervin said at the time.[31]

There was widespread opposition to the bill from renowned former executive branch lawyers, including Archibald Cox, Lloyd Cutler, Nicholas Katzenbach, Herbert Wechsler, Ramsey Clark, Burke Marshall, former Justice Arthur Goldberg, J. Lee Rankin, and Theodore Sorensen. Many doubted that the bill was constitutional. They noted that an independent Justice Department might jeopardize the vigorous enforcement of national policies as reflected in elections. Many worried that an "independent" Justice Department would be captured by interest groups or Congress. They noted how often the department engaged in controversial prosecution or law enforcement efforts, and that the decisions to undertake and defend those actions must lie in a politically accountable actor. And they believed that Watergate showed that a vigorous press, robust congressional oversight (including confirmation hearings), and a strong public ethic were the best antidotes to the problems of political corruption of the Justice Department's tools. Although these former officials opposed making the department formally independent, they offered various smaller-scale reforms, and many of them supported an independent counsel for conflicts of interest with the White House.

THE TRUMP ERA

President Trump "has engaged in a scorched-earth assault on the pillars of the criminal justice system in a way that no other occupant of the White House has done," noted the *New York Times*, accurately, in February 2018.[32] Matters have grown worse since then. We assess both what the president said and did, and how officials in the White House and Justice Department responded to his provocations. (We set aside until Chapter Eight the president's very serious norm violations when he interfered in Special Counsel Robert Mueller's investigation.)

Trump from the beginning made clear that he either did not understand or did not respect the norms that had governed White House relations with the Justice Department since the 1970s. He pined for an attorney general who would protect him from legal jeopardy. And he expressed dismay that he could not have his way with the Justice Department. Trump famously stated that he had an "absolute right" to do what he wanted with the Justice Department.[33] This is an overstatement even of the president's formidable power under Article II to control Justice Department initiatives.

But what is more interesting is the distance between Trump's formal powers and the norms that got in the way of his exercising them. "You know, the saddest thing is that because I'm the president of the United States, I am not supposed to be involved with the Justice Department," Trump said in late 2017.[34] "I am not supposed to be involved with the F.B.I. I'm not supposed to be doing the kind of things that I would love to be doing."[35] Trump reportedly did not understand "why he cannot simply give orders to 'my guys' at what he sometimes calls the 'Trump Justice Department.'"[36]

Trump frequently defied the settled norms at the level of rhetoric, especially with regard to those he regarded as adversaries. He called for the Justice Department to reopen the Hillary Clinton email investigation and related issues, and for new investigations into what he described as "the illegal acts that took place in the Clinton campaign & Obama Administration."[37] He also called for investigations of the origins and use of the "Steele dossier," Democratic Party opposition research that came into the possession of the FBI and was used in the investigation of Trump-Russia connections; the Clinton Foundation's involvement in a Russian agency's acquisition of the Uranium One mining company; and Clinton aide Huma Abedin for her alleged actions related to official emails found on her husband's computer. Trump suggested that the Justice Department should criminally investigate former FBI Director James Comey for leaking documents and allegedly lying to Congress; that John Kerry should be prosecuted for talking to Iranian leaders; and that former CIA Director John Brennan, Justice Department officials Lisa Page, Andrew McCabe, Peter Strzok, and Bruce Ohr, and Fusion GPS, a research firm involved with the production of the Steele dossier, should be investigated as well. Trump also broke norms when he commented on pending prosecutions that did not involve political enemies, including the military prosecutions of Bowe Bergdahl and Edward Gallagher, and the criminal prosecution of alleged terrorist Sayfullo Saipov.

In addition to these public threats, Trump allegedly pressured White House officials to order the Justice Department to prosecute Comey and Clinton. The department did not prosecute Comey. Comey *was* subject to three Justice Department inspector general investigations, which found fault with some of his actions related to the Hillary Clinton email investigation and the investigations of Trump and his campaign (all of which we discuss in detail in Chapter Nine). These investigations and their fruits were broadly accepted, since the inspector general, Michael Horowitz, has a reputation for independence and integrity, and because his reports were comprehensive and even handed. Horowitz also investigated and criticized McCabe, Strzok, and Page, but the Justice Department declined Trump's entreaties to do more. (The department considered prosecuting McCabe for lying to the FBI but never did so. A large hurdle to prosecution was that the president's incessant criticism of McCabe tainted the matter.)

As for Clinton, the department appears not to have heeded the president's calls for a new, full-fledged investigation. In 2017, Rep. Bob Goodlatte urged the Justice Department to appoint a special counsel for allegedly unlawful actions of the Clinton Foundation, including in the Uranium One matter.[38] Then–Attorney General Jeff Sessions responded in a letter that he would have senior prosecutors "evaluate" the issue, a step that does not, in Justice Department jargon, constitute an investigation.[39] It is hard to tell if this was a standard noncommittal letter of the type the Justice Department often sends in response to a congressional request, or an effort to assuage Trump and perhaps pressure Clinton. In any event, Sessions turned the matter over to a Utah federal prosecutor, John Huber, who was first appointed by President Obama. In 2019, Attorney General Barr announced that Huber's work related to the Clinton matter was "winding down and hopefully we'll be in a position to bring those to fruition."[40] Yet, even if the department takes no action against Clinton, as seems likely, and even if Sessions's letter to Congress was not a response to pressure from Trump, the "evaluation" of the matter was generally and understandably seen as politicized and retaliatory due to Trump's rhetoric.

Concerns that the Justice Department is in the president's pocket on law enforcement matters related to his political agenda has only grown in the last year of his presidency. Trump has dozens of times complained about Special Counsel Robert Mueller's treatment of three close allies: former National Security Adviser Michael Flynn, who pleaded guilty to lying to the FBI; Trump's ally Roger Stone, who was convicted of obstruction of justice and lying under oath (and whose sentence was later commuted by Trump); and former Trump campaign manager Paul Manafort, who was convicted of tax and bank fraud.

Barr subsequently took actions related to two of these convictions— overruling career prosecutors to seek a more lenient sentence for Stone, and successfully moving to dismiss the case against Flynn even though Flynn pleaded guilty—that were largely viewed as caving to pressure from Trump. This critique took hold even more firmly when, after Barr's decision in the Stone case, Trump tweeted, "Congratulations to Attorney General Bill Barr for taking charge of a case that was totally out of control and perhaps should not have even been brought."[41]

Barr appeared to recognize that the president's tweets tainted his decisions and made them seem political. "I'm not going to be bullied or influenced by anybody ... whether it's Congress, newspaper editorial boards, or the president," Barr told ABC News following Trump's congratulations.[42] Barr insisted that Trump "has never asked me to do anything in a criminal case" but emphasized that the president's interference via tweets made it "impossible" for him to perform his role as attorney general. "I cannot do my job here at the department with a constant background commentary that undercuts me," he said, articulating one important reason for the norms in this area. "I think it's time to stop the tweeting about Department of Justice criminal cases," Barr added. But Barr's public statements did not stop the president's tweets and norm breaking through other channels, and the attorney general did not make further critical public comment.

Another prominent example of Trump's interference was his attacks on John Bolton in connection with Bolton's tell-all memoir about his time as national security adviser. Prior to publication, Trump described the book, which was very critical of him, as "highly inappropriate" and said that "if the book gets out, he's broken the law and I would think he would have criminal problems. I hope so." Trump said he discussed the matter with Barr even while emphasizing that it was Barr's call. When Barr's Justice Department filed a lawsuit a few days later seeking to enjoin publication, the *New York Times* reported that "the aggressive move is the latest instance in which the Justice Department under his watch has appeared to wield its law enforcement power in ways that align with Mr. Trump's views of perceived political allies or adversaries."[43] The department lost its motion but won some important points in the ruling. But win or lose, once again Trump's intervention made it seem likely that the Justice Department was acting at the president's behest to serve his political and personal goals.

Another episode that raised serious questions about politicization involved Trump's firing of the acting U.S. attorney for the Southern District of New York, Geoffrey Berman. Berman was a career prosecutor appointed by a federal court to replace Preet Bharara, whom Trump fired in 2017. Bharara had investigated matters close to Trump that Trump often complained about. One focus was Michael Cohen, Trump's former lawyer. Cohen pleaded guilty to (among other things) campaign law violations related to the Trump presidential campaign, and he alleged in court that Trump directed his actions in the commission of one of those crimes involving payments to two women to keep them quiet during the campaign. Berman was also investigating Trump lawyer Rudy Giuliani and had filed charges against two Giuliani associates related to the Ukraine matter. In addition, he was investigating a state-owned bank in Turkey, and Trump had reportedly pledged to Turkish president Recep Tayyip Erdoğan that he would intervene in the case.

Barr originally announced that Berman would be stepping down (not fired) and replaced by Trump friend Jay Clayton, the chairman of the Securities and Exchange Commission. When Berman balked, Trump fired him. After a day of intense controversy in which many observers suspected that Trump or Barr was improperly intervening in cases that affected the president, Barr shifted course and announced that Berman would be replaced by his chief deputy, career prosecutor Audrey Strauss. Berman announced that the "proud legacy" of his office could be in "no better hands" than Strauss's.[44]

Barr's letter announcing the change then affirmed "the Department's applicable standards, policies, and guidance," which included an acknowledgment of a norm against "improper interference with a case."[45] Barr stated further that

> [g]oing forward, if any actions or decisions are taken that office supervisors conclude are improper interference with a case, that information should be provided immediately to Michael Horowitz, the Department of Justice's Inspector General, whom I am authorizing to review any such claim. The Inspector General's monitoring of the situation will provide additional confidence that all cases will continue to be decided on the law and the facts.

It is impossible to know whether Barr reiterated the department's norms of law enforcement on principle, or whether he was retreating to this ground in the face of intense criticism and the notable absence of support from Republican allies in Congress. The reaffirmation of the norm in this context was in any event especially notable.

And then there was the investigation by John Durham, under the close supervision of Barr, of the origins of the 2016 investigation into the Trump campaign and the 2017 criminal and counterintelligence investigations of the president. An investigation of the investigators can be viewed as appropriate in the sense that the investigations of Trump and his campaign was unprecedented and politically fraught in ways that implicate long-held concerns about the impact of secret government surveillance on democratic processes. The public needs to know how the investigations transpired so that it can have confidence that the power exercised by the FBI was not abused and also so that the FBI can learn how to approach these problems better in the future (issues we take up fully in Chapter Nine). But here too the president's incessant aggressive criticism of the FBI investigation against him has contaminated the legitimacy of the investigation. And in this instance, Barr exacerbated the problem by violating norms—the breach of which he decried in others in analogous circumstances—when he often prejudged the case through insinuation and innuendo.[46]

President Trump has also taken aim at American companies that have drawn his ire. There are numerous allegations that the president attempted to intervene directly in the merger of AT&T and Time Warner, due to his animus toward a Time Warner subsidiary, CNN. Google and Facebook have both found themselves in the president's crosshairs as well: Trump suggested in June 2019 that they should be sued.[47] Trump has claimed that Google is "trying to rig the [2020] election"[48] and has claimed repeatedly that Facebook and other social media companies are biased against conservatives.

The record of Trump's attempts to bend the Justice Department to serve his will is troubling but, in the end, the results were mixed. On the one hand, there were remarkable instances when Trump failed to accomplish his aims to direct Justice Department action—an ineffectiveness that Trump frequently bemoaned, in public and private. Trump's appointees did not carry out his wishes to prosecute his enemies; and legal rules and norms often operated to check untoward department actions that seemed to serve Trump's interests, especially in the Mueller investigation, which we examine fully in Chapter Eight. But, especially over the fourth year of his term, Trump appeared to succeed in influencing the Justice Department in self-serving ways. So, while the norms and laws withstood Trump's unprecedented onslaught for much of this time, there were clear signs by 2020 that they were under serious strain. And by any measure, Trump's attacks on Justice Department independence did enormous damage to the department's reputation and to the legitimacy of many of its actions.

REFORM

The question in the aftermath of the Trump presidency will be whether it is enough to rely on the relative resilience of law and norms, and Trump's eventual departure from office, to guarantee a return to a presidency that maintains the principles of independence that should govern the relationship between the president and the White House, on the one hand, and the Department of Justice, on the other.

Trump and Nixon, their presidencies separated by fifty years, could be viewed as outlier presidents whose abuses did not cause the collapse of norms of independence but instead served to test them and, eventually, prove their durability. Some observers might argue that the experience of the Trump presidency, like the "national nightmare of Watergate," is a shock to the system from which it emerged challenged but stronger.

Maybe. But as we explained in Chapter One, developments in national politics have weakened, and threaten to continue to weaken, the norms of independence. Intense polarization and the rise of populism pose a heightened risk that, in a bitter battle between partisans, the executive branch may weaponize the law enforcement process. Those same features feed the toxic suspicion that the press is being abused. Donald Trump's taste for weaponizing law enforcement is open and notorious, and his expression of it is crude.

We cannot assume that this tendency will remain limited to Trump, or will always be so crude. Democratic candidates competing to face Trump in the general election professed an analogous willingness to do what is necessary, with less solicitude for norms, to meet the threat, as they perceive it, of the Trump presidency. For example, some pledged to direct the prosecution of Trump if they succeed him in the White House or have prejudged the merits of the legal case against him. Even allowing for a measure of hyperbole on both sides of the political divide, unduly politicized law enforcement—and, nearly as important, its appearance—has become an increasingly large question about the operation of the criminal justice system.

That said, reform in this area is hard for two reasons. First, it is impossible to muzzle a president who insists on breaching norms of noninterference in Justice Department actions through his public pronouncements. And second, as noted earlier and explained further in the remainder of this chapter, there is no sharp line between acceptable political factors that inform law enforcement decisions and unacceptable politicization of law enforcement.

With these problems and challenges in mind, we propose three main areas for reforms.

Stronger Protections Against Improperly Politicized Law Enforcement

Dannehy insisted that nonlegal Justice Department "principles" of "fairness and justice" weigh strongly against "undue sensitivity to politics" even in cases where the law does not forbid it. While these principles, or norms, are no doubt prevalent in the Justice Department, Dannehy cited no written source, and there is no obvious one. We propose reforms within the executive branch to strengthen these norms by making them explicit.

First, we propose to amend the "Supplemental Standards of Ethical Conduct for Employees of the Department of Justice" that apply on top of the ethical rules that apply to all executive branch officials.[49] The new section would be directed specifically to "Improper Political Considerations" and would draw practically word-for-word from the Dannehy letter. As we present it more fully in the appendix, the regulation should prohibit department employees from acting "in the performance of their duties on the basis of the improper partisan political purpose of influencing an election to public office" and should expressly reiterate that these employees "answer in all their actions not to partisan politics but to principles of fairness and justice." The regulation should also define "improper partisan political purposes to influence an election" to include the definitions specified by Dannehy.

Second, we propose to amend the guidance supplied by the Justice Department's "Principles of Federal Prosecution" in the department's *Justice Manual*, and its more specific "Federal Prosecution of Election Offenses," in order to bring the Dannehy principles to the attention of law enforcement officials involved in such cases. The manual's discussion of the principles governing the exercise of prosecutorial discretion now defines an "impermissible consideration" in investigations and prosecutions to include decisions improperly based on a "person's ... political association, activities, or beliefs."[50] The revision we propose would supplement and expand on this guidance with a discussion of the U.S. attorneys firing case and its resolution. That discussion would mirror our proposed revisions to the Justice Department's "Supplemental Standards of Ethical Conduct," and it would fit naturally in the section of the manual currently entitled "Federal Role: Prosecution, Not Intervention."[51] Under our proposals, the Dannehy principles would be incorporated into both the specific guidelines for the investigation and prosecution of election offenses and, more generally, the department's ethical standards.

Third, and finally, 5 C.F.R. § 2635.702 prohibits all federal employees—not just Justice Department or White House officials—from using a position of authority to "coerce or induce another person, including a subordinate, to provide any benefit, financial or otherwise, to himself ...

or persons with whom the employee is affiliated in a nongovernmental capacity."[52] The regulation is structured to apply broadly to prohibit the use of office for "private gain"[53] or to give "preferential treatment."[54] Although it focuses most specifically on the illicit service of "financial interests," it also extends to "any benefit, financial *or otherwise*" (emphasis added). Actions within the Justice Department, or external pressure on the department, to initiate a prosecution, or influence its course, for the partisan political purpose of affecting an election certainly confer a "benefit" on the political party in a position to seek this advantage. The same party obtains this benefit and also "preferential treatment" if, because of this same improper intervention, its escapes legal accountability for actions that would normally be investigated and prosecuted.

The regulations are nonetheless not as clear as required on this point. We propose that Section 2635.702 be revised to deal specifically with the "improper partisan political purpose of influencing an election to public office." The proposed revisions appear in relation to the current prohibition on the "use of public office for private gain." Improper partisan political purposes are one such misuse of official authority. The prohibition we would add in clear terms is cabined along the lines discussed previously: It is not partisan political considerations more generally that the reformed ethical proscription would reach, given the difficulties we have suggested of applying a standard that is too broadly cast. The reform's focus is the impropriety of partisan political motivation to influence the outcome of an election to public office.

Obstruction of Justice

As Dannehy made clear, the primary obstruction of justice statute, 18 U.S.C. § 1503, applies to the law enforcement actions of executive branch officials, including the attorney general and his or her subordinates. (It is a harder question, addressed in Chapter Eight, whether and how the statute applies to the president.) While impossible to show, there are good reasons to believe that the possibility of criminal obstruction of justice had an impact on executive branch officials who resisted President Trump's various efforts to use law enforcement tools to serve his personal interests. The best example of this, as we lay out in Chapter Eight, is the remarkable and indeed uniform resistance by Trump's senior aides and political appointees to his efforts to fire Special Counsel Robert Mueller or to influence Mueller's investigation.

That said, we think that the obstruction of justice statutes operate mainly as a feared caution sign against corrupt law enforcement rather than as a tool that can be wielded readily in investigations against executive branch officials absent extreme circumstances. This is so because: Article II gives executive branch officials broad discretion over law enforcement; political considerations in the broadest sense of the term often properly inform this discretion; and it is hard to identify and weed out law enforcement actions that are "corruptly" politically motivated without unduly burdening, and chilling, standard executive branch prerogatives.

The Dannehy analysis about obstruction in the electoral interference context hints at some of these problems. She read extant law to apply to interventions by executive branch officials to accelerate a charging decision or initiate an investigation for the *sole* purpose of influencing a specific election. The rub comes in "mixed-motives" cases, where Dannehy interpreted the obstruction statutes not to apply to politically motivated action to influence an election when there is also present a good-faith belief in the merits of the action. In fact, mixed-motives cases may involve not merely a good-faith but a mistaken belief in the merits: The action based in part on anticipated political benefits could be the better or even the best choice on the merits.

Dannehy's approach to mixed motives is the right standard for at least two reasons. First, the line between mixed-motives cases and those with only a "bad motive" will not always be clear, but even as Dannehy construes it, the main obstruction statute should still have a deterrent effect on unduly partisan law enforcement actions even in cases where motives are mixed. Second, the alternative standard—where the mere presence of an illicit motive constitutes obstruction, regardless of proper law enforcement aims—would pose a significant burden on the president's (and the Justice Department's) constitutional authority to enforce the law.

There is a broader dimension to politicized law enforcement, not tied to a particular election, that is challenging to conceptualize within an obstruction of justice rubric. Presidents and their political teams invariably keep an eye on the political significance of executive branch policies and actions, and their impact on key constituencies or voting blocs. Assume that the Justice Department is evaluating the potential prosecution of an individual or a company within an industry or the nonprofit community that has been supportive of the president. Assume further that the case is a hard one, the decision to proceed could go either way, and the administration weighs in the balance the political fallout from proceeding. Perhaps its concern is that bringing charges will damage the president politically within a specific community of supporters. The political assessment may include projections of harm to the president's stable of reliable political donors in that community, or it may be that he or she is trying to reward loyalty for past political support.

A legal standard designed to preclude that sort of "politics" presents major issues of both administrability and constitutionality. In endless contexts like these, there is no clear line between politics of the kind that presidents and their subordinates have long practiced and actions that threaten the administration of justice. A more demanding standard than the one in the Dannehy analysis would impose significant burdens on executive branch prerogatives to make discretionary judgments when these may involve political considerations in this broader sense.[55] And it would surely invite political opposition to frequently weaponize vague claims that executive branch officials were corruptly motivated by partisan political considerations in the performance of their duties. Again, there is reason to think that the obstruction of justice statute as currently construed has an impact on official conduct.

These are some of the reasons we do not propose alterations to the current obstruction of justice statutes as a mechanism to tamp down on the possibility of politicized law enforcement by Justice Department officials and White House officials other than the president and vice president. Those statutes are already doing work, though it is hard to see. As we explain in Chapter Eight, however, we do favor altering the primary obstruction of justice statute for certain actions by the president and vice president. We believe that this change will have nontrivial additional downstream effects, beyond the current operation of the obstruction of justice statutes, on the behavior of executive branch officials below the president and vice president.

Legislation to Specify Qualifications for Senior Justice Department Positions

A first line of defense against political interference in the law enforcement process obviously rests with Justice Department officials. The Trump experience is the case in point. As noted earlier, and as made clear in Chapter Eight's discussion of the special counsel experience, the department for the most part held firm in the face of the president's incessant efforts to protect him and his friends, or to prosecute his enemies.

Future presidents may learn the wrong lesson from this experience and decide they need more dependable friends in office who are more responsive to their needs. They might look to fill senior Justice Department positions with political allies whose primary appeal is their background and loyalty, rather than special professional qualifications for the job. Trump appeared to try to do this with the appointment of Matthew Whitaker as acting attorney general. Whitaker did not act as some critics of his appointment had feared he might by, for example, acting as Trump's agent in discrediting or undermining the Mueller investigation. It may be that, in fact, Whitaker subscribed strongly to the norms of independence or that he concluded that he should not challenge those within the department who did. In any event, Whitaker's tenure as acting attorney general was a further testament to the resilience of those norms. But we should not assume that Whitaker's failure to give in to Trump on several matters will mean that presidents won't try harder and better succeed in the future. Many people think Trump has done just that in his selection of William Barr as attorney general.

Other than the potential for adverse public opinion, Senate resistance to confirmation, and impeachment, there are limits to what can be done about this problem. A president who goes about this task with subtlety can choose a nominally respectable lawyer who is also a strong political supporter whom the president is confident will go great lengths to collaborate in unsavory if not illegal political initiatives, or who holds such broad views of executive power as to effectively enable the president to do what he or she wants. Indeed, with few exceptions, presidents for many decades—going back at least to Franklin D. Roosevelt and, indeed, even earlier—have chosen attorneys general who are close friends, committed political allies, or relatives. There is perhaps no more definitive evidence of presidential sensitivity to the political opportunities and dangers of law enforcement than this fact.

While no reform can eliminate the possibility of presidential nomination of an attorney general or other senior Justice Department official who is guided in his or her actions by a misplaced, excessive standard of political loyalty or who lacks adequate integrity, we propose statutory qualifications for senior Justice Department officials that can rule out some of the most dangerous cases and might influence a norm about acceptable nominees.

First, Congress should reinstate its original qualification for attorney general and apply it as well to the positions of the deputy and associate attorney general, and assistant attorneys general. The Judiciary Act of 1789 required the attorney general to be "a meet person, learned in the law."[56] We would add to the traditional requirement that the attorney general also be a person of integrity, so that the formulation would read: "a meet person of integrity, learned in the law." Even with the addition, this may seem like a trivial requirement, since "meet," which in this context means "appropriate," is underspecified; "learned in the law" might not rule out anyone with a law degree; and "integrity," which connotes honesty and strong moral principles, might be contested in practice. Indeed, this qualification might not have precluded the appointment of Whitaker, a former U.S. attorney and chief of staff to the attorney general who was nonetheless widely seen as unqualified for his three-month stint as acting attorney general.

We believe that this requirement could have an impact on the Senate confirmation process and thus on executive branch deliberations about whom to nominate. The requirements to be "meet," a person of "integrity," and "learned in the law" would sharpen the Senate discussion and place a burden on the candidate to explain why he or she is appropriate and adequately learned and has an unblemished reputation for probity. They would also temper claims that the choice is purely one of presidential prerogative. Especially when the Senate is closely divided, this more focused discussion can have an impact.

Consider Whitaker's case. It was easy enough for Trump to appoint him as acting attorney general. But if Whitaker were in a confirmation process, he would have faced serious questions about his qualifications for the job. Under our proposal, the question would be forthrightly presented by statute—whether by experience and accomplishment, he was meet, learned in the law, and a person of integrity.

Second, Congress should bar the president from appointing to senior Justice Department positions individuals who within two years of appointment were engaged in identified forms of partisan political activity. Individuals within this category include those who held in the preceding presidential election cycle positions of trust or responsibility in the president's personal campaign organizations; in a national, state, or local political party; or in other political organizations that supported the president for election. This proposal would exclude the most overt partisans from top Justice Department jobs, which is important not just in fact but in appearance as well. To be sure, it would not prevent a president from nominating someone who is fiercely partisan and loyal but who did not engage in proscribed political activity. But again, it would exclude some who might otherwise be considered and could favorably shape the norm surrounding appropriate nominees.

Qualification requirements are commonplace for agency heads and other inferior officer positions in the executive branch. Even principal officers, including some Cabinet heads, have qualification requirements. The secretary of defense, for example, must be "appointed from civilian life" and "may not" be appointed "within seven years after" after serving in the armed forces.[57] Despite the prevalence of qualification requirements, there is a question about how far Congress can go in burdening the president's appointment power. The Supreme Court has never been clear on this issue, and the Office of Legal Counsel has acknowledged that "[t]here is no settled constitutional rule" here.[58] Supreme Court and Office of Legal Counsel opinions both emphasize, somewhat unhelpfully, that the main question is the degree to which the qualification burdens the president's appointment power.[59]

There is little doubt that the qualification requirement from the Judiciary Act of 1789 is constitutional. That qualification for attorney general prevailed from 1789 until 1870 and has been a qualification for the solicitor general ever since.[60] Adding the integrity criterion to this traditional requirement almost certainly does not go too far. It is harder to predict whether the "political activity" bar is constitutional. But it satisfies a central Office of Legal Counsel requirement, since it clearly does not "rul[e] out a large portion of those ... persons best qualified by experience and knowledge to fill a particular office."[61] The "political activity" bar would rule out relatively few otherwise qualified people. It is also at least as material to the attorney general's job as the civilian qualification is for the secretary of defense, and its time bar is shorter. Only litigation in this discrete context can settle the question, but the proposal is plausibly constitutional.

THE SPECIAL COUNSEL

One of the defining events of the Trump presidency was Special Counsel Robert Mueller's investigation of Russian contacts with the 2016 Trump presidential campaign, which led to the opening of an investigation of Trump himself. The Mueller investigation was the first extended experience with special counsel regulations adopted to succeed the controversial 1970s independent counsel statute, which expired with bipartisan approval in 1999. Under any circumstances, a special counsel investigation on the scale of Mueller's would have provided a lot of important information about how the regulations performed and how they might be improved. But the Mueller investigation was also characterized by unprecedented opposition and interference by the president, which put maximum stress on the already-difficult task of the executive branch investigating the president.

That task is difficult because the Constitution vests "the executive Power" in the president, but the president and senior executive officials cannot be fully trusted to investigate themselves when credible evidence of criminal wrongdoing emerges. The appointment of a special counsel with some independence from the president and the attorney general has been the traditional response to this situation. And this response has always run the risk that the special counsel's "independence" would translate as a practical matter into a loss of political accountability, which would leave too much room for enforcement of the law in a politicized or otherwise unfair manner and thereby replicate the very problem the special counsel was designed to avoid. In this chapter, we examine how these factors have played out in history and especially during the Trump presidency before offering lessons learned and proposing reforms.

BACKGROUND

The history of special counsel investigations of high-level executive branch officials divides into five periods: pre-Watergate (1876–1972), Watergate (1973–1975), the independent counsel statute regime (1978–1999), the special counsel regulations regime (1999–2016), and the Mueller investigation pursuant to these regulations (2017–2019). The semi-independent investigators have had different names during these different periods—special counsel, independent counsel, or special prosecutor. We refer to the general category as "special counsel" but will use the appropriate name when speaking about particular investigators.

Pre-Watergate

During the long first period, the president or attorney general appointed nine special counsels during five presidencies—Ulysses S. Grant, James A. Garfield, Theodore Roosevelt, Calvin Coolidge, and Harry S. Truman—in connection with six different executive branch scandals.[1] In every instance, the president or attorney general appointed special counsels under public pressure to establish a credible and independent investigation of alleged executive branch wrongdoing. The president or attorney general appointed these special counsels pursuant to general statutory or constitutional authorities, and in one instance (the Teapot Dome scandal) the Senate confirmed the special counsel. The president during this first period was never the target of a special counsel. But the special counsels' success sometimes turned on the support or resistance of the president, which often reflected the political context and political constraints, if any, of the moment.

Consider the fate of the first special counsel, John Henderson. Grant appointed him to investigate a scheme between whiskey producers and federal officials to underreport whiskey production and divvy up the tax savings. Henderson had success prosecuting "Whiskey Ring" conspirators in St. Louis until he zeroed in on Grant's friend, Orville Babcock, who was up to his eyeballs in the scandal. Grant was not involved in the scandal or under investigation, but he was loyal to Babcock and duped by him. Grant tried to slow Henderson's investigation of Babcock. When Henderson in the course of the trial of another Ring member accused Babcock of obstruction and implied that Grant might be involved in the scandal, the president fired Henderson.

Grant then appointed a new special counsel, James Broadhead. Grant and his attorney general also put up hurdles to Broadhead's investigation of Babcock, who was eventually acquitted (in part due to Grant's supportive testimony). As Andrew Coan has noted, "Grant paid no personal political price for scuttling the prosecution of Babcock."[2] In part this was because "the American public maintained faith in [Grant's] personal integrity," according to Ron Chernow.[3] And in part it was because partisan newspapers "relentlessly attack[ed] Henderson's motives and actions," with the result that Henderson more than Grant was delegitimated, says Coan.

Watergate

Contrast this episode with the second landmark in the history of special counsels, and the first to focus on the president: Watergate. As the scandal increasingly implicated Richard Nixon by spring 1973, Elliot Richardson—as a condition of receiving Senate consent to become attorney general—appointed a special prosecutor, Archibald Cox, and gave him extraordinary independence. Nixon's proxies, like Grant's, attacked the special prosecutor as biased and vindictive. But the attacks lost steam after former Nixon White House Counsel John Dean's damning June testimony and the revelation about Nixon's taping system. Cox subpoenaed the tapes and refused a compromise proposal from Nixon. Nixon then directed Richardson to fire Cox on Oct. 23. Richardson (and his deputy) resigned instead, but Solicitor General Robert Bork carried out the order.

This "Saturday Night Massacre" sparked a hostile public reaction and a significant loss of support among Republicans. Nixon's vice presidential nominee, Gerald Ford, implored the House of Representatives to "carry on" with its impeachment inquiry and pledged support for removing the Watergate investigation from Department of Justice purview. At that point, Nixon pledged "total cooperation" to Bork's replacement for Cox,

Leon Jaworski, who was given greater independence than Cox. Jaworski pursued the subpoena case to the Supreme Court, which affirmed the subpoena's validity and led to Nixon's resignation.

Watergate was in a sense the high-water mark for special counsels. The institution of the special prosecutor asserted and maintained extraordinary independence, even in the aftermath of Nixon's firing of Cox, and successfully investigated the White House and the president to uncover multiple crimes. It did so, formally, entirely within the structure of the executive branch. But it was aided by several convergent external factors. Various congressional committees investigating aspects of Watergate provided strong support. The press famously uncovered and published accounts of many White House sins. Starting in spring 1973, the American public grew increasingly interested in, and increasingly supportive of, the special prosecutor's work, and the Nixon-proxy attacks on the special prosecutor faltered due to increasing public evidence of White House complicity and the Saturday Night Massacre. The courts played a crucial supportive role in several respects, most notably in upholding the special prosecutor's subpoena of the tapes. So too did executive branch officials, in particular Mark Felt ("Deep Throat").

The Ethics in Government Act

The third period of special counsels concerns the experience under the Ethics in Government Act of 1978.[4] The act grew out of congressional efforts in the days after the Saturday Night Massacre to establish a mechanism for investigating the president that was to some degree independent of the Justice Department. Even though the system "worked" during Watergate, many commentators noted after the scandal that it almost didn't work or that it might not work in the future. So Congress for the first time placed the appointment of a special counsel outside the executive branch and tied such appointments to easy-to-meet criteria.

The statute in its final amended form gave the federal judiciary a key role in guaranteeing investigatory independence. It required the attorney general to report to a special federal court when he or she determined, after an initial brief investigation, that there were "reasonable grounds to believe that further investigation or prosecution is warranted" of certain high-ranking government officials who "*may* have violated any

Federal criminal law."[5] The court was then charged with appointing an "independent counsel" vested with "full power and independent authority to exercise all investigative and prosecutorial functions" of the Justice Department and attorney general, and with defining his or her jurisdiction.[6]

The attorney general could remove the independent counsel for "good cause" or some debilitating disability, and with notice to the court and Congress.[7] The independent counsel was required to send the appointing federal court occasional reports on his or her activities, including a final report on the conclusion of the investigation, and was required to inform the House of Representatives of "substantial and credible information ... that may constitute grounds for an impeachment."[8] And the congressional judiciary committees, and certain subcommittees, could request that the attorney general appoint an independent counsel.

The independent counsel statute attracted bipartisan support in Congress and broad support among legal and journalistic elites in 1978. By 1999, even after several amendments, the bipartisan conventional wisdom had reversed entirely, and there was bipartisan support for allowing the statute to expire and for returning control over special counsels to the Justice Department. In the interim, courts had appointed independent counsels in twenty cases. Most of these cases were successful in the sense that the independent counsel cleared senior officials of allegations of wrongdoing without controversy, and in a few cases prosecuted or reached plea deals with executive officials, all without serious controversy.

But several cases under the independent counsel statute were politically contested and controversial. The two most controversial cases focused on the White House and the presidency. First, the Iran-Contra scandal traversed the Ronald Reagan and George H.W. Bush administrations and resulted in (among other things) an indictment of Defense Secretary Caspar Weinberger and other officials on the eve of the 1992 election (later mooted by presidential pardons). Second, the Whitewater investigation of the Clinton administration ultimately shifted to a focus on the president's affair with an intern and ended in President Clinton's impeachment following Special Prosecutor Ken Starr's submission of a long impeachment report to Congress in 1998 regarding Clinton's alleged misdeeds.

These cases made plain that in high-profile investigations, the desired enhanced credibility of an "independent" counsel is difficult if not impossible to attain. Both Starr and Lawrence Walsh, the special prosecutor in the Iran-Contra case, drew fierce partisan attacks on their credibility, and their alleged partisanship and indiscipline were exacerbated, in the eyes of their critics, precisely because they were acting with minimal political accountability. Stated differently, in high-profile cases under the independent counsel statute, "independence" became synonymous with "rogue" even before the present era of intensified polarization.

Many lessons about the experience with the independent counsel statute emerged from two lengthy hearings in 1999 on whether the statute should be modified or allowed to expire.[9] These lessons are worth keeping in mind in efforts to reform the regulations that replaced the statute. The most salient lessons for our purposes are the following:

- There is no perfect arrangement for ensuring investigatory independence, prosecutorial accountability, public confidence, and fairness to the target of the investigation. Trade-offs are inevitable.

- The one identified virtue of an independent counsel, as opposed to an investigation conducted within the Justice Department, is that the independent counsel, all things being equal, has more credibility when he or she clears or vindicates the target of an investigation.

- However, in higher profile investigations, especially ones focusing on the White House, the independent counsel statute did not ameliorate the problem of the politicization of investigations and did not enhance the American people's confidence in government. If anything, in the high-profile contexts it exacerbated the problems. There were many reasons for this, including the invariably sharp political attacks on the independent counsel mentioned previously. Other reasons included the practical unaccountability of the independent counsel to any branch of the government, which sometimes led to prosecutorial zeal; and the attorney general's still-controversial residual role in supervising the independent counsel, which often led to actual or perceived conflicts between these two senior officials that did not achieve the statutory objective of bolstered public confidence in the law enforcement process.

- Placing responsibility for selecting the independent counsel in the Special Division, an Article III court, also did not reduce the problem of politicization. Indeed, as one witness noted, "selection by the Special Division, far from providing an [independent counsel] cover against political attack, may actually aggravate the problem because partisans may call into question the impartiality of that body."[10] Most notably, the circumstances of the Special Division's appointment of Ken Starr to replace Robert Fiske drew the panel into a sharp controversy over partisan motivation.

- Returning control over special counsels to the attorney general would not reduce political controversy, though it would change it by inviting political heat on an actor (the attorney general) who is accountable to politically elected actors: Congress (through confirmation, oversight, and impeachment) and the president (through direction and firing). As then–Attorney General Janet Reno noted, such accountability "goes to the very heart of our constitutional scheme" and is important so that "the blame [for prosecutorial decisions] can be assigned to someone who can be punished."[11] Many witnesses agreed with this conclusion, and (like Reno) cited and praised Justice Antonin Scalia's dissent in *Morrison v. Olson* for presciently assessing these and other problems with the independent counsel statute.

- The independent counsel tended to be unfair to targets in this sense: Due to the lack of budgetary constraints, a charge to pursue a single issue, the final report requirement, and a lack of traditional accountability, the independent counsel was incentivized to over-investigate the target and to bring indictments that an ordinary prosecutor, out of the spotlight and burdened with resource constraints, would not bring.

- The trigger for an independent counsel was too low and, together with the predictable political pressures from the press and political opposition for an "independent" inquiry, it led to unwarranted investigations.

- The final report requirement was unfair to targets because, contrary to standard Justice Department practice, they aired facts and allegations even though no prosecution was brought, making it hard for the target to refute. The impeachment referral provision had the same effect and also diminished Congress's Article I responsibilities for impeachment.

On the basis of these generally accepted propositions, Congress allowed the independent counsel statute to lapse. This was not merely the outcome of a political deal between the two major political parties after each separately concluded that it lost more than it gained from the keeping the law alive. Independent analysis of the experience with the independent counsel yielded much the same bipartisan consensus that the attorney general should control the appointment and supervision of the special counsel. In 1999, for example, former Senate Democratic and Republican leaders George Mitchell and Robert Dole headed a bipartisan task force to examine the independent counsel experience. The members included senior lawyers with executive branch and Justice Department experience, including former Solicitor General Drew S. Days and future Supreme Court Chief Justice John Roberts. Their unanimous recommendations foreshadowed many of the key elements of the special counsel regulations, such as the more central role and enhanced control of the attorney general. Of particular note is the members' observation that "[w]hen regular Justice Department authority is displaced, we risk uneven application of the law and a weakening of the Department."[12]

Special Counsel Regulations

The Reno Justice Department embraced these views and promulgated regulations—still in force today—for a special counsel centered in the executive branch.[13] This marks the fourth period in the history of special counsels. The regulations (in the words of their introduction) sought "to strike a balance between independence and accountability in certain sensitive investigations, recognizing that there is no perfect solution to the problem."[14] The main balance struck was to give the special counsel "day-to-day independence" but to place "ultimate responsibility for the matter and how it is handled" in the attorney general.

The regulations authorize the attorney general to appoint a special counsel when a criminal investigation raises a conflict of interest or "other extraordinary circumstance," and when appointing a special counsel is in the public interest. This is a higher bar that gives the attorney general much more discretion than did the lapsed statute.[15] The regulations also authorized the attorney general to determine the special counsel's jurisdiction, to overrule an "inappropriate or unwarranted" investigative or prosecutorial action by the special counsel, to discipline or remove the special counsel for specified bad acts, and to control the special counsel's budget.[16]

The regulations eliminated the final report provision of the independent counsel statute because it "provide[d] an incentive to over-investigate, in order to avoid potential public criticism for not having turned over every stone, and create[d] potential harm to individual privacy interests."[17] They also eliminated the impeachment referral provision. In their place, the regulations contemplate "a limited reporting requirement ... in the form of a summary final report to the Attorney General" that should be handled as "a confidential document, as are internal documents relating to any federal criminal investigation."[18] The attorney general has a duty to "notify the Chairman and Ranking Minority Member of the Judiciary Committees of each House of Congress" upon the appointment and removal of a special counsel, and "[u]pon conclusion of the Special Counsel's investigation."[19] Finally, the attorney general has discretion to "determine that public release of these reports would be in the public interest, to the extent that release would comply with applicable legal restrictions."[20]

These regulations have been on the books for more than two decades. Yet, in contrast to the twenty investigations authorized under the independent counsel statute over its twenty-two years (1978–1999), only one special counsel has been appointed pursuant to the special counsel regulations in the twenty-one years of their existence—in 1999, to investigate government actions at the Branch Davidian compound in Waco, Texas.

The stark difference in numbers is probably not explained altogether by higher ethical standards or compliance in administrations during the latter period. The main explanation is surely that the jurisdictional trigger for an investigation is harder to satisfy under the regulations than the statute and is entirely under the control of the attorney general. In addition, after 1999, presidents of both parties—perhaps wary of the dangers of special counsels based on the experiences of the 1980s and 1990s—were especially careful to return to the tradition of appointing attorneys general who were political loyalists. There have been no Edward Levis or Janet Renos appointed since the 1990s, and there likely will not be again.

There is another explanation for the rare invocation of the regulations: The attorney general (or acting attorney general) has an alternate route to appoint a special counsel. In 2003, Deputy Attorney General (and Acting Attorney General) James Comey appointed U.S. Attorney Patrick Fitzgerald to investigate the unauthorized disclosure of CIA employee Valerie Plame's identity. (Attorney General John Ashcroft was recused.) Comey invoked Sections 509, 510, and 515 of Title 28 of the U.S. Code, which together authorize the attorney general to appoint a Justice Department officer, "or any attorney specially appointed," to "conduct any kind of legal proceeding, civil or criminal," which U.S. attorneys are authorized to conduct.[21] This appointment, like so many other special counsel investigations of the White House, proved controversial, especially when Fitzgerald subpoenaed reporters, jailed *New York Times* reporter Judith Miller, and indicted and later convicted the vice president's chief of staff, Scooter Libby, for perjury.

The Fitzgerald appointment shows that the special counsel regulations promulgated in 1999 are in many respects *optional*, and that an attorney general often has an alternative to appointing a special counsel under the regulations.[22] Comey said he chose this route because Fitzgerald, a sitting U.S. attorney, could move forward with the investigation "immediately" without the delays that would attend an outside special counsel's initial staffing and clearance process.[23] This route also enabled Comey to confer more independence, at least in some respects, on Fitzgerald than he could have conferred on a special counsel under the regulations. Comey's charge to Fitzgerald gave him broader leeway and subject him to less attorney general supervision than did the regulations, and made clear that Fitzgerald's authorities were not limited by the regulations. That said, Fitzgerald might be deemed to have had less independence than a special counsel under the regulations, since he was a Justice Department employee and was not protected by the regulations' for-cause removal provision.

The Mueller Investigation

The Mueller investigation grew out of concerns about Russian interference in the 2016 presidential election and possible Trump campaign involvement in that interference. The matter had been under investigation in normal Justice Department channels since July 2016. When then–Attorney General Jeff Sessions recused himself from the investigation, Deputy Attorney General Rod Rosenstein became acting attorney general for that purpose. After President Trump fired FBI Director James Comey on May 9, 2017—and under pressure following news reports of Comey's damning memos about the president's conduct toward the investigation—Rosenstein appointed Mueller as special counsel.

Rosenstein did not appoint Mueller pursuant to the special counsel regulations. Rather, he appointed Mueller pursuant to the same general Justice Department authorities under which Comey appointed Fitzgerald in 2003.[24] He likely did so because the special counsel regulations apply by their terms to a "criminal investigation," and the focus of the Russia matter, at the time Mueller was appointed, was on counterintelligence. Rosenstein's order nonetheless incorporated by reference and made "applicable" Sections 600.40–600.10 of the regulations—concerning, primarily, the relationship between the acting attorney general and the special counsel. And Rosenstein defined Mueller's jurisdiction to cover "(i) any links and/or coordination between the Russian government and individuals associated with the campaign of President Donald Trump; and (ii) any matters that arose or may arise directly from the investigation; and (iii) any other matters within the scope of 28 C.F.R. § 600.4(a)."[25]

Mueller came to the task of special counsel with bipartisan credibility as a law enforcement officer of unimpeachable integrity. Like all previous special counsels investigating the White House, he was soon subject to criticism from the president's proxies for his alleged bias or alleged malfeasance. Unlike every previous special counsel, however, he was also subject to direct public criticism by the president. The criticism was not mild or restrained. Rather, Trump's criticism— of Mueller, his staff, Sessions, Rosenstein, and others involved in or related to the investigation—was incessant, vicious, inflammatory, and personal. In its scale, tone, and authorship, Trump's criticism was entirely unprecedented in American history. Trump also on numerous occasions publicly threatened to fire Mueller, and behind the scenes (as we learned from the Mueller Report) he tried but failed to direct subordinates to fire him.

Mueller submitted his 448-page, two-volume "final report" to Attorney General William Barr on March 22, 2019. Barr released the report in lightly redacted form on April 18, 2019. Volume I showed in great detail how Russia interfered in the 2016 election. As to the Trump campaign's involvement, the report "established that the Russian government perceived it would benefit from a Trump presidency and worked to secure that outcome" and "that the Campaign expected it would benefit electorally from information stolen and released through Russian efforts" but "did not establish that members of the Trump Campaign conspired or coordinated with the Russian government in its election interference activities."[26]

Volume II addressed the president's actions toward the FBI's original investigation of the Trump campaign and the Mueller investigation that commenced in 2017. It laid out ten episodes that the Mueller team believed potentially implicated the president in obstruction of justice. The special counsel declined to make "a traditional prosecution or declination decision" about these episodes, because he determined "not to apply an approach that could potentially result in a judgment that the President committed crimes." He explained that fairness dictated this result in light of the Justice Department position banning indictment or prosecution of a sitting president, since the president would have no adversarial forum during the presidency to contest a conclusion of his guilt. The report's authors added, however, that "if we had confidence after a thorough investigation of the facts that the President clearly did not commit obstruction of justice, we would so state." The report did not, however, "conclusively determin[e] that no criminal conduct occurred." Therefore, "while this report does not conclude that the President committed a crime, it also does not exonerate him."[27]

The Mueller investigation provides the most extensive evidence to date about how the regulations operate.[28] Mueller's report acknowledged that he was bound by the regulations, as well as by department legal interpretations and policies, in conducting his investigation. Yet there were several instances in which Mueller and Barr disagreed on legal and policy matters, or where Mueller appeared to depart from the regulations and Justice Department rules and policies, at least as understood by the attorney general.

Mueller's lengthy report was clearly intended for public dissemination. The regulations had eliminated the impeachment referral provision of the expired independent counsel statute and contemplated only a "confidential report explaining the prosecution or declination decisions reached by the Special Counsel"—a report that the Justice Department defined upon adoption as a "limited reporting requirement."[29] Mueller was perhaps justified in laying out his detailed findings in Volume I of his report nonetheless, since the main aim of his investigation—which was originally conceived as a counterintelligence investigation, even if not conducted as one—was to uncover links between Russia and the Trump campaign. The hundreds of pages of factual and legal discussion in Volume II about the president's potential criminal culpability on obstruction of justice were more controversial under the regulations.

Mueller also acted in tension with the regulations when he sent a letter to Barr, soon made public, to object to the way the attorney general had summarized his report after receiving it from Mueller. Barr had been widely criticized on the grounds that this summary was misleading. These criticisms aside, the regulations make clear that the special counsel's job is complete when he or she transmits the report to the attorney general and that the attorney general has full discretion under the rules to decide on the extent and shape of any public release.

Volume II was also notable for the dissonance it produced between the special counsel and the attorney general on legal interpretive matters. The regulations state that the attorney general maintains "ultimate responsibility" for the special counsel investigation. Further, they require the special counsel to "comply with the rules, regulations, procedures, practices and policies of the Department of Justice" and to "consult with appropriate offices within the Department for guidance with respect to established practices, policies and procedures of the Department."[30]

Mueller accepted—correctly in our view—that he was bound by the Office of Legal Counsel opinions in the course of making his decisions. And of course the Office of Legal Counsel exercises interpretive authority delegated by and subject to the views of the attorney general. The regulations thus appear to contemplate that the special counsel is subordinate to the attorney general on legal interpretive matters.[31]

Despite these prescriptions, Attorney General Barr stated that he "didn't agree with ... a lot of the legal analysis" in the Mueller Report, which, Barr believed, "did not reflect the views of the department."[32] There seem to be at least three matters on which Barr believed that Mueller departed from the "views" of the department.

First, the regulations call for the special counsel in the final report to explain "prosecution or declination decisions." But on the obstruction of justice issue, Mueller laid out the relevant facts as he found them and opted against making any decision. Mueller explained that he declined to apply the normal "Justice Manual standards governing prosecution and declination decisions," because making a traditional prosecutorial decision that might result in conclusions that the president acted criminally would raise "fairness concerns" to the president in light of the Office of Legal Counsel ruling that a sitting president cannot be indicted.[33] The attorney general, by contrast, believed that the proper reading of the Office of Legal Counsel opinions, the regulations, and department policy was that Mueller could have and should have reached a decision to prosecute or decline prosecution, even if the president could not be indicted while in office.[34]

Second, Barr objected to Mueller's statements that he "could not conclusively determine" whether the president committed a crime and that his report "did not exonerate" the president. Barr stated that this is "not the standard we use at the department" and added that the department's standard was "to determine whether there is a clear violation of the law" and, if not, to decline prosecution.[35] Third, Barr disagreed with how Mueller interpreted the "clear statement rule" as interpreted in Office of Legal Counsel opinions, in reaching his conclusion that the obstruction of justice statutes reach "facially valid exercise of core presidential authority or official authority."[36]

We do not here endorse Barr's legal interpretations on these matters. The important point for present purposes is that the open legal disagreements between Barr and Mueller represent a breakdown of the regulations. The regulations subordinate the special counsel to Justice Department policy and the attorney general's (or acting attorney general's) legal views and ultimate review, and give to the attorney general the final decision on "any investigative or prosecutorial step," the removal of special counsel, and the shape of any public report. It should not have been possible under the regulations for the special counsel to issue a report that embodied so many matters of department legal interpretation and policy to which the attorney general objected. The Mueller investigation showed that if a special counsel resists the attorney general review mandated by the regulations, the attorney general can be deprived of the contemplated mechanism of supervisory control. Regardless of whether Mueller and his team consciously adopted this strategy, this was the result.

While Mueller did not always strictly follow the regulations, it is important to keep in mind the extraordinary context in which he worked. The Russian interference in the 2016 election, and the possible involvement by a presidential campaign that benefited from that interference, was unlike anything the regulations contemplated. The regulations also did not contemplate a criminal investigation that implicated the legitimacy of a presidential election. Nor did they contemplate a president who would be hostile to the investigation beyond anything ever seen or even imagined in American history.

The Mueller investigation was in many ways a success despite these unusual circumstances. Volume I of the Mueller Report is the definitive account of Russian interference in the 2016 election. Absent an aggressive investigation using the full array of evidence-gathering techniques that only a prosecutor with full Justice Department backing possesses, this account would not have been possible. Moreover, while few politicians and journalists seemed happy with the overall outcome of Mueller's investigation, the American people (in some polls, more than two-thirds) approved in various ways of Mueller's conduct of the investigation.[37] The general public support for the Mueller investigation is remarkable in light of the unprecedented ways that the president and some of his allies went after Mueller and the infrastructure supporting him. It is impossible to say how much this support was attributable to Mueller himself—his sterling reputation when he entered the job, and how he conducted the investigation—and how much was attributable other factors, including the complex outcome of the investigation.

Finally, it is a testament to post-Watergate norms that Mueller was able to complete his investigation and report despite the president's strident criticisms, threats, and efforts to have him fired. These norms guided Trump's political appointees—including Rosenstein and Comey's successor as FBI director, Christopher Wray, both of whom faced presidential pressure and threats—in seeing through the Mueller investigation. They might also have informed Barr's decision to release the report relatively quickly and with relatively few redactions despite disagreeing with Mueller's legal analysis and his pass on a definitive prosecutorial judgment.

As Volume II of the Mueller Report makes clear, these norms also guided Trump subordinates and allies, who in various ways resisted the president's attempts to interfere with the investigation. And at crucial points, even many of the president's Republican allies in Congress supported Mueller in the face of the president's threats. We don't know how these norms will operate in the future—whether, for example, Trump's failures to manipulate his appointees to stop the special counsel will provide a road map to opportunities for more competent future presidents. But in this instance, with respect to almost everyone in the executive branch save the president, the norms seemed to have had real bite.

BACKGROUND PRINCIPLES FOR REFORM

Any reform of the special counsel regulations will be politically charged and thus controversial. Memories of the Mueller investigation, and of Trump's behavior in connection with that investigation, remain fresh. And for many observers, the main reform focus—like the main focus after Watergate, which led to the independent counsel statute—will be to enhance special counsel independence and narrow the attorney general's and the president's control. We take a different view. We think that proper reform requires enhancing special counsel independence in some respects but narrowing it, and enhancing the attorney general's authority, in other respects.

We also believe that the overriding objectives to be served by a special counsel can be effectuated primarily by regulation, adopted by the Justice

Department, and not by statute. A substantial question is the extent to which Congress can regulate the manner in which the president or attorney general conduct the core executive law enforcement function. The Supreme Court upheld the constitutionality of the independent counsel statute in *Morrison v. Olson*, but the continuing force of that decision was questioned even before the Supreme Court began to cut back on its foundations in recent years.[38] A recent Supreme Court decision pointedly quoted Madison's dictum that "if any power whatsoever is in its nature Executive, it is the power of appointing, overseeing, and controlling those who execute the laws."[39] Despite these points, Congress still has a role to play in our scheme. We propose a statutory "good cause" restriction on the attorney general's removal of a special counsel—though, as we note, even this is subject to constitutional challenge. The rest of our redesign depends on self-regulation, namely, a president and an attorney general committed to reform in this area. Two background principles should guide the reforms that we describe below.

The Special Counsel's Accountability Function

Mike Rappaport distinguishes between the Criminal Prosecution Model and the Accountability Model for special counsels.[40] The Criminal Prosecution Model "views the special counsel as an institution necessary to ensure that high executive officials have not violated the laws, especially the criminal laws." On this view, the special counsel's role is to determine in a credible way whether senior executive officials violated the law. The special counsel makes an up-or-down decision on criminality and, like a typical prosecutor, offers no public explanation for decisions not to prosecute.

The Accountability Model, by contrast, "views the special counsel as an institution necessary to determine what actions were taken by high executive officials." The principal goal of this model is "to reveal to the public and other institutions what happened, so that those officials can be held accountable through elections, removal, or impeachment." On this model, the special counsel's main goal is to collect and release to the public facts that will allow other institutions—Congress, the press, the American people—to hold senior executive officials accountable for their actions.

The independent counsel statute's final report and impeachment referral provisions emphasized accountability in addition to criminal prosecution. This emphasis was criticized in the 1999 hearings. The special counsel regulations that replaced the statute sought to diminish the accountability function of special counsels by enhancing attorney general control, by eliminating the impeachment referral provision, by insisting that the special counsel's final report on prosecution or declination decisions be "confidential," and by giving the attorney general discretion (but no mandate) to release the special counsel's report "to the extent that release would comply with applicable legal restrictions."[41]

But as the Mueller investigation made plain, the regulations did not eliminate the accountability function. While Mueller obtained numerous indictments and convictions, the main function of his final report was to collect important information—about Russian interference, the Trump campaign's role, and the president's possible obstruction of justice. With regard to obstruction, Mueller believed, plausibly, that since the Justice Department had ruled out an indictment of the president while in office, it was important to collect and preserve possible evidence of a crime for when the president left office. Barr had the discretion under the regulations not to disclose, or to selectively disclose, the contents of Volume II. But the overwhelming public expectation was that Mueller's report should be disclosed as fully as possible. The result was something similar to what the independent counsel statute required and the regulations sought to eliminate: an extensive public airing of facts and potentially damning legal analysis that did not result in indictment.

The Mueller investigation—like the experience with the Nixon special prosecutor, and the Whitewater independent counsel—shows that a special counsel will always play an accountability function to some degree, especially when he or she investigates the president and vice president. If the president or vice president has acted in a fashion that warrants appointment of a special counsel, there will be tremendous public interest in knowing facts related to corrupt or at least controversially norm-busting actions that do not rise to the level of illegality. This is unfair to the subjects and, in some instances, even witnesses of the investigation, at least from a traditional prosecutorial perspective. But it is inevitable, and we think appropriate, in the context of high-level executive branch misdeeds. Our reforms propose ways to accommodate this reality.

Transparency

We have explained why we—along with the drafters of the 1999 regulations—believe that the attorney general must remain in charge of the legal interpretation and prosecution decisions for the Justice Department. And we propose additional mechanisms to enhance attorney general authority. This raises the large challenge of ensuring that the attorney general acts with integrity in all elements related to the special counsel's job—from appointment, to supervision, to legal interpretation, to the ultimate prosecutorial decision, to the release of information related to the investigation after it is complete. In every difficult case, most if not all of these decisions will be contested. Many observers will view the attorney general to have acted tendentiously, and in some instances he or she might have done so. As the various experiences since Watergate have shown, there is no perfect solution to this problem. Even the independent counsel statute gave the attorney general unreviewable authority to make law-informed but discretion-infused prior decisions before the Special Division could appoint an independent counsel.

The most important tool against attorney general abuse is transparency of decision-making so that the other elements of our constitutional democracy—Congress, the press, voters—can assess the actions of the attorney general, the special counsel, and the persons under investigation, and then pass judgment. As noted earlier, transparency-induced political constraints, including by Republicans in Congress and the executive branch, were important safeguards against Trump moving from attacks on the special counsel to his firing, and in checking other untoward or norm-breaking actions by the administration. Such transparency was a primary strategy of the 1999 regulations, and we propose additional transparency mechanisms in the next section.

As we have acknowledged throughout this book, such transparency ultimately works only if other institutions in the political system, and the American people, act on the information to check an abusive president or attorney general. This mechanism operated much more extensively during the Trump administration than has been appreciated. But there is no guarantee that it will continue to work. If a political system becomes so degraded and fragmented that political checks lose all or most of their bite, then no legal reform can help prevent abuse in this context.

REFORM

Our reform proposals concern six topics: (1) the jurisdictional trigger, (2) the relationship between the attorney general and the special counsel, (3) the statute of limitations problem, (4) impeachment, (5) protection of the special counsel, and (6) obstruction of justice. A common feature of many of the proposals is to enhance transparency to Congress and the public about decisions of and about the special counsel.

Jurisdictional Trigger

The regulations currently in force vest the attorney general with considerable discretion, and the final say, in deciding whether to appoint a special counsel. According to the regulations, the attorney general "will appoint a Special Counsel when he or she determines that criminal investigation of a person or matter is warranted," but only if the attorney general additionally determines that a normal investigation by the Justice Department "would present a conflict of interest or other extraordinary circumstances," with no further detail or guidance on what those circumstances might be.[42] The regulations do not specify the threshold for when a criminal investigation is warranted. They do not explain the circumstances that justify a "conflict of interest," though it seems that credible allegations of misconduct against a senior government official, and in particular the president and vice president, invariably raise the specter of conflict of interest and compel an appointment. And they do not give meaningful guidance about the public interest concern that would dictate appointment.

This vagueness in standards for appointment is guaranteed to generate significant controversy in application. The main danger is that the attorney general will protect a senior executive branch official by declining to appoint a special counsel when one is warranted. It is no accident that the two White House–focused special counsel investigations since the 1999 regulations were promulgated—the Fitzgerald investigation of the Valerie Plame matter, and the Mueller investigation—were initiated and appointed by deputy attorneys general (Comey and Rosenstein, respectively) who were previously career prosecutors and who were charged with the matter only because the attorneys general were recused.

It is also no accident that special counsels since 1999, in contrast to the period before, have been exceedingly rare. Especially going forward, we must worry about the danger that an unrecused attorney general will read the regulations or relevant law opportunistically to protect senior executive branch officials from a special counsel investigation.

Two solutions to this problem have been tried and rejected, both in the lapsed independent counsel statute. One is to have a lower or tighter threshold for the appointment of a special counsel. We are not opposed to such a change if it can be achieved without inviting the evil that was present from 1978 to 1999: a too easily weaponized special counsel who over-investigates the executive branch and thereby lessens rather than enhances confidence in law enforcement. We doubt that a change without those risks is achievable. Another approach is to place the decision to appoint the special counsel in an independent body outside the executive branch. The latter approach was rejected in 1999, for reasons already canvassed, with which we agree.

To address this problem, we propose to maintain the current standard for the appointment of a special counsel, but to impose five important requirements on attorney general decision-making.

First, we would clarify that for the attorney general to conclude whether an investigation is warranted, he or she would have to make that determination on the basis of "credible information or allegations."

Second, we would add a transparency and reporting requirement when the attorney general declines to appoint a special counsel in the face of credible allegations of criminal wrongdoing. The attorney general would be required to submit written reasons for the decision, including a factual and legal analysis, to the House and Senate Judiciary committees that would also be made public. The difficult issue here is to specify what level of allegation is credible enough to trigger the reporting requirement. There is a danger that the attorney general would be flooded with allegations just to trigger the duty to report. We propose that the attorney general be given the discretion to determine which allegations are credible enough to trigger such reporting.

Third, to underscore the special counsel's accountability function, the regulations should put squarely in the balance the public's need to know the facts related to possibly criminal activity in determining whether a criminal investigation is warranted. We thus propose that the attorney general must take into account the need for an independent factual inquiry in assessing whether, under the regulations, the "public interest" is served by the appointment of a special counsel.

Fourth, the special counsel may believe that his or her jurisdiction should be expanded to include new matters that may have come to light during the investigation. At present the special counsel is required to consult with the attorney general, who is empowered to determine whether to proceed with the expansion of jurisdiction or "assign [the new matters] elsewhere."[43] We propose that if this consultation results in the attorney general's deciding against a grant of additional jurisdiction, then the attorney general should have to notify the House and Senate Judiciary committees of the special counsel's views and the reasons for this determination. We would create an exception to this duty to report and allow the attorney general to delay the report, if the attorney general makes a finding in writing that such a report would compromise the ongoing investigation, and he or she reports this fact to the majority and ranking minority members of the committees.

Fifth, we would require the attorney general to use the special counsel mechanism in any investigation of the president or vice president if he or she determines that a criminal investigation is warranted. As the Fitzgerald investigation of the Plame matter shows, the current regulations give the attorney general discretion to use "normal" Justice Department mechanisms in place of the special counsel mechanism, presumably under the rationale or determination that the public interest requires it or the risk of conflict is low. We would disallow that option. In short, only a duly-appointed special counsel should have the authority to investigate the president or vice president.

The Relationship Between the Attorney General and the Special Counsel

The 1999 special counsel regulations sought to make the special counsel "free to structure the investigation as he or she wishes and to exercise independent prosecutorial discretion to decide whether charges should be brought, within the context of the established procedures of the Department" and under the "ultimate responsibility" of the attorney general.[44] The Mueller investigation demonstrated that this allocation is not as clear as it could be under the regulations. The lack of clarity affected the public debate and contributed to a sense of irregularity in the process.

Our basic approach is to maintain but significantly clarify the 1999 regulation's basic allocation of authority between the attorney general and the special counsel, but also to give the special counsel a more clearly delineated and protected role in finding facts needed for the accountability function.

Reforms Concerning Special Counsel Fact-Finding

We propose that the special counsel's fact-finding role be clarified and protected, and that opportunistic attorney general decision-making be deterred, as follows.

First, as already noted, the regulations should provide that the public interest in the appointment of a special counsel includes an assessment of the need for an independent factual inquiry.

Second, as noted, the regulations should require the appointment of a special counsel in all cases involving the president and vice president (if the attorney general determines that there is credible information or allegations to support the inquiry).

Third, the special counsel should have wide latitude to conduct his or her investigation, and the attorney general should have to satisfy certain requirements before interfering with the special counsel's specific investigative decisions and, in the event that he or she takes any such action, report it to Congress. Had Mueller elected to subpoena Trump's testimony and provoke a legal test in the courts, Barr could have blocked that action under the current rules if Mueller's subpoena was "inappropriate or unwarranted under established Department practices."[45] The triggers for any such blocking action—an "inappropriate" or "unwarranted" investigative step—are insufficiently precise to protect the special counsel's fact-finding role, which is a central feature of our proposal. We would tighten this standard by providing that "the attorney general shall not direct the special counsel to omit or abandon pursuit of any investigative step, except where any such step is plainly inconsistent with law or established department practices." Moreover, if the attorney general concludes that those standards have been met and blocks any investigative step, he or she must notify the leadership of the House and Senate Judiciary committees in a final report upon the investigation's conclusion.

Fourth, upon the special counsel's conclusion of an investigation, or earlier if the attorney general closes the investigation upon dismissal of a special counsel, the special counsel would be authorized to provide the public and Congress with the facts found within the jurisdiction of the investigation. Whatever controversy may follow a declination or a dismissal, there should not also be a dispute about the special counsel's fact-finding process. The "cover-up" most feared in these cases involves the concealment of facts by those politically close to the president. The special counsel has a unique role in protecting against those concerns, and with ensuring that the American people and Congress will learn the basic facts uncovered in the investigation, so that they can judge for themselves, through public argument, the appropriate non-prosecutorial responses (including oversight and impeachment) to those facts, if any. This is functionally what happened with the Mueller Report, but the legitimacy of this function and its consistency with the regulations were contested under the current regulations. We propose to make this role for special counsel unambiguous.

The special counsel's protected role in fact-finding will supply a check on the attorney general's decision to decline prosecution or to end an investigation by firing the special counsel. But the special counsel's role too is subject to abuse, especially since the special counsel in this context will operate with a freer hand from normal accountability checks. And the facts found and reported—like the ones included in the Mueller Report and the Starr Report—will be untested by a grand jury, a trial process, or any other adversarial process. There is thus a danger of the special counsel's fact-finding getting out of control. The regulations should limit the special counsel fact-finding role to the scope of the approved criminal investigation and should require special counsel expressly to consider and not disclose facts that unduly harm privacy interests. But beyond these limitations, we believe the risk of special counsel abuse in this context is outweighed by the benefits described earlier.

The special counsel would be required to redact the publicly released report to avoid disclosure of grand jury material protected under Section 6(e) of the Federal Rules of Criminal Procedure. We do not believe that the redaction of this material would seriously undermine the informational value of the special counsel's reporting function. The Mueller Report was redacted for this purpose but provided more than 400 pages of detailed information about the investigation. Moreover, Congress may have the option upon receiving the report to seek the omitted material upon application to the court.

An additional and special set of issues arises as a result of standing Office of Legal Counsel opinions that conclude that the president cannot be prosecuted while in office. The issue would arise if a special counsel concludes, and the attorney general agrees, that the president *did* violate the law and that indictment was warranted but could not be issued until after the president's term ends. Even in this difficult circumstance, the special counsel should retain the obligation to issue a factual report to Congress and the public. There is a powerful public interest in information about the facts of the president's conduct, as found by the special counsel. And if a known investigation comes to an end with the special counsel's factual findings somehow withheld, an administration would face toxic suspicion and runaway speculation. There would surely be leaks of information, of varying degrees of accuracy, about what the special counsel found, often via the counsel to witnesses, even if the special counsel's office is scrupulous in keeping its distance from the press. Moreover, Congress will have a strong constitutional claim to the information in order to determine whether the facts as found warrant impeachment. For all these reasons, the special counsel's office should issue its fact-finding and leave no question about what it found—or did not find.

This approach raises a legitimate concern about the unfairness to the president of charges leveled but not tried, since it leaves him without the means of a defense. Mueller cited this concern in declining to reach a "traditional prosecutorial judgment" about presidential obstruction in the Russia matter. However, the complex issues surrounding the investigation and prosecution of the president necessarily present hard choices and trade-offs. While there is unquestionably unfairness in a fact-finding coupled with a prosecutorial judgment but only a deferred prosecution, or fact-finding in a case that is not prosecuted, the public interest and Congress's need for the information weigh in favor of disclosure. The president also has a vast communications apparatus available to contest the facts and argue his innocence, and recent experience, especially the investigations of Clinton and Trump, demonstrates the power of the public defenses that presidents can mount outside of formal legal process.

Reforms Concerning Attorney General Legal and Prosecutorial Control

We also propose that the attorney general's control over legal and prosecutorial decisions be clarified.

First, we would expand the attorney general's authority to supervise the investigation overall. Under the current rules, it is up to "the special counsel [to] determine whether and to what extent to inform or consult with the Attorney General or others within the department about the conduct of his or her duties and responsibilities."[46] We would give the attorney general express authority to seek information as he or she sees fit, including requests for periodic updates by the special counsel on the course of the investigation.

Second, consistent with the attorney general's authority to receive, review, and either affirm or reject prosecution or declination decisions by the special counsel, the attorney general should have the ability to superintend the development of the special counsel's legal positions. This end can be achieved by requiring the special counsel to submit his or her legal conclusions on prosecution or declination for the attorney general's review prior to issuing a decision. Or the regulations could give the attorney general the discretion, in case of concern, to direct that, on any pertinent legal question, the special counsel must consult with the Office of Legal Counsel and be bound by its decision, subject (as is always the case with Office of Legal Counsel decisions) to the attorney general's final decision. We support the latter approach.

In either case, in order to clarify the lines of decision-making authority, the regulations should specify that the attorney general retains final responsibility for the legal conclusions, while, as described, the special counsel is responsible for the fact-finding unless plainly inconsistent with law or established department practice. In the event that the special counsel and the attorney general disagree about the applicable law, the attorney general directs that a question be referred to the Office of Legal Counsel, or the attorney general directs the special counsel not to pursue an investigative step, the attorney general must notify Congress in a final report upon the investigation's conclusion.

Third, the regulations should constrain the special counsel from straying into legal argumentation in the course of performing his or her fact-finding mission. In a report upon dismissal or at the investigation's conclusion, the special counsel should avoid any commentary on the legal significance of the facts reported. We propose that the regulations be amended to bar the inclusion in any such fact-finding document of "any discussion of whether the evidence tended to support prosecution or declination." Relatedly, the regulations should clarify that the special counsel is strictly bound by the regulations' review and approval procedures. The current regulations make such compliance mandatory. But they create an ambiguity by acknowledging extraordinary circumstances that "would render inappropriate compliance with required review and approval procedures," and by giving the special counsel the option ("may") on this question to "consult directly with the attorney general."[47] We propose that the rules be clear on the point and require that the attorney general be consulted and specify that he or she "shall make the final determination" on prosecution and declination of charges.

We appreciate that concentrating power in the attorney general in this way risks the possibility that an ill-motivated or feckless attorney general will ignore or purposefully misinterpret the law. This concern can be addressed only, if at all, through enhanced transparency and political checks. We have proposed several new requirements to make the attorney general's decision-making function subject to greater public scrutiny. In sum, these include notice (with reasons) to Congress and the public:

- If the attorney general concludes that a criminal investigation of the president or vice president is not warranted and a special counsel need not be appointed;

- If the attorney general rejects a request by the special counsel for additional jurisdiction;

- If the attorney general determines before the beginning of a fiscal year that an ongoing special counsel investigation should not continue; and

- If the attorney general and the special counsel disagree on a question of law, including any such question that the attorney general directed the special counsel to refer to the Office of Legal Counsel.

As noted many times, there is no guarantee that transparency-induced political checks will work here, but in the end that is all there is.

In assessing how to control an ill-motivated attorney general, it is important to keep in mind the problem of unaccountable law enforcement. As noted earlier, the "independence" of a particular independent or special counsel has turned out to be highly contested in practice in high-profile cases, with the result that both parties in different cases passionately believed and complained that the president was the victim of both a biased and an unaccountable law enforcement official. In these cases, there was no agreement about the outcome somehow dictated by the "law." Many Democrats rejected any notion that Ken Starr upheld the rule of law with the case he built for obstruction of justice. Republicans reacted with similar indignation to the Mueller theories of obstruction and even the premise that there was any such thing as "collusion" that warranted investigation. Our view is that political accountability is especially important when prosecutorial judgment must be made in the hard or controversial case.

Tolling the Statute of Limitations

The Office of Legal Counsel has issued two opinions, in 1973 and 2000, concluding that the president cannot be prosecuted while in office. As noted earlier, we propose that in these circumstances, unlike in other cases of nonprosecution, the special counsel would issue to Congress and to the public his or her factual findings.

The Office of Legal Counsel opinions present but do not answer the question of whether a president's immunity while in office could result in a statute of limitations bar on a criminal prosecution once the president's term or terms end. The 2000 opinion notes the possibility (but no more than the possibility) that the statute could be subject to tolling by judicial decision, "either as a constitutional implication of temporary immunity or under equitable principles."[48] But it acknowledges that in any event, "Congress could overcome any such obstacle by imposing its own tolling rule."[49]

In the wake of the Mueller Report, the chairman of the House Judiciary Committee introduced a bill to establish such a rule, entitled the "No President Is Above the Law Act."[50] It provides that in "the case of any person serving as President of the United States," the statute of limitations would be tolled for the "duration of [the president's] tenure in office." It would also apply to "offenses committed during any period preceding such tenure in office."

Congress should at a minimum enact a tolling statute for criminal acts the president commits while in office. The Office of Legal Counsel emphasized in its 2000 opinion that presidential immunity was only temporary and that one important alternative means to "securing the rule of law" was prosecution upon leaving office.[51] For this to be a real alternative, all uncertainty about time bars on the applicability of the criminal law the president violated should be removed.

Whether the tolling statute should extend to offenses that precede office is a tougher question. On the one hand, one might think the president should not escape trial for crimes committed before taking office but discovered while in office just because a temporary immunity allowed the statute of limitations to run. On the other hand, the main focus of a special counsel should be on crimes that constitute abuse of office, and extending the tolling statute to crimes committed before taking office enhances incentives for mischief in looking for and alleging such crimes in a context—the prosecution of a former president—that is inherently dangerous in a constitutional democracy. We have seen this before: The "Whitewater" investigation into President Clinton's financial affairs concerned an Arkansas real estate transaction the Clintons entered into fourteen years before he became president. However, the tolling statute could be applied to offenses committed by the president in the course of seeking election to the presidency. A president engaged in those election-related offenses may incur corrupt obligations that, if he is elected, could influence the conduct of official duties. In this case, there is a clear potential connection between the period prior to assuming office and abuse of power.

Indeed, the nation would take a step in a dangerous direction by merely setting up legal structures that overtly contemplate the prosecution of former presidents, especially since it will often be the case that a president and attorney general of one party will be making decisions about prosecuting former presidents of another party. Such structures, once in place, will enhance the legitimacy of political discourse about prosecuting former presidents, and will make it more likely that such prosecutions will occur. The case for a tolling statute is to enhance ex ante clarity about presidential accountability in the hope of deterring bad presidential acts.

Impeachment and the Role of Congress

The independent counsel statute required the independent counsel to report to Congress any credible evidence of the commission of impeachment offenses. The special counsel rules were designed to omit any such requirement. Yet as noted earlier, the Mueller case generated significant expectation that Mueller would find a way to communicate to Congress any information potentially relevant to impeachment. This appeared to be Mueller's expectation as well, since he produced a 448-page report—including 187 pages on the president's possible obstruction of justice—that he was well aware would be made public.

We do not support a revision of the rules to empower the special counsel to assess the evidence under the constitutional standards for impeachment. As a prosecutor within the executive branch, the special counsel has no special capacity for making even a preliminary judgment of this kind. Impeachment is a political process, and the evaluation of the grounds for impeachment, including the assessment of the constitutional precedents, is laden with political implications and necessarily influenced by the politics of the moment. The special counsel's credibility depends heavily on the perception that he or she is a law enforcement professional working at a safe distance from the political battlefield.

Moreover, the special counsel's direct involvement in impeachment issues presents a high risk of distorting the constitutional process. The indication that he or she finds evidence of impeachable offenses alters the debate by introducing a purportedly "professional" or independent view that could be assigned far too much weight. Partisans favoring impeachment will point to the special counsel as a singularly reliable voice. Partisans in opposition will have the incentive to relentlessly attack the special counsel's credibility. Independent Counsel Ken Starr's experience in the Clinton case is instructive in this respect. The House Republicans relied virtually entirely on his report to Congress, and Starr became the leading witness on their behalf in the House. The Democrats made it their mission to discredit his arguments and his motives. No single episode had more impact in moving public opinion against the renewal of the independent counsel statute.

This is not to say that Congress should not have access to the special counsel's findings of fact, which our proposal calls for. Its formal purpose is to ensure that the public and its elected representatives have access to the answers to the question "What actually happened?" Consistent with our view that the fact-finding and the legal analytic functions should treated separately in constructing the role of the special counsel, we would argue for the reports to Congress to be limited to the facts—and leave it to the lawmakers to judge the constitutional meaning of that record.

Protection of the Special Counsel

During Mueller's service as special counsel, he came under persistent attack from the president, who also took steps to fire him but did not do so. The fear that Mueller might be dismissed and the investigation derailed or ended led to a number of proposals for legislation to protect him.

As Watergate showed, the president can order the attorney general, on pain of dismissal, to fire a special counsel. Congress can, of course, pressure the president to desist from a dismissal. In the Mueller case, even the Republican congressional leadership signaled that the president should leave Mueller in place to finish his work. The Senate Judiciary Committee also reported out a bill, with bipartisan support, that would authorize a special counsel to contest his or her dismissal in the U.S. District Court for the District of Columbia. Congress has other tools, of course: It can also threaten to hold up nominations or action on pending legislation important to the president.

We propose statutory codification of the removal provisions currently contained in the special counsel regulations, which allow for dismissal for "misconduct, dereliction of duty, incapacity, conflict of interest, or for other good cause, including violation of Departmental policies."[52] The codification would further include the requirement that "the Attorney General shall inform the Special Counsel in writing of the specific reason for his or her removal."[53] As we have noted, there are constitutional questions of how far Congress can go to tie the executive's hands in matters like this, and Supreme Court jurisprudence on this question is in flux. But a targeted restriction of this kind is worth testing, and it may survive scrutiny if the court retains in significant part the analysis in *Morrison v. Olsen* that upheld a "good cause" restriction on the removal of an independent counsel because it "did not see how the President's need to control the exercise of that discretion is so central to the functioning of the executive branch as to require as a matter of constitutional law that the counsel be terminable at will by the President."[54]

We would not go further to authorize the special counsel to appeal dismissal to the courts. As we discussed in reviewing the experience with the independent counsel statute, there are serious costs to bringing courts into the resolution of what are inevitably, at bottom, intensely political disputes over the sensitive exercises of executive discretion. If the attorney general bears responsibility for the appointment and supervision of the special counsel, then the attorney general should have responsibility for making and answering for the decision to dismiss. Accountability for that decision is best left to the political process and, in the end, Congress, which can act in a variety of ways to ensure that the attorney general must account for this action if taken.

Congress may, however, enact measures to discourage a special counsel's firing while also, and critically, ensuring that it does not impede access to the record he or she compiled while still in office. One proposal is legislation to provide that, in the event that the special counsel is removed, he or she would provide a report to Congress on factual findings through the date of dismissal. The president would be prevented from using the firing to cover up the special counsel's work. With this trigger for reporting requirements in place, the president might also think twice about removal for any other than the most substantial grounds. We propose a revision to the rules to provide that upon dismissal, the special counsel would be afforded access to the investigative record for no less than thirty days for purposes of preparing and submitting a report to Congress.

Obstruction of Justice

Finally, and vitally, Congress must make plain the extent to which the obstruction of justice statute applies to the president.

There is significant uncertainty over whether and to what degree the president is subject to the current array of federal obstruction of justice statutes. Several Office of Legal Counsel opinions dating back decades hold that "statutes that do not expressly apply to the President must be construed as not applying to the President if such application would involve a possible conflict with the President's constitutional prerogatives."[55] The Office of Legal Counsel in dicta has stated an exception to this rule for the bribery statute, which it reasoned "raises no separation of powers questions were it to be applied to the President" because the Constitution "confers no power in the President to receive bribes."[56]

The Office of Legal Counsel's clear statement rule is controversial because it goes further than the Supreme Court precedents on which it relies. Even accepting the rule, which Mueller did, its impact on whether the president can obstruct justice is unclear. Simplifying only a bit, Barr thought the plain statement rule precluded application of the obstruction of justice statutes to most if not all of the ten episodes in Volume II of the Mueller Report. By contrast, Mueller thought the rule would be no hurdle to a conclusion that the president violated the statutes for all ten episodes (though Mueller did not reach this conclusion). Legal academics hold an array of intermediate positions.

It is an intolerable state of affairs for the president, Congress, and the American people not to have a clearer sense of whether and under what circumstances the president can obstruct justice, and especially how the exercise of undoubted Article II powers such as removal and supervision of prosecutions constitutes obstruction of justice. We can expect administrations of different parties to take very different views on the interpretation of the current statutes going forward. Only Congress can fix this problem, at least in the first instance, with a plain statement of presidential liability.

Two related questions arise: First, what presidential acts should Congress criminalize? And, second, what are the constitutional limits on Congress in criminalizing presidential actions through obstruction of justice?

Begin with the constitutional question first. The basic issue, as Mueller noted, is when the application of the obstruction of justice statute to presidential actions would unduly burden a presidential power. To put it mildly, this is not a determinate inquiry. Mueller believed that the obstruction statute's corrupt intent standard provided a good test: "Congress can validly make obstruction of justice statutes applicable to corruptly motivated official acts of the President without impermissibly undermining his Article II functions."[57] When a president acts corruptly, Article II is no barrier.

This formulation begs the question of what Article II actions are done with corrupt intent. Setting aside the facts of the Trump case, does a president act with corrupt intent if he or she fires the FBI director in order to slow an investigation that he or she believed was concocted and was having a negative impact on U.S. foreign policy? What if this president also thought it was hurting him or her politically? What if he or she also worried that the FBI director might uncover that he or she had engaged in criminal conduct? Surely that would be a corrupt intent. But what if the president was motivated by all of these concerns? Should the normal judicial standard for mixed-motive cases—the presence of bad motives suffices for liability even if legitimate motives are also present, and even dominate—be applied straightforwardly to the president, or does Article II demand a more forgiving standard?[58]

All Mueller said about how the corrupt intent standard would apply to the president is as follows:

> Direct or indirect action by the President to end a criminal investigation into his own or his family members' conduct to protect against personal embarrassment or legal liability would constitute a core example of corruptly motivated conduct. So too would action to halt an enforcement proceeding that directly and adversely affected the President's financial interests for the purpose of protecting those interests. In those examples, official power is being used for the purpose of protecting the President's personal interests. In contrast, the President's actions to serve political or policy interests would not qualify as corrupt. The President's role as head of the

government necessarily requires him to take into account political factors in making policy decisions that affect law-enforcement actions and proceedings. For instance, the President's decision to curtail a law-enforcement investigation to avoid international friction would not implicate the obstruction-of-justice statutes. The criminal law does not seek to regulate the consideration of such political or policy factors in the conduct of government. And when legitimate interests animate the President's conduct, those interests will almost invariably be readily identifiable based on objective factors. Because the President's conduct in those instances will obviously fall outside the zone of obstruction law, no chilling concern should arise.[59]

This is fine as far as it goes, but it avoids all the hard questions, including hard cases about mixed motives.

Against this background, we propose that Congress amend the obstruction of justice statute to specify that presidents commit the crime of obstruction of justice when they commit an obstructive act, with a nexus to an official proceeding, and with a corrupt intent, in three specific cases: (1) intervention to affect the outcome of elections; (2) protection of family members; and (3) self-protection, when the president is either the "subject" or the "target" of a criminal investigation. We do not think it is fruitful for Congress to further specify precisely what counts as "corrupt intent" in these contexts, except to specify, for reasons we explained in Chapter Seven, that presidents do not act with corrupt intent under the statute if they are motivated in part to carry out legitimate Article II functions.

We close by emphasizing two points related to obstruction of justice. First, it is clear from the Mueller Report that Trump's subordinates would not carry out his orders to obstruct justice. Whether they did this because of a sense of governing norms or because they worried about obstruction of justice, or some combination of the two, is hard to figure out. As the Trump experience shows, it is hard for the president to obstruct justice without the cooperation of subordinates. Subordinate criminal liability for obstruction of justice is thus vital to keeping presidents in check—it may be just as important in practice, if not more, than applying the obstruction statute to presidents themselves. To clear away (or at least reduce) constitutional questions of whether subordinates can be liable under the obstruction statutes if they are carrying out the president's orders in the exercise of his or her Article II powers, we propose that subordinate criminal liability be made explicit.

Second, everyone should be clear-eyed about the fact that a future attorney general who holds views akin to the current attorney general might conclude that our statutory proposals are unconstitutional, and thus not allow the Justice Department, including the special counsel, to even investigate the president for these actions, much less conclude that the president committed obstruction of justice. Here we meet the nub of attorney general (and ultimately presidential) control over legal interpretive matters underlying law enforcement actions. At the end of the day, this problem cannot be avoided without amending the Constitution in ways that we think would introduce more problems and uncertainty than gain, even assuming it were possible.

As we have emphasized throughout this chapter and Chapter Seven, political processes and political pressure (including the confirmation process) are ultimately all that can keep the attorney general in check. These background political forces were the ultimate sources of power and protection for both the Watergate special prosecutor and Robert Mueller. Whether and to what degree these forces will continue to work is hard to know. But the prospects of politics serving this checking function can be improved, we hope, through the comprehensive, well-targeted transparency requirements that we have proposed.

★

THE BUREAUCRACY AGAINST
THE PRESIDENT

We have thus far focused on reforms of the presidency to redress inadequate legal and norm-based checks, or accountability constraints, on presidents themselves and on their close aides in the White House and Justice Department. That is the main topic of subsequent chapters as well. In this chapter we focus not on problems for the presidency posed by presidents and their aides but, rather, on problems posed by executive branch officials, and especially by those in the FBI, who may investigate presidents, presidential campaigns, or presidential candidates. These problems have involved both Democratic and Republican presidential candidates and also a president, and all proved very controversial.

The problems fall roughly into two baskets. The first is inadequate guidance for and supervision of the FBI for three types of investigations: criminal investigations of the president, counterintelligence investigations of the president, and both types of investigations of presidential campaigns. All three types of investigations occurred in 2016 and 2017, and they were all unprecedented in one way or another. As we explain, a large part of the controversy resulted from an absence of concrete rules about when such investigations should be opened, who should approve and manage them, and how they should proceed. This is one focus of reform.

The second basket of problems resulted from investigators who defied relevant policies and norms in the course of the investigations.

Such behavior—often justified on the ground that "unusual times call for unusual measures"—has been a common phenomenon in recent years. But, as we explain, it has proved to be an especially unfortunate practice when engaged in by executive branch officials in high-stakes contexts.

BACKGROUND

Unlike in most chapters in this book, here we combine into one discussion the historical background to these problems (much of which has already been discussed in Chapters Seven and Eight) and the events of the Trump era. We first briefly describe the history of FBI investigations in political contexts. We then recount the basic facts of the FBI's investigations of Hillary Clinton's use of a private email server, of links between Donald Trump's campaign and Russian interference in the 2016 election, and of President Trump's possible obstruction of justice and actions triggering counterintelligence concerns. Along the way, we discuss some of the many problems that arose in these investigations that are relevant to reform.

J. Edgar Hoover's FBI

The FBI under J. Edgar Hoover long used investigations and secret surveillance against U.S. citizens for political ends, or to serve the Bureau's interests at the expense or in defiance of elected officials. The latter practice—the FBI's historical use of law enforcement and surveillance techniques to influence or control politicians, including in the executive branch—is the background relevant to this chapter.

"The moment [Hoover] would get something on a senator he'd send one of the errand boys up and advise the senator that we're in the course of an investigation and we by chance happened to come up with this data on your daughter," according to William Sullivan, who led the FBI's domestic intelligence division under Hoover.[1] "From that time on, the senator's right in his pocket." Hoover did the same with senior executive branch officials, including presidents, all of whom tended to give Hoover what he wanted and not to cross him. The FBI also covertly leaked its political intelligence to the news media in order "to influence social policy and political action" in accord with its preferences, according to the Church Committee, a Senate intelligence committee formed in 1975 to study intelligence abuses.[2] Sometimes the FBI conveyed "distorted and exaggerated facts" to the media to support its political goals.[3]

These and related practices, when disclosed publicly in the 1960s and 1970s, almost destroyed the bureau. The FBI survived because its powerful investigatory and surveillance powers were made subject to a number of legal and norm-based restrictions. We have in prior chapters mentioned some of these restrictions, including the Foreign Intelligence Surveillance Act (FISA), the Attorney General's Guidelines for Domestic FBI Operations (AG Guidelines), the FBI Domestic Investigations and Operations Guide (DIOG), various Justice Department law enforcement norms, the White House contacts policy, and restrictions on access to IRS tax records. One point of these arrangements was to assure the American people that the FBI (among other intelligence agencies) did not *in fact* use its powers for political ends. Another point was to ensure that the FBI did not *appear* to use its powers for these ends. The appearance of nonpolitical law enforcement is important because if enough people believe that the FBI is a "political instrument of those in power to be used against opponents, it actually doesn't matter if it's untrue," as one of us wrote previously.[4]

FBI Investigations of Presidential Campaigns and the President

The system worked reasonably well prior to 2016—both in fact and in appearance. But 2016 witnessed several discombobulating events that called the system's legitimacy into question. Here we describe the elements of recent investigations that are relevant to reform: those of Hillary Clinton's use of an email server, the Trump campaign, and President Trump himself.

Investigation of Hillary Clinton's Use of an Email Server

On July 10, 2015, the FBI opened an investigation, code-named "Midyear Exam" or "Midyear," into Hillary Clinton's use of a private email server located at her home in New York during her time as secretary of state. The investigation was a response to a referral from the inspector general of the intelligence community. It focused on Clinton's "potential unauthorized storage of classified information on an unauthorized" server in her home in New York and on "Clinton's intent in setting up and using her private e-mail server."[5]

The Clinton investigation was a "sensitive investigative matter" (SIM) under the FBI's DIOG. A SIM is defined to include investigations "involving the activities of a domestic public official or domestic political candidate (involving corruption or a threat to the national security)," as well as "any other matter which, in the judgment of the official authorizing the investigation, should be brought to the attention of FBI Headquarters and other [Department of Justice] officials."[6] The predicate for a SIM is the same as for any other investigation. But if a matter is designated a SIM, it must be reviewed in advance by senior FBI officials, and an "appropriate" official in the Justice Department receives notification after the fact.[7] The FBI notified Deputy Attorney General Sally Yates about the investigation thirteen days after the bureau opened it, on July 23, 2015.

At 11 a.m. on July 5, 2016, in the middle of the presidential campaign, FBI Director James Comey held a press conference to announce the FBI's view of the email investigation. Comey informed senior leadership in the Justice Department about the press conference a few hours before it occurred but after they had learned about it from the press. He did not inform them about what he would say prior to the press conference. When Attorney General Loretta Lynch asked Comey to advise her of the conclusions he was preparing to disclose to the press, he declined. Nor did he consult with the career prosecutors on the case.

At the press conference, Comey acknowledged that "the Department of Justice makes final decisions on matters like this" but stated that he would advise the department "that no charges are appropriate in this case."[8] He then explained why. Despite "evidence of potential violations of the statutes regarding the handling of classified information," he said, "our judgment is that no reasonable prosecutor would bring such a case." Comey added that Clinton and her colleagues "were extremely careless in their handling of very sensitive, highly classified information" and that "in similar circumstances, a person who engaged in this activity ... often [would be] subject to security or administrative sanctions." The day after Comey's press conference, Lynch announced that she had accepted the recommendation from the FBI and career prosecutors to close the investigation without any charges.

In his subsequent report reviewing the FBI and Justice Department's conduct of the Midyear investigation, Justice Department Inspector General Michael Horowitz criticized Comey's July 5 announcement on two grounds. First was "Comey's decision to depart from longstanding Department practice and publicly announce the FBI's declination recommendation without coordinating with the Department."[9] Horowitz concluded that this was an "unjustified usurpation" of the attorney general's authority that violated several regulations and norms.[10] Comey gave five reasons why he departed from department policy: (1) President Obama had made statements that appeared to prejudge the case, (2) Lynch had acted in ways that made Comey worry she was "carrying water" for the Clinton campaign, (3) Lynch's twenty-minute meeting with Bill Clinton on a tarmac in Arizona on June 27, 2016, might have tainted the case, (4) Comey feared that "highly classified information" might be released that "would impact [Lynch's] credibility," and (5) a Democratic president had appointed Lynch. Horowitz "found none of these reasons persuasive … as a basis for deviating from well-established Department policies and acting unilaterally in a way intentionally designed to avoid supervision by Department leadership over his actions."

Horowitz's second criticism of Comey concerned the content of Comey's July 5 statement. One problem was that "Comey included criticism of former Secretary Clinton's uncharged conduct, including calling her 'extremely careless,' thereby violating longstanding Department practice to avoid what others described as 'trash[ing] people we're not charging.'" Horowitz could not find any basis in a written regulation or policy for Comey's departure from this "practice and protocol." Another problem, according to the prosecutors and other Justice Department officials on the case, was that Comey's statement was "factually and legally incomplete" in ways that caused controversy and confusion in the public.

Midyear might have ended there but for the discovery by the FBI's New York field office on September 26 of emails on a laptop owned by Anthony Weiner during the FBI's investigation of Weiner for various sex crimes. Weiner was married to Huma Abedin, one of Clinton's closest aides, and the laptop contained nearly 350,000 emails, including some from email addresses associated with Clinton. Senior FBI officials—including

Comey and FBI Deputy Director Andrew McCabe—were informed about the laptop within several days. But for reasons that Horowitz found "unpersuasive," the FBI failed to investigate those emails for nearly a month. The bureau finally recognized the potential significance of the laptop to the Midyear investigation on October 26, thirteen days before the presidential election. Two days later, Comey sent a letter to Congress notifying it, and the public, about the emails.

Horowitz concluded that Comey's letter to Congress violated two "longstanding Department and FBI policies, norms, and practices." First, Comey violated the department's "stay silent" principle of not commenting "publicly or to Congress regarding ongoing investigative activity," which was embodied in several Department instruments.[11] Second, Comey departed from an unwritten "norm against taking an action during the run-up to an election that could impact an election."[12] Comey's decision resulted from three concerns, according to Horowitz: (1) "failing to send the letter would harm the FBI and his ability to lead it," (2) failure to send the letter could render a Clinton presidency—Comey says he assumed she would win— illegitimate, and (3) Comey believed that the investigation could not be completed before the election. Horowitz questioned the trade-offs Comey made in what Horowitz described as "ad hoc decisionmaking." But his ultimate judgment was that ad hoc decision-making was inappropriate in general in light of established norms, policies, and precedents, which Comey should have followed.

Comey denied to the inspector general that he sent the letter to Congress because of threatened leaks by the FBI's New York field office, but several other senior FBI officials noted that the threat of leaks was discussed prior to the decision and informed it. Attorney General Lynch informed the inspector general that Comey told her that senior people in the New York field office "have a deep and visceral hatred of Secretary Clinton," a dynamic that caused Comey to worry about leaks. There were powerful reasons to believe that the New York field office was indeed leaking information about the investigation in October 2016 to Trump's lawyer, Rudy Giuliani, and his political ally, Rep. Devin Nunes. Both men publicly alluded to elements of the investigation in ways that sought to advantage Trump, and Nunes said that he got his information about the Wiener laptop from "good FBI agents."[13] Comey told Congress that the FBI investigated the leaks, which violated clear FBI policy, but the results of the investigation were never disclosed.

Horowitz also commented on the poor communication between Comey and senior Justice Department leadership about his decision to send the letter to Congress. The day before Comey sent the letter, he informed the Justice Department about his plan by having his chief of staff tell Yates's deputy. In response, neither Lynch nor Yates contacted Comey or ordered him to stand down. They believed, according to Yates, that they could not stop Comey. So instead, as Horowitz recounted, Lynch told Yates's deputy to tell Comey's chief of staff that "we don't want this letter to go out." Comey said that the message he received was that the department "didn't wish to speak to" him but "recommend[ed] against'" the congressional notification and thought it was "a bad idea." Comey disagreed with the advice and believed Lynch left the call to him since she did not engage him directly or order him to stop. Horowitz said it was "extraordinary" that Comey chose not to speak directly with Lynch and Yates, and that Lynch and Yates believed "it would be counterproductive to speak directly with the FBI Director" about the issue. "We believe that open and candid communication among leaders in the Department and its components is essential for the effective functioning of the Department," concluded Horowitz.

Investigations of Russian Interference in the 2016 Presidential Campaign and of the President

The FBI was also investigating the Trump presidential campaign in 2016. The investigation was a response to Russian interference in the 2016 election, which we described in Chapter Eight.

Soon after WikiLeaks released its first batch of stolen documents in July 2016, the FBI learned that, a few months earlier, Trump campaign adviser George Papadopoulos had suggested to an Australian diplomat that the campaign had received outreach from the Russian government offering to release damaging information about Clinton. On July 31, 2016, FBI Assistant Director for the Counterintelligence Division E.W. "Bill" Priestap opened a counterintelligence investigation, "Crossfire Hurricane," into whether individuals associated with the Trump campaign were coordinating with the Russian government in its interference activities. As Horowitz recounted in a different inspector general report, the stated purpose of the investigation was "to determine whether individual(s) associated with the Trump campaign are witting of and/ or coordinating activities with the Government of Russia."[14] Prior to opening the matter, Priestap consulted with several officials in the Counterintelligence Division, with the FBI General Counsel's Office, and with Deputy Director McCabe.

The Trump campaign investigation was, like the Clinton email investigation, a sensitive investigative matter because it concerned "the activities of a … domestic political organization [and] individual[s] prominent in such an organization." Priestap garnered the appropriate approval up the FBI chain of command and notified the department's National Security Division in an oral briefing on August 2. In his report evaluating the investigation, Inspector General Horowitz concluded that the investigation was properly predicated under "the low threshold for predication in the AG Guidelines and the DIOG." Subsequent to the opening of the investigation, the FBI opened individual investigations on Trump campaign manager Paul Manafort, senior adviser Michael Flynn, and two other campaign advisers, Carter Page and George Papadopoulos.

In addition to the counterintelligence investigation of the Trump *campaign*, the FBI in May 2017 opened up both a counterintelligence investigation and a criminal investigation of President Trump. The details have not officially been made public, but the following can be gathered from newspaper reporting and memoirs.

The criminal investigation centered on Trump's possible obstruction of justice with respect to the campaign investigation that had begun in 2016. The FBI had apparently been considering such an investigation after Trump twice asked FBI Director Comey to drop the FBI's investigation of former National Security Adviser Michael Flynn, and in light of Trump's disparaging references to the investigation. Then Trump fired Comey on May 9, 2017. The next day, Trump told senior Russian officials in the Oval Office that he faced "great pressure" due to the Russia investigation that he had "taken off" due to Comey's firing.[15] On May 11, Trump explained to Lester Holt of NBC News that his decision to fire Comey was a response to the Russia investigation. The Holt interview apparently triggered both the opening of the criminal obstruction of justice investigation of the president and Deputy Attorney General Rod Rosenstein's appointment on May 17 of Robert Mueller as special counsel.

The Holt interview also precipitated the counterintelligence investigation of the president. Between January and May 2017, Comey had represented to Trump that he was not under investigation in connection with the investigation of his campaign. According to McCabe, during this period senior FBI officials discussed whether this was an appropriate representation since, "as the leader of his campaign, by definition some of [Trump's] activity and behavior would be within the scope of the investigation."[16] The FBI eventually began to see Trump's perceived interference with the campaign investigation as evidence of possible collusion with the Russians. After the Holt interview, the FBI formally opened a counterintelligence investigation of the president to determine, according to the *New York Times*, "whether he had been working on behalf of Russia against American interests."[17]

In congressional testimony in October 2018, James Baker, who was FBI general counsel at the time of these events, explained why the FBI thought it was lawful and appropriate to open the criminal and counterintelligence investigations of President Trump. Part of Baker's testimony focused on whether the president had the constitutional authority to fire Comey or to end a criminal investigation. Baker answered that Trump could do so under Article II as long as the action "is not otherwise in contravention of his other responsibilities under the Constitution," including "his oath of office to preserve, protect, and defend the Constitution" and his "solemn obligation under the Constitution to take care that the laws are faithfully executed, all of the laws simultaneously."[18] Baker did not discuss whether and, if so, when the obstruction of justice statutes could lawfully apply to the president. He said there was a legal analysis of whether the FBI could open up the investigation of the president after the firing of Comey but stated that it took place in "conversations and perhaps some e-mails, that type of thing; not like a formal memo or anything like that."[19]

Baker also explained the legal basis for opening a counterintelligence investigation of the president. FBI counterintelligence investigations "address threats related to national security" from "espionage and other [related] intelligence activities ... conducted by, for, or on behalf of foreign powers, organizations, or persons."[20] Baker explained that the counterintelligence investigation was proper because Trump's firing of Comey constituted a "threat to national security."[21] When asked to elaborate, he stated:

> We were trying to investigate what the Russians did and ... whether there were any Americans or others who had done things in support of those efforts ... so that we could understand the full nature and scope of what the Russians had attempted to do. And so to the extent that this action of firing Director Comey may have been caused by or was the result of a decision to shut down that investigation, which I thought was a legitimate investigation, then that would frustrate our ability to some degree to ascertain what the Russians as well as any other Americans or others had done in furtherance of the objectives of the Russian Federation. So not only ... would it be an issue about obstructing an investigation, but the obstruction itself would hurt our ability to figure out what the Russians had done, and that is what would be the threat to the national security. Our inability or our—the inability or the delays, the difficulties that we might have with respect to trying to figure out what the Russians were doing, because our main objective was to thwart them.

Baker appears to be saying here that the FBI believed the president was a proper target of a counterintelligence investigation because his firing of Comey hurt the FBI's ability to ascertain Russian involvement in the presidential election and was in that sense a "threat to the national security."

The FBI and Justice Department's conduct of the Crossfire Hurricane investigation, and its investigations of President Trump beginning in 2017, are well documented in the public record and in three inspector general reports.[22] Inspector General Horowitz identified numerous problems, all of which have been aired extensively. We focus here on three problems that are central to our reform proposals.[23] As we explain, some of these problems also surfaced in ways the inspector general did not address.

First, Horowitz questioned FBI standards for opening and conducting sensitive investigative matters in the context of presidential campaign investigations and investigations of the president. He made four points that are relevant to our proposed reforms. First, he noted that the threshold for opening such an investigation was "low" and did not "provide heightened predication standards for sensitive matters, or allegations potentially impacting constitutionally protected activity, such as First Amendment rights."[24] Second, he expressed concern that the FBI was not required to notify or consult with the Justice Department "before opening an investigation such as the one here involving the alleged conduct of individuals associated with a major party presidential campaign." Third, he expressed concern about the FBI's "limited notice requirements before using more intrusive investigative techniques that could impact constitutionally protected activity" in the presidential election context. And fourth, he noted that the Bureau lacked a policy on whether to notify campaigns that, like Trump's, are targets of an investigation.

Second, Horowitz criticized the erosion of political accountability within the Department of Justice. He focused primarily on the failure by former Associate Deputy Attorney General Bruce Ohr, a career official, to report to his superiors about meetings with the FBI related to the investigation of the Trump campaign, which was an area outside his formal responsibility. Ohr justified his failure to report these activities to his boss, Yates, because she might tell him to stop, and because the matter was best decided by "career people." Another career official in the Criminal Division, Bruce Schwartz, justified his failure to keep his superiors in the loop on a related investigation on the ground that he was trying to prevent the investigation from being "politicized" and he wanted to protect "the Department from allegations that its investigation of Manafort was politically motivated."[25]

Horowitz wrote that Ohr and other officials "fundamentally misconstrued who is ultimately responsible and accountable for the Department's work." He continued that "Department leaders cannot fulfill their management responsibilities, and be held accountable for the Department's actions, if subordinates intentionally withhold information from them in such circumstances."

Political accountability broke down in Crossfire Hurricane in other ways that Horowitz did not examine. The FBI had opened a counterintelligence investigation on Trump campaign foreign policy adviser Michael Flynn in August 2016. It was planning to close the investigation until it learned that Flynn, by then Trump's designee to be national security adviser, had communicated with Russian ambassador Sergey Kislyak in late December 2016. In January 2017, near the end of the transition, the deputy attorney general, the director of national intelligence, and the CIA director advised FBI Director Comey to notify incoming Trump administration officials about the Flynn-Kislyak communications. Comey refused on the ground that he needed to protect his investigation. Comey and others in the FBI began planning to interview Flynn and did not intend to notify the department or the White House. On the morning of January 24, Yates, then acting attorney general, contacted Comey to demand that he notify the White House about the Kislyak calls. Comey returned the call that afternoon to advise her that agents were on the way to the White House to interview Flynn. Yates was "flabbergasted" and "dumbfounded" because "an interview of Flynn should have been coordinated with [the Justice Department]."[26]

The third systemic problem that emerged from Crossfire Hurricane concerned leaks, including on the part of senior FBI officials or former officials. Horowitz in particular criticized Comey's handling of seven memoranda that he wrote about interactions that he had with Trump, both as president-elect and as president. One criticism focused on Comey's providing a copy of one memorandum to an attorney (and a friend), after he had been fired, with instructions to share its contents with a reporter for the New York Times. Comey explained that he did this to put "extraordinary pressure on the leadership of the Department of Justice, which [he did] not trust" to appoint a special counsel to investigate Trump's actions and statements regarding the Flynn investigation.[27] Comey thought the issue was of "incredible importance to the Nation" and told the inspector general he took the action because of his love for the country, the Justice Department, and the FBI.

Horowitz criticized Comey's actions and reasoning. He determined that the memos were FBI records and that the leak violated Comey's employment agreement and prepublication review obligations and was not justified by "Comey's own, personal conception of what was necessary," especially "given the other lawful and appropriate actions he could have taken to achieve his desired end." Horowitz concluded that "Comey set a dangerous example for the over 35,000 current FBI employees" and "failed to live up to" the responsibility of the FBI to protect sensitive information.

There were other leaks in connection with Crossfire Hurricane, including unprecedented leaks of foreign intelligence intercepts.[28] The first leak of this type occurred in February 2017 and was about Flynn's calls to Kislyak. This was the leak that led to the FBI's renewed interest in Flynn and ultimately led to his resignation and indictment. Other leaks by what newspapers described as current and former intelligence officials involved intercepts of Russian government officials discussing "derogatory" information about Trump and his campaign staff; of other Russian officials bragging that they could use their relationship with Flynn to influence Trump; of Kislyak claiming to have discussed campaign-related issues with then-Sen. Jeff Sessions; and of Kislyak reporting to Moscow that Trump's son-in-law, Jared Kushner, wanted to establish a secure communication channel.

We do not know the source of these leaks—though especially this early in the administration, they almost certainly came from the bureaucracy and not Trump appointees. Whoever the source, the leaks threatened to compromise sources and methods of intelligence collection, violated criminal law, and abused the privacy rights of the American citizens involved. But for present purposes the core offense involved in these leaks was the strategic release of intelligence information for political purposes.

Those who leaked the information probably believed they were taking extraordinary action to sound the alarm about Russian influence in the government. But, as happens so often in these situations, these actions inevitably appear to others to be designed to influence democratic politics in what—regardless of whether the leaks came from the FBI or some other agency—seemed like a throwback to the days of J. Edgar Hoover. This perception of political manipulation had galled Democrats who protested leaks and threatened leaks concerning the investigation of Weiner's laptop in the Clinton email investigation. Republicans who were silent about these abuses were vocal in their complaint about the Crossfire Hurricane leaks. And vice versa. The general point, however, is that the 2016 and 2017 experiences show that the problem of leaks in highly sensitive investigations of this kind, like the problem more generally of FBI norm-breaking, crossed party lines and administrations.

REFORM: FBI INVESTIGATIONS OF PRESIDENTIAL CANDIDATES AND CAMPAIGNS

We propose several concrete rules for FBI investigations of presidential candidates or "campaigns," a term that for present purposes includes all officials, employees, and others who act in coordination with a campaign organization or are authorized to act on its behalf.[29] We also propose rules for FBI investigations of the president. The reforms focus primarily on specific guidance for various aspects of these investigations. If investigations are conducted pursuant to concrete and well-crafted guidance—which the investigations recounted earlier were not—then concerns about politicization and illegitimacy can be tempered. Such guidance can establish a process to ensure that controversial steps are properly vetted in ways that minimize mistakes and maximize political accountability. This, in turn, can help to avoid controversy later, either because the Justice Department and FBI declined to take unnecessarily controversial investigatory steps, or because they took necessarily controversial steps but can point to clear guidance and accountability for legitimation. Such concrete guidance will also redress some of the norm-breaking episodes of the past few years.

The reforms we propose should be implemented by the executive branch with guidance provided by the attorney general. It is possible that Congress will want to weigh in on some of these issues.

The FBI opened a "full investigation" against candidate Hillary Clinton in 2015 and another one on Trump campaign officials in 2016.[30] In a full investigation, the FBI can use all of its prodigious surveillance and intelligence-gathering techniques. It need satisfy only two requirements to open a full investigation. First, it must have an "authorized purpose" (such as detecting a federal crime or threat to national security). Second, it must have an "articulable factual basis" that "reasonably indicates" that a federal crime or threat to national security "*may* have occurred" or "*may* occur," and that the investigation *may* obtain relevant information. As Horowitz noted, this is a "low" threshold. The FBI thus has enormous leeway in opening an investigation of political candidates and campaigns.

There is one additional rule. As noted earlier, an investigation involving a political candidate or campaign is a sensitive investigative matter. An FBI agent considering opening a sensitive investigative matter must consult and receive approval up the FBI chain of command to various degrees depending on the type of assessment or investigation at issue. This requirement applies to *all* political candidates and public officials— a presidential candidate as well as a candidate running for local public office. As noted, consistent with the DIOG, the FBI notified the Justice Department about the Clinton and Trump campaign investigations *after* they were opened. Beyond notice after the fact, the DIOG urges caution in opening such investigations of political candidates, but it does not require any heightened predication beyond the "low" predication needed for other investigations. After an investigation is opened, the DIOG generally does not require the FBI to get senior department approval for its investigative steps in this context.

In the proposals that follow to address the inadequacies in this system, we draw two distinctions: first, between a criminal and a counterintelligence investigation; and, second, between investigations conducted before inauguration and after inauguration (that is, between the end of the campaign and the beginning of the presidential administration).

With regard to the former distinction, the AG Guidelines currently state that "all of the FBI's legal authorities are available for deployment in all cases" in order to "protect the public from crimes and threats to the national security and to further the United States' foreign intelligence objectives." This means that as a general presumptive matter, the FBI need not label investigations and information-gathering activities in those investigations differently or use different rules for different types of investigations. "In many cases," the guidelines explain, "a single investigation will be supportable as an exercise of a number of these authorities—i.e., as an investigation of a federal crime or crimes, as an investigation of a threat to the national security, and/or as a collection of foreign intelligence." This "braided" approach to investigations was a post-9/11 innovation that accompanied the lowering of the "wall" between the FBI's criminal and counterintelligence functions.[31] Although the braided approach makes sense as a general matter, for reasons explained in the discussion that follows we propose to reject it in the context of campaign and presidential investigations.

A final note before turning to reforms. We acknowledge that the procedural and substantive rules and guidelines that follow, taken together, will make it more cumbersome to investigate presidential campaigns than under the current rules, and could invite risk aversion that leaves undetected criminal or adverse national-security activity related to a campaign. This problem requires particularly close attention in an era likely to be marked by increased activity to illicitly influence the political process in the United States. But we believe these risks, which we do not think are large, are justified. The experience of the past three years has exposed the large costs of unguided investigations, which has fueled the weaponization of the law enforcement process. For these reasons, we conclude that the need for greater guidance and more accountability outweighs the introduction of more checks and limits into these investigations.

Preinauguration Criminal Investigations

Any criminal investigation of a presidential candidate or presidential campaign threatens to distort or undermine the electoral process. Word of the investigation can leak out, often misleadingly, from within the government or from witnesses, subjects, or targets. Independent of leaks, the campaign would be required to allocate resources and attention to its legal defense. The individuals under investigation have to arrange legal representation and assume its costs. They will experience disruption in their work for the campaign. This means disruption to the campaign as well. And the investigation can in various ways influence voters and cause outcry over the perceived abuse of law enforcement to affect an election's outcome.

An investigation may warrant these potential costs, but the costs must be considered in crafting rules for the investigation.

Review and Approval of the Investigation

Horowitz's 2019 report on the Carter Page FISA applications expressed surprise about deficiencies in the DIOG guidance in the context of opening and conducting investigations related to political campaigns. It noted that for some investigative steps in other sensitive contexts that touch on civil liberties—such as subpoenas to the news media and nonconsensual monitoring of senior executive branch officials—the FBI must get prior approval from a senior Justice Department official. Horowitz recommended that before opening an investigation that implicates "core First

Amendment activity and a national political campaign," the FBI should give "advance notice to Department senior management officials" such as the deputy attorney general.

We agree with Horowitz's recommendation that the FBI provide notice to senior department leadership of any investigation of a presidential candidate or campaign. But because of the momentousness of such an investigation, we would go further and propose that in addition to notice to senior department officials, the bureau obtain *approval from the attorney general* prior to proceeding.

We propose review prior to a final decision by the attorney general at two specific levels of the Department of Justice: the FBI director and the assistant attorney general in charge of the Criminal Division. By requiring two layers of review before the attorney general, this reform can strengthen protection against the problem created by the FBI's unilateralism. The attorney general will have the benefit of multiple perspectives, and the officials who provide him or her with their views will be accountable for the quality and rigor of their analysis and judgment.

Senior Senate-confirmed Justice Department officials will typically take a broader view of the matter than the bureau. They would be, as Horowitz noted, in a better position to "consider the potential constitutional and prudential implications in advance of these activities" and to consider "enterprise risk" to the department and the bureau. The attorney general would make the ultimate call. In the event that the attorney general exercises poor judgment, he or she, and not the FBI, should answer to Congress and the public for the department.

One downside of allocating responsibility in this way is that the department might be accused of bias if a decision either favors a candidate or campaign of the attorney general's party *or* disfavors a candidate or campaign of another party. But as we learned in recent years, analogous accusations can fly, with all the connotations and concerns of the Hoover era, if the decision is made within the FBI, including by the director.

The argument for placing the decision in the FBI is that it is independent and professional, and not "political." We buy this argument in many contexts. But for the same reasons that the DIOG requires Justice Department involvement before taking investigative steps in other extremely sensitive circumstances, we believe that senior department decision-making should be the rule in presidential elections. Legal and prudential judgment from outside the bureau should be brought to bear on these most consequential of decisions. Especially since that judgment touches on the fate of our democracy, the decision, for better or worse, needs to be made by an actor who is more politically accountable than the FBI director. One problem in some of the FBI's controversial investigative decisions is that the attorney general or acting attorney general appeared to shirk or shy away from making decisions on hard questions. The rules we propose will not permit this in the campaign investigation context.

Review and Approval of Investigative Techniques

We propose reforms to address important gaps that Horowitz identified in FBI guidance about the use of investigative techniques as they apply to investigations of presidential candidates and campaigns. Such techniques include the use of electronic surveillance, confidential human sources, and undercover employees for "consensual monitoring." As a general matter, the FBI should propose a plan of the investigation to the Justice Department's senior leadership for the attorney general's approval, and it should regularly notify senior department leadership about the use of such techniques and the progress of the investigation.

We believe that a more concrete and restrictive rule is needed for using undercover employees in the context of investigations of presidential candidates and campaigns. Horowitz "found it concerning" that undercover monitoring of Trump campaign affiliates, including one who was not a subject of the investigation, was "permitted under Department and FBI policy" with only the approval of a first-level supervisor, without any requirement to notify senior Justice Department officials. These policies, he concluded, "are not sufficient to ensure appropriate oversight and accountability." Horowitz recommended a requirement that there be "consultation, at a minimum," with the Justice Department, before using these techniques in the context of presidential campaigns.

We would go further. It would be extraordinary for an administration to use an undercover employee in an ongoing presidential campaign, where the investigation does not involve significant national security concerns. (We propose different investigative standards for counterintelligence threats, as discussed in the next section.) It would be difficult to justify planting a "spy" in any campaign. It would be most difficult do so when the administration is headed by a president of the opposing party. It would also be hard in cases where the administration and the campaign are affiliated with the same party, such as an investigation of a primary opponent of the president.

At a minimum, the Justice Department should establish a rule of attorney general approval, akin to attorney general sign-off for the FBI to seek a FISA warrant from the FISA Court, before using this technique in the context of a presidential campaign. We would accompany this requirement with a presumption against using this technique in this context. There is a powerful argument that the concerns we laid out earlier warrant a stronger rule—an absolute ban on the practice. Whether this step is appropriate would depend on an assessment of whether there are plausible scenarios where the failure to use this technique will present a high likelihood of significant criminal activity going unredressed, and whether the attorney general's discretion over the use of this technique would suffice to meet this concern.

Public Discussion of the Investigation, or Other Steps Likely to Draw Public Attention

The inspector general's Clinton email investigation report made three recommendations to protect against the political impact of investigations into an ongoing presidential campaign:

- "We recommend that the Department consider making explicit that, except in situations where the law requires or permits disclosure, an investigating agency cannot publicly announce its recommended charging decision prior to consulting with the Attorney General, Deputy Attorney General, U.S. Attorney, or his or her designee, and cannot proceed without the approval of one of these officials."

- "We recommend that the Department and the FBI consider adopting a policy addressing the appropriateness of Department employees discussing the conduct of uncharged individuals in public statements."

- We recommend that the Department consider providing guidance to agents and prosecutors concerning the taking of overt investigative steps, indictments, public announcements, or other actions that could impact an election."

We propose that given the very high stakes in presidential campaigns and the serious consequences of soft or nonexistent policies in this area in 2016, the department should transform these three recommendations into concrete guidance in the context of investigations related to presidential campaigns.

First, the department should establish an absolute rule against an investigating agency, including the FBI, announcing recommended charging decisions related to presidential candidates or campaigns. This is the normal presumption in law enforcement, and one that has special force in the context of the most important event in our democracy, presidential elections.

Second, in the context of presidential campaigns, we see no reason why any official in the Justice Department, other than the top two department officials, should ever have discretion to discuss publicly the conduct of uncharged presidential candidates or campaign officials. We propose an absolute ban in this context below the level of attorney general and deputy attorney general, and guidance that these top two officials can discuss uncharged conduct in this context only in exceptional circumstances, as the public interest requires.

Third, we propose to make the so-called 60-day "rule" a concrete policy in the context of presidential campaigns. Horowitz defined the rule in this way: "[P]rosecutors avoid public disclosure of investigative steps related to electoral matters or the return of indictments against a candidate for office within 60 days of a primary or general election." The 60-day rule, however, "is not written or described in any Department policy or regulation," said Horowitz. Ray Hulser, who was once the section chief of the Justice Department's Public Integrity Section, told Horowitz that a general codification of the 60-day rule was "unworkable." Perhaps so, due to the wide array of elections and circumstances in which criminal investigations may intersect with elections. But in the context of presidential campaigns, specific guidance is appropriate.

The 60-day rule should thus be embodied in a firm prohibition, with an exception for only the attorney general or deputy attorney general in exceptional circumstances. Moreover, the rule should be established as a floor, not a ceiling. The department should adopt, as it has in its *Federal Prosecution of Election Offenses* in the case of voting fraud cases, the "general policy of the Department not to conduct overt investigations … until after the outcome of the election is certified."[32] The purpose of this requirement is to "minimize the likelihood that the investigation itself may become a factor in the election."[33]

The Logan Act

The Logan Act is a statute enacted in 1799. It currently makes it a crime for "any citizen" to carry on "any correspondence or intercourse" with a foreign government or officer with intent to influence their conduct "in relation to any disputes or controversies with the United States, or to defeat the measures of the United States."[34] Most but not all scholars believe that the Logan Act is unconstitutionally vague. The U.S. government has brought only two prosecutions under the act, "in 1803 and 1852, neither of which resulted in a conviction."[35] In early January 2016, the FBI considered opening up a criminal investigation of designated National Security Adviser Michael Flynn under the Logan Act in connection with his phone calls with Russian ambassador Sergey Kislyak during the presidential transition. The Obama Justice Department's view at the time was that it would be "difficult to prosecute" Flynn for such conversations.[36]

Given the desuetude of the statute, its uncertain scope, its constitutional problems, and especially its imprecise basis for investigating campaigns, we propose that Congress abrogate the statute, at least as it applies to members of presidential campaigns and transitions. As we explained in Chapter Two, campaign contacts with foreign officials are commonplace and often important. A variety of laws other than the Logan Act regulate relations between campaign officials and foreign governments. And in Chapter Two we have proposed ways to revise the laws to regulate those aspects of these communications and relationships that present particularly serious threats to the American electoral process. Beyond these revised laws, and other laws (such as a criminal conspiracy, for example), communications between campaigns (including transition teams) and foreign governments should not be regulated.

Preinauguration Counterintelligence Investigations of Presidential Candidates and Campaigns

Counterintelligence investigations of presidential candidates and campaigns raise many of the same issues as criminal investigations in this context, but they also raise different issues. The main difference—and one that requires somewhat different rules—is that a counterintelligence investigation seeks to understand and possibly counteract a threat to national security.

Review and Approval of the Investigation

We propose a multilayered review procedure for opening a counterintelligence investigation in this context, culminating in final approval required by the attorney general. But unlike in the criminal investigation context, the assistant attorney general heading the National Security Division rather than the assistant attorney general in charge of the Criminal Division would be required to review the request. The director of national intelligence should also participate in this formal review to clarify intelligence community equities.

Review and Approval of Investigative Techniques

As with criminal investigations of presidential candidates and campaigns, the FBI should be required to propose a plan of the investigation to the Justice Department's senior leadership for the attorney general's approval, and should regularly notify senior department leadership about the use of such techniques and the progress of the investigation. All investigative techniques should be available in a counterintelligence investigation. We mentioned earlier that the executive branch might consider ruling out the use of undercover employees for "consensual monitoring" in criminal investigations of presidential candidates and campaigns. Because of the higher stakes, undercover employees should be available in a counterintelligence investigation, with the approval of the attorney general.

Report to Congress

The executive branch has a general obligation to keep the congressional intelligence committees (or, for very sensitive intelligence activities, their top four members) "fully and currently informed" of U.S. "intelligence activities," including "significant anticipated intelligence activity."[37] This obligation probably includes significant counterintelligence activities, but Congress should clarify the matter and craft special rules for counterintelligence activities involving presidential campaigns.

The main aim of notice, in our view, is to inject discipline and accountability into the attorney general's decision whether to open and how to conduct a counterintelligence investigation of a campaign. The notice should be triggered either by the opening of such an investigation, or by the failure to do so upon the recommendation of either the director of national intelligence or the FBI director. In the case of an opened investigation, the notice should explain its basis, including any disagreement in the recommendation to open it between the FBI director and the director of national intelligence. In the case of an attorney general's refusal to open an investigation, the notice should explain what the director of national intelligence and the FBI director recommended, and the basis for the attorney general's decision.

Notice to the Campaign

We propose reforms that will clarify the question of whether and when a campaign subject to a counterintelligence investigation should be so notified. The FBI gave the Clinton administration a defensive briefing on the Russian threat to its campaign, but it did not give the Trump campaign a defensive briefing on the possible counterintelligence threats in or related to its campaign. The judgment not to notify the Trump campaign came from an assistant director, who concluded that informing the campaign might prohibit the Bureau from "finding the truth."[38] The different approaches on the surface perhaps made sense, since the Clinton campaign was the target of the threat and members of the Trump campaign were subjects of the counterintelligence investigation. But matters are more complex than that.

In our view, the question turns on whether the investigation plausibly includes the candidate or senior management, or is instead directed toward an individual employed by or associated with the campaign, and there is no evidence that the actions under investigation were directed by the campaign or the candidate. That distinction will not always be easy to discern, and the final call should rest with the attorney general in consultation with the FBI director and the director of national intelligence. In this latter case, the campaign should be afforded the opportunity to cooperate with the investigation. It should also be able to protect itself against any infiltration or similar activity presenting legitimate security concerns. An example would be a campaign notified that an individual on the campaign's payroll or closely associated with it in an advisory capacity is reporting directly to a foreign power interested in influencing the outcome of the election.

REFORM: FBI INVESTIGATIONS OF PRESIDENTS

A decision to open and conduct a criminal or counterintelligence investigation of a president is obviously a momentous and difficult event. We have already explained in Chapter Eight why such a criminal investigation would need to be conducted by a special counsel, and we proposed a series of reforms in that chapter to improve that process. One reform concerned the need for legal clarity about when and how the president can obstruct justice. Another reform, offered in Chapter Six, addressed the need for clarity on the circumstances in which the president is liable for bribery in the doling out of pardons. A president can of course be investigated for other crimes, including crimes unrelated to officeholding, such as violence against another person or financial improprieties. All of these investigations must take place within the framework of a special counsel, which we have already analyzed.

A counterintelligence investigation of a president is a much trickier proposition, for many reasons. The special counsel regulations do not even contemplate counterintelligence concerns as a jurisdictional trigger. They are currently limited to situations where a "criminal investigation of a person or matter is warranted" but presents a conflict of interest or other extraordinary circumstance.[39] That is why, as we noted in Chapter Eight, the Mueller investigation of Russian contacts with the Trump campaign was technically not opened pursuant to the special counsel regulations. Rather, Acting Attorney General Rod Rosenstein opened the investigation pursuant to the attorney general's broader authority to appoint legal counsel for special purposes, and he incorporated the special counsel rules by reference to govern the matter.

One hopes that a situation never again appears where the FBI has plausible reasons to suspect a president as a counterintelligence threat. But after the events of recent years, and given the likelihood of increased efforts at foreign interference in U.S. elections, the government must contemplate the possibility. Our initial proposal in this context is thus to expand the special counsel regulations to include as a jurisdictional trigger counterintelligence investigations of executive branch officials that present a conflict of interest or other extraordinary circumstance. The investigation of a president would be deemed to satisfy these criteria and require the appointment of a special counsel. However, any system for investigating the president for counterintelligence concerns must face at least three hard questions.

The first question is about the precise criterion for opening a counterintelligence investigation of the president. The FBI defines its counterintelligence responsibilities as "countering actions of foreign intelligence services and organizations that employ human and technical means to gather information about the U.S. *that adversely affects our national interests*" (emphasis added). The bureau sees its counterintelligence mission as "identifying and neutralizing ongoing *national security threats*" (emphasis added). Based on news reports and testimony, it appears that the FBI opened a counterintelligence investigation of the president because, after Trump fired Comey, the FBI feared that Trump was a threat to the national security interests of the United States, likely because he was opposed to the investigation of Russian interference in the election.

This is a fraught judgment for the FBI to make about the president of the United States. It is fraught because of the FBI's history of secret intelligence operations against the president and other elected officials to influence the behavior of those officials and democratic politics. And it is fraught because under the U.S. Constitution, the president is charged with determining what constitutes the national security interest and national security threats, at least for the executive branch and subject to valid congressional restrictions. Because the president defines what a national security threat is, it is hard for a subordinate agency like the FBI to determine that he or she is a national security threat for purposes of opening a counterintelligence investigation. Presidents often engage in controversial contacts with foreign leaders that lead to sharp changes in the direction of U.S. foreign policy, and some critics charge that these contacts constitute a threat to national security. Think of how some critics viewed Nixon's opening with China or Obama's with Iran and Cuba.

To be sure, Trump was an extreme and unprecedented case. Among other things, he often showed apparent fealty to Russian President Vladimir Putin, he disclosed classified information to the Russian ambassador in the Oval Office, he persistently refused to acknowledge what his director of national intelligence described as Russia's "ongoing, pervasive efforts to undermine our democracy," he fired Comey because of the Russia investigation, and he took many other controversial and sometimes bizarre—and, some also believed, suspicious and troubling—actions and postures toward Russia. These are all presidential prerogatives, but in the aggregate they present understandable concern. And it is easy to imagine evidence that would make the president appear very much like a Manchurian candidate—for example, unambiguous evidence that the president is compromised, and acting on behalf of a foreign power, and has pledged to that foreign power to expose U.S. intelligence methods or assets.

It is hard to specify the precise trigger for opening a counterintelligence investigation of a president, but the criterion must be more specific than a mere conclusion that the president presents a threat to U.S. national security interests. The criterion must be specified in advance, after a thorough legal analysis by the Justice Department about where the outer bounds of presidential prerogatives to determine the national security interests of the United States end and where unjustifiably harmful collusion or collaboration begins.

The decision to open such an investigation should not be made by the FBI alone, as happened in 2017. FBI leaders understood the predicament they faced, and they notified the acting attorney general and relevant congressional leaders. As with counterintelligence investigations of campaigns, we would take this decision out of the hands of the FBI and place it in the hands of the attorney general after input from the director of national intelligence, the FBI director, and the head of the National Security Division.

We also believe that such a multilayered and contextualized review, more than a precise definition of what constitutes a presidential counterintelligence threat, should result in more rigorous consideration of the factors supporting an investigation. We also believe that mandatory reporting to the congressional intelligence committees, akin to the reporting outlined for counterintelligence investigations of presidential campaigns, is vital in this context. As in that case, the reporting requirement should include any decision by the attorney general to reject the advice of either the FBI director or the director of national intelligence to open a counterintelligence investigation of the president, along with the attorney general's reasons for the declination.

NORMS AND ACCOUNTABILITY

The concrete rules and procedures we prescribe in this chapter will go a long way toward preventing the most harmful types of norm-breaking or under-guided decision-making that have occurred during the past few years in investigations of presidential candidates and campaigns and the president himself. For example, the following would be expressly prohibited under our proposals: Comey's announcement of his recommendation not to prosecute Clinton for the email matter; Comey's decision to send a letter to Congress within weeks of the election about reopening the investigation; the FBI's failure to coordinate with the acting attorney general before interviewing incoming National Security Adviser Michael Flynn; and the FBI's opening of a counterintelligence investigation of the president without a greater showing of counterintelligence threat, more thorough legal analysis, and ex ante approval by the attorney general. Our proposals would tamp down on unaccountable actions by the FBI not just by regulating certain investigative steps more heavily but also by making clear that the attorney general cannot eschew responsibility for these steps, since these calls would necessarily be his or hers, and not the FBI's.

Specific guidance can help avert some of the controversies of recent years, but compliance with even clear rules depends on norms, culture, and threats of punishment or termination. In the post-Trump era, it will be vital for leaders in the Justice Department to reemphasize the norm of rule-following even in crisis situations. This was a common theme in all of Horowitz's reports. Horowitz quoted from a Justice Department veteran whose views we share on this point:

[The Justice Department] has principles and there's always an urge when something important or different pops up to say, we should do it differently or ... we might want to deviate because this is so different. But the comfort that we get as people, as lawyers, as representatives, as employees and as an institution, the comfort we get from those institutional policies, protocols, ... is an unbelievable thing through whatever storm, you know whatever storm hits us, when you are within the norm of the way the institution behaves, you can weather any of it because you stand on the principle. And once you deviate, even in a minor way, and you're always going to want to deviate. It's always going to be something important and some big deal that makes you think, oh let's do this a little differently. But once you do that, you have removed yourself from the comfort of saying this institution has a way of doing things and then every decision is another ad hoc decision that may be informed by our policy and our protocol and principles, but it's never going to be squarely within them.

One element of norm-breaking that will not be solved by the preceding reform proposals, and that we do not propose to address through reforms, is the problem of leaks. Leaks from the executive branch, including leaks of highly classified information, did not begin with the Trump administration. Authorized or semiauthorized leaks have long been deployed opportunistically by presidential administrations to shape the political environment. And unauthorized leaks of various sorts have long plagued the presidency. Unauthorized leaks can expose an embarrassing comment, document, or email that a government official did not intend for the light of day—perhaps with the purpose of diminishing his or her influence or inducing a firing or resignation. They can affect or influence a policy deliberation by alerting potential critics of an option under consideration and giving them time to mobilize opposition to it. And, of course, leaks can also function as vital acts of whistleblowing and accountability by bringing to the attention of Congress and the press questionable or illegal conduct that would otherwise remain concealed.

Whether a leak serves a salutary or harmful purpose can be the subject of intense disagreement. This is especially so when the leaks involve classified or sensitive national security information. Depending on the observer's standpoint, such leaks can be a heroic blow struck for civil liberties and executive branch accountability, or the reckless endangerment of the public. Unauthorized leaks of classified national security information have grown much more prevalent since 9/11 due to several factors: a bloated secrecy bureaucracy, the huge growth in secrets, controversial secret actions in a seemingly endless war, and the digitalization of secrets. Every presidency bemoans the problem of leaks, especially national security leaks. The Bush and Obama administrations took novel steps to stem the flow of such leaks, and largely failed. The Trump administration tried even harder, and also failed.

This is not the place to try to fix the general problem of leaks. But even accepting that leaks are commonplace and can serve salutary purposes, the past four years have presented two new, related concerns about leaks that warrant special attention.

The first is the perception that bureaucrats are leaking information in ways that aim to shape the outcomes of democratic electoral politics. Most leaks aim to shape politics, and unauthorized leakers tend to be confident that they are justified in doing so. But leaks since 2016 have involved unusually high political stakes related to presidential elections. The first were the leaks by the FBI's New York field office concerning the Hillary Clinton investigation in 2016, and the worries about further such leaks, which informed the FBI's decision to notify Congress about its reopened investigation of Clinton weeks before the election. The second were the leaks by FBI Director Comey with the aim of forcing appointment of a special counsel, and leaks by other unnamed officials in 2017 that suggested that Trump and his senior advisers were colluding with the Russians.

Whether these leaks were "justified" invariably depends on where one sits, and we do not here adjudicate that question. We simply make two points. First, these leaks demonstrate the extraordinary power that leakers have over the fate of democratic politics, and over the political agenda that informs presidential electoral choice, both before and after the election. The strategic release of executive branch secrets at this level calls to mind the Hoover era at the FBI and should at least give pause to the frequent glorification of leaks as a bulwark of a free society. Second, and relatedly, an important impact of these leaks is to discredit the legitimacy of career officials who are widely perceived, justifiably or not, to be the source of the leaks. This is another underappreciated cost of leaks of this sort.

The second and related concern involves the sheer scale of the "daily barrage of leaks that [have] poured out of Trump's executive branch."[40] The leaks have been extraordinary in volume and in kind beyond the point just noted. Sensitive intelligence information secretly gleaned from the conversations of foreign officials leaked for the first time during the Trump administration—not once, but several times. Some of these leaks breached a different taboo against revealing information about U.S. citizens "incidentally collected" during surveillance of a foreign agent. Even in an era when leaks were commonplace, leaks of these types of information were unprecedented. Other unprecedented types of leaks included the disclosure of the transcripts of Trump's telephone calls with foreign leaders, and the September 2018 op-ed by a "senior official" of the Trump administration that proclaimed that many like him or her in the executive branch "are working diligently from within to frustrate parts of his agenda and his worst inclinations."[41] This official argued that this extraordinary venture—a "resistance inside the administration"—was imperative in defending against a presidential "leadership style" that was "impetuous, adversarial, petty and ineffective."

As we have noted, Trump's erratic, feckless, and self-regarding behavior; his proclivity for brazen norm-busting; and his disdain for institutional norms and constraints undoubtedly provoked these extreme responses from within the executive branch—presumably, but not nec-essarily, from bureaucrats as opposed to Trump political appointees. Under these conditions, it is not surprising that executive branch officials developed the view that, as the anonymous op-ed author put it, the "deep state" was really the "steady state." It was widely believed that desperate times called for desperate measures. The concern, however, is that once the norms shift dramatically to address the exceptional case, it is possible, if not predictable, that the shift will become more of a transformation, and a different "resistance" to a different president will believe itself justified to adopt the same course. Donald Trump will always bear a fair measure of the responsibility for what one of us (Goldsmith) has called a bureaucratic "immune response" to his most outlandish conduct.[42]

But the immune response could become uncontrolled and set a new, even more permissive and accepted standard for leaking, with corrosive impacts on the presidency. At some level, the presidency cannot serve its constitutional role in fashioning and successfully executing policy without significant confidentiality. Setting aside the difficult and highly controversial legal questions presented by leaks and executive branch responses to leaks, particularly in national security affairs, the question of concern is whether a heightened respect for confidentiality can be recovered and restored to a more commanding position in the ethos of federal government service. We hope, but are not confident, that the novel forms of leaking witnessed in the past four years will dissipate in a presidential administration that is more respectful of widely accepted norms.

In closing, we note that the Code of Ethics for Government Service sets out as a core ethical principle that a "person in government" should "never use any information coming to him confidentially in performance of his official duties as a means of making a profit."[43] Congress passed the code unanimously, and President Jimmy Carter signed it, in 1980. It provides that "each agency shall display [a copy] in appropriate areas of Federal buildings[.]"[44] A modest step, certainly short of a major reform, would be a revision to this principle, broadening it beyond the misuse of confidential government information for financial return, to include an emphasis on the observance of confidentiality more generally as a vital element of the conception of "public office [as] a public trust."

★

INVESTIGATING PAST ADMINISTRATIONS

This chapter assesses how a new administration should think about investigation of and accountability for the outgoing administration. This is a growing problem in the U.S. legal system, and one that is sure to be front and center once Trump leaves office. Our analysis focuses on two different ways that an administration might examine the actions in office of senior executive branch officials of the prior administration. The first concerns an investigation and possible prosecution, or pardon, of a former president for acts committed in office. The second focuses on the new administration's investigation of the counterintelligence or criminal investigations conducted by a prior administration. This occurred with Attorney General William Barr's broad investigation of the investigation of the Trump campaign, and it may arise in a different guise once Trump leaves office.

What a new administration should do in these contexts raises thorny issues about how to ensure executive branch accountability, legitimate law enforcement, and peaceful and legitimate transfers of power in a democracy.

A PARDON FOR TRUMP?

Donald Trump's presidency has been shadowed from the very beginning by charges, investigations, and prosecutions that—in one way or another, directly or indirectly—raise questions about his potential liability for violations of federal and state law. Most prominent is the report of Special Counsel Robert Mueller, who considered at length whether the president committed obstruction of justice in the course of the Russia investigation. Mueller declined to "exonerate" the president but also refused to reach a definitive conclusion. Attorney General Barr resolved the issue in the president's favor, but the next presidential administration could revisit it.

Moreover, Trump may face other inquiries into possible obstruction. His former national security adviser, John Bolton, has claimed that Trump appeared to engage in "obstruction of justice as a way of life."[1] Bolton suggests that the Trump impeachment inquiry missed additional episodes of obstruction that arose out of promises made to foreign leaders to intervene in the criminal enforcement process to protect banks or businesses under investigation. As of late July 2020, Congress was preparing to investigate the allegations, and a new administration may also do so.

In addition, the U.S. attorney for the Southern District of New York has an ongoing investigation that has already resulted in the conviction and imprisonment of the president's former lawyer and close aide, Michael Cohen, for campaign finance violations committed in connection with "hush money" payments to women with whom the president was allegedly involved. Court filings in that case identify the president as "Individual No. 1" who, as Cohen has also testified, directed his lawyer's actions. Once Trump leaves office, he loses the immunity from prosecution for federal crimes conferred on sitting presidents by standing Office of Legal Counsel opinions and is clearly exposed to potential indictment in that case.

The disposition of these matters became a recurring topic of debate on the Democratic side in 2020. During the presidential primary campaign, Senator Elizabeth Warren pledged that, if elected, she would establish an independent task force within the Department of Justice to "investigate violations of specific anti-corruption and public integrity laws during the Trump administration, with independent authority to pursue any substantiated violations."[2] Another candidate, eventual nominee for vice president, Senator Kamala Harris, when asked if prosecutors in the next administration should bring a case against Trump, said, "I believe that they would have no choice and that they should, yes."[3] Former Vice President Biden, now the Democratic nominee for president, offered that he would give his Justice Department no specific direction but would expect it to decide the president's legal responsibility on a fully independent basis. It is clear that if Donald Trump loses the election, many Democrats and perhaps others will demand a definitive accounting of the president's alleged misconduct in office.

In the course of the 2020 presidential primaries, Democratic presidential candidates were pressed on whether, if elected, they would pardon Trump for any federal crimes he may have committed. With one exception, Andrew Yang, all rejected the possibility of any exercise of clemency on the president's behalf. Yang expressed concern that the United States should not fall into the "very nasty pattern" in some other countries "where a new president ends up throwing the president before them in jail."[4] But more representative of the class of candidates was Biden. When asked if he would commit not to pardon Trump "under the pretense of healing the nation," he replied, "I commit."[5]

If Trump wins the 2020 election, these issues will not be on the table anytime soon, and the issues will likely look different, almost certainly worse, in 2025. But whether Trump loses in 2020 or leaves office at the end of a second term, very hard questions will arise about how his successor in the Oval Office should go about assessing criminal legal liability and a possible pardon of Trump. Rather than lay out one proposal, what follows are what we see as the best cases for two basic approaches: One, favored by Bauer, argues that Trump should face a full investigation as determined by the merits of the matter and that he should not receive a blanket prospective pardon; and the other, favored by Goldsmith, argues for extreme caution in a criminal investigation of a prior president for acts done in office.

THE CASE FOR ENSURING THAT NO PRESIDENT IS—OR APPEARS TO BE—ABOVE THE LAW

Criminal prosecution of an ex-president, especially by a successor who defeated him or her at the polls, is an event without precedent in U.S. history and carries a significant risk of inflaming the already-deep partisan divisions in the country. On the other side is the comparable, if not weightier, risk of establishing a "norm" that president is "above the law." The president who enjoys immunity while in office on the theory that prosecution would destabilize the *government* should not *also* escape accountability after his or her term concludes on the closely related claim that prosecution would then destabilize the *country*—by creating a public spectacle that would seriously hinder the next administration in refocusing the nation's attention to major domestic and international issues. One is reminded of the old tale about the sign that reads in bold letters: "Knock Before Entering," below which is a further command: "Never Knock."

Any notion of routine clemency for an ex-president's wrongdoing is problematic for another reason: the "bite-back effect" of encouraging state prosecutorial actions to provide the accountability that the federal government will not. A president can grant clemency only for federal crimes, of course. Depending on the facts and circumstances, state and local prosecutors can pursue investigations under state law. We have seen this in Trump's case, as the district attorney for New York County has been conducting a vigorous criminal inquiry into the Trump Organization's finances and allegations that Trump directed the payment of "hush money" on the eve of the 2016 election to cover up extramarital relationships. Any charges or convictions arising out of this investigation, or any other state law investigation, are not subject to a presidential grant of clemency. Of course, these separately tracked investigations can, and might, occur regardless of whether the president issues a pardon for related or other federal offenses. But a "norm" of pardoning ex-presidents might also in some cases generate pressure on state and local prosecutors to rush into the vacuum.

This is not to suggest that all the dangers of the prosecution of an ex-president should be discounted. Prosecutions driven by demands for political retribution, or that seem more an expression of political difference than a vindication of the legal process, are a threat to constitutional government in just the way that Andrew Yang described. Sound prosecutorial judgment and tightly developed and presented cases are essential to dispel to the extent possible any suspicion that the law has been weaponized for political purposes. Essential to achieving these goals is the operation of law enforcement on a fully independent basis, free of partisan influence or pressures.

The same rigor should be brought to the president's explanation of a decision to pardon, or not pardon, a predecessor. The one experience in our history with this kind of pardon decision was President Gerald Ford's grant to Richard Nixon of a "full, free, and absolute pardon" for crimes he "has committed or may have committed."[6] The decision, announced on a Sunday one month after Ford took office, was met with resounding public disapproval at the time. Ford, who had ridden high in the polls after assuming office, suffered the "largest single [poll to poll] drop in history."[7] Troubled that he had not been informed that the president was considering a pardon, but also strongly objecting on the merits to the decision, the president's press secretary resigned.

Under this intense criticism, Ford agreed to the exceptional act of explaining this decision in sworn testimony to a House Judiciary subcommittee. At that time, Ford endeavored to meet congressional, press, and public demands that he explain in detail a pardon that was "negotiated in secret, created on advice from [his] inner circle, and given on terms clearly in Nixon's favor."[8] Members of Congress specifically demanded to know how the decision was reached, who was consulted, and whether there was a "deal" by which Nixon resigned, elevating Ford to the presidency, in exchange for a pardon.

There was no evidence of a deal, and none has surfaced since. But there were fierce objections to the *process* by which Ford had concluded he should grant a pardon. At Ford's direction, White House aides consulted the special Watergate prosecutor on the offenses Nixon may have committed, and the time required to prepare for and conduct a trial. The president surveyed a small group of aides on the wisdom of a pardon but did not seek the views of the attorney general. The consultations extended to Nixon and his lawyer as Ford sought to encourage, but without setting as conditions for a pardon, a statement of contrition and the settlement of an outstanding dispute over ownership and control of Nixon's White House tapes and records. All of this was conducted in the secrecy on which Ford insisted: "I want no leaks."[9]

There were two other aspects to this process that caused Ford trouble. First, Ford had testified during his vice presidential confirmation hearings that he would not issue a pardon because the country "wouldn't stand for it."[10] Once he became president, he said at a press conference that he would not rule out a pardon. But after noting that "there has been no action by the court ... no action by any jury," he stated that "until any legal process has been undertaken I think it's unwise and untimely for me to make any commitment."[11] But he then issued a pardon in the face of his testimony that he would not—and before Nixon had been charged with any crimes.

Second, Ford's explanation to the country of his decision roamed over various rationales: the problems for Nixon in securing a fair and speedy trial, concerns about Nixon's health, the "ugly passions" in the country that a prosecution would unleash, the extent to which Nixon had suffered enough by losing his office, and Ford's own Christian duty to show "mercy."[12] It was unclear what relative weight any one or more of these factors carried in the final decision. In the end, it was very much an explanation on the order of "then there was this consideration, and then there was this other," and the scattershot, unfocused defense of the pardon served primarily to stimulate suspicion that there must have been a *real* reason—possibly, a "deal."

Years later, Ford came to enjoy more favorable consideration of the decision. In 2001, the Kennedy family conferred on him a Profile in Courage Award, and Senator Edward Kennedy, a critic of the pardon at the time it was granted, now concluded that Ford had been "right" in making it "possible for us to begin the process of healing and put the tragedy of Watergate behind us."[13] Kennedy conceded that he was moved to reconsider his views by the "whole impeachment furor" involving Bill Clinton, which "drove from political debate all national and international concerns."

But it cannot be assumed that all pardons of all presidents in the name of national healing will strike future generations as sound and in the best interests of the polity. In Ford's case, the pardon may have won over skeptics as the years passed. In another future case, the nature of the offense or offenses, and the particular process by which the pardon is considered and then granted or rejected, will determine whether the public judgment of the president's decision shifts over time. And there is always the problem of speculating about, but not being able to know, how it all would have turned out if Ford had decided the matter the other way.

The strong, critical reaction to Ford's pardon, and especially the process by which it was considered and then granted, did not dissipate for years. It damaged Ford's credibility when he most needed to preserve it after the shock of Watergate sapped trust in government. Close students of the period have concluded that the sour taste it left in the electorate's mouth "made Jimmy Carter's victory possible."[14]

As the Democratic primary debates indicated, a Democratic president who succeeds Trump will be hard-pressed to justify a pardon and perhaps, even after trial and conviction, a commutation. More likely, he or she will face demands to reject any possibility of clemency.

It will likely and plausibly be argued that the Nixon pardon proved disastrous for Ford, more than the electorate could bear, and that by any measure, Trump is even *less* deserving of consideration for clemency. Nixon lost his bearings completely as he faced the 1972 reelection campaign, and the result was the Watergate scandal. Trump's presidency has been characterized by a wide range of charges of investigable or illegal conduct from the time of his candidacy throughout the four years that followed. Nixon made every effort to subvert the investigations that brought him down, but in the end, he gave up the damning "smoking gun" tapes. Trump may not have fired Robert Mueller, but he attacked Mueller's prosecution team ceaselessly, publicly, and recklessly, and he refused to sit for an in-person interview with Mueller and his investigators.

So, those rejecting out-of-hand any consideration of clemency for Donald Trump will argue that if the rule of law means anything, and if any president should have to answer in full to the legal process in order to vindicate the principle that the highest elected and law enforcement official in the land is not "above the law," it is Donald Trump.

It is impossible to predict what, with the passage of time and the unfolding of events, the next president may do when confronted with a clemency decision of some sort about Trump. A Ford-type pardon, issued virtually upon assuming office, seems highly improbable. Perhaps after years of investigation, trial, and appeals, and in the event of conviction, a Democratic (or even Republican president) might grant some measure of clemency—such as a commutation of sentence, even if the convicted ex-president at an advanced age must serve some time.

What is critically important is that a president making this decision avoid Ford's fatal error of process. It is on this ground that a president should take a clear and firm stand, setting out in advance the criteria that will be applied and the procedures that will be followed in any such decision. This is essential to a pardon process that is governed by rule-of-law principles.

The component parts of such a process would be built from the following:

The Process

The ex-president should not receive consideration for a pardon until after offenses have been charged.

- The president should have to apply for a pardon or commutation and specify the offenses for which the clemency is sought and the grounds for a grant. It should not become the norm that, by virtue of the office he or she once held, a president is *entitled* to consideration for clemency.

- The president should direct the attorney general to develop a clemency recommendation based on criteria that the president provides in writing and makes public.

- The attorney general's recommendation should be made public.

- Following the receipt of the attorney general's recommendation, the president should consult with congressional leaders, elected leaders at the state and local levels, and others at his or her discretion, and disclose publicly those with whom he or she has consulted.

- When the president announces the decision, he or she should provide a full statement in writing of the reasons for the grant or denial of clemency.

The Criteria

The criteria the president will consider include but are not limited to the nature of the offenses charged; the number of offenses charged; whether the offenses were committed prior to or during the ex-president's candidacy for office, the presidential transition, or the term of office; whether others have been charged or convicted for the same offenses who are alleged to have acted at the direction of the president, or as co-conspirators; the complexity of the issues presented by the charges, including any constitutional defenses the ex-president may raise; and any other special considerations bearing on the grant or denial of the pardon in the public welfare.

THE CASE FOR CAUTION IN CRIMINALLY INVESTIGATING A FORMER PRESIDENT FOR ACTS IN OFFICE

Of all the allegations leveled against Donald Trump over his four years as president, perhaps none was more damning than former National Security Adviser John Bolton's claim that Trump appeared to engage in "obstruction of justice as a way of life."[15] The most remarkable thing about Bolton's charge was that it was not surprising. Trump's presidency has been characterized by his incessant and often-public interference in law enforcement matters that affect his personal interests, by his disregard for legal and norm-based constraints on presidential action, and by his open search for lawyers who will "protect" him from a legal process that he has no scruples about undermining.

As the Trump-era events recounted in Chapters Seven and Eight show, Trump has not really tried to hide his obstruction of justice. Whether any of these activities and other similar ones amount to criminal law violations is a much harder question. As we explained in Chapter Eight, the current obstruction of justice statutes do not specify their application to the president. Absent such a plain statement (which will be unavailable for any prosecution of Trump), a prosecution for obstruction of justice for a president's actions while in office will raise serious constitutional hurdles; in some and possibly most instances in which Trump has been accused of obstruction, those hurdles will be insurmountable.

Tightly developed and presented charges will be hard in this context because the legal issues are so muddled, even before one considers contested factual questions. Any investigation and prosecution would take many years to sort out through the criminal trial and appellate process. Perhaps Trump committed other crimes while in office that might be easier to prosecute—bribery, for example. But it is not obvious yet that this has happened. And again, it too would take enormous time and resources to investigate the facts before one could make a judgment on the law. The process of a new administration poring over the actions in office of a just-ousted president, and of his administration, looking for crimes, would be a first in American history. It cannot help but be deeply politically divisive, even (and perhaps especially) if a repudiated Trump is the target.

Given these known challenges—and there are many others, discussed below—what, if anything, should the presidential administration that succeeds Trump do about his possible crimes while in office? Two principles must be kept in mind. The first is the meaning of accountability. Trump must be held accountable for wrongdoing in office. But appropriate accountability does not necessarily mean criminal liability, even if crimes were committed. Accountability in this context means that the former president's actions are made public, examined, and judged. Criminal process is one form of accountability, one of the more extreme. But elections, hearings, public scrutiny and condemnation, "9/11-style" truth commissions, ostracization, and the like are also forms of accountability.

The second principle is that instrumental calculations sometimes trump—no pun intended—criminal liability for crimes. Prosecutors very often, and legitimately, consider the adverse impact on the community in exercising prosecutorial discretion not to prosecute someone who committed a crime, or to strike a relatively favorable plea deal. And the pardon power was designed in part to allow the president to wipe out the consequences of a crime for the sake of national healing—a justification invoked by Washington in the Whiskey Rebellion, Ford in his pardon of Nixon, and many pardons and amnesties in between.

These principles in combination mean that sometimes criminal prosecution is not the right form of accountability, even, and perhaps especially, for a president. These principles also complicate the trope that "no one is (or should be) above the law." In fact, sometimes alleged criminals, including criminals who serve in high office, escape criminal prosecution because more important countervailing principles should and do win out. Ford's pardon of Nixon is again a good example—one criticized at the time but viewed more favorably later.

How these factors play out in Trump's case is obviously hard to determine and will surely be contested. There are significant costs, benefits, and uncertainties to each approach. It might seem strange to give a president immunity from criminal prosecution for public crimes while in office to avoid destabilizing the presidency, and then to give him a pass on the criminal law after office in order to avoid destabilizing the nation. But this approach is neither inconsistent nor incoherent. Nonprosecution of a president while in office is a rule that has its own justification and that for now at least is settled; nonprosecution or pardon after the president leaves office has to be justified independently on a different, contextual cost-benefit basis at the time of decision.

Nor would refusing to investigate or prosecute Trump, or pardoning him, incentivize future presidents to commit crimes in office, any more than it did for Nixon's successors. (Trump's aberrant behavior is certainly not a response to Ford's pardon of Nixon.) Whether it does depends entirely on what other punishments—that is, what other forms of accountability—are brought to bear on Trump for his actions in office: how thoroughly he is repudiated at the polls (if he is), and what other costs he and his family suffer after office (ostracization, business decline, criminal investigation for private or pre-presidential acts, and the like). Even in the absence of post-presidential prosecution, it seems doubtful that a future president will look at Trump's difficult time in office, and his fate after office, and feel incentivized to commit crimes.

Nor is it clear which approach is better for the governing agenda of the next presidency. The polar possibilities are a criminal process aimed at figuring out Trump's crimes in office, and what to do about them, at one end; and something like a quick decision to pardon or not prosecute Trump on instrumental grounds, at the other. (There are many possibilities in between.) The argument that the latter approach will make it difficult to impossible for the next administration to govern turns on the notion that the new president's party would react to Trump's effective immunity by refusing to cooperate in the new president's agenda, or would be torn asunder.

But even if the new president controls both houses in the next Congress, a criminal investigation of Trump's time in office will be a consuming spectacle for the new administration. The very act of opening the investigation—especially if obstruction of justice is the main focus—is politically fraught. Even if the investigation is conducted with strict integrity, the Justice Department of one administration viewing the actions of the president and others through a criminal lens will invariably appear political to a large chunk of the country—especially since Republicans, including Trump, will be spinning up the nation at every turn. This part of the country will see the investigation as political retribution, just as the Barr review of the Trump campaign investigation (discussed in the next section) has been seen as political retribution. The investigation will be viewed through the same politically polarized Twitter/cable news lens through which the investigations and counter-investigations during the Trump era have been seen.

Inevitably, the Justice Department will do things that confirm the politicization narrative. History shows that once a specialized Justice Department investigation starts, it is hard to cabin. The investigation of Trump's actions in office will necessarily focus on more than Trump. Many dozens of former administration officials will need to be interviewed and investigated. Many of them will resist, grand jury subpoenas will fly, collateral investigations and charges will ensue, and Washington lawyers will rack up fees. Huge process issues—taking years of litigation—will arise about one administration's examination and use of another's internal deliberations against the former president.

Over time the investigation will become scorched-earth because the scorched-earth defenses of the president and his subordinates will require a proportionate response. Trump can be expected to fully participate in the spectacle, which will keep him and his tweets in the spotlight. The unprecedented investigation and possible subsequent prosecution will surely take up the next president's term, and will dominate the news cycle. It will also dominate the agenda of the next attorney general, consume huge swaths of Justice Department resources that could be put to better use, and render impossible the already-hard task of restoring the department's integrity and relative detachment from politics.

There is no guarantee at all that a prosecution of the president will succeed, no matter how firm the evidence and law (and the law will be doubtful on obstruction of justice). A trial of a president following years of battle and ending in acquittal will cause the country tremendous pain for no good end and will likely create numerous unfortunate precedents along the way. No matter how it comes out, the whole episode poses an obvious threat to democratic process even if Trump committed crimes. The investigation of Trump on top of the Mueller investigation and the impeachment trial and (by hypothesis) his defeat at the polls will keep very much alive the narrative about an elite left-wing coup against him and his presidency. And most corrosively of all, the entire enterprise threatens to begin a tit-for-tat cycle of recriminations across administrations.

These considerations call to mind why Barack Obama chose to "look forward as opposed to looking backwards" on a full examination of the interrogation and black-site program of the Bush administration.[16] In explaining why the Obama administration did not take the truth commission route, a senior official explained: "[Obama's] concern was that would ratchet the whole thing up. His whole thing is, I banned all this. This chapter is over. What we don't need now is to become a sort of feeding frenzy where we go back and re-litigate all this."[17] Obama was and continues to be criticized for this decision. But these criticisms neglect (among other things) the counterfactual world in which the administration might not have been able to achieve health care reform (won by a whisker) and other accomplishments had it expended more resources and political capital legally scrutinizing the actions of its predecessors.

The pragmatic case for not investigating or prosecuting Trump, in sum, is that the likely aggregate benefits of doing so are outweighed by the likely aggregate costs. On this view, the least bad course of action for the next administration—a course that is admittedly not cost-free—is to not look back. The case for this approach is strengthened by two factors. First, there will inevitably be a thorough vetting of Trump's presidential term by Congress, the press, and the public, and it will not be pretty for Trump. These forms of accountability diminish the need for additional Justice Department accountability.

Second, two investigations have long been underway that implicate Trump. The U.S. attorney for the Southern District of New York has an ongoing investigation that potentially implicates Trump in many ways. This investigation primarily if not exclusively implicates pre-presidential behavior. And the Manhattan district attorney's office has long been scrutinizing the Trump Organization for crimes, and again presumably concerns mainly pre-2017 actions. Investigations of the president for crimes committed before the presidency or in a private capacity raise fewer hard legal issues and are easier to justify once the president leaves office—especially since both investigations began during the prior administration (and the federal investigation was opened and conducted by Trump's Justice Department). Trump will face criminal investigative scrutiny upon leaving office even if the Justice Department does not look at his time in office.

The pragmatic case for noninvestigation or a pardon of Trump for actions he took in office admittedly rests on assumptions about the future that are unknowable. The same is true of the case for investigation and prosecution. But even if we knew more about the future that would make the case for noninvestigation or a pardon more certain, it is doubtful that this course is a live option for the next president. The demands for retribution against Trump are too loud; the illusion that the case against Trump will be easy, and a definitive rebuke to Trump, is too enticing; and in the current Washington environment, short-term political calculations predominate too much over longer-term structural ones. The Ford precedent is less powerful than it seems, at least for decisions that may need to be made in 2021, because he was pardoning someone from his own party. Ford nonetheless suffered in the short run for his pardon of Nixon. A nonprosecution or pardon of Trump may be even more damaging politically in the short run for the next president. And so the dire predictions outlined here may well be tested.

EXAMINATION OF CRIMES BY OFFICIALS IN THE PRIOR ADMINISTRATION

One administration's examination of the possible crimes of a prior president is an unusual and—beyond Ford's quick review of Nixon's sins and his subsequent pardon of Nixon—unprecedented event. It is commonplace, by contrast, for one administration to review and alter the legal actions taken by the prior administration. For example, the new administration typically reviews the prior administration's federal court legal stances and prosecution priorities, pending regulations, and an array of executive branch policies—all with an eye toward adjustment or reversal.

Sometimes, a new administration uses the criminal investigation process to examine, reexamine, or continue examining actions by officials in prior administrations. The Ford and Carter administrations continued

Watergate-related prosecutions of Nixon officials that began during the Nixon administration. The Dannehy investigation of the U.S. attorney firing scandal (see Chapter Seven) began under the Bush administration but carried over into the Obama administration. Obama's attorney general, Eric Holder, reinvestigated actions taken by CIA officers during the Bush administration that had been previously deemed not to warrant prosecution by career Justice Department officials. In 2008, Bush's Attorney General, Michael Mukasey, had tasked a Connecticut prosecutor, then-Assistant U.S. Attorney John Durham, with investigating the CIA's destruction of interrogation videotapes. A year later Holder expanded Durham's mandate to reexamine allegations related to CIA black sites.

Attorney General Barr took processes of this sort to new levels. On April 10, 2019, he announced that he would review "both the genesis and the conduct of intelligence activities directed at the Trump campaign during 2016."[18] In late March 2019, he tapped Durham, now the U.S. attorney in Connecticut, for the task. On May 23, 2019, President Trump announced that, at Barr's request, he had "directed the intelligence community to quickly and fully cooperate with the Attorney General's investigation into surveillance activities during the 2016 Presidential election." Trump also authorized Barr to "declassify, downgrade, or direct the declassification or downgrading of information or intelligence that relates [to the investigation]."

The investigation run by Durham and supervised by Barr began as a "review" of the Trump campaign investigation, which meant that Durham lacked the power to subpoena documents or compel testimony. But it soon grew in significance and scope. Over the course of the summer of 2019 it was reported that Durham, with significant assistance and sometimes participation by Barr, was seeking the cooperation of multiple foreign governments and their intelligence services that were involved—or alleged to have been involved—in the FBI's Crossfire Hurricane investigation. He had also by that point interviewed dozens of current and former officials in the FBI and other intelligence agencies related to the investigation.

And then on October 24, 2019, news reports revealed that Durham's probe had expanded into a criminal investigation, which meant he was given authority to subpoena witness testimony and documents, and to seek criminal charges before a grand jury. The criminal investigation was opened at least in part due to a criminal referral from Justice Department Inspector General Michael Horowitz, who had since before Durham's investigation been investigating elements of the Crossfire Hurricane investigation. Apparently, Horowitz referred to Durham his finding that an FBI lawyer altered an email that officials used in an application to surveil former Trump campaign adviser Carter Page. Whatever the reason, from that point on, Durham, at least in discrete areas of his investigation, was invested with the department's coercive criminal investigatory powers.

Horowitz issued his report on the Trump campaign investigation on December 9, 2019. The aspect of the report most relevant to Durham's probe was its conclusion that Crossfire Hurricane was adequately authorized and predicated under Justice Department and FBI policy. On the same day that Horowitz released the report, Barr stated in a press release: "The Inspector General's report now makes clear that the FBI launched an intrusive investigation of a U.S. presidential campaign on the thinnest of suspicions that, in my view, were insufficient to justify the steps taken." About thirty minutes later, Durham offered his own statement on the matter: "Last month, we advised the inspector general that we do not agree with some of the report's conclusions as to predication and how the F.B.I. case was opened." Durham added that, unlike the inspector general, his team had access to "developing information from other persons and entities, both in the U.S. and outside of the U.S."

In 2020, Durham's investigation continued to expand. By then it had focused on the so-called "Steele dossier," which contained opposition research financed by the Democratic Party and used by the FBI to support the Carter Page FISA surveillance applications. It had also focused on how other intelligence related to the Trump campaign investigation was processed and shared in the community. Durham also appeared to be looking into the details of how intelligence officials developed their assessment that Russia sought to aid Trump in 2016, as opposed to simply sowing confusion. Durham also seemed to be focusing in particular on the role and judgments of former CIA Director John Brennan in the Trump campaign investigation. (Brennan was often a focus of Trump's vicious tweets, and often attacked the president in sharp terms on cable news shows.) In this and other instances, Durham was examining the work of former officials who had drawn Trump's ire over the Crossfire Hurricane investigation.

Durham's portfolio also expanded to include leaks of classified information early in the Trump administration, the "unmasking" by many Obama administration officials of then-national security adviser designee Michael Flynn in intelligence intercepts, and other issues related to the subsequent investigation and prosecution of Flynn. In February 2020, Barr took the extraordinary step of appointing the U.S. attorney in St. Louis, Jeff Jensen, to thoroughly scrutinize the criminal case against Flynn. (This review resulted in the Justice Department moving to dismiss the criminal information that the Mueller investigation team filed against Flynn.) In May 2020, Justice Department spokesperson Kerri Kupec announced Durham's expansion into the unmasking issues on the Sean Hannity program on Fox, and that Durham would be assisted in this regard by U.S. attorney in the Western District of Texas, John Bash.

Throughout these events, in testimony and interviews, Barr has offered a running public commentary on where he thinks the Durham and related investigations are leading. Barr frequently and publicly prejudged the Durham and related inquiries and insinuated that officials on the Crossfire Hurricane investigation engaged in wrongdoing and possible criminal activity. We lack space to capture all of Barr's conclusions, but here is a sampling:

- *May 31, 2019.* When asked whether the people under review by Durham had committed "treason," Barr replied, "Not as a legal matter, no" in a way that suggested they acted treasonably even if not illegally so. Barr then implied that the officials who investigated the Trump campaign, and were under review by Durham, had a "Praetorian Guard mentality" and engaged in malfeasance or were biased even if they were not acting on purpose with "conscious, nefarious motives."[19]

- *December 2019.* After the Horowitz report came out, Barr stated that he believed the report "le[ft] open the possibility that there was bad faith [by the FBI.]"[20] When questioned ten days later on whether it was appropriate for an attorney general to speculate about such bad faith in the context of an ongoing investigation,

Barr stated: "I think there are episodes there that simply cannot be squared with innocent mistakes. And I think people have to come to terms with that."[21]

- *April 10, 2020.* Barr said that Durham "is looking to bring to justice people who are engaged in abuses if he can show that they were criminal violations." He added: "My own view is that the evidence shows that we're not dealing with just mistakes or sloppiness. There is something far more troubling here. We're going to get to the bottom of it. And if people broke the law and we can establish that with the evidence, they will be prosecuted."[22]

- *June 1, 2020.* Barr stated that Durham is looking for "who should be held accountable for" Trump's unfair treatment in the Trump campaign investigation. "I think Comey has cast himself as being seven layers above the decision-making. I don't think that holds water. The record will be clear that that's not the case."[23]

Barr's public commentary on the Durham investigation violated Justice Department regulations and norms.[24] The department's media contacts policy, which applies to "all DOJ personnel," prohibits "respon[ses] to questions about the existence of an ongoing investigation or comment[s] on its nature or progress before charges are publicly filed."[25] None of the exceptions, such as for public safety, apply to the Durham investigation.[26] Another rule states that "federal prosecutors should remain sensitive to the privacy and reputation interests of uncharged third-parties."[27] Department regulations also prohibit the disclosure of information "relating to the circumstances of an ... investigation [that] would be highly prejudicial or where the release thereof would serve no law enforcement function...."[28] It is hard to see the law enforcement function of Barr's public commentary.

REFORM

There may have been good reasons for a comprehensive inquiry into the investigations of the Trump campaign's links with Russia's 2016 electoral interference, and of the president himself. As we noted in

Chapter Nine, the Crossfire Hurricane investigation was in many ways unprecedented. It suffered from a lack of legal and policy guidance, and Inspector General Horowitz uncovered a pattern of serious errors in certain aspects of the investigation even as he also concluded that the investigation was properly predicated at the outset. The opening of the criminal and obstruction of justice investigations against the president also suffered from a lack of adequate guidance and raised many novel issues, as we noted in Chapter Nine. If politics could be removed from the process and public debate—something that, as we showed earlier, has not happened—the nation would benefit from an understanding of what happened in these investigations, so that it could do better next time, if there is one.

In saying that an examination of the prior investigations may have been justified, we definitely do not subscribe to the view that, as Trump regularly proclaims, these investigations were "hoaxes" or otherwise illegitimate. The investigations concerned serious allegations that uncovered significant wrongdoing. As set out in Chapter Two, they also revealed weaknesses in current legal protections against foreign national electoral interference, and against political alliances between American campaigns and foreign state interests, that should lead to reforms.

Nor do we think that a probe by a prosecutor under the close supervision of the attorney general was the right way to examine these investigations. As we write these words, we do not know the fruits of Durham's work. But whatever wrongdoing Durham may find or allege will invariably be tainted. It will be tainted by the fact that the president has persistently, publicly, and tendentiously prejudged the investigation of his campaign for years. And it will be tainted by Attorney General Barr's unprecedented, opinionated, and norm-violative public commentary on the subject matter of Durham's investigation.

Moreover, now that we understand better Durham's focus, it is clear that it is not a task appropriate for a prosecutor using the tools of criminal investigation. (In a better world, it would have been a task for Congress or a congressional commission.) The review began as an effort to understand what happened in the genesis and conduct of the Crossfire Hurricane investigation. There was no inkling at the time that crimes had been committed; Durham's initial probe was a mere "review" to gather and assess facts. This is a core responsibility of inspectors general and falls within their expertise. Prosecutors of course can and do develop and assess facts, but they do so in the criminal investigation process. The proper approach would have been for inspectors general across the government to review and comprehensively assess Crossfire Hurricane, as Horowitz did for a slice of it. If evidence of crimes arose in such an investigation, it could have been referred to a prosecutor—again, as happened with Horowitz's investigation.

An investigation by a prosecutor threatening to use the coercive tools of criminal law enforcement is especially inappropriate for what appears to be one large focus of Durham's investigation: the nature and validity of the intelligence assessment that the Russian intervention in the 2016 election sought to aid Trump rather than merely sow confusion. Durham has experience examining the intelligence world due to his investigation of the CIA tape destruction and black site program. But he is neither personally nor institutionally expert in intelligence assessments or the intelligence assessment process, and a prosecutorial lens is not the right one to understand the basis for the assessment.

There are obvious dangers in one administration using the prosecutorial process to examine a counterintelligence and related investigation of the prior administration. Durham himself began this process as a credible figure, even if one not fully qualified or positioned for the task given to him, especially as it developed. But his investigation was politically fraught from the beginning due to the context. And it grew politicized due to the actions of the president and the attorney general.

In response to this episode, we propose three reforms.

First, the Justice Department should make clear that the department's media policy and rules for prosecutors about discussing a pending case extend to the attorney general. This is already implicit in the rules. But the next attorney general should make it explicit in an effort to reestablish the norm.

Second, a "what happened?" investigation of a counterintelligence or related criminal probe by a prior administration should be conducted in the first instance by the inspector general of the Justice Department, not by a prosecutor. If a government-wide investigation is needed, it can be conducted on a government-wide basis by inspectors general in coordination, as occurred in the Stellarwind investigation.[29] If the input of foreign governments is necessary, that can be arranged by the State

Department or by the agency whose foreign counterpart possesses the relevant information (for example, by the director of national intelligence if information from foreign intelligence services is needed).

As with all inspector general investigations, former employees can cooperate voluntarily but cannot typically be coerced through legal process into cooperation. If the inspector general uncovers evidence of criminal wrongdoing, he or she should refer the matter to the attorney general, who (see below) would be required to invoke the procedures of the special counsel, as amended. This is an extension of the "conflict of interest" theory behind the special counsel rules. Those regulations now locate the potential conflict in one administration's enforcement of the law against its own senior personnel. Here the conflict to be addressed is the real and apparent conflict between an administration's duty to enforce the law impartially, and any pressures to investigate and bring charges against senior officials of the other party.

Third, an administration's criminal investigation of the president or senior officials of the preceding administration for violations of law arising from the conduct of their official duties should be subject to the appointment of a special counsel. The use of U.S. attorneys to conduct special-purpose inquiries of the kind Attorney General Barr favors should be ruled out, as they only foment or heighten suspicions of a political vendetta—especially when those selected to conduct these inquiries are political appointees of the incumbent president. A prominent virtue of the special counsel procedure is the requirement that the attorney general account with greater transparency and thoroughness to Congress and the public for the manner in which these investigations are justified, conducted, and concluded. A policy of resort to the special counsel rules for these cases may encourage an administration to determine with particular care whether to pursue them.

★

THE WHITE HOUSE COUNSEL

In the preceding four chapters, we focused primarily on the Justice Department side of White House–Justice Department relations. In this chapter, we reverse the lens and focus on the counsel to the president, or "White House counsel," as the office is commonly called.

The president has almost ten thousand lawyers in the Justice Department, and tens of thousands more throughout the executive branch, to help him or her exercise constitutional responsibilities and duties, including the duty to "take care that the laws be faithfully executed." But only one, the White House counsel, is commonly described today as "the president's lawyer." The counsel has a suite of offices located in the West Wing of the White House, a floor above the Oval Office. He or she heads what is in effect a small law firm, the Office of White House Counsel, whose members spill over into offices in the adjacent Eisenhower Executive Office Building. The counsel is a member of the president's senior staff.

The White House counsel's power over legal issues has been growing steadily for many decades and has been accompanied by a steady stream of criticism and concern. The concerns about the office grew under Trump and now justify, we argue, a major restructuring of the office.

BACKGROUND

In its current form, the Office of White House Counsel is relatively new. Franklin D. Roosevelt created the office in 1943 to assist him with managing the fast-growing executive branch. The earliest White House counsels were counselors in the widest sense. They advised the president on policy and carried out other chores for the president, such as writing speeches. During this early period, the attorney general, aided after 1953 by the assistant attorney general in charge of the Office of Legal Counsel (OLC), was viewed by the president and the Department of Justice as "the president's lawyer" who advised the president on constitutional and other legal matters.

Beginning in the Eisenhower administration, the president began to charge the counsel with a handful of strictly legal advisory duties. White House counsels in the Kennedy and Johnson administrations also performed legal services, but they focused primarily, to one degree or another, on policy development, congressional relations, and communications strategies. As DeVier Pierson, counsel to President Lyndon Johnson, stated, the general understanding at the time was that the Justice Department and its OLC remained "the real lawyers of the White House."[1]

It was during the Nixon administration that the office began to develop more fully into what it has remained through succeeding administrations to the present time: the functional equivalent of a law firm charged with providing legal advice to the president and the senior staff on a discrete range of subjects. A White House counsel to Ronald Reagan defined the role as it came to be in the 1980s: "80 to 85 percent of [the Office of White House Counsel's] work has to do with pure legal work. We generally are not policy-makers."[2] Especially influential counsels, and ones who came to the job with pronounced interests in policy, might participate in purely policy matters. However, the basic definition of the job called for systematic, day-to-day attention to legal matters.

The office's growing legal advice–giving role reflected developments in the 1970s. First there was Watergate, an unprecedented investigation by the Justice Department into the president and the presidency, followed by the first impeachment proceedings against a president in a century. Nixon's White House counsel, John Dean, became heavily involved in managing the crisis for the president. His services to the president also took a dark turn: He was instrumental in assisting the president and his senior staff in covering up the crimes committed in connection with the break-in at the Democratic National Committee headquarters. He became a critical witness against the president, was convicted of obstruction of justice, and subsequently served prison time. Dean's involvement in the

Watergate affair was rooted in the assumption that the White House counsel should play a leading role as a president's crisis manager, a role that White House counsels have played ever since.

Then came the post-Watergate reforms that were intended to hold an "imperial presidency" in check. Presidents had to address new obligations under statutes compelling the president, vice president, and senior officials to make personal financial disclosures and comply with other standards of "ethical" official conduct. This period of reaction to the Watergate scandal, some of it building on relatively long-standing reform proposals, included mandatory presidential record-keeping and transparency requirements. The independent counsel statute subjected the president and senior executive branch officials to special procedures for inquiry into allegations of criminal wrongdoing. Watergate effectively placed the Justice Department, Congress, and the press on high alert for potential surreptitious presidential wrongdoing. Presidential scandal became a recurring threat to the standing and governing agenda of presidential administrations. And the White House counsel grew in stature to address and guard against both the threats and the other institutions' scrutiny.

Much of this growth in power came at the expense, at least formally, of the attorney general's traditional role as the president's chief legal adviser. As law and scrutiny enveloped the president like never before, the president needed "more convenient advice closer to home."[3] Another reason for the growth of the White House counsel's influence, ironically, was the post-Watergate aim of protecting Justice Department independence from the White House. The demand for more of an arm's length, detached relationship devolved into the assumption of a legal advisory role for the White House counsel on matters more closely related to "politics." This new role did not mean counseling on partisan political matters, like directly supporting reelection campaigns. But it did encompass matters that were central to the president's governing program and were therefore intertwined with questions, in the broadest sense, of popular appeal and political impact.

The White House counsel came to hold a portfolio of responsibilities that has been much the same from administration to administration:

- Screening and recommending candidates for judicial nominations, especially for appellate courts and the Supreme Court.

- "Vetting" major presidential nominees to senior executive appointments and, for those requiring Senate confirmation, engaging with Congress as required to facilitate successful outcomes.

- Advising on the legally enforceable "ethics" requirements for holding official positions, such as ensuring that senior officials complied with the law governing potential conflicts of interest or the limits on political activity by federal employees while on or off duty, or in the workplace.

- Providing the first line of defense for the president in responding to congressional oversight and investigations, and coordinating lawyers across agencies and departments in that effort.

- Managing "scandal" crises that might break out in the media and then move to congressional and criminal investigations of the president or his or her administration.

- Supporting the president with advice on national security matters along with other legal specialists in the National Security Council, departments, and agencies.

- Routinely advising the president on the constitutional issues raised by proposed legislation and addressing them as required with "signing statements" expressing presidential reservations.

- Reviewing executive orders, presidential memoranda, or presidential proclamations for proper form and legality.

- Advising the president on executive clemency.

The White House counsel today typically commands a staff of twenty to thirty lawyers, sometimes exceeding forty in intense periods of oversight or congressional investigation. Beyond the areas of control, the White House counsel exercises influence in another crucial way. The president has the final call on legal decisions for the executive branch on any issue where he chooses to intervene—regardless of whether the advice that informs his judgment comes from the attorney general or OLC. Typically, the White House counsel is the last lawyer in the government to have the president's ear, and thus to advise him, before he or she decides. This close advisory relationship—often rooted in shared personal and political history, and institutionalized through membership in the White House senior staff and a suite in the West Wing— is the key to the White House counsel's power.

And the president surely benefits from having such counsel at close quarters. A legal staff within the building can respond quickly and efficiently to demands or questions from the president or senior presidential staff. The president's appointment of lawyers with whom he or she has prior political or personal associations is not necessarily problematic. These relationships can mean that the president reposes that much more trust and confidence in the counsel. On the strength of this relationship, the counsel may enjoy more credibility and influence within the West Wing and can more effectively ensure that legal questions are promptly identified and resolved. In this sense, the counsel is in a position to bring the law and its imperatives into the heart of the operation of the presidential office.

Yet despite these potential virtues, the role and performance of the White House counsel has been controversial from the start. When Franklin Roosevelt prepared to appoint the first White House counsel, Samuel Rosenman, the attorney general, Francis Biddle, objected. Roosevelt responded by naming Rosenman a "special counsel" and assigning him nonlegal duties. The anxieties triggered by the president's appointment of his "own" legal staff have never subsided. At the heart of this complaint is the danger that the president may retain a personally chosen legal adviser to give the advice he wants to hear, not honestly rendered, accurate advice. It has long been feared that, in bypassing the corps of more detached lawyers in the Justice Department, the president has more influence over selective legal issues and a better chance at putting politics and preferred policies above the law as reasonably interpreted by less biased lawyers.

As one prominent former head of OLC, Antonin Scalia, framed the issue: "The White House will accept distasteful advice from a lawyer who is unquestionably 'on the team;' it will reject it, and indeed not even seek it, from an outsider—when more permissive and congenial advice can be obtained closer to home."[4] Scalia noted that the White House counsel was one source of "permissive and congenial advice" to whom the president could turn. Just as modern White Houses have expanded the National Security Council to centralize control over foreign policy and national security from the departments in these fields, the White House counsel can become a resource by which the president can expand his or her legal power over the administration—not just vis-à-vis the Justice Department, but in connection with legal policies throughout the government.

This unflattering picture of the White House counsel has acquired considerable plausibility because presidents since Roosevelt have very often selected counsel from the circle of personal friends or intense political supporters. This was often (though somewhat less often) true of the attorney general as well, of course. But unlike the attorney general, the White House counsel is neither vetted nor approved by the Senate, nor surrounded by a huge staff of experienced career officials, nor embedded in a culture of independence that proved relatively though not entirely resilient even to Trump's unprecedented onslaughts.

The personal or political history behind these appointments, and the imperatives of the office, raise the question of whether the White House counsel can maintain the professional distance necessary to serve as a lead *government* attorney, rather than personal attorney, for the president. The counsel is paid by the taxpayers to assist the president in his official capacity only. To the extent that the president seeks counsel on matters of personal legal liability, as he might if faced with a criminal inquiry, he would need a personal lawyer retained in a separate attorney-client relationship. But since the White House counsel works in close proximity to the president and the president knows the counsel well and often chooses him or her on the basis of a shared political or personal history, or both, it is natural for the president to seek advice from the White House counsel on questions that should have been referred to personal counsel. This same confusion of role can arise if the counsel so identifies with the president's political or policy goals that it affects his or her capacity for fully dispassionate legal analysis and judgment.

One of President Ronald Reagan's White House counsels, Peter Wallison, went so far as to question "the implication … that you can tell the difference [between the institutional president and the person occupying the office]." His view was that "when the going gets rough, you really can't."[5]

It is thus inevitable that the counsel on whom presidents rely to stave off or address controversy might end up in the middle of the controversy. One early and disastrous case was that of Nixon's White House counsel, John Dean, as noted earlier. Other counsel ran into less severe trouble but also had tenures marked by sharp criticism of their performance. President Clinton's first White House counsel, Bernard Nussbaum, came under attack for playing too much the role of the president's personal defense lawyer in contending with various high-profile controversies and allegations of wrongdoing leveled at the president. When a deputy White House counsel, Vince Foster, died by suicide, Nussbaum would not allow the FBI access to Foster's office until he had reviewed its contents and removed files deemed "personal" to the president and first lady. Nussbaum's view of his role also drew attention when it was discovered that he had met with the official of the regulatory agency at the center of the "Whitewater" scandal, an investigation of the Clintons' personal financial dealings in Arkansas in the years prior to Bill Clinton's election.

Nussbaum's credibility came into question, and he resigned. Yet he insisted that, in critical respects, the distinction between the institutional and personal presidency was illusory. The increasingly routine investigations of the president—and Nussbaum took many of these investigations to be "phony," motivated by partisanship—could not be addressed apart from their disruptive effect on the president's capacity to govern.[6] In this respect, the personal and the official did not sort into neat categories. Attacks on the president could not fail to undermine the functioning presidency, and the White House counsel's defense of the president in this context was also a defense of the presidency as an institution.

Other counsel came under scrutiny for their roles in the issuance of controversial pardons, as in the final year of the Clinton administration, or in politically motivated firings of U.S. attorneys, as in the George W. Bush administration. Numerous counsels have been called upon to testify before Congress, and a number did so after the president waived claims of executive privilege. In defending President Clinton in the course of criminal investigations, White House counsels sought unsuccessfully to rely on the attorney-client privilege to protect presidential communications or the production of "work product" documents. The courts had the opportunity in this context to define the personal-official boundary and found that, as a government and not personal lawyer, a White House counsel has an obligation to give evidence in legal proceedings concerned with allegations of presidential (or other official) wrongdoing.

Outside the sphere of scandal or congressional investigation, counsels were the targets of complaints about the quality of their professional legal advice. Once again, the concern was that the counsel was enabling presidential initiatives by conforming legal advice to the president's practical and political requirements. One former White House counsel conceded that "[t]here's hardly ever a time that I can imagine where the Counsel would actually oppose the President's desire to do something that the President honestly wants to do, even though it doesn't work for the institution of the Presidency quite as well."[7] Critics see the counsel as usurping the role of more professionally dispassionate legal advisers elsewhere in the government and doling out permissive advice that happens to match what the president hopes to hear.

This fairly constant critique has, among many examples, been directed at one author of this book (Bauer) for rendering a disputed interpretation of President Obama's obligations under the War Powers Resolution at the time of a U.S.-led NATO coalition military engagement in Libya in 2011. Lawyers within the government were divided on the key legal question, and the Justice Department's Office of Legal Counsel did not share the White House counsel's conclusion. But the president adopted and proceeded on the basis of the latter's advice (shared by the legal adviser to the State Department). It is fair to note that the other author of this book was critical at the time of the counsel's advice. Goldsmith wrote, "It is interesting and unusual enough that President Obama, of all people, would take an aggressive view of his war authorities and interpret the WPR [War Powers Resolution] very narrowly. But the lawyers he relied on to reach this conclusion make the situation even more interesting and unusual." He continued: "I discount the legal input of the White House Counsel; Bob Bauer is a smart man but neither he nor his office is expert in war powers or situated to offer thorough legal advice on the issue."[8]

The Libya case and others like it underscore the basic concern that the White House counsel operates, on issues the president most cares about, to disrupt the normal processes by which professional government lawyers develop advice squarely on the merits for the president's eventual consideration. Within the Justice Department, OLC bears the overall responsibility to provide definitive legal interpretations for the executive branch on the widest range of legal issues. It abides by principles and practices that call for reaching its "best understanding of what the law requires," even as it is committed to developing, where possible, legal positions that facilitate the president's achievement of his or her objectives.[9] Yet, in Libya and other cases, White House counsel may seek OLC's views and yet manage the flow of advice to the president and structure the presentation of the various views, including his or her own. The counsel has the last word even if, ultimately, it is the president's call.

Commentators have come to observe not only tension between OLC and the White House counsel but also shifts of power from the former to the latter, especially during periods when presidents were served by "very powerful, centralizing White House Counsels."[10] If presidents seek control of their legal advice on the matters most critical to their governing and political agenda, it would not be surprising that they would turn increasingly to "their lawyers." Also, OLC has confronted legitimacy crises of its own after the discovery of deficiencies of process and legal craftsmanship in many national security–related memoranda after 9/11. OLC is now more routinely under pressure to disclose its opinions, whether by congressional demand or Freedom of Information Act suits, which is a further reason for presidents to pull into the West Wing and protect with broad claims of privilege the legal deliberations of core issues.

Despite its growth in influence, the Office of White House Counsel is not set up to address the range of questions on which OLC and other legal specialists in government have expertise. The office is typically filled with strong lawyers, some of whom have expertise in discrete areas, such as national security law. But the office does not rival in numbers, depth of experience, or command of specific issue areas either OLC or many other executive branch legal departments.

This is one reason why the White House counsel has not supplanted OLC in its day-to-day legal advisory role within the executive branch. Other than those issues of particular importance to the president's governing agenda, OLC does its work with limited engagement with, much less challenge from, the White House counsel. OLC guides other executive branch agencies on issues large and small. And it possesses the authority that the White House counsel formally lacks to issue opinions binding on executive branch actors.

Moreover, if agency personnel are seeking opinions on issues that involve personal legal liability, and especially criminal liability, OLC or some other Justice Department component is best positioned to provide guidance that can ensure practical immunity from subsequent prosecution. In the George W. Bush administration, CIA lawyers, policymakers, and operatives involved in the agency's "enhanced interrogation techniques" program viewed OLC opinions approving their actions as a "golden shield" from later prosecution.[11] A similar phenomenon was in play with the Bush-era Stellarwind surveillance program, which was governed by law that contained criminal restrictions. Then–FBI Director Robert Mueller was prepared to resign when President Bush reapproved the program based only on the advice and approval of the White House counsel, without the narrowing changes proposed by the Justice Department, and without the department's approval. Mueller told the president that the FBI "could not participate in operations that Justice held to be in breach of criminal law."[12]

Yet on so many issues, especially those near-and-dear to the president and often those that impact the president at the intersection of his or her personal, political, and public roles, the White House counsel retains extraordinary legal power. Long prior to the Trump administration, history had shown that it was reasonable to worry that the legal advice given by the White House counsel was unduly influenced by political judgments. We do not suggest, as some commentators have, that White House counsels have invariably performed poorly under these pressures and have functioned, as their most severe critics allege, much like lackeys or lapdogs. There is no evidence in the day-in to-day outflow of legal advice within the Executive Office of the President that supports this depiction of gross professional responsibility. Routine legal advice is not, however, the issue. The test for the White House counsel is whether he or she renders the best legal advice consistent with the president's objectives and yet also with high professional standards when the president's policy and political interests are keenest. In those cases, the public may have reason to believe that the White House counsel is not consistently or reliably meeting this test.

THE TRUMP ERA

Donald Trump's career as a business executive required him to have lawyers at his side. His conceptions of their role and the uses of law are what has set him apart from other prominent executives who must manage legal risk and compliance. For Trump, law has been a weapon, a tool, that he has used with abandon to advance his interests and attack those of others. "I know lots about litigation," he once declared. On another occasion, he restated the point colorfully: "I'm like a Ph.D. in litigation."[13] By the time Trump became the presumptive 2016 Republican nominee for the presidency, he had been involved in, by one count, 4,096 lawsuits.

Trump has not been selective in the choice of targets or reluctant to pursue suits of dubious merit. The range of his targets over time is exceptional:

> He has sued people over unpaid royalties in licensing deals. He has sued Miss Pennsylvania. He has sued Bill Maher. He has sued the creator of Jeopardy! and Wheel of Fortune. He has sued Scotland. He has sued New Jersey. He has sued New York City, and he has sued New York state. He has sued Palm Beach. He has sued an architecture critic from Chicago. He has sued the secretary of the Interior and the National Indian Gaming Commission. He has sued people for using his surname in businesses...even though it was also their surname .... He has sued and been sued by longtime business partners .... He has threatened to file countless lawsuits he then hasn't filed.[14]

And this is just the tip of the iceberg. A legal program this vast in scale and pursued with this degree of relentlessness is impossible without willing lawyers. Trump, as client, needed lawyers who were prepared to do what he wanted done, proving themselves loyally committed to his goals and open to rough-and-tumble tactics and strategies.

Trump made no secret of the quality he prized first and foremost in his counsel: "loyalty." His model, and for years his trusted legal adviser, was Roy Cohn, who acquired notoriety as lead counsel for Senator Joseph

McCarthy and throughout his career for questionable professional conduct that culminated in his disbarment. In 1986, Trump testified on behalf of Cohn at the debarment proceeding and singled out the quality he most valued in Cohn as legal professional: "If I summed it up in one word, I think the primary word I'd use is his loyalty."[15] Later, Trump boasted that while Cohn was "brutal," and someone who "brutalized" for his client, "he was a very loyal guy."[16] Trump added: "[H]e's been vicious to others in his protection of me."[17]

Trump's personal lawyer of many years, Michael Cohen, did not join the administration, but his lawyering became a big issue for the president. He was, if nothing else, loyal to Trump, at least until he wasn't. "I'm the guy who would take a bullet for the president," Cohen once declared.[18] He lamented that when Trump became president, "high-ranking individuals" made a "concerted effort … to keep out [of the White House] loyalists."[19]

Cohen was one loyalist disappointed to discover he would not enter the government with his client. And Cohen's loyalty proved costly to him. On January 12, 2018, the *Wall Street Journal* reported that he "brokered a $130,000 payment" to Stephanie Clifford ("Stormy Daniels") in October 2016 in order to prevent her from publicly discussing an alleged affair she had with Trump in 2006.[20] On August 21, 2018, Cohen surrendered to the FBI and pleaded guilty to eight counts, including campaign finance violations involving payments of hush money to Clifford.[21] According to the court filings, Cohen submitted bank statements from Essential Consultants LLC, the shell company he created to mask the payment's connection to Trump. On December 12, 2018, Cohen was sentenced to three years in prison. At his sentencing, Cohen said that his "weakness" in engaging in this course of criminal conduct "can be characterized as a blind loyalty to Donald Trump."[22]

Trump's preoccupation with "loyalty," as he understood it, drew intense public attention from the beginning of his administration. Most famously, the president pressed FBI Director James Comey for loyalty, and received in return a commitment to "honest loyalty." In the report on this conversation, Special Counsel Mueller found substantial evidence that, contrary to Trump's denials, the president had, as Comey related the episode, stressed the premium he placed on loyalty. "'I need loyalty,' the president advised Comey, 'I expect loyalty.'"[23]

Trump expected this brand of loyalty no less from his administration lawyers than from other senior aides. More than once, when expressing deep frustration with his government counsel, including his White House counsel, Trump exclaimed: "Where's my Roy Cohn?"[24] Trump's entirely instrumental understanding of that role, shaped by his notion of the personal "loyalty" lawyers owed him, brought out vividly, more so than at any time since Watergate, the problems associated with the small law firm now entrenched in the White House.

White House Counsel Don McGahn

Don McGahn was the Trump presidential campaign's general counsel and then became the first White House counsel in the Trump administration. Few White House counsels became so prominent so quickly for clashing on major matters with the president. From the beginning of McGahn's tenure, the president professed dissatisfaction with his performance—and with his loyalty.

The first clash appeared to be over Attorney General Jeff Sessions's recusal from the Russia investigation after it was disclosed that, during the Trump transition, Sessions had met and discussed the policies of the incoming administration with the Russian ambassador to the United States. Sessions was advised by career officials, and agreed, that Justice Department regulations left him no choice in the matter. Trump was infuriated because he believed that, as attorney general, Sessions was obligated to protect him. Trump directed McGahn to persuade Sessions to reconsider the recusal. McGahn conveyed the president's views to Sessions, but Sessions refused to unrecuse. According to Mueller, Trump criticized McGahn for failing to persuade Sessions to reverse his position and assailed Sessions as "weak." At an Oval Office meeting, he complained that "I don't have a lawyer" and "brought up Roy Cohn, stating that he wished Cohn was his attorney." In a later meeting with Sessions, according to the former attorney general, the president admonished him: "'[Y]ou were supposed to protect me,' or words to that effect." The president had told his chief of staff, Reince Priebus, that he wanted a "bulldog" for a lawyer, and neither Sessions nor McGahn met the test.

In June 2017, Trump and McGahn struggled once more over the counsel's response to the president's instructions for dealing with the special counsel investigation. On June 14, the *Washington Post* reported that Mueller had come to focus on potential misconduct by the president himself. Three days later, citing what he believed to be Mueller "conflicts of interests," the president ordered McGahn to arrange with Acting Attorney General Rod Rosenstein to fire Mueller. McGahn declined to comply. He testified to Mueller that he considered the claim of conflicts to be "silly," and he also thought it inappropriate for the White House counsel to be involved in advancing any argument for Mueller's dismissal. According to Mueller's report, McGahn believed that "the President should consult with his personal counsel if he wished to raise conflicts." But Mueller found that the president, "instead of relying on his personal counsel[,] … sought to use his official powers to remove the Special Counsel."

The president continued to make demands on McGahn to arrange Mueller's dismissal. McGahn concluded that he had no choice but to resign and informed Priebus and senior aide Steve Bannon, both of whom urged him to reconsider. McGahn did, and he remained on the job. McGahn apparently did not raise directly with the president his intention to resign.

The conflict between the president and McGahn over the Mueller firing came to public attention in press reports in January 2018. The president denied that he had given any such order. He asked White House Staff Secretary Rob Porter to relay his directive that McGahn publicly deny any order for Mueller's dismissal. McGahn refused, advising first Porter and subsequently the president, that he clearly recalled the dismissal order. The president insisted that he intended only that McGahn raise the conflict issues with Justice Department officials for their consideration. McGahn disagreed with this version of events.

In the course of this Oval Office discussion, the president and McGahn had a revealing exchange, recounted in the Mueller Report, in which Trump reflected on his expectations of lawyers. Trump challenged McGahn's practice of taking notes: "What about these notes? Why do you take notes? Lawyers don't take notes. I never had a lawyer who took notes." McGahn replied that he was a "real lawyer" who did, in fact, take notes. The president responded with a reference again to his model of a lawyer: "I have had a lot of great lawyers, like Roy Cohn. He did not take notes." Apart from a demand for a public denial, the president added an order, relayed through Porter, that McGahn create a "letter to the file" of the counsel's office affirming that he had not been directed to arrange for the firing of Mueller. According to Porter, the president told him that "[i]f he [McGahn] doesn't write a letter, then maybe I'll have to get rid of him." McGahn also refused this request.

McGahn's role in these events later made him a key witness in the special counsel's inquiry. McGahn spent at least thirty hours in interviews with the special counsel's investigators, with much of the focus on Trump's attempt to remove Mueller. McGahn's exceptional level of cooperation stemmed in part from his concern, as reported in the *New York Times*, that "Mr. Trump was setting up Mr. McGahn to take the blame for any possible illegal acts of obstruction."[25] McGahn became determined "to do as much as possible to cooperate with Mr. Mueller to demonstrate that Mr. McGahn did nothing wrong." McGahn's relationship with Trump was already strained, with Trump questioning McGahn's loyalty, and McGahn referring to Trump as "King Kong," a reference to his volcanic temper.

As the extent of McGahn's cooperation with Mueller became clear, Trump surprised his counsel by announcing on Twitter that McGahn would leave the White House following the Senate's confirmation of Supreme Court nominee Brett Kavanaugh. Trump tweeted that he was "[n]ever a big fan" of McGahn, and implied that he might have been even more frustrated with McGahn than with Mueller.[26]

On occasion, McGahn did placate the president, as he did in agreeing to relay to Attorney General Sessions the president's unhappiness with his recusal in the Russia investigation and Trump's wish that he reverse course. And he had lapses on the job as well. He overreached when he unsuccessfully asserted the Office of White House Counsel's authority to issue authoritative constructions of the controversial "travel ban" executive order that the president issued shortly after taking office. The U.S. Court of Appeals for the Ninth Circuit had choice words in trimming back the White House counsel's ambitious definition of his role: "The White House Counsel is not the President, and he is not known to be in the chain of command for any of the Executive Departments."[27] And McGahn failed to anticipate or contain the significant ethics and conflicts of interests problems that characterized the first year of the Trump White House and that were largely his responsibility.[28]

But what most defined McGahn's years as White House counsel was his resistance to the president's relentless pressure to have him act like Roy Cohn, especially where Trump's most intense personal and political interests were at issue.

White House Counsel Pat Cipollone

The tenure of Pat Cipollone, McGahn's successor as White House counsel, began in October 2018. Less than a year later, in September 2019, Speaker of the House Nancy Pelosi announced that the House would initiate an impeachment inquiry focused on evidence that the president had pressured the government of Ukraine to open a criminal investigation of former Vice President Joe Biden, a potential Democratic nominee to oppose Trump in the 2020 election. Cipollone became the lead defense lawyer for the president, sharing this responsibility with the president's personal counsel. It is in this very public role that Cipollone had choices to make about how to manage his institutional responsibilities and still maintain "loyalty" to the president in the defense of his reputation and incumbency. It does not minimize the challenge that he faced in addressing these pressures to conclude that some of his choices seriously damaged the institutional standing of the Office of White House Counsel.

A White House counsel's defense of a president in an impeachment process is not unusual. President Clinton also relied on his White House counsel, Charles Ruff, for advice and public defense in the 1998 House impeachment and 1999 Senate trial. A president may appropriately treat impeachment as a legal challenge requiring both personal and government counsel. Personal misconduct is typically at issue in allegations of impeachable offenses—the charge that the president committed "high Crimes and Misdemeanors"—and a president may face legal consequences upon leaving office. At the same time, Congress' determination of whether the evidence meets the constitutional standard for removing a president from office fully justifies the White House counsel's involvement in the defense in his or her institutional role, that is, in defending of the long-term interests of the presidency.

Cipollone and his colleagues did not entirely neglect this institutional defense, but they drew the most attention for the ways that their defense endorsed and in some ways mimicked the president's incendiary rhetoric. Trump's incessant attacks on the impeachment process on Twitter included the charge that it was nothing less than a "COUP,"[29] and the "[m]ost unfair and corrupt hearing in Congressional history!"[30] And in a letter to Speaker Pelosi that in tone and content went far beyond anything in modern presidential communications to Congress, Trump referred to Pelosi's "spiteful actions," "egregious conduct," "illegal, partisan attempted coup," and to impeachment proceedings as "a Star Chamber of partisan persecution," a "perversion of justice," and designed to "undo the election of 2016 and steal the election of 2020!"[31]

That was par for the course for Trump. But it was surprising when his White House counsel leveled similar charges in a letter to the House that announced that Trump would refuse all cooperation with the House. Cipollone accused the Democrats of a "naked political strategy" for the same purpose the president identified: "to overturn the results of the 2016 election" and "influence the next election."[32] In the Senate trial, Cipollone took up the claim that Democrats were "stealing" elections, both the last and the next, and described their aims further as "the most massive interference in an election in American history."[33] And, as the president did, the White House counsel in its trial memorandum suggested that the Democrats were unable to compete on fair terms with a president who had compiled a supposedly impressive record of achievement in his first three years in office.

It was unusual for the White House counsel to make a legal case structured much like the scorched-earth political one heard from the president, his political supporters, and his personal counsel. A senior government lawyer's representation of the presidency should call for an argument focused more on the constitutional merits of the claims against the president and not on the imputed partisan motivations of his accusers. This is essential in addressing the larger critique of White House counsels as "lawyers selected for their loyalty to the president."[34] The counsel assisting in the defense against an impeachment bears the burden of taking the long view, answering the question of how this impeachment stacks up against the constitutional precedent, and arguing the insufficiency of the particular case for ousting a president—*any* president—from office. The counsel's choice of tone and language should be appropriate to his or her institutional role, bringing clarity to the constitutional and institutional stakes, and leaving to others reinforcement of the president's primarily political message. In impeachments, as in all constitutional controversies engulfing a president's conduct and use of power, there is inevitably and necessarily a political argument, but it is not the one a White House counsel should participate in making.

There is a further and more consequential risk that a White House counsel runs when drawn as a leading actor into high political drama. Acceptance of this role means that fundamental institutional interests may go inadequately represented, sacrificed, or subordinated to the president's political strategy. It may have worked for Trump's politics to refuse engagement with the House and to stand by while the process unfolded without his participation. And his lawyers did complain that he was denied "due process," pitching their case at the most general level. But the heart of their argument was that, because the charges against him were supposedly bogus, he had done nothing wrong, so questions of process were beside the point. It was an "invalid" impeachment, corruptly motivated, and thus he would not engage. So Cipollone and his team aided Donald Trump with the political case he wished to make. But in subordinating constitutional lawyering to this political argument, the counsel left major long-term institutional equities unaddressed. The flat refusal to engage with the House meant that Trump failed to define, not just for himself, but as a matter of precedent for his successors, what core set of procedural protections a president should be provided as a constitutional matter.

This was good enough for Trump, however. After his acquittal, Trump spoke from the East Room of the White House with his personal lawyers and White House counsel Cipollone seated before him in the first row. "You guys stand up, please," the president commanded. "Great job."[35] This president, who demands full "loyalty" from his lawyers and was so often disappointed by them, felt that this time it was given.

Another episode in the tenure of Trump White House counsel Pat Cipollone illustrates how lawyers in this job who may have no intention of being embroiled in controversy will be unable to escape it. As a member of the senior staff, a White House counsel attends meetings, participates in discussions, or advises on matters that entangle them in political conflict. The House impeachment managers concluded in the course of the Trump impeachment process that Cipollone was a "material witness" who had "extensive knowledge" of key events and discussions bearing on the president's conduct at the heart of the inquiry.[36] They contended that under the ethical rules, he could not properly serve as both advocate and witness. The controversy over his role widened after press reports emerged that, along with the White House chief of staff and one of the president's personal lawyers, Cipollone had attended a meeting at which the president had directed his national security adviser, John Bolton, to advance his efforts to pressure the government of Ukraine to help with a political "hit" on former Vice President Biden.[37]

For our purposes, we would stress that, granting the exceptional circumstances of Cipollone's involvement in meetings relevant to a presidential impeachment, the White House counsel *routinely* attends Oval Office meetings and participates in the most sensitive matters involving the president. This daily, intensive engagement with the president and his senior staff is laden with the potential for roping the counsel into at least controversy and, often enough, alleged "scandal."

REFORM

It might seem that Trump and his crudely instrumental view of lawyers is the extreme case and that his experience with Don McGahn, who appeared to resist inappropriate directives, is reassuring. The counsel stood firm on many issues, and the president backed down (or lost interest). We think there is limited comfort to be taken from this episode.

First, the history of the Office of White House Counsel shows that counsels come regularly under pressure to do the president's bidding—to be the "president's lawyer" in the narrowest personal rather than the broadest institutional sense. Several counsels before McGahn did not—or did not appear to—hold up as well under that pressure. McGahn's successor, we have argued, should be included in that category. Second, McGahn had exceptional support from congressional Republican leadership. He was a strong partner in their successful efforts to move hundreds of judicial nominations. They wanted him to stay in place; they were openly sorry to see him go, when he decided after two years to do so. In this respect, McGahn was dealing with Trump from a position of independent political strength that few, if any, White House counsels have enjoyed.

Any consideration of reform of the institution of the White House counsel runs up against clear limitations. A president can get legal advice from whomever he or she wishes, inside or outside the government. And the vesting of the executive power in the president in Article II gives the president significant control over his or her own legal advisory process. There is no legal solution available, or desirable, to meaningfully constrain those choices. But, as we have noted throughout this book, while we focus on statutory reform where feasible, we also argue for reform internal to the executive branch that presidents could adopt to influence the restoration or development of norms. A structural alternative for the provision of legal advice is open for any future president to consider; if one does and it proves to be workable and effective, then others may follow.

In that spirit, we propose one such structural reform: that the White House counsel be bound closer to the Justice Department and not so tightly woven into the West Wing culture. To this end, we suggest that the White House counsel remain a member of the president's senior staff, with an office in the White House, and with a minimal staff of two or so deputies. But the larger group of lawyers who provide this small Office of White House Counsel its direct support would be located in the Justice Department—primarily in the Office of Legal Counsel, but also, as we explain below, in other Justice Department components. The Justice Department, reorganized as necessary for this purpose, would provide the research and analysis on which the Office of White House Counsel depends.

OLC would be the component most affected by this shift, but the shift would not constitute a dramatic change in its formal mission. At present, OLC understands its charge to include "advice in response to requests from the Counsel to the President," especially on "legal issues of particular complexity and importance."[38] OLC cites as examples advice on the "constitutionality of pending legislation" and approval of "the form and legality of executive orders and substantive proclamations issued by the President." Its overall mission has always been to help "the President [to] fulfill his or her constitutional duties."[39] Under our proposal, much of the White House counsel's "small law firm" would be merged into the Office of Legal Counsel. OLC might have to add another political deputy to its cadre of deputies to supervise the new work from the White House, but we expect that the rest of the additional personnel would come at the nonpolitical line attorney level. With this scheme, we see significant benefits and little if any harm done to the basic arrangement through which the president receives prompt attention and support from a dedicated corps of lawyers.

Culture

The reorganization we propose offers advantages for the culture of professionalism in the provision of legal advice to the president. It matters to the culture of the Office of White House Counsel where its lawyers are situated—near the White House Press Office, just a few steps from the senior advisers to the president who are responsible for policy decisions or public communications strategies, or a mile down Pennsylvania Avenue at the Justice Department. The White House counsel and his or her small staff would still be near to the president and available at a moment's notice to be brought into a matter that requires legal counsel. But the lawyers in this very reduced office would rely for the development of that counsel on Justice Department lawyers.

The Justice Department, of course, is far from immune to political influences from the White House—nor should it be in many contexts. We also recognize the serious questions that have been raised about the erosion in the department's independence from improper political pressures. Yet it remains the case that the Justice Department, for reasons already given, is typically more detached from political pressures than the Office of White House Counsel. We argued in earlier chapters that the department's culture and supporting norms of independence require reaffirmation and reinforcement. But the department still serves—and will continue to serve—as a counterweight to a White House consumed daily with political and policy pressures and the related demands of public communication. The lawyers supporting the White House counsel but working from and within the Justice Department would be subject to resilient departmental norms and would benefit in their work from distance from the political hothouse that is the West Wing. And a higher percentage of nonpolitical lawyers in the Justice Department will ultimately work on White House matters than occurred when the bulk of the work was done within the White House.

Our proposal should also be weighed against the alternative possibility that the Office of White House Counsel will continue to grow in influence, jurisdictional ambition, and even size. It is already a small law firm, not really just the "office" of the White House counsel. It has developed that way, for the reasons we have described, as a reflection of the growth in presidential power, the demands on the office, and the complexity of the legal landscape that presidents must navigate. These are all reasons for the president to have accessible legal advice, but no less a cause for concern that the legal advisory functions may come to be commandeered by the West Wing. Further movement in this direction will prove costly to the professional culture of executive branch lawyering.

The White House counsel cannot escape the hothouse and attend meetings each day on the whole range of issues with which the president is concerned. The counsel is immersed in the administration's policy and political focuses and priorities, and in the environment in which these are discussed. As Lyndon Johnson's senior aide and presidential press secretary, George Reedy tartly described these working conditions, "the atmosphere of the White House" could be a combination of "sycophancy and a belief in the efficacy of closely held knowledge." The life of the White House is "the life of a court, ... a structure designed for one purpose and one purpose only—to serve the material needs and desires of a single man."[40]

This may be overstated, but there is more than a grain of truth in it. Yet this need not be the working environment for *all* the lawyers, typically numbering well over twenty, who staff the Office of White House Counsel. By relying on Justice Department lawyers, who are required to think of themselves as department lawyers, our proposal ensures that the legal counsel given to the president is more clearly within the law dimension of the complex interplay of law, politics, and policy in any administration. The effect may be subtle and yet significant. This arrangement would also, we think, serve the White House counsel in maintaining the balance necessary to resist being too much "on the team."

Functionality

This proposed reorganization does not present a threat to the efficient delivery of legal services to the president.

First, the president would retain the ability to meet face to face with the White House counsel at any time.

Second, the counsel's assignment of research or written work product does not require proximity to the staff lawyers. OLC and other Justice Department components can be organized so that specific lawyers assist the White House counsel with continuity and dispatch in the management of the White House legal workload. If staff needs to meet with the counsel, the department is a mile away from the White House. This would not mean constant local travel. Most White House associate counsels meet only as needed with the counsel, for all-staff meetings or as specific projects require, and these lawyers attend meetings with the president even less frequently.

Third, not all current White House counsel legal and legal policy functions would be doled out to the Office of Legal Counsel. OLC would be limited to addressing strictly legal questions related to the counsel's work. But other tasks could be divided between the White House counsel and other Justice Department components. The task of screening and vetting judicial nominees and major executive branch nominees should be allocated between the Justice Department's Office of Legal Policy (which has performed this task, at least for judicial nominees, in some administrations) and the White House legislative liaison and communications staffs. The White House counsel or a deputy counsel could also be involved. In administration responses to congressional oversight and investigations, OLC would provide the primary legal advice, as it does today on issues such as executive privilege, though the White House counsel might continue to coordinate lawyers and others across agencies and departments in that effort. Something similar would happen to the White House counsel's ethics function. The White House counsel and other White House officials would continue to organize and conduct White House briefings, but OLC would provide the legal advice, perhaps with input from other Justice Department components.

Some issues would be more complicated. Consider scandal crises that implicate large media coverage and then possibly congressional and criminal investigations of the president or his or her administration. The White House counsel currently plays a central role in this response. In our proposal, *legal* support would come from OLC—for example, legal analysis of issues that arise in connection with the administration's response to congressional oversight or investigations.

The White House counsel would be responsible for making sure the legal work was assigned, and he or she would review it and have the final word with the president. The counsel would also support as necessary the senior White House staff on the various elements of crisis management—the integration of legal, political, and communications strategies; assisting with responses to press inquiries; and demands from Capitol Hill for testimony or information. The wider Office of White House Counsel, the bulk of its lawyers located in the Department of Justice and concerned solely with analysis and advice on legal issues, would not be involved in this aspect of the White House response. Once again, it involves too much politics, which risks affecting the quality and integrity of the legal work.

This general allocation of responsibilities would resemble the relationship of the White House counsel to the Justice Department in the development of recommendations to the president for executive clemency. Since the nineteenth century, the department's pardon attorney has reviewed the vast majority of the petitions for pardons and commutations, and the White House counsel is now the point of contact in receiving and evaluating the department's proposed grants and denials and making final recommendations to the president. The department's role has conferred significant credibility and legitimacy on the president's exercise of the pardon power. As discussed in Chapter Six, the most controversial pardons have involved presidential decisions taken outside the normal process, when the department is excluded from participation and the White House counsel simply assists the president in doing what he wishes. We believe that systematic department support of the White House counsel in other areas, through an enhanced function for OLC, will bolster rule-of-law values.

The concrete suggestions made here are tentative. Working out the details of a large shift of legal capacity from the Office of White House Counsel to the Justice Department would be complicated, and some tasks are more segregable and easier to allocate properly than others. Problems would surely arise in practice that would require adjustment. But the basic move makes sense: Legal interpretation and analysis should be shifted from the Office of White House Counsel to the Justice Department, and the execution of policies should remain in the White House.

Rule-of-Law Commitment

Moving the White House counsel's supporting lawyers to the Justice Department cannot decisively answer all the concerns about a legal advisory process under the president's thumb. A president determined to prize loyalty and results-oriented advice can get his way with appointments to all senior legal positions, from the attorney general all the way down (and across, to other agencies). What is different about the White House counsel is the distinctiveness of the role. The counsel is right by the president's side, building up and managing a group of what appears to critics to be primarily loyalists and only secondarily lawyers. The choice and then performance of White House counsels is now instrumental in setting the tone and standard for the rule of law in the operation of the executive branch. A presidential decision to have the Justice Department support the White House in the ways we propose would, we believe, signal a major change in how the president would approach rule-of-law issues.

One objection certain to be raised is that moving the president's dedicated corps of lawyers to the Justice Department would worsen the problem of the politicization of law interpretation and enforcement. In the strongest formulation of this concern, the president would simply have dispatched political and personal cronies into the heart of the Justice Department. But we doubt that the problem we are seeking to address would simply be moving down the street. In the end, we are looking to achieve both physical and cultural separation. Even if the White House counsel has a say in who is hired for this White House support function, it matters whether these lawyers are located in the West Wing and their colleagues are White House staff, or they work day-to-day as—and in the company of—Justice Department lawyers.

★

PART III

THE PRESIDENT AND CONGRESS

We live in an era of presidential governance because of congressional abdication and delegation. Across every conceivable issue area, Congress has given the executive branch broad powers to take various actions and to make regulations and issue executive orders with the force of law. Moreover, presidents have tended to interpret these conferrals of authority aggressively, thus expanding presidential power even more. The issue obviously did not originate with Donald Trump. But Trump exercised power, or threatened to, in ways that have amplified the issue and, in some instances, have led to bipartisan calls for reform.

The chapters in this part focus only selectively on this very large problem and, in particular, on four problems that became especially salient during the Trump presidency:

- *The President's War Powers.* Presidents have since the Founding slowly expanded their authorities to use military force abroad without congressional authorization. With the notable exception of the War Powers Resolution, Congress has gone along with this trend by giving the president an ever-larger standing military service with few restrictions on its use, and with little meaningful oversight. As a practical matter, there are few domestic legal restrictions on the president's power to use force militarily. This problem proved most worrisome during the Trump administration when the president casually threatened to use nuclear weapons.

- *Executive Branch Vacancies.* One of Trump's most significant innovations is to circumvent, or ignore, the Senate confirmation process for top executive branch appointments and, relatedly, to exploit gaps and uncertainties in the statutes that govern how senior-level executive branch vacancies must be filled. Like most of Trump's norm-breaking practices, these had precursors in prior administrations, but Trump took them to new extremes.

- *The Insurrection Act and Emergency Powers.* Trump's threat to use military forces in the homeland to quell protests shone new and troubling light on the Insurrection Act. This 1807 statute authorizes the president in very broad terms to use the armed forces when (among other situations) unlawful activity or "rebellion" impedes the enforcement of federal law or where an outbreak of "domestic violence" infringes on the constitutional rights of citizens and state authorities are "unable, fail, or refuse" to protect those rights. The statute has thin substantive limitations and even thinner procedural ones. So do too the broad array of emergency powers that Congress has conferred on the president.

- *Congressional Subpoenas.* One of the chief tools that Congress has to exercise a constitutional check on presidential action is the issuance of subpoenas to compel information and testimony. Presidents have a number of traditional arguments for resisting and delaying (and thus undermining) the effectiveness of these subpoenas, but Trump took these arguments to a new level of confrontation with Congress, eschewing traditional avenues of negotiation and accommodation.

WAR POWERS AND NUCLEAR WEAPONS

There is a perennial debate in the United States about the legality and wisdom of presidential unilateralism in the deployment of U.S. military force abroad. On this issue perhaps more than any in this book, the most dangerous expansions of presidential power took place prior to Trump. However, the significance of and hazards in this expansion—especially with regard to presidential control over nuclear weapons—became crystal clear under Trump due to his undisciplined rhetoric, mercurial judgment, and indifference to facts and expert judgment. Trump, in short, was the lit match that made clear the dangerousness of the badly packed explosives in the presidential woodhouse.

BACKGROUND

As background, we first summarize the legal doctrine governing the president's use of force generally and then turn to the law, policies, protocols, and past practices related to nuclear weapons.

General Legal Principles Governing War Powers

Article II designates the president as the "Commander in Chief of the Army and Navy of the United States." Alexander Hamilton stated in *Federalist* No. 69 that this designation "would amount to nothing more than the supreme command and direction of the military and naval forces, as first general and admiral of the Confederacy," and he noted that this power fell far short of the analogous power in the king of England, who had the power to declare war and raise and regulate the army and navy.[1] Article I of the Constitution allocated these latter powers, and many others related to the conduct and control of the military, to Congress.

The Framers believed that the Constitution required presidents to receive authorization from Congress before they could use significant military force abroad, though it remains unclear whether this requirement was grounded in the Declare War Clause, or in Congress's control of the purse, or both. The Framers also believed that presidents would retain the authority, without congressional authorization, to "repel sudden attacks," a principle that the Supreme Court recognized in 1863.[2] This understanding of the allocation of war powers proved unstable as the United States grew in global power and as Congress approved a larger and larger standing Army and Navy (and later Air Force).

Through presidential practice, the "repel sudden attacks" rationale morphed into a broad "self-defense" rationale. Presidents on dozens of occasions unilaterally deployed military forces abroad to protect U.S. persons, property, and interests from ever-more-distant threats outside the United States. The broadest self-defense (and related) rationales came in two Office of Legal Counsel (OLC) opinions written in connection with the 9/11 attacks and the 2003 invasion of Iraq.

The first opinion was issued a few weeks after the 9/11 attacks. In it OLC collected and read expansively all the significant precedents on unilateral presidential uses of force.[3] It ruled that independent of Congress's statutory authorization for the president to use force, the president under Article II can use force "both to retaliate for those attacks, and to prevent and deter future assaults on the Nation." The president, OLC reasoned, was not limited to uses of force against the terrorist organizations that attacked the United States. Instead, it concluded, "the Constitution vests the President with the power to strike terrorist groups or organizations that cannot be demonstrably linked to the September 11 incidents, but that, nonetheless, pose a similar threat to the security of the United States and the lives of its people, whether at home or overseas." The analysis in the opinion was directed at threats from terrorist organizations, but its logic applied to threats from states as well.

OLC's second opinion was issued on October 16, 2002. It concluded that Article II authorized the president to use force against Iraq if he concluded that "Iraq's development of WMD [weapons of mass destruction] might endanger our national security because of the risk that such weapons either would be targeted against the United States, or would be used to destabilize the region."[4] OLC added that a preemptive use of military force against Iraq's supposed WMD capabilities would be consistent with the U.N. Charter. The factors OLC considered were "the probability of an attack; the likelihood that this probability will increase, and therefore the need to take advantage of a window of opportunity; whether diplomatic alternatives are practical; and the magnitude of the harm that could result from the threat."

Applying these factors, OLC concluded that "even if the probability that Iraq itself would attack the United States with WMD … were relatively low, the exceptionally high degree of harm that would result, combined with a limited window of opportunity and the likelihood that if we do not use force, the threat will increase, could lead the President to conclude that military action is necessary to defend the United States." OLC added that "[a] proportionate response might include destruction of Iraq's WMD capability or removing Saddam Hussein from power."

Both of these Bush-era opinions were technically unnecessary to the matters at hand since Congress had previously authorized military force concerning the issues for which OLC claimed there was independent Article II authority. Nonetheless, although more than a dozen Bush-era OLC opinions were withdrawn, these two remain on the Justice Department books. And although the Obama administration never purported to rely on either opinion, it developed its own broad conception of the president's authority to use military force in self-defense against terrorist organizations, including a broad notion of anticipatory self-defense, under both Article II and international law.[5]

Presidents have also used force without congressional authorization in circumstances that implicate "national interests" other than self-defense. This trend culminated in the pre-Trump years in two opinions written during the Obama administration, one concerning the military force deployed in Libya, and the other supporting military force, largely for humanitarian reasons, in Iraq.[6] The opinions recognized a number

of broad national interests that would justify presidential unilateralism, such as promoting regional stability, assisting allies or strategic
partners, and preventing a worsening of humanitarian atrocities. OLC
recognized only one possible limit on this permissive "national interest"
test for presidential unilateralism. If the planned military engagement
is "prolonged and substantial," it involves "exposure of U.S. military
personnel to significant risk over a substantial period," and the scale of
the expected hostilities are large, then the action constitutes "war" that
requires prior congressional authorization.

These opinions mean that, without congressional authorization, the
president can use U.S. military force in any situation where he or she determines that doing so would serve the "national interest," loosely conceived,
as long as the force does not pose a great risk of American casualties or
significant escalation. In addition, the Obama administration read the
1973 War Powers Resolution not to apply to the Libya conflict after that
conflict exceeded the statute's sixty-day limitation on "hostilities" not supported by congressional authorization. Many prior presidents had claimed
that the resolution's sixty-day trigger was unconstitutional. The Obama
administration did not, but it instead read the "hostilities" trigger not to
apply to war from a distance that did not pose a serious risk of harm to
U.S. troops or a serious risk of escalation. On these understandings, the
president can conduct "war from a distance" (manned and unmanned
air power, long-range-missiles, and cyberattacks) without congressional
authorization and outside the strictures of the War Powers Resolution.

These permissive understandings of the president's lawful unilateral
presidential authority to use force represent only the executive branch's
view and are not shared by many in Congress or by many scholars,
including scholars of international law. Nonetheless, this legal understanding is highly relevant to any account of presidential war powers
because presidential uses of force are not generally subject to judicial
review, and thus the executive branch view of the law will govern the
actual use of force absent some binding intervention by Congress that
the executive branch accepts.

Against this legal background, the following controversies over
unilateral presidential action related to conventional forces arose in the
decades prior to the Trump presidency:

- The Bush administration embraced the unprecedentedly broad conceptions of unilateral military power described in the 2001 and 2002 OLC opinions.

- The Bush administration unilaterally expanded Congress's 2001 Authorization for Use of Military Force (AUMF), which was aimed at the perpetrators of the 9/11 attacks, to include all manner of al-Qaeda-associated forces. The Obama administration interpreted the AUMF to include the Islamic State, which is not an associated force of al-Qaeda. These interpretations allowed presidents to use significant military force in almost ten nations against many terrorist groups that were not in existence on 9/11.

- The Obama administration, building on past practice, engaged in humanitarian interventions in Iraq and Libya without congressional authorization. These actions did not concern the safety or property of U.S persons or the defense of allies. And they stretched the "national interest" test for unilateral war powers to its furthest point yet.

- The Bush and Obama administrations stretched the "self-defense" rationale for unilateral war powers to include broader and broader conceptions of self-defense, including a generous multifactored test for anticipatory self-defense, and a broad notion of "unit self-protection" that expands unilateral presidential authority since U.S. troops are deployed in many war zones around the world.

- Presidents have on their own authority involved the United States in various forms of military and intelligence support for other nations' wars. A prominent recent example is the United States' support since 2015 of a coalition of nations led by Saudi Arabia, in the war in Yemen.

There are three reasons why the nation's military policies, as reflected in the president's decision on when and how to use military force, came to rest almost entirely on the president's discretion alone. First, Congress provided the president with a two-million-strong armed force (1.2 million service members on active duty) and an astonishing array of weapons systems. Whatever practical constraints inhered in a small standing army dissipated long ago, and unilateral presidential uses of forces have in general risen with the growth in the permanent military's size.

Second, the presidency grew in size and responsibility, especially after the Civil War. As the nation also grew in power and responsibility on the international stage, presidents perceived ever-widening national interests that required deployments of U.S. troops.

Third, Congress failed to exercise its constitutional authorities to constrain presidents from using the troops and weapons it provided. As early as 1804, the Supreme Court upheld congressional restrictions on the circumstances in which the U.S. Navy could seize enemy ships during the Quasi-War with France.[7] Congress can also check or shape presidential uses of force after the fact by prohibiting or limiting spending on continuing uses of force. In 1983 and 1993, Congress forced presidents to change missions (in Lebanon and Somalia, respectively) through the use of conditional funding restrictions. Congress's funding restrictions were also a major contribution to the end of the Vietnam War. But Congress has constrained the presidency very little in military affairs in recent decades.

One reason Congress has difficulty exercising its prodigious war powers is that after a president deploys force unilaterally, the political pressure to "rally around the troops" makes it hard for many members to oppose the action. Second, Congress must muster veto-proof majorities to reverse or check unilateral presidential uses of force. Third, and most importantly, most members of Congress do not want to take public responsibility for war powers decisions. They prefer to remain quiet so that they can take credit or allocate blame, depending on how things work out. Consider the nineteen-year war that Congress ostensibly authorized in the 2001 AUMF and that presidents have persistently expanded through interpretation. Many members of Congress have complained about these unilateral presidential extensions of the statute. And there have been numerous calls (including, notably, by President Obama during his term) for Congress to update and refresh the 2001 AUMF to take greater responsibility for how the conflict has developed. But Congress has failed to act, at least in a public way, although it has by large majorities quietly enacted appropriations that aim precisely to support the conflict against the Islamic State.

Congress's major effort at reform of presidential war powers—the 1973 War Powers Resolution—has been a failure. The resolution requires the president to cease unilateral military actions after sixty days in any situation where U.S. forces are engaged in hostilities or likely hostilities, unless Congress authorizes the mission. It has been a failure for a number of reasons. First, most presidents have not accepted its constitutionality. Second, the executive branch has interpreted the sixty-day window before it needed to secure congressional authorization as an effective authorization to use force within that window. Third, as noted earlier, presidents have interpreted the "hostilities" trigger for requiring congressional authorization opportunistically to cover, at most, only extended engagements of U.S. troops that pose a serious risk of U.S. casualties and escalation. Fourth, Congress has acquiesced in almost every context where the executive branch has emasculated the War Powers Resolution through interpretation or defiance.

Nuclear Weapons

Nuclear weapons present a special case of the general war powers problem. They have a unique capacity to kill many millions in a single detonation, and their use, even tactically, threatens to spark an existential escalatory spiral and to create long-term and widespread damage to health and the environment. Because of their uniquely devastating power, specific law, policies, and protocols have developed to govern their use.

Law

A 2013 Department of Defense report accurately states the conventional wisdom about the president and nuclear weapons: "Consistent with decades-long practice, the President, as Commander in Chief of the U.S. Armed Forces, *has the sole authority to order the employment of U.S. nuclear forces.*"[8] This sentence needs unpacking. The main idea is civilian control: The president alone has authority to order deployment of nuclear weapons. A related idea, more contested, is that the president alone is *currently authorized* to deploy nuclear weapons.

There is no published Justice Department opinion that explains how OLC jurisprudence on Article II war powers applies to nuclear weapons. It seems clear that the president has the authority to launch nuclear weapons in self-defense in the face of an incoming nuclear attack—a much-planned-for scenario since the early days of the Cold War. Matters become more complex if the president orders a first-use nuclear strike in a situation short of an incoming nuclear attack. Some observers have reasoned that the OLC's "national interest" opinions require congressional authorization for the use of nuclear weapons in this situation, since any such nuclear attack would be on a scale that implicated prolonged and substantial hostilities and the exposure of U.S. troops (and civilians) to significant risk. But two factors complicate this analysis.

First, the "national interest" opinions written in contexts other than self-defense (such as the recent interventions in Syria and Libya) may not be relevant when the president deploys military force *in self-defense*, including anticipatory self-defense. The president's unilateral military power is at its height when he or she exercises force to protect the nation. And as noted, OLC currently takes a very broad view of the president's authority to use force in self-defense, including anticipatory self-defense. There are a number of plausible scenarios short of an incoming nuclear attack—including verbal threats to use nuclear weapons, and intelligence indicating preparation to use such weapons—that might suffice under extant OLC opinions to authorize the president to use force. North Korea, which undoubtedly has a nuclear capacity, has taken many threatening actions toward the United States, and uttered many more threatening words. Based on the OLC opinions written to justify the invasion of Iraq, and other broad self-defense opinions, the Justice Department could conclude that Article II would authorize the president to deploy nuclear weapons necessary and proportional to the threat to eliminate Kim Jong Un's nuclear threats against the United States.

Second, there is a weak argument that Congress has already authorized the president to use nuclear weapons at his or her discretion. The Atomic Energy Act (AEA) of 1946 (amended in 1954) provides that the president "may direct" the Atomic Energy Commission "to deliver such quantities of fissionable materials or weapons to the armed forces *for such use as he deems necessary in the interest of national defense.*"[9] This language almost certainly aimed to secure civilian control over all applications of nuclear technology, and not to authorize presidential use of nuclear weapons against an adversary.[10] But it could be read as an authorization to use force, and such an authorization would have been consistent with the widespread understanding at the time that the use of nuclear weapons was a question of presidential discretion.[11] Finally, a 1989 OLC opinion cites this passage when it states in dicta that "[t]he President is authorized by the Act to require the Commission to deliver nuclear material and to authorize its use for military purposes."[12] A final legal uncertainty concerns international law. In the 2002 opinion sketched earlier, OLC interpreted *jus ad bellum* principles—ones derived from the U.N. Charter and related customary international law—to allow the president to use conventional air, naval, and ground power in anticipatory self-defense, conceived very broadly. However, OLC has never opined on how the U.N. Charter applies to the use of nuclear weapons, and there is considerable uncertainty on this point. The proportionality component of the anticipatory self-defense test would almost certainly operate differently, and with greater restriction, in the context of using nuclear weapons.

Moreover, there is another body of international law—the law governing the conduct of war, known as the law of war, or *jus in bello*—that governs the legality of targeting. The Justice Department has not said much about how this body of law applies to presidential uses of force. But the Defense Department takes this body of law seriously. It has made clear that "[t]he law of war governs the use of nuclear weapons, just as it governs the use of conventional weapons"; that "nuclear weapons must be directed against military objectives," not civilian targets; and that "attacks using nuclear weapons must not be conducted when the expected incidental harm to civilians is excessive compared to the military advantage expected to be gained."[13]

Nuclear Declaratory Posture

The Nuclear Posture Review (NPR) is a document prepared by the Defense Department that assesses and states U.S. policy and posture on nuclear weapons. (It is notable that an executive branch agency and not Congress prepares this review.) Modern NPRs began in 1994, during the Clinton administration, to assess the United States' nuclear posture after the end of the Cold War. The George W. Bush, Obama, and Trump administrations also promulgated nuclear posture reviews. (The Bush and Obama NPRs were mandated by Congress.) Among other things, NPRs aim to examine and explain the role of nuclear weapons in U.S. security and to tell the American public, allies, and adversaries about the U.S. nuclear deterrent posture and the circumstances in which the United States will deploy nuclear weapons.

Of most relevance to legal reform are the NPR's stated circumstances under which the United States will deploy nuclear weapons. President Obama was famously committed to reducing U.S. nuclear stockpiles and U.S. reliance on the use of nuclear weapons. The key elements of his declaratory policy were the following:

- The United States will continue to strengthen conventional capabilities and reduce the role of nuclear weapons in deterring non-nuclear attacks, with the objective of making deterrence of nuclear attack on the United States or our allies and partners the sole purpose of U.S. nuclear weapons.

- The United States would only consider the use of nuclear weapons in extreme circumstances to defend the vital interests of the United States or its allies and partners.

- The United States will not use or threaten to use nuclear weapons against non-nuclear weapons states that are party to the Nuclear Non-Proliferation Treaty (NPT) and in compliance with their nuclear nonproliferation obligations.[14]

This policy maintained the option of using nuclear weapons in a first-use situation. It also maintained the possibility of using nuclear weapons to deter "non-nuclear attacks," and declined to spell out the circumstances under which the United States might do so. But it was noteworthy for expressing the aims of eventually eliminating this role for nuclear weapons and limiting their use to deterring nuclear attacks. The Obama NPR also continued U.S. ambiguity on what "vital interests" of the United States would justify in extreme circumstances the use of nuclear weapons. President Trump's NPR declaratory policy was somewhat different:

The United States would only consider the employment of nuclear weapons in extreme circumstances to defend the vital interests of the United States, its allies, and partners. Extreme circumstances could include significant non-nuclear strategic attacks. Significant non-nuclear strategic attacks include, but are not limited to, attacks on the U.S., allied, or partner civilian population or infrastructure, and attacks on U.S. or allied nuclear forces, their command and control, or warning and attack assessment capabilities. The United States will not use or threaten to use nuclear weapons against non-nuclear weapons states that are party to the NPT and in compliance with their nuclear non-proliferation obligations. Given the potential of significant non-nuclear strategic attacks, the United States reserves the right to make any adjustment in the assurance that may be warranted by the evolution and proliferation of non-nuclear strategic attack technologies and U.S. capabilities to counter that threat.[15]

The Trump NPR maintains the option of first-use and is explicit about it: "To help preserve deterrence and the assurance of allies and partners, the United States has never adopted a 'no first use' policy and, given the contemporary threat environment, such a policy is not justified today." It is also explicit about the strategic ambiguity that has historically characterized U.S. nuclear policy: "It remains the policy of the United States to retain some ambiguity regarding the precise circumstances that might lead to a U.S. nuclear response." The Trump NPR departs in other notable ways from the Obama NPR. One is that the Trump NPR spells out the types of "significant non-nuclear strategic attacks" for which the United States is prepared to use nuclear weapons. The Trump NPR also walks back somewhat the pledge not to threaten or use nuclear weapons against NPT parties in light of the development of "non-nuclear strategic attack technologies," including, presumably, cyberattacks.

Process

A central concern during the Cold War was that the U.S. government needed to be able to retaliate in the face of a Soviet first-strike before the incoming Soviet missiles destroyed U.S. land-based missiles. To respond to such a first-strike, and also to deter it, the United States needed a credible way to respond during the approximately twenty-five to thirty minutes it would take from launch for a Soviet missile to reach the United States.

The executive branch thus developed an elaborate nuclear command-and-control system—much of it classified—that consists of people, procedures, capabilities, communication systems, and protocols to ensure that the president can make the decision to use nuclear weapons quickly in a variety of circumstances, and also with assurance that it is the president who issues the order. Simplifying a great deal, the system works as follows. The president is accompanied at all times by military aides who carry the Emergency Satchel (or "football"), which contains strike options and a system of secure communications. The order is communicated from the president to the National Military Command Center at the Pentagon, which authenticates the message and then communicates the order securely, through Strategic Command, to the entity launching the intercontinental or submarine-launched ballistic missile.

The system places a premium on authentication and speed. It is not designed to check unreasonable, irrational, or impulsive presidential commands. The existence of any such check would be antithetical to the quick and definitive decision-making that is necessary to meet the incoming attack, and that is central to credible nuclear deterrence. (It is an open question, discussed below, whether and to what extent such decision-making speed is needed in situations short of an incoming nuclear attack.)

There is, however, one potential check in the system that has risen in prominence during the Trump era: legality. Military personnel in the chain of command have a duty, on pain of court martial or termination, to comply with a *lawful* presidential order. But the military subordinate—be it a combatant commander or the captain of a nuclear-armed submarine—also has a duty not to obey an illegal order. The decision lies in the subordinate's discretion, and that decision's validity can be fully adjudicated only after the fact in a court martial. In the meantime, the president can fire a uniformed officer who fails to carry out an order that the officer believed was unlawful. And the president can keep firing people until he or she finds someone to carry out the command. The president remains in control as a legal matter. But people in the chain of command can use deliberations and objections related to legality as a basis for slowing the implementation of an exceedingly unreasonable presidential order related to nuclear weapons.[16]

There are at least four drawbacks to relying on legality as a possible basis for slowing presidential decision-making related to the use of nuclear weapons. First, subordinate deliberation about legality is antithetical to the needed speed of attack. Second, the subordinate might be wrong about illegality in a situation in which the president has good reason to order the deployment of nuclear weapons. Third, empowering or encouraging those in the chain of command to make independent legal judgments about presidential orders to use nuclear weapons could hinder the effectiveness and credibility of U.S. nuclear forces—especially since many areas of international law related to the use of nuclear weapons are unclear or contested. Fourth, not every unreasonable presidential order to use nuclear weapons would be plausibly illegal. As noted earlier, an order to fire tactical nuclear weapons at military targets in North Korea in response to a serious provocation would not obviously be illegal under legal positions that currently prevail in the executive branch.

An unstable president issuing an exceedingly unreasonable order to use nuclear weapons can be slowed in another way. There are many human beings in the loop in the chain of command between the president who gives the order to fire a nuclear weapon and the men or women who launch the weapon, and any one of them, starting with the secretary of defense or the head of Strategic Command, could simply act in an insubordinate manner, on risk of termination or court martial. In 1974, for example, President Nixon's secretary of defense, James Schlesinger, reportedly ordered the chairman of the Joint Chiefs of Staff not to execute the president's military orders without checking with him, or (in a different version) ordered military commanders to "check with either him or Secretary of State Henry Kissinger before executing" a nuclear launch order from Nixon. (The historical record on this point remains contested.)[17]

Past Presidents

Presidents prior to Trump often spoke about the dangers of nuclear weapons but rarely spoke publicly about using or threatening to use nuclear weapons.

On November 30, 1950, in the midst of the Korean War, President Harry S. Truman had the following exchange with a journalist during a press conference:

> *The President:* We will take whatever steps are necessary to meet the military situation, just as we always have.
>
> *Q:* Will that include the atomic bomb?
>
> *The President:* That includes every weapon that we have.
>
> *Q:* Mr. President, you said "every weapon that we have." Does that mean that there is active consideration of the use of the atomic bomb?
>
> *The President:* There has always been active consideration of its use. I don't want to see it used. It is a terrible weapon, and it should not be used on innocent men, women, and children who have nothing whatever to do with this military aggression. That happens when it is used.

Afterward, the White House issued a press release that stated that while "[c]onsideration of the use of any weapon is always implicit in the very possession of that weapon, ... only the President can authorize the use of the atom bomb, and no such authorization has been given."[18]

In a 1954 press conference, President Dwight D. Eisenhower spoke implicitly about using nuclear weapons:

> [T]here are weapons now in being that give more than ever to the attacker a tremendous advantage, the man who attacks by surprise. The element of surprise, always important in war, has been multiplied by the possibility of creating such widespread destruction quickly. Therefore, any president should be worse than impeached, he should be hanged, I should say, if he didn't do what all America would demand that he do to protect them in an emergency.[19]

In an effort to end the Korean War, Ike also communicated privately to the Chinese and North Korean governments in May 1953 that he was authorized and prepared to use strategic and tactical weapons. Ike and his subordinates also threatened to deploy nuclear weapons in a dispute with the People's Republic of China over Taiwan. Indeed, Secretary of State John Foster Dulles gave a speech entitled "The Strategy of Massive Retaliation" that publicized the Eisenhower administration policy that "atomic weapons would be used at the outset of a general war."[20]

President John F. Kennedy often spoke about the threat or danger of nuclear weapons, including the possibility of their use "by accident or miscalculation or by madness."[21] On October 22, 1962, at the height of the Cuban Missile Crisis, Kennedy stated to the nation:

> Nuclear weapons are so destructive and ballistic missiles are so swift, that any substantially increased possibility of their use or any sudden change in their deployment may well be regarded as a definite threat to peace …. We will not prematurely or unnecessarily risk the costs of worldwide nuclear war in which even the fruits of victory would be ashes in our mouth—but neither will we shrink from that risk at any time it must be faced …. It shall be the policy of this Nation to regard any nuclear missile launched from Cuba against any nation in the Western Hemisphere as an attack by the Soviet Union on the United States, requiring a full retaliatory response upon the Soviet Union.[22]

President Richard Nixon never publicly threatened to use nuclear weapons. He once stated in a meeting with members of Congress that "I can go in my office and pick up a telephone, and in 25 minutes, millions of people will be dead."[23] And in the summer and fall of 1969, he and National Security Adviser Henry Kissinger did self-consciously deploy a "madman" theory against the Soviet Union that implicitly relied on that possibility. They let it be known to the North Vietnamese government that they would "take measures of the greatest consequence" if the North Vietnamese did not take steps toward peace. "We'll just slip the word to them that 'For God's sake, you know Nixon is obsessed about

Communism,'" Nixon told White House Chief of Staff H. R. Haldeman, explaining the theory. "'We can't restrain him when he's angry—and he has his hand on the nuclear button.'" Nixon also ordered his secretary of defense to conduct a series of alert measures for U.S. strategic forces as part of the bluff.

None of the other presidents in the nuclear age—Johnson, Ford, Carter, Reagan, Bush, Clinton, Bush, or Obama—ever overtly threatened to use nuclear weapons, at least outside the official U.S. statement of its nuclear declaratory policy. (President George W. Bush came close when he was asked if his claim that "all options are on the table" regarding Iran implied the possibility of a nuclear strike. Bush reiterated, "All options are on the table."[24]) These presidents made general statements on the danger of the weapons, on the need for non-proliferation, and sometimes on the need for nuclear weapons reduction.

THE TRUMP ERA

Against the baseline of Obama administration practices, the Trump administration ramped up the use of drones and loosened the rules of engagement in the fight against the Islamic State. This resulted in geographic victory over that terrorist organization, though the threat clearly persists. Trump twice used force against Syria for its use of chemical weapons, but the OLC opinion in support of the second strike was basically in line with legal precedents for humanitarian intervention set by Trump's predecessors. Trump's targeted killing of Iranian Gen. Qassem Soleimani was high stakes and dangerous in the sense that it easily could have sparked a much broader conflict with Iran (though as of this writing, it has not). The killing probably did not exceed the generous precedents established by prior presidents, though Trump's failure to vet the strike fully, the high risk of the strike, and the executive branch's confused public explanation for its legality led to widespread criticism and concern. Trump continued U.S. military and intelligence support for a coalition of nations, led by Saudi Arabia, in the war in Yemen. He also tried, but had only middling success, in reducing the numbers of U.S. troops in Afghanistan, Syria, and Iraq.

The Trump administration has not developed novel legal theories on the use of conventional forces. But Trump's ad hoc decision-making process, his apparent indifference to facts, and his disrespect for senior military figures, whom he reportedly attacked as "losers" and "a bunch of dopes and babies," caused concern about the scale of unilateral presidential control over the use of military force.[25] Congress tried to push back against some of Trump's military decisions. It twice enacted legislation, vetoed by the president, to block billions of dollars in sales of arms to Saudi Arabia in connection with its war with Yemen. And after the strike against Soleimani, Congress passed a statute that required the president to seek congressional authorization before further uses of force against Iran. President Trump vetoed this law as well, on May 6, 2020.

Trump caused most concern, however, when he threatened to use nuclear weapons. Most notably, between January 2017 and July 2018, he made a number of menacing statements toward North Korean leader Kim Jong Un. During the first half of 2017, Trump issued numerous veiled or abstract threats to halt or reverse North Korea's nuclear weapons capability.[26] On August 8, 2017, Trump pledged that North Korean threats "will be met with fire and fury like the world has never seen."[27] On August 10, he said that if Kim attacks Guam, "it will be an event the likes of which nobody's seen before, what will happen in North Korea."[28] A few days earlier, Trump's national security advisor, H. R. McMaster, implied that the United States was prepared to launch a preventive strike against North Korea in the face of its nuclear threats. On September 19, Trump first referred to Kim as "Rocket Man" in an address to the U.N. General Assembly in New York City.[29] The vague threats continued throughout the fall, as did threats by North Korea to use force against the United States.

In his speech to the United Nations on September 19, Trump also stated: "The United States has great strength and patience, but if it is forced to defend itself or its allies, we will have no choice but to totally destroy North Korea." Addressing the South Korean National Assembly on November 7, he said: "The longer we wait, the greater the danger grows, and the fewer the options become."[30] And on January 2, 2018, in response to Kim's claim to have a nuclear button on his desk, Trump tweeted: "I too have a Nuclear Button, but it is a much bigger & more powerful one than his, and my Button works!"[31]

Many observers inside the United States, and presumably abroad as well, interpreted these words "to mean that the President is actively considering the use of nuclear weapons in order to deal with the threat of North Korea," as Senator Ben Cardin put it in November 2017.[32] The Trump administration's statements did little to assuage Cardin's and others' concerns: Trump's Nuclear Posture Review called for the development of "low-yield [nuclear] options,"[33] and then–Secretary of Defense James Mattis testified in response to questioning from Senator Ed Markey that "he could imagine the president ordering a first strike" nuclear attack.[34]

These statements, combined with Trump's apparent impulsiveness, his indifference to (or perhaps weak grasp of) military and legal advice, and his frequent inversion of traditional U.S. interests abroad on a number of fronts, led to several proposals in Congress to check the president's control over nuclear weapons. The proposals tended not to question the president's authority to respond to an incoming nuclear attack, where the need for reactive speed and his constitutional authority are at their height. Instead, the proposals focus on the president's ability to use nuclear weapons in a first-use context.

The most prominent bill to restrict the president's first-strike nuclear authorities came from Rep. Ted Lieu and Senator Markey. Their bill proposed to declare it "the policy of the United States that no first-use nuclear strike should be conducted absent a declaration of war by Congress."[35] It then provided that "[n]otwithstanding any other provision of law, the President may not use the Armed Forces of the United States to conduct a first-use nuclear strike unless such strike is conducted pursuant to a declaration of war by Congress that expressly authorizes such strike."

REFORM: CONVENTIONAL FORCES

Trump's tenure has sparked a renewed national debate about why the president possesses unilateral authority to deploy nuclear weapons without any express restraint. Trump has not obviously extended the bounds of presidential war powers with respect to conventional forces, though he has continued to exercise the broad unilateral powers staked out by his predecessors. But in Trump's hands, these powers have for many observers seemed more worrisome than ever. We propose reforms in both contexts, starting with nonnuclear issues.

The president has too much unchecked discretion to use military force to start new conflicts or to significantly expand extant conflicts beyond originally stated objectives or geographic limits. Such broad discretion to use military force is not necessary to protect vital national interests, and in many contexts the exercise of this discretion has harmed the national interest. One person should not have plenary power to decide for the nation when and against which countries to go to war. As we explain in this section, we believe that the president should possess the authority to use military force without congressional authorization in self-defense and related scenarios. But there is no normative justification for placing essentially unchecked offensive military power in the discretion of a single person.

There is no way to reform the president's unilateral military authority without a dramatic change in congressional responsibility and engagement to the point where veto-proof supermajorities of Congress are interested in major reform. (This is what happened in 1973 when Congress enacted the War Powers Resolution over Richard Nixon's veto.) We do not know when, if ever, that will happen. But consistent with the aims of this book, here we set out several discrete reforms, from least to most ambitious, that Congress (and in some instances the executive branch) should consider and that together we believe would help restore the constitutional balance.

Withdraw Prior Office of Legal Counsel Opinions

The executive branch should withdraw the 2001 and 2002 OLC opinions discussed earlier. These opinions take historically, and in our view excessively, broad views of the president's authority to use force in anticipatory self-defense. Neither opinion was written to authorize an actual use of force, since Congress had previously authorized the conflicts in question. Both were in a real sense dicta, and remarkably overbroad and under-analyzed dicta that in effect say that there are no legal limitations at all on even large-scale presidential uses of force. We believe that these opinions can be withdrawn without affecting the president's needed self-defensive powers. The opinions are loaded guns that should be unloaded and stored safely. They should, in short, be abrogated.

Repeal the 2002 Authorization for Use of Military Force

In 2002 Congress authorized the president "to use the Armed Forces of the United States as he determines to be necessary and appropriate in order to ... defend the national security of the United States against the continuing threat posed by Iraq."[36] The purpose of this authorization was, as the preambular language made clear, to meet the threat posed by Iraq's past aggression, international law violations, and supposed threat of weapons of mass destruction. But the language of the authorization sweeps more broadly and has been construed imaginatively in a number of circumstances as authorization to use force that was unrelated to the threat actually posed by the government of Iraq. For example, the Obama administration invoked it as one basis for using force against the Islamic State in Iraq. And the Trump administration used it in 2019 as a basis for killing Soleimani in Iraq.

These uses of force over a decade (and in one case almost two decades) after the 2002 AUMF was enacted, for reasons entirely removed from what Congress had in mind, show that it is an undisciplined authorization for any needed use of force related to Iraq. Congress should repeal the law to make clear that presidential uses of force in and related to Iraq have to be justified by either the 2001 AUMF or the president's Article II self-defense powers. This likely will not have a material impact on the president's authorities in the area, since every use of force in which the 2002 AUMF was invoked likely could have been authorized independently by some combination of the 2001 AUMF and Article II—bases of authority for which we propose reforms below. But the statute has outlived its purpose and should be repealed as part of tidying up presidential military authorities after Trump.

Repeal and Update the 2001 Authorization
for Use of Military Force

Congress must become more involved in the sprawling two-decade war that began on 9/11. There appears to be a general consensus in the executive branch (through action and interpretation) and Congress (through acquiescence and appropriation) that the president can use military force against al-Qaeda, the Taliban, the Islamic State, and associates. But Congress should repeal the 2001 AUMF and enact a new one in order to make this authorization express in accordance with the following principles:

Specify the Enemy

The 2001 AUMF was drafted before it was clear who was responsible for the 9/11 attacks, and so the enemy was described in vague terms as the "nations, organizations, or persons [the president] determines planned, authorized, committed, or aided the terrorist attacks that occurred on September 11, 2001, or harbored such organizations or persons."[37] This lack of specificity is one factor that has allowed presidents to expand the AUMF through interpretation. Congress can and should be more specific. The replacement AUMF should name the enemies (at the moment, al-Qaeda, the Taliban, and the Islamic State), including all current associated forces (such as al-Shabab) against whom Congress wishes to authorize force.

Update Associated Forces

Congress needs to provide a rigorous mechanism for updating the list of associated forces against which the president can use force. Terrorist organizational boundaries are fluid, and related forces that are not formally or obviously part of the groups against whom force is authorized can be excluded from a too-rigid definition of "associated forces." The worry, however, is that presidential administrations have interpreted the phrase "associated forces"—a phrase not found within the 2001 AUMF but that has been added through interpretive gloss—without transparency and on occasion opportunistically. The "associated forces" extension of the 2001 AUMF is easily subject to manipulation and abuse, and has been the basis for expanding a war far beyond what Congress formally authorized, and sometimes outside of public (or even congressional) knowledge.

One solution to this problem is for Congress to expressly authorize force against associated forces but to define the term and require the president to notify Congress and the public when new groups are added to the list. The definition that three presidents have used for associated forces, and that we think is appropriate, is as follows: An associated force is one that "has entered the fight alongside" and "is a co-belligerent with" al-Qaeda, the Taliban, or the Islamic State "in hostilities against the United States or its coalition partners."[38]

As for notice, we draw on an idea in the AUMF that Senators Corker, Kaine, Flake, Coons, and Nelson proposed in 2018.[39] That bill authorizes the president to identify new groups of associated forces, but it also requires him or her to notify Congress of the designation within thirty days. It then provides for an expedited review mechanism by Congress and guaranteed congressional debate on whether the designation should be repealed. To be sure, repeal would be hard for Congress to accomplish since it would need to overcome a presidential veto. One could thus argue for the opposite presumption: The president should have to return to Congress and get affirmative approval before adding any terrorist organization to the list. We think ex post notice, transparency, and debate would discipline the president's addition of associated forces and hold him or her accountable for those extensions, and we doubt that Congress would ever embrace responsibility for fine-grained approval of associated forces in the first instance. But reasonable minds can differ.

Sunset Provision

Presidents have interpreted and stretched the AUMF for two decades to meet the changing terrorist threat. Congress has failed to revisit the 2001 AUMF with regard to use-of-force issues during this period, despite these many presidential changes. In light of the irresponsibility and lack of discipline this failure reflects, we think it is vital that, when Congress finally musters the capacity to revisit the 2001 AUMF, it establishes a forcing mechanism to ensure its future engagement and review.

The forcing mechanism we propose is a two- to three-year sunset clause. A sunset clause is a provision that in advance terminates, or "sunsets," the authority in question and thus requires its affirmative renewal. A sunset in a new AUMF would commit Congress and the president to revisit the nature and scope of the war against Islamic terrorists on a regular basis. It would require the president to publicly explain and defend the nature of the conflict and the reasons why it must continue (and how). It would force Congress to exercise its constitutional and democratic responsibilities to deliberate about and vote on (or at least face) the issue. And it would prevent the situation that has prevailed for two decades: a sprawling, lengthy, morphing, long-term war without congressional involvement beyond appropriations.

A sunset clause in an authorization to use military force poses risks. The main one is that Congress will not renew the authorization, or not renew it to the president's liking, thus forcing the president to rely on his or her less-certain and politically riskier Article II authority to continue the conflict, or to narrow the conflict further than he or she would like, and perhaps end it. We believe it is unlikely that Congress will refuse to renew authority if the president makes the case forcefully that it is necessary to meet a real threat to U.S. national security. If history is any guide, political pressures tend to push Congress toward rather than away from authorizing force that a president requests. And in any event, the nation should not shy away from the possible consequences of democratic deliberation on a vital question like war.

Some critics of sunset clauses have claimed that they send a signal to the enemy of weakness or a lack of resolve. We disagree. The constitutional requirement that congressional military appropriations last no longer than two years does not signal that Congress or the nation lacks the resolve to continue a fight. All that a sunset signals, and means, is that Congress must exercise its constitutional responsibilities and reconvene to assess and update the president's authorities to use force every few years in light of new conditions.

An alternative to a sunset clause is the forcing mechanism in the Corker-Kaine bill. The senators proposed to require Congress to have a floor debate on a regular basis (every four years) about the continued validity of the AUMF but do not make continued authority under the AUMF turn on affirmative approval. This is better than the current situation because Congress would at least have to deliberate about the shape of the conflict as a body every four years. But it is far short of the type of engagement that Congress should have in an ongoing war, and so in our view it does not suffice.

Revise or Replace the War Powers Resolution

As noted earlier, the 1973 War Powers Resolution, Congress's last and indeed only effort to assert its constitutional responsibilities related to war in a general way, has been a failure. The fundamental reason for its failure is that Congress eschewed responsibility for direct oversight of presidential uses of force, and instead tried to create an acontextual, self-enforcing legal mechanism that, without discrete congressional engagement, required a president to cease using force after sixty (or, with an extension, ninety) days.

We believe that Congress must go beyond such a passive mechanism by placing affirmative limits on presidential unilateralism and by enforcing those limits with appropriations restrictions. Abstracting away from many important details, we believe that any such revision should embrace the following general principles:

Define and Limit Inherent Presidential Power

Congress should define the circumstances in which the president can use force under Article II without congressional authorization and limit his or her authority to those circumstances. Trump and other presidents may disagree, but it is important for Congress to put down a clear marker. We propose, based roughly on two bills from then-Senator Biden in the 1990s, the following authorized bases for unilateral presidential use of force, which are basically variations on the self-defense theme:

> In the absence of a declaration of war or statutory authorization for a specific use of force, the President, through powers vested by the Constitution of the United States, is authorized to use force abroad only in the following circumstances—
>
> (1) to repel an attack upon the United States or its armed forces;
> (2) to respond to a foreign military threat that severely and directly jeopardizes the vital national interests of the United States under emergency conditions that do not permit sufficient time for Congress to consider statutory authorization or a declaration of war;
> (3) to extricate citizens and nationals of the United States located abroad from situations involving a direct and imminent threat to their lives;

(4) to forestall an imminent act of international terrorism directed at citizens or nationals of the United States or to retaliate against the perpetrators of a specific act of international terrorism directed at such citizens or nationals; and

(5) to protect internationally recognized rights of innocent and free passage in the air and on the seas in circumstances where the violation, or threat of violation, of such rights poses a substantial danger to the safety of American citizens or the national security of the United States.[40]

Prohibit Humanitarian Intervention Without Congressional Authorization

Humanitarian intervention is the constitutionally least-justified basis for the president to use the U.S. military, since by definition it is not designed to assist or protect U.S. persons or property and thus is furthest away from the president's core power to use military force in self-defense. For the same reason, humanitarian intervention is also the ground on which congressional control is constitutionally most sound. Even though a morally powerful case for humanitarian intervention can be made in particular circumstances, it is a vast expansion of the president's unilateral power to deploy force, it often makes the situation on the ground worse, and it always has unforeseen consequences.

The availability of this form of unilateral presidential action also opens the door to an administration's assertion of humanitarian aims as rhetorical cover for pursuit of other objectives. Even in the most straightforward cases, this kind of intervention can begin with the most honorable intentions and end in a major and sustained military presence overseas. While humanitarian intervention is implicitly prohibited by the preceding principles, Congress should expressly rule it out. We do not oppose humanitarian intervention in all cases and do not believe the American people do either. But should the president determine such an intervention is required as an expression of American values and standing on the world stage, he or she should take such action only after making the case to Congress and receiving explicit authorization.

Consultation

In situations (1) and (3)–(5) above, where the president is authorized to use force, but not in situations where an emergency exists that does not permit sufficient time to consult Congress (such as in situation (2)), the president must inform and seek the advice of a specially identified group of members of Congress before any use of force abroad.

Reporting

Not later than forty-eight hours after commencing a use of force abroad, the president shall submit to the speaker of the House of Representatives and to the president pro tempore of the Senate a report stating (1) the objective of such use of force and (2) in the absence of a declaration of war or specific statutory authorization for such use of force, the specific sections of this law that authorize the use of force.

Sixty-Day Requirement

The president may not under any circumstances continue the use of force beyond sixty days unless one of the following three circumstances exists: (1) Congress has declared war or provided specific statutory authorization for the use of force abroad beyond such period; (2) the president has requested that Congress enact a joint resolution constituting a declaration of war or statutory authorization but such joint resolution has not been subject to a vote in each House of Congress; or (3) the president has determined and certified to the speaker of the House of Representatives and the president pro tempore of the Senate that an emergency exists that threatens the supreme national interests of the United States and requires the president to exceed such period of limitation.

Congress should be required to debate the appropriateness of time limitations on any authorizations to use military force in the face of presidential requests. And if the president certifies that an emergency exists and extends the deployment beyond the original sixty days, he or she must within this additional sixty days seek and receive congressional authorization to continue using force. The request will be subject to expedited consideration, and the use of force would be terminated if Congress then failed to authorize it. We think it unlikely that Congress would not approve force in a situation that threatens supreme national interests, and in any event, in such a context it is unclear whether the termination would be constitutional in the face of the president's core Article II self-defense powers.

Funding Restrictions

No funds made available under any provision of law may be obligated or expended for any use of force abroad inconsistent with the provisions of this act.

REFORM: NUCLEAR WEAPONS

The United States may not suffer the misfortune of another president as unstable, mercurial, and indifferent to facts and informed advice as Trump. But as noted in the introduction to this book, reforms of the presidency must take into account the serious possibility of demagogic, norm-breaking presidents as far as the eye can see. This brand of politics does not necessarily entail erratic speech and action related to the most destructive weapons on the planet. But it may involve a dangerous blend of inexperience, aggressiveness, and theatrical bravado that is far from ideal in leaders with nuclear weaponry at their command. If future presidents are much less likely than Trump to possess his aberrational attitude toward nuclear weapons, this has implications for reform because, as we explain in this section, placing checks on a president's ability to authorize the use of nuclear weapons can have adverse implications for the effectiveness of U.S. nuclear deterrence. To the extent that future presidents are likely to possess Trumpian volatility, the costs to deterrence of checking an impulsive and irrational president may be warranted by the need to prevent unjustified nuclear war.

There are three basic scenarios to consider in the context of reforming presidential authority to launch nuclear weapons.

First is the classic Cold War worry: a response to an incoming nuclear attack. This scenario may seem less likely now than during the Cold War, but it is not. Russia still possesses a huge array of nuclear weapons and often threatens to deploy them in a first-use, North Korea is pursuing the capacity to threaten the U.S. homeland with nuclear weapons, China will soon have ballistic missile submarines, and Iran is attempting to develop nuclear weapons and ballistic missile capabilities.[41] Nuclear threats clearly remain. And since they are diffused among several countries with various and changing interests, they might be more worrisome today than in the Cold War, which was characterized by bilateral and relatively stable and predictable threats.

For these reasons, it remains vital that the president be able to quickly, effectively, and unilaterally authorize the deployment of nuclear weapons in response to an incoming attack. Such unfettered authority is needed to respond to the attack itself but also, more importantly, to establish credible deterrence of any such attacks in the first place. This scenario is not one in which an unstable or irrational president is waking up the military to launch a difficult-to-understand attack in the face of no incoming threat. It is the opposite—here the military is waking up the president and asking for permission to respond to an incoming attack. In this situation both the functional need for exclusive presidential authority and the constitutional arguments for unilateral presidential power are at their height. It is thus no surprise that no one in Congress has seriously proposed to eliminate presidential authority in this context.

Scenarios two and three involve variations of first-use. The second is at the other extreme from a response to an incoming nuclear attack: The president orders a nuclear attack that is outside U.S. declaratory policy and that seems to reasonable observers to be outlandish and inappropriate. For example, Trump is well known to have an obsessive hatred of Ukraine and its government. Imagine that, in a fit of pique over some nonthreatening military operation or troop movement by Ukraine, Trump orders the use of nuclear weapons against that country. Such an order would not come (as declaratory policy requires) in "extreme circumstances" and would not address "the vital interests of the United States, its allies, and partners." The attack would also likely exceed presidential authority under even the permissive OLC opinions.

This is the scenario in which the case for reform is obviously strongest. The nation should not have to rely on the courage and systemic noncooperation of military officials to prevent or slow an entirely illegal and unjustified nuclear war. And yet a congressional prohibition on the use of force in just this circumstance is definitionally tricky. Later in this section we propose a statute that would outlaw the use of nuclear force in this and other circumstances. Note that a congressional prohibition on the use of nuclear weapons in even these extreme circumstances still depends on executive branch bureaucrats for its efficacy. If a president is unstable or irrational enough to order deployment of nuclear weapons in the imagined circumstances, he or she likely won't be dissuaded by a legal prohibition on the weapons' use. But perhaps such a prohibition would embolden actors in the chain of command to resist.

Scenario three falls in the broad spectrum of possibilities between the extremes of scenarios one and two. In this scenario, there is at least a plausible strategic or legal case for the use of nuclear weapons, and the use is not obviously ruled out by U.S. declaratory policy, but it would be controversial nonetheless. This scenario is also characterized by time for deliberation—many hours and possibly days or weeks. But these cases are also the hardest to regulate as a matter of substance. Consider two possible fact-patterns:

- There is a real threat—perhaps nuclear, perhaps conventional—that is growing but has not yet culminated in a launch or an attack. Perhaps Iran is moving masses of troops in a threatening way that portends a huge conventional attack on U.S. or allied civilians. Or perhaps the United States has unambiguous intelligence that North Korea plans to launch a nuclear attack on South Korea next week. In response, a president orders the use of nuclear weapons on the adversary's military assets to prevent the threatened attack.

- A president orders a nuclear attack on North Korea in response to one of Kim's verbal provocations but in the absence of concrete intelligence of plans for a North Korean attack on U.S. or allied vital interests. Such an order—against the background of North Korea's nuclear build-up and many threats to use nuclear weapons against the United States—could conceivably be deemed lawful under the domestic law principles articulated by OLC. It might also be deemed lawful under OLC's view of the U.N. Charter and might depend on whether the use of nuclear force was proportionate to the threat. And under *jus in bello* principles, the primary legal question under Defense Department doctrine would be whether the use of nuclear force was aimed at military targets and whether the expected harm to civilians was justified by the military advantage gained.

The first fact-pattern above presents a stronger case, legally and otherwise, for the use of nuclear weapons. But neither is obviously ruled out by U.S. nuclear declaratory policy. The United States has always declined to define the circumstances in which it would deploy nuclear weapons in a first-use against nuclear states.

Such strategic ambiguity about whether and when it would use nuclear weapons in first-use against nuclear states is thought to be central to the deterrence impact of nuclear weapons. At a 2017 hearing on the president's authority to use nuclear weapons, Senator Marco Rubio posited that "calculated ambiguity" about the use of nuclear weapons was an important element of deterrence in the face of the Warsaw Pact's conventional forces superiority, and might have deterred Saddam Hussein from using chemical and biological weapons in the First Gulf War.[42] He asked whether the concept was still relevant. Gen. Robert Kehler, the retired commander of Strategic Command, stated that calculated ambiguity remained crucial because it "enhances our deterrence to have some doubt in the mind of an adversary about under what conditions we would use a nuclear weapon." Peter Feaver, who worked on nuclear policy in the Clinton and second Bush administrations, agreed. He noted that "President Obama, who was no fan of nuclear weapons ..., nevertheless left in place calculated ambiguity in precisely these scenarios." Brian McKeon, who was chief Democratic counsel on the Senate Foreign Relations Committee for a dozen years, and a senior official in the Obama administration in several positions related to nuclear policy, concurred.

Against this background, we turn to reform possibilities. First we assess the case for no reform. One might think that any constraint on the president in this context is an unnecessary overreaction. Trump is an unusually inexperienced, impatient, and temperamentally volatile president the likes of which we may never see again. Perhaps we should not tie his successor's hands to meet a problem that may not recur, especially since doing so might weaken the U.S. strategic deterrence posture. The whole point of strategic ambiguity in the hands of the president is to achieve maximum deterrence and thereby to ensure that nuclear weapons are never used. On this view, the best check against a low-probability, deeply unreasonable action by a future president that at the same time preserves strategic ambiguity is the men and women in the chain of command who can invoke legal or other principles in resisting or delaying a seemingly irrational presidential order to use nuclear force.

Our answer to this fair challenge is that it requires only one president who is poorly equipped to assume these vast responsibilities to produce a catastrophic result. Once that president is elected, it is too late to impose reasonable restrictions. It requires the most optimistic of outlooks to imagine that all presidents in the future will have the capacity for rational deliberation and good judgment that is critical to the wise management of all elements of such an awesome responsibility. And we believe that prudent reforms to presidential control over the use of nuclear weapons can be achieved to temper the dangers of the worst-case scenarios without adversely affecting U.S. nuclear deterrence.

At least three major considerations inform possible reform, in the guise of legal limitations, on the president's first-use nuclear authority: (1) what, precisely, the limitations should be, (2) what impact such limitations would have on strategic ambiguity and nuclear deterrence, and (3) how effective such legal limitations would be.

The case for more robust reform to constrain presidents' uses of nuclear weapons can take many variations—too many to analyze comprehensively. One possibility we do not consider here is an absolute ban on first-use of nuclear weapons in any circumstances. This is a perfectly coherent position with many adherents. But at the moment, it lacks broad support in both Congress and the defense community, and it has profound implications for U.S. nuclear policy and strategic nuclear deterrence that go far beyond our present concerns.

Major reforms that pose less of a threat to traditional U.S. nuclear policy build on the fact that in every version of scenario three, there is time, and perhaps significant time, for deliberation before using nuclear weapons. In this context, the reform argument goes, the consequences to the nation and the world are too great for there not to be some form of legally required check on the president's unilateral discretion. Many reform proposals require a sign-off within the executive branch. For example, Richard Betts and Matthew Waxman propose a requirement of certification from the secretary of defense that the president's launch order is valid (that is, from the commander in chief) and from the attorney general that it is lawful.[43]

It is unclear whether this proposal is constitutional or why it would help check the president's discretion in one of the hard scenario-three cases, especially since current executive branch understandings of the law are so permissive. Nor is it clear how much this check would help in scenario-two cases involving a mad president ordering an irrational launch of nuclear weapons. The secretary of defense, without or without certification, could, under the current arrangement, slow execution of the launch order by (among other means) consulting the attorney general on whether the launch is lawful. Of course, a mad president might have a defense secretary and attorney general under his or her control, or might fire them during the deliberation period in order to find other more pliant officials.

Another potential reform, one involving a truly adversarial institution, would require the president to consult with Congress and seek and receive congressional authorization for certain presidential uses of nuclear weapons. The strongest case for this check occurs when the Constitution demands authorization for the use of nuclear weapons. Unfortunately, the circumstances in which this is so are contested. Even the pro-executive OLC opinions, however, likely would not permit unilateral presidential authorization for using nuclear weapons in a fit of pique against Ukraine, as in the earlier example. Congress could define the circumstances in which it believes the Constitution permits unilateral action and the circumstances in which it requires congressional authorization prior to a use of nuclear weapons, and in the process could calibrate the check to minimize impact on U.S. deterrence. Especially if it did so in a way that limited the requirement to non-self-defense situations, this approach might raise few constitutional questions and have little impact on deterrence.

Here is our proposal to serve all of these goals, and to bar a president from ordering nuclear attacks in the exceedingly unreasonable context of scenario two. The basic idea is for Congress to enact a statute that acknowledges the president's unilateral power to use nuclear weapons in ways that track the common ground in the Obama and Trump nuclear declaratory policies. Simplifying a great deal, the elements of such a statute would be as follows:

- Congress notes, consistent with the War Powers Resolution, that the president has the constitutional power to introduce "United

States Armed Forces into hostilities, or into situations where imminent involvement in hostilities is clearly indicated by the circumstances" pursuant to "a national emergency created by attack upon the United States, its territories or possessions, or its armed forces."[44] This would acknowledge that the president has Article II authority to respond to an incoming nuclear attack.

- Congress further notes that the president's constitutional power to defend against an attack on the United States, its territories or possessions, or its armed forces includes the power to use nuclear weapons in self-defense *in extreme circumstances to defend the vital interests of the United States or its allies*. This would acknowledge that the president's constitutional power matches current U.S. declaratory policy without specifying the degree of imminence that is needed before using these weapons. This approach aims to impose limits on the president's use of nuclear weapons with minimal damage to U.S. strategic ambiguity and deterrence. The self-defense standard here is open ended and for some would be controversial, but it is the current U.S. posture to which Congress has acquiesced to date.

- Congress specifies that only it can declare or authorize war in the constitutional sense and specifies further that use of nuclear weapons beyond a response to an incoming nuclear attack or in self-defense in extreme circumstances to defend the vital interests of the United States or its allies would constitute an act of war in the constitutional sense. In short, any use of nuclear weapons beyond the elements of U.S. nuclear declaratory policy common to Obama and Trump would be unlawful absent congressional authorization.

- Congress could impose a consultation requirement. It could, for example, declare it the policy of the United States that whenever the executive branch receives intelligence indicating extreme circumstances demanding the use of nuclear weapons in defense of the vital interests of the United States or its allies, it must consult with identified senior congressional leadership before authorizing the use of such weapons.

Even such a statute that aims to limit the uses of nuclear force to current declaratory policy might have an adverse impact on U.S. deterrence by slowing the circumstances under which the president can order a launch. On the plus side, this statute embeds U.S. declaratory policy in statutory form with congressional buy-in and authority, and it makes it clearly unlawful to use force outside that policy.

Of course, Congress can if it wishes try to limit presidential authority beyond current declaratory policy. It could, for example, limit presidential uses of nuclear forces to responses to actual or imminent attacks, and could define imminence to make the notion tighter than current executive branch understandings. Such an approach would raise harder constitutional questions about Congress's power and would involve a much greater disruption to U.S. nuclear deterrence.

Finally, we suggest that Congress make clear that Section 6 of the Atomic Energy Act is *not* a blanket authorization to use nuclear weapons as the president sees fit. This will tamp down a tad on possibly unwarranted overconfidence in the executive branch's legal authority to use nuclear weapons outside of self-defense scenarios.

VACANCIES REFORM

One of Donald Trump's signature governmental initiatives has been to circumvent, or ignore, the Senate confirmation process for top executive branch appointments. Trump's most consequential gambit has been to terminate or force out confirmed officials at the senior levels of Cabinet departments and agencies and then either replace them with unconfirmed "acting" officials or delegate their powers to other officials. This conduct had precursors in prior administrations, but Trump took it to new extremes. Trump's manipulation of the vacancies system skirts the check of the constitutional appointments process and denigrates the values underlying that process, which include ensuring competence and quality control, public vetting of appointees' views, securing public commitments by appointees, and the legitimation of Article I confirmation. These problems and concerns can be fixed through statutory reforms.

BACKGROUND

The Constitution addresses appointments of executive officials primarily in two provisions. The Appointments Clause specifies that certain executive branch officials, "Officers of the United States," must be appointed by the president and confirmed by the Senate, while "inferior Officers" can be appointed by many bodies, depending on what Congress prescribes.[1] And the Recess Appointments Clause provides that the president "shall have Power to fill up all Vacancies that may happen during the Recess of the Senate, by granting Commissions which shall expire at the End of their next Session."[2]

From the beginning, presidents faced a problem when they needed to fill a vacant office temporarily but the president and Senate could not agree quickly on a replacement and a recess appointment was not possible because the Senate was in session. Congress addressed this issue in 1792 when it authorized the president to designate "any person" to act as an officer at the departments of State, Treasury, and War until a permanent replacement could fill the job.[3] Congress shortly thereafter placed a six-month limit on acting officials.[4] The next big innovation came in the Vacancies Act of 1868, which expanded the number of offices the president could fill with acting officials, while restricting who could serve as an acting official, and for how long.[5]

As the federal executive branch (and thus the number of federal officers) expanded enormously over the course of the twentieth century, the challenge of dealing with the growing number of temporary vacancies became more acute. This was especially true after Watergate, when the Senate began to demand more detailed background inquiries into nominees' professional and personal histories and the length of the confirmation process expanded accordingly. The modern confirmation process also allowed Congress, and especially the party in opposition, to deliver "political payback ... as partisans look to settle scores from early confirmation defeats," to cause the nominee to pay "for the prior political sins of unpopular presidents," or in some other way to "send a message to the president."[6] The Senate's power was enhanced further by the fact that any senator could place a hold on a nomination, a weapon used regularly in executive-legislative power struggles unrelated to the merits of the affected nomination.

This more difficult confirmation process led to more vacancies in important executive branch positions. Governance problems arose because the number of executive officials who required Senate confirmation grew steadily. To take one benchmark, President John F. Kennedy had to fill 196 Senate-confirmed positions at the secretary, deputy secretary, under secretary, assistant secretary, and deputy assistant secretary levels. Almost four decades later, President Bill Clinton, in his second term, had to make more than 1,000 such nominations.[7] Today that number is around 1,200.[8]

Presidents responded to these challenges in part by increasingly use so-called "czars"—individuals appointed to a White House position, without any Senate confirmation, who wield authority in various policy areas in ways often indistinguishable from that of a Cabinet secretary. They also sought to evade congressional restrictions on temporary "acting" officials for vacant offices. For example, the executive branch maintained that a department head could ignore the strictures of the then-extant vacancies law and appoint acting officials for Senate-confirmed slots for an indefinite period when (as was typically the case) a department's "organic act vests the powers and functions of the department in its head and authorizes that officer to delegate such powers and functions to subordinate officials."[9]

Through the use of this "delegation strategy" and through exploitation of other loopholes in the vacancies law in force at the time, the executive branch got in the habit of skipping the Senate confirmation process for many sub-secretary appointments. By 1998, around 20 percent of all Senate-confirmed positions across fourteen departments were held by acting officials, most of whom were serving beyond the 120-day limit authorized by the then-governing statute.[10] The Senate grew especially furious about this circumvention of its constitutional prerogatives when Bill Lann Lee served as acting assistant attorney general for civil rights for more than two years beginning in late 1997 even though the Senate had rejected his nomination for that very position.[11]

To redress presidential manipulation of the vacancies process, Congress in 1998 enacted the Federal Vacancies Reform Act, or FVRA.[12] The FVRA establishes rules for presidents to appoint temporary acting officials to positions for which Senate advice and consent is otherwise needed. By its terms the FVRA sometimes operates in conjunction with statutes that provide agency-specific rules for the appointment of acting officials.

The FVRA applies when an officer whose appointment requires advice and consent "dies, resigns, or is otherwise unable to perform the functions and duties of the office."[13] When this happens, the first assistant to the vacated office automatically assumes the role on an acting basis, unless the president selects either a Senate-confirmed officer elsewhere in the administration or a senior employee (defined by reference to the employee's pay grade and time in the department) within the same agency.

All the acting appointments under the FVRA are subject to time limitations. The basic limit is 210 days, but the clock stops running if the president has submitted a nomination still pending before the Senate. If the Senate rejects or returns the president's nomination, or the nomination is withdrawn, the time period is reset at 210 days and begins to run again. A second nomination also tolls the 210-day period of permitted acting service. If the second nomination also fails, then one more and final 210-day period begins to run. As Anne O'Connell has noted, this scheme in theory permits an acting official to serve for more than two and a half years.[14]

The FVRA prohibits the president from nominating someone for an advice-and-consent office who is filling the office on an acting basis. In other words, one may be either the acting official or the nominee to the post, but not both. The FVRA provides one exception to this restriction: The president may nominate a first assistant whose position required Senate confirmation and who had served in that role for ninety days or more. Another provision reflects the same focus on protecting the Senate's advice-and-consent role. It allows the president to direct an official whose confirmed term had already expired to continue to serve on an acting basis if nominated again to the same post. The statute also provides that any actions taken by a person who has not assumed interim authority as prescribed by the statute "shall have no force or effect." It also created for agencies a duty to report vacancies, the appointment of acting officials, and nominations to fill vacant posts to the Government Accountability Office.

The FVRA did not end heavy presidential reliance on nonconfirmed officials in offices that require Senate confirmation. It gives the president pretty broad discretion, with fairly long time periods, to appoint acting officials for vacant Senate-confirmable slots. And presidents have used this authority as they saw fit. The need to do so grew after the Supreme Court's decision in *NLRB v. Noel Canning*[15] and the Senate practice of conducting pro forma sessions practically killed the possibility of recess appointments.

Another reason the FVRA was not a high hurdle to heavy reliance on nonconfirmed officials is that the executive branch read the FVRA to permit it to "continue[] to invoke the delegation strategy, effectively creating a cadre of shadow acting officials ... [by] delegat[ing] power to people who would be ineligible to 'act' under the FVRA's qualifications requirements, time limitations, or both."[16] On this view, the department or agency basically has discretion to delegate all powers not assigned by law *exclusively* to the vacant office—which in most cases are most if not all powers of that office.

The two administrations before Trump's used this strategy despite the FVRA. The Bush administration's deputy head of the Office of Legal Counsel (OLC), Steven Bradbury, was nominated at least four times to the top post at OLC but the Democratic-controlled Senate never confirmed him. Yet he continued to lead the office and sign OLC opinions through delegated power and other maneuvers.[17] Similarly, the Obama administration never nominated anyone to replace the director of the Bureau of Alcohol, Tobacco, Firearms, and Explosives (ATF) when he stepped down in April 2015. It instead gave the job to the nonconfirmed career deputy under the FVRA. When the 210-day clock ran out, the deputy continued to serve in the same role, without the "acting" title, through delegated authority. *Politico* reported that the administration did this "to avoid a nasty confirmation hearing" before the Republican-controlled Senate for an agency that had been "troubled" by the "Fast and Furious" scandal—a controversial ATF program that used illegal guns to track the sellers and purchasers.[18]

An analysis of the Obama administration at the dawn of its eighth year found that "dozens of crucial [Cabinet agency jobs] ... are either totally empty or run by an acting deputy," and that "[m]ore than a quarter of the administration's most senior jobs, more than 100 overall, are missing permanent occupants."[19] The George W. Bush administration also used acting officials extensively. A report near the end of Bush's sixth year in office found that three Cabinet secretary positions (including the attorney general) were occupied by acting officials, and that the second and third positions at the Justice Department, as well as more than 25 percent of U.S. attorney positions, were filled with acting appointees.[20] More broadly, "the vacancy rate for senior jobs" in the Bush administration was reportedly "far higher at the end of the Bush administration than it was at the same point in the terms of Mr. Bush's recent predecessors."[21]

In short, despite the FVRA, presidents before Trump relied heavily on non-Senate-confirmed officials in offices that require Senate confirmation. A factor contributing to this practice was surely the Senate's more aggressive use of procedural mechanisms—holds, filibusters, and the like—to stall or block the confirmation of presidential nominees. As one analysis noted, "George W. Bush faced the most procedural hurdles and filibusters to his nominees until Barack Obama was elected and faced historic blockades."[22] Bush faced thirty-nine filibusters on nominees over eight years, and Obama faced 175 over the same number of years.

THE TRUMP ERA

"I like acting," President Trump once declared. "It gives me more flexibility."[23] Unsurprisingly, Trump has surpassed his predecessors in running an "acting" government. The data suggest that Trump has had much greater turnover in top positions, and exploits vacant offices with temporary officials more frequently, than his predecessors. Once again, a contributing factor to this pattern was the Senate, which by June 2020 had conducted an unprecedented 314 filibusters of Trump's nominations. But the Trump administration's vacancies practice was much more than a response to these filibusters. The administration often used the gaps and loopholes in vacancies law—in combination with firings, forced resignations, unusually high turnover rates, and failures to nominate candidates for vacant positions—to gain flexibility and control over the executive branch.

As of April 2019, just over two years into Trump's term in office, fifteen people who had served in his Cabinet had left the administration. The comparative numbers for Presidents Obama and George W. Bush for their two terms were seven and four, respectively.[24] For only about four months of Trump's first two and a half years in office did he have a fully confirmed Cabinet in place.[25] One study found that from the Carter through Obama administrations, three in ten Cabinet members whose positions were subject to confirmation served on an acting basis. In Trump's executive branch, those numbers have risen to a little more than half: twenty-two of forty-two.[26] As of January 2020, Trump had thirty acting Cabinet secretaries during his three years in office. By comparison, President Clinton had twenty-seven across his eight years, President Bush had twenty-two across eight years, and President Obama had twenty-three across eight years.[27] Trump's acting officials serve in office much longer, on average, than those of his predecessors.

The evidence also suggests that Trump has used acting officials below the secretary level, and in sub-Cabinet agencies, more than his predecessors.[28]

A deeper dive into some of Trump's more prominent uses of the FVRA shows how he has exploited the vacancies system to his advantage. In late 2017, Trump installed Mick Mulvaney, the Senate-confirmed director of the Office of Management and Budget (OMB), as acting head of the Consumer Financial Protection Bureau (CFPB), an agency Trump despises. The CFPB's organic statute stated that the deputy director, then Leandra English, "shall … serve as acting Director" when the director is absent or unavailable.[29] English sued for her job. The Trump administration argued that the FVRA's authorization of the president to appoint a Senate-confirmed officer controlled, a federal district court agreed, and English eventually dropped the lawsuit.

Something similar happened in early 2018, when Trump fired Secretary of Veterans Affairs David Shulkin and replaced him with Robert Wilkie, who had been confirmed as undersecretary of defense for personnel and readiness. Several veterans' groups filed suit. Their argument—one that became an important point of contestation under the FVRA during the Trump administration—was that a vacancy created by presidential firing did not implicate the FVRA because a fired official is not someone who "dies, resigns, or is otherwise unable to perform the functions and duties of the office." When Trump nominated Wilkie for the permanent role (and appointed a new acting secretary in the interim), the groups withdrew the suit.

When Trump pushed out Secretary of Defense James Mattis, Deputy Secretary of Defense Patrick Shanahan became acting secretary under both the Defense Department succession statute and the FVRA.[30] After Shanahan served six months as acting secretary, Trump appointed Army Secretary Mark Esper to the acting position but then quickly nominated Esper for the permanent post. Because the statute would not allow Esper to continue in an acting role while his nomination was pending, Trump was required to appoint a third acting defense secretary.

In early 2020, when conflict between the United States and Iran over nuclear arms control and clashing regional interests intensified, the Trump administration had no confirmed official in these relevant positions: director of national intelligence, deputy director of national intelligence, commissioner of U.S. Customs and Border Protection, under secretary of state for arms control, assistant secretary of state for Europe, secretary of the Navy, or director of Immigration and Customs Enforcement.[31] The year before, in early 2019, the Department of Homeland Security, the Department of the Interior, the Environmental Protection Agency, and the Social Security Administration were also headed by acting officials.[32] Throughout its term the administration was full of similar vacancies at lower levels. Some of these vacancies resulted from Senate recalcitrance (especially the filibuster), and some from the administration simply not nominating anyone.

One of Trump's most high-profile vacancy moves was his replacement of fired Attorney General Jeff Sessions with Sessions's unconfirmed chief of staff, Matthew Whitaker. Deputy Attorney General Rod Rosenstein became the acting attorney general after Sessions was fired under a statute on Justice Department governance that specified succession at the senior levels. But OLC concluded that this statute did not supplant the president's discretion under the FVRA, which Trump used to appoint Whitaker as acting attorney general.[33] The appointment allowed Trump to put the department under the control of an unconfirmed officer to whom senior confirmed officials, including the deputy and associate attorneys general, would report. This raised concerns that Trump would use his leverage over Whitaker, and Whitaker's authority over Rosenstein (who under department rules still supervised Special Counsel Robert Mueller) to limit, if not end, Mueller's Russia investigation. This fear proved unfounded, but many people, including several Republicans, believed that the Mueller investigation is what motivated the move. Several lawsuits challenged the validity of the Whitaker appointment, but they all failed.

Trump also sought to enhance his grip on border and immigration issues through the vacancies process. Trump forced Secretary of Homeland Security Kirstjen Nielsen, who disappointed him, to resign. He then appointed as acting secretary the Senate-confirmed commissioner for Customs and Border Protection, Kevin McAleenan, who satisfied the criteria for actings under the FVRA. This appointment initially didn't work because Congress, in a Homeland-Security-specific statute that expressly trumped the FVRA, designated the under secretary of management at the time, Claire Grady, to serve as acting secretary when the secretary and deputy secretary positions are vacant. Trump solved his problem by having Nielsen withdraw her resignation and then demanding that Grady resign. When she did so, Nielsen resigned once more, and the statute no longer applied (since the under secretary of management slot was vacant). Under the FVRA, the president then successfully made McAleenan the acting department secretary.

In another maneuver to install the acting of his choice, the president in May 2019 asked for and received the resignation of the head of the U.S. Citizenship and Immigration Services (USCIS), Lee Cissna. Trump wanted to replace Cissna on an acting basis with former Virginia Attorney General Ken Cuccinelli. But Cuccinelli was not serving in the administration and thus did not even nominally qualify for acting appointment under the FVRA. To overcome this hurdle, the agency created a "principal deputy position" and the president hired Cuccinelli for that position. With that step, Cuccinelli became the "first assistant" and then, under the FVRA, the acting director of USCIS.[34] However, a federal court later ruled that Cuccinelli's appointment was unlawful, and the court thus invalidated several directives he had issued while in office.[35] Judge Randolph Moss held that Cuccinelli's office never was second in command to the director, since it was created after the vacancy arose and would cease to exist once the vacancy was filled. As a result, the agency had created a deputy position for Cuccinelli to fill that was "second in command in name only" and thus unlawful under the FVRA.

Most recently, Trump has fired several agency inspectors general and used his FVRA authority to appoint acting inspectors general more to his liking. The slew of inspector general removals began on April 3, 2020, when Trump removed Intelligence Community Inspector General Michael Atkinson. Under a separate statute, presidents must give Congress thirty days' notice before firing an inspector general.[36] So Trump fired Atkinson, effective in thirty days, and placed him on administrative leave in the interim. As soon as Trump placed Atkinson on administrative leave, he appointed an acting replacement. Over the next month and a half, Trump removed three acting inspectors general (at the Department of Defense, the Department of Health and Human Services, and the Department of Transportation). These removals illustrated the added flexibility that attaches with acting officials, since, unlike Atkinson's firing, Trump did not need to provide Congress with advance notice before removing an acting. And then on May 15, Trump fired State Department Inspector General Steve Linick. As with Atkinson, Trump apparently placed Linick on leave in the intervening thirty days and appointed an acting replacement.

Trump also relied heavily on the delegation strategy to fill vacant offices that require Senate confirmation. To take one of many examples, between January 2017 and May 2020, the secretary of the interior frequently delegated to other individuals the powers of "vacant non-career Presidentially appointed and Senate-confirmed positions for which there is no Principal Deputy that would automatically become acting[.]"[37] The May 2020 version of the order doing so delegated "[a]ll functions, duties, and responsibilities" of five vacant offices requiring Senate confirmation to various nonconfirmed officials.[38] An analysis of Trump administration vacancies in April 2019 suggested that almost twice as many vacant offices were being carried out by officials exercising delegated authority as by acting officials under the FVRA.[39]

To give a different view of the Trump administration and vacancies, consider an analysis by the *Washington Post* and the Partnership for Public Service, which together have followed 755 key executive branch positions that require Senate confirmation.[40] On July 13, 2020, a month before this book went to press, only 513 (68 percent) of these slots were filled. Almost a third were vacant, and 19 percent didn't even have a nominee. The Department of Homeland Security had only 35 percent of its officials confirmed, and no one had been nominated for any of the vacancies, including the offices of secretary (empty since April 24, 2019), deputy secretary (empty since April 15, 2018), and general counsel (empty since September 17, 2019). The Justice Department was operating at 45 percent of its Senate-confirmed capacity, and the Defense Department at two-thirds capacity.

This necessarily selective overview reveals several characteristics of the Trump administration's uses and abuses of vacancies law and processes. First, the Trump administration more than its predecessors relies on acting officials to fill vacant executive branch positions requiring Senate consent. It has done so by exploiting the FVRA and aggressively using the delegation strategy. Second, Trump, more than his predecessors, uses the president's power to terminate or push out officials (or to not nominate them), in combination with the FVRA and other mechanisms, to skirt the confirmation process and ensure greater control over agencies. The Whitaker example shows that the president could have used such control to ensure that confirmed officials supervising a supposedly independent investigation of the president were under the supervision of a nonconfirmed presidential appointee. And other times, as in the case of the CFPB and the inspectors general maneuverings, the president used firings plus FVRA authorities to enhance his power over ostensibly independent entities.

REFORM

The executive branch vacancies problem is too complex to address here comprehensively.[41] We focus mainly on the upper echelon of Senate-confirmed executive branch offices and outline the central tenets that we believe any reform should include. Our reforms aim to restore the balance between the Senate's constitutional prerogative to vet officers of the United States with the president's need for flexibility in keeping the government running during periods of office vacancy. Right now the executive branch has too much discretion to create and fill vacancies in a way that skirts the Senate's check and other public official account-ability mechanisms. But there is always a danger of going too far and allowing a recalcitrant Senate—especially one controlled by a party that opposes the president—to block effective governance through its refusal to confirm nominees. We propose significant reforms of the law of vacancies and also that Congress require Senate confirmation for far fewer executive branch officials.

Before turning to reforms, we explain why Congress has broad author-ity to regulate the president's options for choosing acting appointments. At first glance it might seem like this is a presidential prerogative under the Appointments Clause. But the Appointments Clause is not the source of the president's power to appoint acting officials for temporary vacancies. The Take Care Clause is. And the presidential power to appoint under this clause operates only until Congress specifies a different method, as it has done in the FVRA. As a 1995 OLC opinion explained, the FVRA "constitutes a restriction on the President's authority, as opposed to a source of power. If it applies to a given position, the [FVRA] constitutes the sole means by which a temporary appointment to that position may be made."[42] OLC opinions in administrations of both parties have confirmed this view.[43]

These opinions suggest that there are few if any structural constitutional constraints on Congress's power to guide the president's choices for acting officials. Congress has a long history of providing specific and narrow criteria that presidents must follow in filling vacancies. And it sometimes specifies the official who shall operate as acting when there is a vacancy, leaving the president no discretion.[44] There is a question about whether and for how long it would be consistent with the Appointments Clause for a president to fill a principal office with a non-Senate-confirmed person (such as a Senior Executive Service or GS-15 employee), as happened with the Whitaker appointment. OLC has ruled, in reliance on *United States v. Eaton*, that the Appointments Clause does not bar such arrangements as long as they are "special and temporary."[45] Every lower court that considered Appointments Clause challenges to Whitaker's three-month tenure rejected them.

In sum, Congress has a lot of constitutional room to constrain the president's options for acting replacements for vacant executive branch offices.

Limit the President's Options for Actings Under the FVRA

The FVRA is too promiscuous in giving the president unstructured discretion to fill almost all vacancies of Senate-confirmed offices with *either* the first assistant to the office (who might or might not be Senate confirmed) *or* a Senate-confirmed official elsewhere in the government *or* a non-Senate-confirmed GS-15 or higher in the same agency who has served for more than ninety days. We consider reform of this problem in two steps: vacancies for Cabinet secretaries or agency chiefs who are not part of a Cabinet office (such as the Environmental Protection Agency), and vacancies for positions below those levels.

There is no good reason for a president to have the unstructured discretion conferred by the FVRA to fill vacant Cabinet offices or the offices of agency heads. This discretion is one reason Trump was able to bypass the many Senate-confirmed officers in the Justice Department and appoint the underqualified and underscrutinized Whitaker as acting attorney general. The FVRA should be amended to make clear that in appointing an acting official for a Cabinet secretary or an agency head, the president *must* choose the first assistant, and if the first assistant is absent, then the president *must* choose among Senate-confirmed officials within the department or agency. In other words, the department or agency should be run by a confirmed official from within if at all possible. (The Whitaker appointment, for example, would not be possible under this reform.)

Congress should also structure the FVRA so that, after these options have been exhausted, the president must replace a department secretary or an agency head with a Senate-confirmed official in another agency. With one exception, we do not favor allowing a nonconfirmed official to act as the head of a department or an agency. The exception is that a nonconfirmed official should be able to run the department or agency for the first four months of a president's term, or longer if no other official has been confirmed for that position at the outset of an administration.

Congress should give the president more flexibility for filling lower-level vacancies for Senate-confirmed offices. Commentators have offered many possibilities here. We believe that *in combination with other reforms suggested below*—shortening time frames for actings, limitations on who can be the "first assistant," limitations on delegations, and special rules for independent agency offices—the basic FVRA options (first assistant, Senate-confirmed official, or GS-15 or higher in office) suffice. It is vital that these other reforms be adopted if the FVRA system below the top spot is to be maintained.

We propose different and narrower limitations on the president's options to appoint acting inspectors general. Trump has shown how the FVRA as currently enacted permits a president to gut the quasi-independence of these important offices that Congress sought to protect. He simply fired or pushed out the inspector general, who lacks for-cause protection, and then replaced him or her with someone more congenial from among the wide array of options provided by the FVRA. To address this problem, and to reduce presidential incentives for gamesmanship, we propose that a vacant office of the inspector general can be replaced only by a Senate-confirmed inspector general from another agency, or a GS-15 official or higher official within the office who has been there for more than three years. This will ensure that only a Senate-vetted inspector general or someone with deep experience in the office will run the office on a temporary basis.

Congress could do something similar for agencies to which it wants to give at least quasi-independent status. If there is no confirmed analogue in another agency, Congress could insist that the temporary replacement be limited to a long-term official in the agency pending nomination and confirmation of a replacement.

Shorten Time Limits on Acting Officials

The FVRA's allowed time for acting service is too long. As noted earlier, an acting can serve for several 210-day time periods depending on the pattern of nominations and Senate rejections. Congress should shorten the time limit, but how to do so is a matter of much debate. The precise time limit matters much less if our other reforms are adopted than it does under the FVRA at the moment. But in any event, we believe an acting should be able to serve 120 days in office, with one renewal for a failed nomination, and then no more after that. This proposal is something of a compromise among various reforms offered by expert commentators.

Clarify "First Assistants"

The Cuccinelli example reveals an important potential loophole in the FVRA. The statute gives the president the authority to fill a vacancy with a "first assistant." But it does not define "first assistant" and does not specify whether that first assistant for purposes of the FVRA must be in place at the time of the vacancy. If the first assistant need not be in place at the time of the vacancy, then the president has extraordinary discretion under the FVRA to put in basically whomever he or she wants from inside or outside government to fill a vacant Senate-confirmed office. Judge Moss invalidated Cuccinelli's orders on the ground that his first assistant role was illegitimate because it was temporary, but he did not rule on whether the FVRA permits first assistants to be named after the vacancy opens.

To avoid this problem, Congress should specify that a first assistant within the meaning of the FVRA must be named and in place before the vacancy arises. We agree with O'Connell that this rule should have two exceptions: "The President should be permitted to name a first assistant after the vacancy arises (1) if the vacancy occurs during the first six months of a new administration, and (2) if the first assistant at the time of the vacancy dies (or falls ill) while serving."[46]

Limit Delegations of Power

As noted earlier, the Trump administration appears to be relying on delegated authority even more than actings under the FVRA to fill vacant Senate-confirmed offices. This is an important piece of the vacancies puzzle. But it is hard to address in a simple, general way. Practically every one of the 1,200 or so relevant federal offices has different nonexclusive powers that operate (and can be delegated) in different, context-dependent ways. The government needs to keep running in the face of vacancies, and the FVRA cannot address every vacancies concern that might arise. Eliminating delegated powers would, given the constraints of the FVRA, mean that in some instances basic government functions could not be performed.

One option would be to limit delegations to those in place when the vacancy arises. But this solution might create perverse incentives to over-delegate in the first place, and it would also mean that some functions of government could not be carried out when time limits on actings expired. Another option, but one that requires agency-by-agency statutory amendments that Congress might not have the capacity to execute, would be to increase the number of exclusive functions for an office or impose a limitation on the offices to which tasks can be delegated. At a minimum, Congress should address the executive branch's use of delegated power as a direct affront to the Senate confirmation process. Thus, Congress should specify that someone who has been nominated but not confirmed for a position (like Bradbury at OLC, in the earlier example) cannot thereafter exercise the delegated powers of the office for which he or she was not confirmed. Congress could also prohibit delegations of function for an office for which the president has not nominated someone within a specified time period—say, 120 days.[47]

Enforce the FVRA

Enforcement of the FVRA is lacking in two ways and should be improved. First, agency action that results in violations of the FVRA has "no force or effect." But the only way to enforce this remedy at the moment is for someone to sue. This approach has been successful on a few occasions, but these lawsuits are expensive and standing is a hurdle, especially after a nominee is confirmed. Congress could rectify this problem by expressly conferring a cause of action on anyone adversely affected by an agency action issued by an officer in violation of the FVRA. That would expand the pool of possible plaintiffs and discipline aggressive readings of the FVRA. Congress could also have the Government Accountability Office examine and regularly report on alleged FVRA violations. Second, agencies persistently underreport their vacancies, acting officials, and nominations, as required by the FVRA. Congress should impose stricter, more informative, and quicker notice requirements on agencies and departments, and tie their funding to satisfaction of these requirements.

Specific Applications of the FVRA

The FVRA is ambiguous about how it relates to agency-specific succession statutes. It claims to be the exclusive means for temporarily authorizing an acting official for a Senate-confirmed office unless "a statutory provision expressly" provides another arrangement.[48] OLC has interpreted the FVRA in many cases to be an independent basis for the president to appoint acting officials even when an agency-specific statute provides otherwise. Thus, for example, the Justice Department succession statute provides that the deputy attorney general, and then a series of other Senate-appointed Justice Department officials, "may exercise all of the duties" of the Office of the Attorney General. But OLC interpreted the FVRA as an alternative to this department-specific scheme to allow Whitaker rather than the confirmed Rosenstein to run the Justice Department. Similarly, the president appointed Mulvaney to run the CFPB pursuant to the FVRA and disregarded the agency-specific succession rules—an interpretation upheld by a federal court.

Many aspects of the problem with this ambiguity are resolved by our proposed FVRA amendment to require in every instance a

Senate-confirmed official to act as head of the department or agency. But to clean up this corner of the FVRA, Congress should make clear that agency-specific succession statutes take precedence over the FVRA, as it has done with the Homeland Security statute. Or it could amend the FVRA to list all agency-specific succession statutes that should be given priority over the FVRA. Either way, the FVRA should operate as a backup when the agency-specific statute results in no one being able to serve.

There is also a question of whether the FVRA applies when the president fires someone. Some observers have contended that a terminated official is not one who, under the FVRA's triggering criteria, "dies, resigns, or is otherwise unable to perform the functions and duties of the office."[49] The FVRA is ambiguous on this question. The policy argument for not allowing the FVRA to apply after a termination is that, as currently worded, it gives the president too powerful an incentive to terminate Senate-confirmed officials and exploit the various options allowed by the FVRA and delegation. We believe our reforms, if adopted, adequately temper those incentives by removing the worst avenues of presidential manipulation. We thus propose that, in conjunction with the other reforms, Congress eliminate this ambiguity in the FVRA's scope by making clear that it applies even for vacancies created by presidential termination.

Reduce the Number of Senate-Confirmed Positions

The preceding reforms will, we believe, constrain the president's options to fill vacancies pending confirmation of a replacement without unduly restricting the president's ability to run the government. Right now, as noted, around 1,200 executive positions require Senate confirmation. As also noted, the Senate during the past three administrations has grown more and more aggressive in using procedural mechanisms—holds, filibusters, and the like—to not confirm presidential nominees.

The combination of a huge number of officials who require confirmation, plus a more aggressive use of techniques by minority members of the Senate to block nominees, is one major impetus for presidents to use the tactics described in this chapter to fill vacancies. The incentives for the minority party to use these techniques are overwhelming and growing, since they can delay a nominee significantly and eat up valuable

Senate floor time that could be used on, for example, judicial confirmations (which no longer face these procedural mechanisms to the same degree). This problem can be expected to continue to grow in the future.

It is vital that Congress do something about this problem as part of any comprehensive reform of vacancies law. We do not expect the Senate to give up its filibuster and nominee-hold prerogatives any time soon. But Congress can and should significantly reduce the number of executive branch positions that require confirmation. Hundreds of Senate-confirmed offices are midlevel positions that receive little close scrutiny in any event. In exchange for significant vacancies reform, which will require presidential buy-in to avoid a veto, Congress should eliminate the requirement of Senate consent for hundreds of these midlevel slots.

OTHER REFORMS

In this final chapter, we examine two additional reforms that implicate the relationship between Congress and the president: a narrowing of congressional delegations of emergency powers, with special attention to the Insurrection Act; and an expedited process for the enforcement of congressional subpoenas.

THE INSURRECTION ACT: BACKGROUND

In a "tradition, born in England and developed in the early years of our nation," Americans have expected that the military will not be involved in domestic law enforcement.[1] The Constitution guarantees the states federal protection against "Invasion" and against outbreaks of "domestic Violence" upon "Application of the Legislature, or the Executive (when the Legislature cannot be convened)."[2] The Posse Comitatus Act bars the deployment of the U.S. Armed Forces "to execute the laws" except "in cases and under circumstances expressly authorized by the Constitution or Act of Congress."[3]

The Insurrection Act, enacted in 1807, is the core statutory authorization that defines those "cases" and "circumstances." In brief, the law authorizes the president to order the armed forces and militia into action where states call upon federal assistance in quelling an "insurrection," where unlawful activity or "rebellion" impedes the enforcement of federal law through "the ordinary course of judicial proceedings"; and where an outbreak of "domestic violence" infringes on the constitutional rights of citizens and the state's authorities are "unable, fail, or refuse" to protect those rights.[4]

The act has been "plagued by both broad and undefined terms throughout its two-hundred year history."[5] Even on a strict reading of its provisions, however, it is an extraordinarily broad delegation of power to the president. In more than 200 years, presidents have invoked the law to deploy the U.S. military and the National Guard, sometimes at the request of states and sometimes without such a request. The Supreme Court in *Sterling v. Constantin* suggested that the president should exercise this statute in "good faith, in the face of the emergency and directly related to the quelling of the disorder or the prevention of its continuance."[6] *Sterling* suggested further that the court would give the president some deference on this question. But the court has never resolved other questions about the Insurrection Act, including whether allegations of executive abuse of authority are political questions or justiciable, and, if justiciable, who has standing to bring such claims.

Congress has never interceded to block a president from ordering troops into service pursuant to this statute. Presidents have invoked the act to quell outbreaks of domestic violence, as President George H.W. Bush did in responding to the rioting that broke out in Los Angeles after the acquittal of police officers charged in the beating of Rodney King. President Eisenhower exercised this authority to enforce court-ordered desegregation of public schools in Arkansas, and President Kennedy did the same in Alabama and Mississippi.

However, on one recent occasion, Congress exhibited keen concern that presidents not be given license to overread the Insurrection Act. In the wake of the devastation in New Orleans caused by Hurricane Katrina, President George W. Bush encountered resistance from Louisiana Governor Kathleen Blanco to his offer to send troops and the National Guard to help restore order in a city in which basic public services had collapsed. The Bush administration then dawdled over whether it had the authority to send in troops without Blanco's request or consent. The Justice Department eventually concluded that the Insurrection Act was available for this purpose, but in the end the Bush administration used different authorities and sent to Louisiana the "largest domestic deployment of troops since the Civil War," but only for a defined humanitarian relief role, not a law enforcement role.[7]

In light of the fallout and confusion surrounding Bush's authority under the Insurrection Act, Congress in 2006 quietly enacted an amendment, titled "Enforcement of the Laws to Restore Public Order," to supply presidents with expanded flexibility under the act. The amended law authorized the president to "restore public order" if "the constituted authorities of the State ... are incapable of maintaining public order."[8] The trigger for this authority was "a natural disaster, epidemic, or other serious public health emergency, terrorist attack or incident, or other condition." This law had been tucked away in a large defense authorization measure and soon became controversial for conferring on the president dangerous additional discretion to inject the U.S. military into domestic law enforcement. Congress repealed the amendment in January 2008, restoring the previous version of the law.

THE INSURRECTION ACT: THE TRUMP ERA

In 2020, Donald Trump threatened to use the Insurrection Act in an aggressive way to quell protests that swept through a number of American cities after the death of George Floyd at the hands of Minneapolis police. From the Rose Garden, he announced on June 1 that if the nation's governors did not call up National Guard troops to "dominate the streets," he would "deploy the United States military and quickly solve the problem for them."[9] Trump did not mention the Insurrection Act expressly, but everyone understood that it was the legal basis for the threat. Earlier that day, according to news reports, Chairman of the Joint Chiefs of Staff Mark A. Milley and the president had a "heated discussion in the Oval Office over whether to send troops into the streets."[10] According to the *New York Times*, Milley persuaded Trump not to invoke the Insurrection Act at the time.

Trump took more aggressive action in the District of Columbia. Instead of invoking the Insurrection Act, the president exercised his authority over the D.C. National Guard and directed the mobilization of various components of federal law enforcement to establish a massive presence on the streets of the capital.[11] Just after Trump's Rose Garden appearance, U.S. Park Police officers, assisted by the D.C. National Guard, used force to clear protesters from Lafayette Square, adjacent to the White House. The president then moved through the cleared area in the company of General Milley and Defense Secretary Mike Esper for a press photo opportunity, Bible in hand, in front of St. John's Episcopal Church.

Against the background of these events, Trump's threatened invocation of the Insurrection Act was met with criticism from former military leaders, including former Chairman of the Joint Chiefs of Staff Mike Mullen. Defense Secretary Esper also retreated from association with the president's remarks and actions. Two days after the Lafayette Park episode, Esper declared his opposition to the use of the Insurrection Act in dealing with the unrest that broke out in major cities after Floyd's death.[12] Esper expressed the view that active-duty troops should be deployed within the United States "only in the most urgent and dire of situations" and that "[w]e're not in one of those situations now."[13] That same day, however, Esper "overturned an earlier Pentagon decision to send a couple hundred active-duty soldiers home from the Washington, D.C., region" after he attended a meeting at the White House.[14]

By the evening of June 3, Trump appeared ready to tamp down the controversy. He announced that he would not have to invoke the Insurrection Act because "we have a very powerful National Guard, over 300,000 men and women, and we can do pretty much whatever we want as far as that."[15] On June 7, Attorney General William Barr denied that Trump had directed that "10,000 active-duty troops ... help crack down on protests in D.C. and across the country."[16] Barr then insisted that "[t]he president never asked or suggested that we needed to deploy regular troops at that point."

Congressional leaders continued to press for clarification of the administration's position on the use of the Insurrection Act and the basis for its use of force in the District of Columbia. The chairman of the House Armed Services Committee called for a hearing and dispatched a letter to explore essential questions "about the use of military forces in response to peaceful protestors in the District of Columbia, the movement of active duty troops to staging areas around the country's capital, and plans to deploy active duty troops around the United States should the President invoke the Insurrection Act."[17] Esper and Milley responded that at no time "were [active-duty troops] ever in the District for purposes of civilian law enforcement."[18]

Milley also expressed regret that he had participated in the Lafayette Square events, which "created a perception of the military involve[ment] in domestic politics."[19] "I should not have been there," he told the graduating class of the National Defense University, and he declared that it had been "a mistake that I have learned from[.]" His predecessor, retired General James Mattis, joined the debate with the publication of an extraordinary letter. Mattis wrote that he never imagined that "troops ... would be ordered under any circumstance[s] to violate the Constitutional rights of their fellow citizens—much less to provide a bizarre photo op for the elected commander-in-chief, with military leadership standing alongside."[20] He stressed his commitment to the principles underlying the Posse Comitatus statute: "At home, we should use our military only when requested to do so, on very rare occasions, by state governors .... Keeping public order rests with civilian state and local leaders who best understand their communities and are answerable to them."

Within days of the president's Rose Garden threat to use troops and the Lafayette Park photo op, the norms of military noninvolvement in law enforcement had received powerful affirmation from the chairman of the Joint Chiefs of Staff and the president's former defense secretary, with more unsteady but still remarkable support from the incumbent secretary. It was an unprecedented public rebuke of—and perhaps warning issued to—a sitting president.

But it also prompted reflection on the broad authority that the Insurrection Act confers on the president. The act's multipronged structure, antiquated language, and lack of defined terms are an invitation to abuse by any president, like Trump, who has a weak understanding of and commitment to constitutional norms. Apart from the 2006 amendment, enacted and then quickly repealed, the Insurrection Act has not undergone a review for more than 200 years.

REFORM: THE INSURRECTION ACT

As noted earlier, presidents have often used the Insurrection Act in contexts where a real breakdown of federal law enforcement in the states warranted such intervention. But the statute is old and vague, and the prospect in June 2020 of a president with Trump's demeanor and impulsiveness exercising this authority raised the question of whether the law should be reviewed and clarified. We believe so.

One proposal for reform was introduced in the Senate in the immediate aftermath of the George Floyd protests and Lafayette Park episode. Senate bill 3902 would amend the Insurrection Act to limit presidential authority and provide for controls on potential abuse. It would require the president to consult with Congress before invoking his or her authority under the statute; require the president, the secretary of defense, and the attorney general to jointly certify to Congress that the state is unable or unwilling to enforce federal law; and "sunset" any deployment after fourteen days unless it is specifically extended by a joint congressional resolution. Active-duty troops deployed pursuant to the statute would participate in law enforcement activity only if expressly authorized by law. Governors would be authorized to request presidential invocation rather than act only if the legislature is unable to convene and call for assistance.

The Senate Armed Services Committee considered and rejected the bill. We believe that on the whole this reform proposal has merit, but our preferred approach, while consistent in some respects, differs in others. Specifically, we propose the following:

1. The law would benefit from revision to clearly delineate the sources of authority for deployment of troops by the president, eliminating, to the extent possible, vague, antiquated, and redundant language. Terms such as "assemblage," "combination," and "unlawful conspiracy," which serve to define conditions in the states that justify federal intervention, should be cut, and other terms such as "insurrection," "ordinary course of judicial proceedings," and "domestic violence" should be defined.

2. We agree that the president should be subject to consultation requirements under the statute, but we would have the consultation take place with the "Governor and other duly constituted State and local authorities" who assist the president in determining whether federal assistance is required to address an "actual, ongoing and serious threat to the safety of citizens of a State."

3. The president would be required to report to Congress that he or she is invoking presidential authority under the act and has consulted with state and local authorities on the need for federal assistance. Moreover, the president would have to make specific findings with respect to the decisions, including the results of state and local consultations. The president would have to identify the threat; the projected use of the military or National Guard to meet that threat; the estimated period during which the federal deployment may be required; the steps to be taken to limit military engagement to indirect aid, rather than troops in the streets; and the concurrence, or any concerns raised, by state and local authorities in the course of consultation.

4. We propose a continuing reporting requirement, every fourteen days, throughout the duration of the deployment, which includes a certification that "the conditions giving rise" to the use of troops or the federalized National Guard still "persist." We also propose a sunset provision such as the one contained in S. 3902, which would require a joint resolution of Congress to authorize a continued deployment after the first thirty days, for an additional thirty days. Every additional thirty days would be subject to the fourteen-day reporting requirement and to a further sunset that would require fresh authorization for each subsequent thirty-day period of deployment.

5. We do not support a mechanism for judicial review. Courts do not have the expertise or capacity to sort out urgent and complex questions of how emergency law enforcement missions should be conducted. The timetable for judicial consideration and decision is also poorly suited to the demands of these situations. The questions likely to arise in these circumstances are most appropriately resolved in the political process, as occurred in June 2020, but reform of the law to set the limits more clearly should better constrain the president and equip Congress to conduct more effective oversight.

6. Reform of the Insurrection Act should also include attention to other statutory authorizations the executive branch would rely on to circumvent the basic principles behind Posse Comitatus. During the June events, the president called on out-of-state National Guard units to support law enforcement in the capital pursuant to a statute authorizing their use to "support ... operations or missions undertaken ... at the request of the President or Secretary of Defense."[21] We propose clarifying that this authority is not an exception to the Posse Comitatus Act, even if the attorney general justified the National Guard's deployment on the purportedly narrow basis that they were needed to support the "mission of protecting federal functions, persons, and property within the District of Columbia."[22]

REFORM: EMERGENCY POWERS GENERALLY

The Insurrection Act confers a type of emergency power on the president in response to domestic disturbances. But it is usually not included in lists of presidential emergency powers since the triggering criterion for its use is not a presidential declaration of an "emergency" per se. However, the president possesses 123 statutory powers that become available when he or she declares a national emergency.[23] Trump has generated some controversy under these authorities, but in general Trump's emergency power declarations have not been more outlandish than those of his predecessors going back to the 1970s. Still, there is a problem with excessive delegation of emergency powers that Trump highlighted, and that Congress should consider reforming.

The National Emergencies Act of 1976 (NEA) establishes procedures for the president to exercise these emergency powers.[24] They include a requirement of a public declaration for every emergency, reporting duties to Congress, and a self-executing termination of the emergency unless the president issues a notice of renewal in the *Federal Register*. Congress believed that the NEA would bring discipline and accountability to presidential emergency power declarations, but it has not. The main disciplining tool under the NEA was a legislative veto that the Supreme Court declared unconstitutional in *INS v. Chadha*. With that threat gone, presidents have declared and extended emergencies in a variety of contexts with little congressional or judicial pushback.

As of July 2020, thirty-eight declared national emergencies were in effect under the NEA.[25] Despite the termination provision in the NEA, it is easy for presidents to renew emergency powers and for emergencies to remain in effect for a long time. For example, the emergency declared by President Carter in 1979 in response to the Iran hostage situation has been renewed annually by every president since and *is still in effect today*. President George W. Bush over two terms declared fourteen national emergencies, eleven of which are still in effect today. President Obama over two terms declared twelve national emergencies, ten of which remain in effect today. As of July 2020, President Trump in his first term declared eleven new national emergencies.

The vast majority of the emergencies in effect today—including the one from the Carter era—were declared under the International Emergency Economic Powers Act of 1977 (IEEPA). IEEPA gives presidents a wide array of economic powers on the basis of their unilateral declaration of an emergency with respect to "any unusual and extraordinary threat, which has its source in whole or substantial part outside the United States."

An "emergency" in ordinary language is a serious or dangerous situation that requires immediate redress. But that is not how presidents have understood their emergency powers as delegated by Congress. For example, President Obama in 2015 declared a national emergency relating to violence and political unrest in Burundi, President George W. Bush in 2003 declared a national emergency related to the sale of Iraqi oil, and President Clinton in 1996 declared a national emergency to address a Cuban military shootdown of unarmed American aircraft in international airspace. One can debate whether these were emergencies in the ordinary-language sense at the time they were declared. But they do not seem like emergencies today, in 2020, even though presidents in the intervening years have renewed all of them, and all remain in effect. As these examples suggest, presidents have extraordinary discretion to proclaim emergencies and (under the National Emergencies Act) to renew them in one-year intervals, thereby extending them indefinitely. And courts have typically upheld Congress's broad delegations of emergency power.

The most controversial emergency declaration under Trump was one to allocate funding for a border wall with Mexico.[26] "The current situation at the southern border presents a border security and humanitarian crisis that threatens core national security interests and constitutes a national emergency" Trump proclaimed, as a predicate for invoking emergency construction authority under 10 U.S.C. § 2808. Many critics questioned whether the emergency at the border was genuine, and the validity of the emergency proclamation is currently being litigated. Presidents have often declared emergencies, whether real or not, in analogous situations in which they identify a threat of some kind.

An analogy is President Clinton's emergency declaration to address the 1996 Cuban military shootdown of two Brothers to the Rescue aircraft. Presidents Bush, Obama, and Trump have modified and reaffirmed the national emergency first declared twenty-four years ago. The "emergency" is still in place. But it has morphed into a navigation policy with the aim—like the one Trump invokes for the wall—of preventing (among other things) "a mass migration from Cuba [that] would endanger our security by posing a disturbance or threatened disturbance of the international relations of the United States." The "threat" posed today by a mass migration from Cuba is not a "real" emergency and is not obviously a greater "threat" than the one posed today by migration from Mexico.

Our point here is not to defend Trump's southern border proclamation but, rather, to highlight how presidents have often used delegated emergency powers in ways that seem to fall short of true emergencies. What Harold Koh and John Yoo correctly said almost three decades ago remains true today: Presidents "have declared national emergencies with little regard to whether a real emergency has actually existed."[27]

The most consequential impact from emergency powers during the Trump era, and the most revealing evidence about the scope of this power, came in international affairs. On May 19, 2019, Trump declared a national emergency under IEEPA that was entitled "Securing the Information and Communications Technology and Services Supply Chain." This declaration, along with the Trump administration's discretionary placement of Huawei, a global Chinese technology company, on a trade blacklist— another discretionary exercise of delegated power—made it hard for Huawei (and other China firms) to maintain its business, since it relied heavily on U.S. components. More broadly, the combined orders—all at Trump's discretion, without any congressional consultation, much less approval—had a hugely disruptive effect on global technology supply chains generally. Trump has also declared emergencies related to (among other things) suspending preferential treatment to Hong Kong, blocking the property of certain persons associated with the International Criminal Court, and initiating various authorities to respond to the coronavirus pandemic.

Finally, Trump threatened to invoke IEEPA to order U.S. companies to leave China. This would be an aggressive use of the IEEPA power that no president has attempted, and Trump has not yet followed through. But it is one indication of IEEPA's scope that Trump could easily declare an emergency and achieve this end, if he wished, in light of IEEPA's extraordinarily weak trigger ("any unusual and extraordinary threat, which has its source in whole or substantial part outside the United States") and its extraordinarily broad powers (including, for example, to "regulate, direct and compel, nullify, void, prevent or prohibit, any acquisition, holding, withholding, use, transfer, withdrawal, transportation, importation or exportation of, or dealing in, or exercising any right, power, or privilege with respect to, or transactions involving, any property in which any foreign country or a national thereof has any interest by any person, or with respect to any property, subject to the jurisdiction of the United States").

We do not have space here to propose a comprehensive plan to rein in the 123 delegations of emergency power to the president. This is an area that obviously demands Congress's serious and extended attention, since the accountability mechanisms that Congress sought to impose in the NEA have clearly failed. The foundation of any reform must be to try to re-create the limitations sought by the NEA but undermined by *Chadha*. The criteria for presidential renewal of emergencies after one year should be tighter and should tighten over time. And the executive branch should be required to explain and defend each renewal each year in written reports to Congress and in hearings before the renewal becomes effective. These two steps alone will bring significant discipline to the practically automatic renewals, and morphing emergency declarations that have become common practice. Congress should also commission a study of all 123 emergency authorizations on the books, with special attention to IEEPA, to ensure that they remain necessary in modern times as written.

CONGRESSIONAL SUBPOENA ENFORCEMENT AUTHORITY: BACKGROUND

In 1791, the House of Representatives launched the "first parliamentary investigation of the executive branch" when it set up a committee of inquiry to examine Gen. Arthur St. Clair's disastrous command of the Army in the Ohio country.[28] President Washington agreed that the House was entitled to some information but not any information "the disclosure of which would injure the public." Later, when the question arose of whether a Cabinet secretary would appear before the House to provide testimony, James Madison expressed his opposition. For the executive to submit to such a demand would contravene the very "principles of government" under the constitutional plan for separated powers.

Ever since the Washington administration, Congress and the executive have periodically clashed over this tension between Congress's investigative and oversight powers, and presidents' concern with overreach and protecting the measure of confidentiality deemed essential to the conduct of government and exercise of executive power. In the extreme case, Congress has acted on its claimed "inherent" constitutional authority to arrest recalcitrant executive branch officials for contempt of its demands for testimony or materials. In 1916, for example, it arrested a U.S. Attorney for the Southern District of New York for issuing an incendiary letter assailing legislators' motives in initiating an investigation of his alleged misconduct. The Supreme Court eventually ordered his release, judging the offense given by the letter to be unrelated to Congress's legitimate legislative concerns. But it did affirm that the House possessed "a power implied to deal with contempt in so far as that authority was necessary to preserve and carry out the [House's] legislative authority."[29]

Congress also developed options other than physical arrest. In 1857, it enacted a law imposing criminal liability for failure to comply with a congressional subpoena. The speaker of the House or the president of the Senate could certify the refusal to the district attorney for the District of Columbia who would have the "duty" to prosecute.[30] Rejecting a challenge to the constitutionality of the law, the Supreme Court expressed sympathy for Congress's frustrations in achieving compliance with its demands: "The history of Congressional investigations demonstrates the difficulties under which the two Houses have labored, respectively, in compelling unwilling witnesses to disclose facts deemed essential to taking definitive action."[31]

The law today remains much as enacted in 1857.[32] But Congress has encountered significant limits on its efficacy. In the case of subpoenas issued to executive branch officials, the Office of Legal Counsel has for decades and across administrations of both parties taken the position that the executive has full discretion to decline prosecution under the 1857 law if the official refusing compliance has invoked executive privilege against the disclosure of the information sought by Congress.[33] The executive branch's legal position is even broader. The Justice Department has suggested that it might refuse to enforce criminal contempt even in situations that do not involve a claim of executive privilege.[34] And the Office of Legal Counsel has questioned whether the House has the inherent authority to directly enforce its subpoenas.

In light of these positions, and the executive branch's control over criminal actions, as a practical and legal matter the "most likely route" for Congress to challenge noncompliance is a "civil action seeking enforcement of the subpoena."[35] Congress has conferred on the federal courts jurisdiction to order compliance with a civil action for enforcement.[36] In cases of this kind, Congress authorizes a committee to sue to demand compliance. The courts must determine whether the subpoena is valid and issued for a valid legislative purpose, and must rule on any claim of executive privilege that would excuse noncompliance. One of many complications presented by this option is the inevitable delay associated with any litigation. "[C]ourts tend to move at a pace that is poorly suited to Congress's need for timely information."[37] Congress thus faces a loss in "both the value of the disclosure and the committee's ability to engage in effective, timely oversight."[38]

The delays can be protracted. A relatively recent action to enforce a subpoena against the attorney general in the Obama administration remains on appeal before the U.S. Court of Appeals for the District of Columbia more than six years after the suit was filed. An earlier suit, to enforce a subpoena against senior aides in the George W. Bush White House, moved slowly and inconclusively through the judicial process for nineteen months before Congress and the executive settled the matter through negotiation.

For many years, negotiated settlement between Congress and the executive branch—as part of what is called an "accommodation process"—was the most common way to resolve these interbranch conflicts. The political branches would bargain over the balance to be struck between legislative need and executive concerns with confidentiality and respect for their co-equal spheres of operation. Courts have encouraged this process as an outcome superior to a resolution imposed by the judiciary and have gone so far as to state a preference that "judicial intervention … be delayed until all possibilities for settlement have been exhausted."[39] In 2008, a federal court could state with confidence that this "process of negotiation and accommodation … most often leads to resolution of disputes between the political branches."[40] The courts had reason to express confidence in the negotiation-and-accommodation process. The 2008 subpoena enforcement action against a George W. Bush administration official asserting privilege was only the second of this kind in the nation's history.

The accommodation process operates on the strength of a norm governing the conduct of interparty and interbranch relations. In the conditions of an intensifying political polarization, the norm has increasingly come under strain. During the Trump presidency, the norm began to fall apart. It left a serious question of whether Congress has any meaningful tools available to vindicate legitimate requests for information for investigative or oversight purposes.

CONGRESSIONAL SUBPOENA ENFORCEMENT AUTHORITY: THE TRUMP ERA

Once the Democrats gained control of the House in the 2018 midterm elections, the relations between the president and the opposition party in the legislature became poisonous—even more so than has been typical in recent decades. The House Democrats had the congressional means to investigate all the controversies that had developed in the prior two years, and it proceeded accordingly. The conflicts escalated and reached their peak when the House undertook an impeachment inquiry in 2019. Trump eventually responded with a "'we're-fighting-all-the-subpoenas' strategy,"[41] which lasted well beyond impeachment and represented the judgment that the House was acting systematically in bad faith and that its demands required all-out resistance.

Those defending the administration blamed the collapse of accommodation on Democratic hostility to Trump, arguing that "[n]ever before have so many congressional committees issued so many subpoenas demanding documents and testimony from so many executive branch officials."[42] A contrary view allocated more of the responsibility to Trump, whose defiance was "different not just in degree but in kind."[43]

How far the administration was prepared to take this defiance was established during the impeachment process. In investigating the potential grounds for impeachment, Congress was presumably acting at the height of its constitutional authority to extract relevant information from the executive branch. The Trump administration refused all cooperation. The White House counsel advised the speaker of the House that the "[a]dministration cannot participate in your partisan and unconstitutional inquiry."[44] Nine administration officials refused to testify; executive departments such as the departments of Defense and State rejected all requests for the production of documents.

The House responded to what it termed the president's "complete defiance of every single impeachment-related subpoena served on the Executive Branch"[45] by fashioning and voting on an article of impeachment charging obstruction of Congress's access to relevant information needed for the conduct of its constitutional responsibility.[46] The president's allies responded by challenging the House to seek civil enforcement of its subpoenas before proceeding to an impeachment vote. With an eye on the calendar as 2019 drew to a close, the Democratic House majority concluded that court action would not be timely enough to allow for a fully litigated resolution of these conflicts. Months would be required for the lawsuits to work their way through the courts, for House investigators to receive and consider whatever information these enforcement actions would yield, and for the House to then vote on articles and transmit them to the Senate for trial before the 2020 presidential election campaign was in full swing. The House concluded formally that judicial review was "unnecessary and impractical."[47]

It might have been true that the House discounted the prospects for successfully urging the courts to expedite review precisely because this was no ordinary case but, rather, a dispute "essential to the ongoing impeachment inquiry."[48] The House was unprepared to take its chances. The administration dug in. Even after the impeachment process concluded, the administration made clear that it would not accommodate the House in any other aspects of its investigative or oversight functions.

By the fourth year of the Trump administration, it became apparent that the problem of delay undermined the utility of this avenue for relief in many circumstances. And as the impeachment episode illustrated, those circumstances could include ones of the greatest consequence. Yet with the accommodation process in tatters, the House unlikely to use its "inherent" authority to enforce by arresting or fining recalcitrant executive branch officers, and the executive branch declining to prosecute criminal enforcement cases referred to the U.S. attorney for the District of Columbia, preserving the role of the courts acquired some urgency.

And then, in 2020, a potential bar arose more fundamental than the slowness of subpoena enforcement. In a case involving the House Judiciary Committee's attempt to enforce a subpoena against former White House Counsel Don McGahn, a divided panel of the D.C. Circuit held that "Article III of the Constitution forbids federal courts from resolving this kind of interbranch information dispute."[49] Cutting through the legal niceties, the decision rests on the view that interbranch disputes are inherently political ones in which courts should not intervene. Each branch has political weapons it might use to gain the advantage in this struggle. Congress has many tools to penalize a noncooperative president and perhaps induce him or her to work harder toward accommodation—such as placing holds on nominations, or delaying or refusing to vote on appropriations for administration priorities. The president, in turn, has tools to fight back, including the "bully pulpit" from which congressional motives or reasonableness can be questioned and public opinion swayed, and discretionary authority over policy and programs it can deploy to recruit allies, reward supporters, and exact costs from adversaries.

The opposite view—again, cutting through legal niceties—is that while courts should encourage the other branches to resolve these disputes by accommodation, they retain an indispensable policing role. A deeply polarized politics diminishes the appetite and limits the room for compromise. If all that remains is "constitutional hardball," an all-out war waged by political means, the risks are high that neither Congress nor the executive will come to the negotiating table in good faith. Each will seek total victory where it can, at considerable cost to the capacity of the branch on the losing end to discharge to some reasonable degree its core constitutional functions. These conflicts take very different shapes, and accommodation is more likely, if both Congress and the executive understand that the other can call on the courts to intervene.

As of this writing it is uncertain whether the D.C. Circuit's view in the *McGahn* case will survive en banc or Supreme Court review. If it survives, it creates a high and perhaps insurmountable constitutional hurdle to Congress enforcing subpoenas against defiant executive branch officials, and there is no point to reform the subpoena enforcement process. The proposed reforms that follow thus assume that the decision will not stand and that Congress will retain the authority to enforce its subpoenas through civil processes in federal court against executive branch officials.

REFORM: CONGRESSIONAL SUBPOENA ENFORCEMENT AUTHORITY

If Congress's enforcement of its subpoenas through civil lawsuits survives constitutional scrutiny, the process should operate in a way that allows courts to intervene in a timely manner to resolve disputes and create normative expectations. In other words, Congress should craft its subpoena enforcement power in a way that is timely and efficacious. To achieve this end, a proposal for expedited, "fast-track" access to the courts in subpoena enforcement cases is needed. One such proposal passed the House by voice vote in 2017 and sets the broad terms for a potentially effective fast-track reform. The proposal would have amended the core jurisdictional statute governing congressional subpoena enforcement by imposing a "duty" on the courts to "advance on the docket and to expedite to the greatest possible extent the disposition of any" civil enforcement lawsuit.[50] Congress could request a three-judge panel with direct appeal to the Supreme Court.

We support this approach. It would provide the opportunity for at least some effectively expedited review. But we would not overstate its benefits. In particular, in legislative-executive conflicts, even an expedited procedure may be unable to yield a judicial decision on the timetable necessary to resolve the dispute. For example, in the impeachment of Donald Trump, the House initiated its investigation in mid-September 2019 and voted on impeachment three months later. The House apparently felt under pressure, as the 2020 election year neared, to complete its investigation, vote, and transmit the articles to the Senate for a trial as soon as possible. On this schedule, the House stood virtually no chance of litigating access to testimony that the administration, asserting immunity on behalf of senior White House aides, had directed that they not provide.

But in other circumstances, involving more protracted oversight and investigative activities, the availability of expedited review could matter. The mere prospect of more timely review could affect the executive's strategic judgments in deciding whether to negotiate toward an accommodation. With expedited review, an administration could not count as confidently on "dragging out" the conflict and perhaps discouraging Congress from persisting in its demands.

Of course, the courts may well rule *against* Congress on the scope of its enforcement power, and on the attendant scope of executive and related privileges. Each time Congress resorts to the courts, it risks losing and setting an institutionally disadvantageous precedent. Depending on the case, this is a consideration for Congress in choosing between litigation and other means of inducing executive cooperation, such as the placing of holds on nominations or adverse action or delay on the administration's policy priorities.

Still, we conclude that if courts will remain open for judicial resolution of these disputes, it is better to have more "teeth" in this alternative. Fast-track authority somewhat neutralizes the factor of extended delay and should prove useful—if not in all cases, at least in some. And it will have some effect on the branches' weighing of the costs and benefits of various strategies, including a resolution by negotiation and accommodation.

The 2017 House-passed bill would also allow for the courts to impose monetary penalties on officials who "willfully" failed to comply with a subpoena. We doubt that this is a constructive element. It would serve only to encourage charges of willfulness and demands for penalties, and it may better serve the orderly resolution of these issues to relieve the courts of the responsibility of arbitrating *these* kinds of disputes.

Finally, it has been suggested that Congress revive the use of its inherent authority to vote contempt and arrest or fine offending officials. Neither the House nor the Senate has shown interest in resorting to these means, and in these times, when partisan conflict is at fever pitch, this seems a prudent act of self-restraint.

CONCLUSION

After the new president delivers an uplifting inaugural address on the steps of the Capitol, he or she will proceed two-and-a-half miles down Pennsylvania Avenue to the White House, where a multitude of onerous problems await. At the top of the list is what tone to set, and what reforms to support, in reconstructing the presidency.

One critic of the presidency, Gene Healy, warned in 2008 that "it's naive to imagine that the office can be put in its proper constitutional place with a carefully designed package of legislative and judicial reforms."[1] The main hurdle to reform, he maintains, is Americans' "romance" with "the Heroic Presidency." If the public continues to envision the president's role in grandiose terms, "even the most well-crafted five-point plan for restoring the constitutional balance of power is likely to fail."

Healy is right that Americans expect much from their presidents— probably even more today than when he wrote those words a dozen years ago. One of the most challenging expectations—then and now—is that the presidency be strong enough to meet the nation's many problems but at the same time remain in a meaningful sense a constitutional presidency that is adequately constrained by laws and norms, both in reality and appearance.

We explained in Chapter One why we believe a strong but restrained presidency is vital to making American government work. And we have endeavored to show throughout this book how a comprehensive program of reform *can* address many of the most pressing concerns about the modern presidency, especially those highlighted during Trump's time in office.

The end of Trump's presidency will not reduce the urgency for reform. It is reasonable to assume, as does Saikrishna Prakash, that the next or a future president "likely will continue to push the boundaries of the office outward and grasp at new powers. After all, every modern president supposes that his agenda is wholly just and absolutely necessary, that he alone enjoys a popular mandate, and that the 'loyal opposition' is in fact obstinately obstructionist."[2] And we worry, for reasons we have discussed, that future presidents will learn from Trump's novel exercise of presidential powers and exploit weaknesses in legal and normative constraints on the presidency even more effectively than he did.

Even had Trump not become president, the case for institutional reform would have been strong. But, as we have tried to show, Trump's conduct of the presidency compellingly clarifies the stakes and has forced certain issues to the forefront of a reform agenda. Trump has declared that Article II of the Constitution "gives me all of these rights at a level that nobody has ever seen before."[3] Whether in the attempt or the execution, Trump has exposed various ways that a president could presume to exercise his untenable version of "Article II" rights "at a level nobody has ever seen before." If the Watergate episode in the Nixon presidency sounded the alarm and summoned the country to reform, so should the Trump presidency.

We have attempted to be very specific about what reforms are needed. The details matter. Both laws and norms are at issue: Norms do work that laws sometimes can't, and reform of the law can reinvigorate norms. Norms will occupy an especially large space in the post-Trump reform program. Other presidents have skirted norms, but Trump has attacked them comprehensively and frequently, and disregarded them openly. He rejects the very constraining role that norms play in bolstering the constitutional balance. Presidents who come after him may not seize the "precedent" Trump has set in his assault on norms, but the nation cannot count on this. Affirmative reform, by statute or executive branch regulation, is needed to reset and extend these norms. So too is a presidential administration committed to them.

It will not be easy for the next president to strike the right balance between reforms needed to contain the presidency and prevent abuses of the office, and the preservation of a strong executive as a vital center of initiative and energy in our constitutional system. These objectives will always be in tension. But we are convinced that the tension can be managed and meaningful reform can be achieved, so long as we recognize that the results will be imperfect, that presidents will sometimes look to throw off the constraints, and that vigilance in maintaining the constraints is vital.

If the new president takes office in 2021, the nation will face one of the most difficult times in its history. It will be a pressing occasion for the new president to reflect on what makes for a "strong" presidency. The strength of the institution, and of a particular presidency, is measured by its capacity for effective executive leadership. Trump's record of feckless leadership was closely related to his unrelenting efforts to defy or destroy constraining institutions. The goal in reconstructing the presidency after Trump must be to ensure that the institution characterized by the energy and initiative championed by Hamilton in *Federalist* No. 70 is nonetheless embedded, as Schlesinger rightly insisted, in a "system of accountability that checks the abuse of executive power."[4]

APPENDIX A

SUMMARIES OF REFORM
PROPOSALS

What follows are summaries of the key points of the reform proposals for each chapter. The details matter, however, and page references for the full discussion of these proposals are noted in brackets.

CHAPTER TWO: FOREIGN STATE INFLUENCE
(PAGES 36–47)

Congress should require campaigns to report to the FBI any contacts from foreign states offering campaign support or assistance. The Justice Department should have enforcement responsibility for reportable foreign contacts and assistance, and the authority to issue advisory opinions to campaigns seeking guidance on the application of the reforms to specific factual circumstances.

Congress also should specifically prohibit mutual aid agreements between presidential campaigns and foreign governments. It should expand the scope of 22 U.S.C. § 219, which now prohibits "public officials" from entering into reportable "agency" relationships with foreign nationals. The amended Section 219 would clearly define presidents as among the public officials who are subject to the statute, and the prohibition would be extended to agreements and offers for assistance between candidates and campaigns and foreign actors, such as foreign states, to collaborate in their mutual interest to influence an election.

Finally, Congress should amend the Federal Election Campaign Act to clarify that a prohibited foreign national contribution to a campaign includes services, materials, or information, such as opposition research, that may not have established market value but that a campaign deems useful. This prohibition should extend to any campaign's solicitation of such a prohibited foreign national contribution.

CHAPTER THREE: FINANCIAL CONFLICTS OF INTEREST (PAGES 61–71)

Congress should bar the president from any active or supervisory role in the oversight of any business, including any formal or informal role. It should also require the president to certify annually, subject to criminal penalties, that he or she has complied with this restriction.

Congress should require the president to account regularly and transparently for his income, holdings, and management of assets and investments. A president should not be required to divest entirely, but to ensure full public transparency, he should be prohibited from establishing a "blind trust." Congress should further require the businesses in which the president has an interest to report publicly those interests, including the names of persons with interests in the firm or other entity, and the value of assets and liabilities.

Congress should prohibit the president from declining his or her statutory salary and thereby relying for his or her living expenses on income from private business income or investments. The president should be further prohibited from taking deductions on the donation of the salary to charity or to the federal government to underwrite official functions.

Congress should require reporting to Congress and the Office of Government Ethics of the president's interests in, and income reasonably anticipated or received from, foreign state investment vehicles or foreign state–controlled businesses. These disclosures would be available to the public. A president-elect would be required to file the first report within thirty days of the date of the election. Should Congress fail within sixty days thereafter to provide affirmative consent, the statute would require the president-elect (or newly sworn president) to sell off the interest. All subsequent reporting requirements would fall on the businesses in which the president held an interest, and Congress would also have to act within sixty days to consent to any reported foreign state income or interests. Absent congressional consent, the business would have to sell off the interest and pay the proceeds to the U.S. Treasury.

The Government Accountability Office (GAO) should conduct and submit to Congress annual audits of the president's compliance with the presidential conflicts of interest rules. The GAO would review the president's annual certifications that he or she did not engage on a consultative or advisory basis with businesses in which he or she had a financial interest, and the office would audit reports filed by the businesses in which the president holds an interest. Congress would use the annual audits to determine whether additional oversight is required and as necessary would refer evidence of noncompliance to the Justice Department.

CHAPTER FOUR: TAX DISCLOSURE
(PAGES 82–86)

Congress should amend the Ethics in Government Act to ensure public disclosure of presidents' (and vice presidents') and presidential (and vice presidential) candidates' tax returns. The public reporting requirement would apply to every president's and vice president's returns for each year in office, to all major-party nominees, and to other presidential candidates who qualify on enough ballots to win a majority of electoral votes. This requirement would also extend to any of the president's or vice president's family members who hold senior executive branch positions.

The Office of Government Ethics should enforce this requirement, and the law should provide that if the president or vice president fails to meet the filing requirement, Congress may direct the Secretary of the Treasury to produce the tax returns and authorize judicial enforcement in the event of the secretary's failure to comply. Congress should also require the public release of the audits of the president's and vice president's returns that the IRS performs annually pursuant to longstanding IRS policy.

CHAPTER FIVE: THE PRESS
(PAGES 101–110)

Congress should amend the Inspector General Act to ensure that the federal government may not devote its investigatory and related resources to punish or retaliate against the press. The amended act should empower inspectors general to investigate "abuse" as defined to include "official acts" that constitute "reprisal against or an attempt to harass or intimidate" news media organizations or individual journalists in their employ." To protect against abuse and political weaponization of this process, media organizations would cooperate only on a voluntary basis. Inspectors general would have the authority to initiate an investigation on a "look-back" basis only and could not proceed if the attorney general certified that the use of investigative tools complied with established and published Justice Department procedures and rules. Any findings of abuse should be transmitted to Congress, and the Justice Department should also report any investigation not pursued because the attorney general certified compliance with department process. Moreover, the inspector general should refer evidence of official retaliatory conduct to the Justice Department for potential criminal investigation.

Congress should amend the Presidential Records Act to explicitly include a president's personal social media accounts or other communication platforms used to communicate and interact with the public about official matters. The amendment would define such accounts as "documentary material" with the effect of disallowing presidential claims that they are personal communication channels from which critical commentary can be blocked.

The next president should also direct the promulgation of a revised regulation governing security reviews of White House press applications. This rule should align the White House's criteria for a "credentialed" journalist with those of the judicial and legislative branches. The Secret Service should be required to review for security clearance any applicant who meets those qualifications, and if there is no basis for exclusion of the applicant on the basis of a security concern, the Secret Service must approve the applicant for the pass. The regulation would also apply due process requirements to initial clearance and any revocation.

Congress should exercise its oversight role to monitor executive branch practices and conduct in the management of press relations, including but not limited to reviewing Inspector General reporting on a "look-back" basis of its investigations into alleged reprisal or harassment. Alternatively, the Senate and the House could create for this purpose a separate subcommittee of their judiciary committees dedicated to the issue of press freedom.

CHAPTER SIX: THE PARDON POWER
(PAGES 125–131)

Congress should amend the bribery statute to establish criminal liability for a president who seeks to obstruct justice through the offer or exercise of the pardon power. The amended statute should specify that the president and vice president are "public officials" within its purview; that an "official act" includes a presidential pardon, commutation, or reprieve provided as part of a corrupt exchange; and that any such grant of clemency is also a "thing of value" if offered or given to influence testimony in any judicial, congressional, or agency proceeding.

Congress should also prohibit self-pardons and specify that such a pardon cannot be the basis for immunity from federal criminal investigation or prosecution.

CHAPTER SEVEN: JUSTICE DEPARTMENT
INDEPENDENCE
(PAGES 153–162)

The Justice Department should amend its internal rules and guidance to emphasize ethical principles that insulate law enforcement decisions from improper partisan political considerations. It should revise the Supplemental Standards of Ethical Conduct for Employees of the Department of Justice and the department's *Principles of Federal Prosecution* and its *Federal Prosecution of Election Offenses* to reflect the principles that the department adopted and formally communicated to Congress in 2009 upon concluding its investigation into allegations of politically motivated firings of U.S. attorneys during the George W. Bush administration. Also, the code of ethics for the executive branch should be amended to include an "improper partisan political purpose of influencing an election to public office" within the prohibition on all federal misuse of official authority.

Congress should bar the president from appointing to senior Justice Department positions individuals who within two years of appointment held senior positions of trust or responsibility in the president's personal campaign organization; in national, state, or local parties; or in other political organizations that supported the president for election or reelection. Congress should also reinstate its original qualification for attorney general that he or she be a "meet person" (that is, appropriate for the position), "learned in the law," with the added requirement of "integrity," and should extend this requirement to the positions of deputy and associate attorney general, assistant attorneys general, and the solicitor general.

CHAPTER EIGHT: THE SPECIAL COUNSEL (PAGES 182–198)

The attorney general should amend the special counsel regulations to tighten the trigger for the appointment of a special counsel by requiring the attorney general to make a determination of whether a criminal investigation is "warranted" on the basis of "credible information or allegations." Should the attorney general decline to appoint a special counsel in the face of credible allegations of criminal wrongdoing, he or she must submit written reasons, including a factual and legal analysis, to Congress. In the event that a criminal investigation of the president or vice president is warranted, the attorney general would have to appoint a special counsel, with no option to proceed through normal department law enforcement process.

The regulations should reflect and protect the public interest in the special counsel's function of finding facts. In any determination of whether the public interest is served by the appointment of a special counsel, the attorney general should take into account the need for an independent factual inquiry. When a special counsel investigation concludes or is terminated by the attorney general, or the attorney general dismisses the special counsel, the special counsel must issue a report of its factual findings to Congress and the public. The attorney general should not direct the special counsel to refrain from taking any investigative step unless it is plainly inconsistent with law or established department practices. If the attorney general disapproves any investigative step after concluding that those standards are satisfied, he or she must include notice of this action in the notification to Congress of a final determination of prosecution or declination. So that a special counsel may prepare a report of factual findings subsequent to a dismissal or the attorney general's decision to terminate an investigation, the special counsel should be given access to the investigative record for a period of thirty days.

The attorney general should maintain clearly allocated supervisory control of the investigation and the final decision on prosecution or declination. The attorney general may direct the special counsel to provide periodic updates on the course of such investigation, may direct the special counsel to seek an opinion from the Office of Legal Counsel on any question of law, and may make the final determination on any such legal question. In the attorney general's final report to Congress, he or she must include notice of any such disputed legal questions, the outcome of Office of Legal Counsel review of those questions, and his or her final determinations.

The attorney general must also report to Congress the basis for any rejection of the special counsel's expansion of the scope of the investigation, or for the attorney general's decision to terminate in connection with the annual review of the special counsel's proposed budget.

Congress should codify the removal provisions currently contained in the special counsel regulations and should further specify that "the Attorney General shall inform the Special Counsel in writing of the specific reason for his or her removal."

Congress should amend the obstruction of justice statute to specify that the president commits the crime of obstruction of justice when he commits an obstructive act, with a nexus to an official proceeding, and with a corrupt intent, in three specific cases: (1) intervention to affect the outcome of elections; (2) protection of family members; and (3) self-protection, when the president is either the "subject" or the "target" of a criminal investigation.

In light of the executive branch legal position that a president cannot be prosecuted while in office, Congress should enact a tolling statute to apply to criminal acts the president commits in office and to offenses committed by the president in the course of seeking election to the presidency.

CHAPTER NINE: THE BUREAUCRACY AGAINST THE PRESIDENT (PAGES 212–229)

Justice Department regulations should require the attorney general to approve any preinauguration investigation of presidential candidates or presidential campaigns, and prior to approving or disapproving such investigation, he or she should have views in writing of the FBI director, the assistant attorney general in charge of the Criminal Division, and the deputy attorney general. The FBI should submit a plan of any such investigation for the attorney general's approval, and should regularly notify senior department leadership about the course of the investigation and the use of electronic surveillance, confidential human sources, or undercover employees. The rule should include a presumption against the use in such investigations of an undercover employee, and the attorney general must approve any such use.

Congress should repeal the Logan Act, at least as it applies to members of presidential campaigns and transitions.

Justice Department regulations should require a multilevel review procedure for opening a preinauguration counterintelligence investigation of a presidential candidate or presidential campaign, culminating in final approval by the attorney general. The FBI director, the assistant attorney general in charge of the National Security Division, and the deputy attorney general should review the basis for any such investigation and make recommendations in writing to the attorney general. The director of national intelligence should also participate in the formal review. The FBI should be required to submit a plan of the investigation for the attorney general's approval, and should regularly notify senior department leadership about the use of investigative techniques and the course of the investigation. All investigative techniques, including the use of undercover employees, should be available in a counterintelligence investigation.

Congress should require the attorney general to notify the congressional intelligence committees of the decision to open any such investigation, or his or her failure to do so, and of the recommendations previously received from the director of national intelligence and the FBI director. In the case of an opened investigation, the notice should explain its basis, including any disagreement between the FBI director and the director of national intelligence about the recommendation to open it. In the case of an attorney general's refusal to open an investigation, the notice should explain what the director of national intelligence and the FBI director recommended, and the basis for the attorney general's decision.

In consultation with the director of national intelligence and the FBI director, the attorney general should have the authority to decide whether to inform a campaign that it is subject to a counterintelligence investigation. The determination should rest on whether the investigation plausibly includes the candidate or senior management or is directed toward an individual or individuals employed by or associated with the campaign where there is no evidence of collusion with the candidate or campaign.

The special counsel regulations should be amended to include a counterintelligence investigation of the president (or vice president) as a jurisdictional trigger for appointment. The criterion for appointment must be specified in advance, after a legal analysis by the Justice Department that takes account of presidential prerogatives to determine U.S. national security interests while establishing a basis for inquiry into harmful collusion or collaboration. The attorney general should make the final decision to open an investigation after obtaining views and recommendations from the director of national intelligence, the FBI director, and the head of the National Security Division. Congress should require notice to the congressional intelligence committees of any decision by the attorney general to reject the advice of the FBI director, the head of the National Security Division, or the director of national intelligence to appoint a special counsel, along with the attorney general's reasons for the declination.

The special counsel regulations should prohibit in clear terms any investigating agency, including the FBI, from announcing recommended charging decisions related to presidential candidates or campaigns. The regulations should also prohibit Justice Department officials from discussing the conduct of uncharged presidential candidates or campaign officials, except for the attorney general and deputy attorney general, who should be able to do so only in exceptional circumstances, as the public interest requires.

The rules should formally incorporate the "sixty-day rule" against the taking of investigative steps related to electoral matters or the return of indictments against a candidate within sixty days of a primary or general election.

Congress should amend the Code of Ethics for Government Service to broaden it beyond an ethical prohibition against the misuse of confidential government information for financial return to include an emphasis on the observance of confidentiality more generally as a vital element of the conception of "public office [as] a public trust."

CHAPTER TEN: INVESTIGATING PAST ADMINISTRATIONS (PAGES 248–251)

Justice Department regulations should make clear that the attorney general is bound by the department's media comment policy and its rules that limit prosecutors from publicly discussing a pending case.

Justice Department policy should specify that if an administration determines that investigation of a counterintelligence or related criminal probe of a prior administration is warranted, such an investigation should be conducted by the inspector general of the Justice Department (or by several agency inspectors general working together), not by a prosecutor. If the inspector general uncovers evidence of criminal wrongdoing, he or she should refer the matter to the attorney general, who would be required to invoke the procedures of the special counsel regulations.

The special counsel rules should provide that, so long as the other triggering criteria for an investigation are satisfied, the attorney general will appoint a special counsel in any investigation of the former president or senior officials of the prior administration for conduct arising from their official duties. Under this policy, the attorney general's use of U.S. attorneys to conduct special-purpose inquiries should be disfavored.

CHAPTER ELEVEN: THE WHITE HOUSE COUNSEL
(PAGES 271–277)

The Justice Department's Office of Legal Counsel should have primary responsibility for legal support for the president. A White House counsel, assisted by a small number of deputies, should continue to be a member of the president's senior staff, available at all times for direct counsel to the president and focused on Senate confirmation issues, congressional oversight and investigations, and other "crisis management" challenges. The Justice Department lawyers dedicated to White House legal support would provide the White House counsel and the president with analysis and opinions on legal issues arising in these and other contexts.

CHAPTER TWELVE: WAR POWERS AND NUCLEAR WEAPONS
(PAGES 298–314)

The executive branch should withdraw the 2001 and 2002 Office of Legal Counsel opinions on war powers issued in the aftermath of 9/11, which took overly broad views of the president's authority to use force in anticipatory self-defense.

Congress should repeal the 2002 AUMF passed to address the threat posed at the time by the regime in Iraq. Congress's repeal of the law would make clear that presidential uses of force in and related to Iraq must be grounded in Article II constitutional authority or a reformed 2001 AUMF.

Congress should replace the 2001 AUMF with an updated version to specify the enemies (at the moment, al-Qaeda, the Taliban, and the Islamic State) and any current "associated forces" (such as al-Shabab) against whom Congress authorizes the use of force. This revised AUMF would require the president to notify Congress of any designation of a new "associated force" and should require expedited congressional review of that designation. Finally, it should include a two- to three-year "sunset" clause and thus require affirmative renewal, which would force

Congress to exercise its constitutional and democratic responsibilities to deliberate about and vote on (or at least address) the issue.

Congress should amend the War Powers Resolution to (1) define and limit inherent presidential powers of self-defense, (2) prohibit unilateral intervention on humanitarian grounds without congressional authorization, (3) require consultation with specifically identified members of Congress for nonemergency use-of-force situations, (4) require a report to the speaker of the House and president pro tempore of the Senate soon after commencing a use of force abroad, (5) set clear restrictions on the circumstances in which a president may continue the use of force beyond sixty days, and (6) forbid any funds from being expended for any use of force abroad inconsistent with the provisions of the reformed statute.

Congress should enact a statute that requires the president to consult with Congress on certain uses of nuclear force. First, the legislation should acknowledge that the president has Article II authority to use nuclear force to respond to an incoming nuclear attack upon the United States, its territories or possessions, or its armed forces, and to act in self-defense in extreme circumstances to defend the vital interests of the U.S. or its allies. Second, Congress should specify that only it can declare or authorize war in the constitutional sense and that use of nuclear weapons beyond a response to an incoming nuclear attack, or in self-defense in extreme circumstances to defend the vital interests of the U.S. or its allies, would constitute an act of war in the constitutional sense. Third, the president should be required to consult, if possible, with identified members of Congress before using nuclear force to respond in self-defense in extreme circumstances to defend the vital interests of the U.S. or its allies.

Congress should make clear that Section 6 of the Atomic Energy Act is not a blanket authorization to use nuclear weapons as the president sees fit.

CHAPTER THIRTEEN: VACANCIES REFORM
(PAGES 325–332)

For a vacancy in Cabinet secretary and agency head positions, Congress should amend the Federal Vacancies Reform Act (FVRA) to require the president to choose in order, as available, (1) a first assistant or (2) a

Senate-confirmed official within the department or agency, or (3) a Senate-confirmed official in another agency. A nonconfirmed official should be able to run the department or agency only if the vacancy has arisen in the first four months of a president's term, or longer if no other official has been confirmed for that position at the outset of an administration. An acting official should be able to serve 120 days in office, with only one renewal of an additional 120 days for a failed nomination.

Congress should make clear that agency-specific succession statutes take precedence over the FVRA, or otherwise ensure that the FVRA operates as a back-up when the agency-specific statute fails to provide for succession.

The FVRA should confer a cause of action on anyone adversely affected by an agency action issued by an officer in violation of the FVRA, require the Government Accountability Office to examine and regularly report on alleged FVRA violations, expand the current requirement that departments and agencies report to Congress on vacancies in order to ensure that they are filled in a more timely manner, and tie agency funding to satisfaction of these requirements.

For a vacant office of an inspector general, Congress should mandate that only a Senate-confirmed inspector general from another agency, or a GS-15 or higher official within the inspector general's office who has been there for more than three years, may fill the role on an acting basis.

In exchange for the president's support for comprehensive FVRA reform, Congress should eliminate the requirement of Senate consent for hundreds of midlevel positions. This would reduce, but not eliminate, senators' use of the filibuster and holds on nominees, which would in turn reduce the incentive for presidents to make aggressive, expansive use of acting appointments.

CHAPTER FOURTEEN: OTHER REFORMS

The Insurrection Act
(pages 337–340)

Congress should amend the Insurrection Act to require the president to consult with the governor and other state and local authorities to assist in determining whether the deployment of troops is necessary to address an "actual, ongoing and serious threat to the safety of the citizens of the State." The amended law should further require that the president report to Congress that he or she is invoking his or her authority under the act and has consulted state and local authorities. The amended act should mandate that such a report contain specific findings with respect to the decision, including the nature of the threat and the projected time period for deployment. It should also establish a continuing reporting requirement and a sunset provision after thirty days' deployment. Finally, Congress should clarify that other statutory authorizations for the executive branch to direct various federal agency components, such as the Drug Enforcement Administration or Immigration and Customs Enforcement, to cooperate in law enforcement are not exceptions to the Posse Comitatus Act.

Emergency Powers Generally
(pages 340–343)

Congress should tighten the criteria for presidential renewal of emergencies after one year and make these criteria even stricter over time. Congress should also require the executive branch to explain and defend each renewal each year in written reports to Congress and in hearings before the renewal becomes effective. Finally, Congress should commission a study of all 123 emergency authorizations on the books, with special attention to the International Emergency Economic Powers Act, to ensure that they remain necessary.

Fast-Track Congressional Subpoena Enforcement Authority
(pages 349–351)

Congress should amend the jurisdictional statute governing congressional subpoena enforcement, by imposing a "duty" on the courts to "advance on the docket and to expedite to the greatest possible extent the disposition of any" civil enforcement lawsuit. The House and the Senate should have the option of requesting a three-judge panel with direct appeal to the Supreme Court.

★

Appendix B

Texts of Selected Proposed Reforms

PROHIBITIONS ON PRESIDENTIAL OBSTRUCTION OF JUSTICE

18 U.S.C. § 1503

(a) Whoever corruptly, or by threats or force, or by any threatening letter or communication, endeavors to influence, intimidate, or impede any grand or petit juror, or officer in or of any court of the United States, or officer who may be serving at any examination or other proceeding before any United States magistrate judge or other committing magistrate, in the discharge of his duty, or injures any such grand or petit juror in his person or property on account of any verdict or indictment assented to by him, or on account of his being or having been such juror, or injures any such officer, magistrate judge, or other committing magistrate in his person or property on account of the performance of his official duties, or corruptly or by threats or force, or by any threatening letter or communication, influences, obstructs, or impedes, or endeavors to influence, obstruct, or impede, the due administration of justice, shall be punished as provided in subsection (b). If the offense under this section occurs in connection with a trial of a criminal case, and the act in violation of this section involves the threat of physical force or physical force, the maximum term of imprisonment which may be imposed for the offense shall be the higher of that otherwise provided by law or the maximum term that could have been imposed for any offense charged in such case.

(b) The President or Vice President of the United States shall not cause, or attempt to cause, a criminal investigation or prosecution to be sought, instituted, or terminated, or influence in any way the conduct of such investigation or prosecution, with respect to

(1) Any candidate for public office or political party organization for the purpose of interfering with or affecting the result of an election;

(2) Any member of his or her immediate family, if

(A) the President or Vice President knows or has reason to know that such immediate family member is a target or subject of any such investigation, or

(B) such immediate family member is a defendant in any such prosecution; or

(3) Any investigation in which the President or Vice President has been notified or advised that he or she is a target or subject of such an investigation, or knows, or has reason to know, that he or she is a subject of the investigation.

The term "immediate family" means a President's or Vice President's father, mother, son, daughter, brother, sister, uncle, aunt, first cousin, nephew, niece, husband, wife, father-in-law, mother-in-law, son-in-law, daughter-in-law, brother-in-law, sister-in-law, stepfather, stepmother, stepson, stepdaughter, stepbrother, stepsister, half brother, or half sister.

(c) The punishment for an offense under this section is—

(1) in the case of a killing, the punishment provided in sections 1111 and 1112;

(2) in the case of an attempted killing, or a case in which the offense was committed against a petit juror and in which a class A or B felony

was charged, imprisonment for not more than 20 years, a fine under this title, or both; and

(3) in any other case, imprisonment for not more than 10 years, a fine under this title, or both.

ABUSE OF THE PARDON POWER

1. Bribery (18 U.S.C. § 201)

(a) For the purpose of this section—

(1) the term "public official" means **the President and Vice President of the United States**, Member of Congress, Delegate, or Resident Commissioner, either before or after such official has qualified, or an officer or employee or person acting for or on behalf of the United States, or any department, agency or branch of Government thereof, including the District of Columbia, in any official function, under or by authority of any such department, agency, or branch of Government, or a juror;

(2) the term "person who has been selected to be a public official" means any person who has been nominated or appointed to be a public official, or has been officially informed that such person will be so nominated or appointed; and

(3) the term "official act" means any decision or action on any question, matter, cause, suit, proceeding or controversy, which may at any time be pending, or which may by law be brought before any public official, in such official's official capacity, or in such official's place of trust or profit, **including any pardon, commutation, or reprieve, or offer of any such pardon, commutation, or reprieve.**

(b) Whoever—

(1) directly or indirectly, corruptly gives, offers or promises anything of value to any public official or person who has been selected to be a public official, or offers or promises any public official or any person who has

been selected to be a public official to give anything of value to any other person or entity, with intent—

(**A**) to influence any official act; or

(**B**) to influence such public official or person who has been selected to be a public official to commit or aid in committing, or collude in, or allow, any fraud, or make opportunity for the commission of any fraud, on the United States; or

(**C**) to induce such public official or such person who has been selected to be a public official to do or omit to do any act in violation of the lawful duty of such official or person;

(**2**) being a public official or person selected to be a public official, directly or indirectly, corruptly demands, seeks, receives, accepts, or agrees to receive or accept anything of value personally or for any other person or entity, in return for:

(**A**) being influenced in the performance of any official act;

(**B**) being influenced to commit or aid in committing, or to collude in, or allow, any fraud, or make opportunity for the commission of any fraud, on the United States; or

(**C**) being induced to do or omit to do any act in violation of the official duty of such official or person;

(**3**) directly or indirectly, corruptly gives, offers, or promises anything of value to any person, or offers or promises such person to give anything of value to any other person or entity, with intent to influence the testimony under oath or affirmation of such first-mentioned person as a witness upon a trial, hearing, or other proceeding, before any court, any committee of either House or both Houses of Congress, or any agency, commission, or officer authorized by the laws of the United States to hear evidence or take testimony, or with intent to influence such person to absent himself therefrom. **For purposes of this subsection, a thing** of value shall include a pardon, commutation, or reprieve, or offer of any such pardon, commutation, or reprieve.

2. Self-Pardons

Whereas Article II, Section 2 of the U.S. Constitution states that the President "shall have power to grant reprieves and pardons for offenses against the United States, except in cases of impeachment";

Whereas Article II, Section 3 of the U.S. Constitution states that the President "shall take Care that the Laws be faithfully executed";

Whereas Article II, Section 3 of the U.S. Constitution provides that a President impeached and convicted "shall nevertheless be liable and subject to Indictment, Trial, Judgment and Punishment, according to Law";

Whereas the Justice Department's Office of Legal Counsel concluded that to the extent that a President is immune from criminal indictment and prosecution while in office, such immunity is "temporary" and results only in "the delay, but not the forbearance, of any criminal trial." Memorandum for the Attorney General (October 16, 2000);

Whereas the Justice Department's Office of Legal Counsel correctly construed the pardon power in concluding that a President may not grant a pardon to himself or herself. Memorandum for the Deputy Attorney General, from the Office of Legal Counsel, Presidential or Legislative Pardon of the President (August 5, 1974);

Whereas, any pardon that a President bestows upon himself or herself is inconsistent with the Constitution's text, structure, and purpose, and no such pardon has any force or effect in any federal criminal investigation or trial;

Now, Therefore, Be it enacted by the Senate and House of Representatives of the United States of America in Congress assembled:

The President's grant of a pardon to himself or herself shall not be accepted by any federal court of the United States nor deprive any such court of jurisdiction over any criminal or civil matter or operate to confer on the President any legal immunity from investigation or prosecution.

WAR POWERS—NUCLEAR FORCE

SECTION 1. SHORT TITLE.

This Act may be cited as the "Nuclear Weapons Use Consultation Act of 2020".

SEC. 2. FINDINGS AND DECLARATION OF POLICY.

(a) FINDINGS. Congress finds the following:

1. Consistent with section 2(c) of the War Powers Resolution (Public Law 93–148; 50 U.S.C. 1541), the President has the constitutional power to introduce "United States Armed Forces into hostilities, or into situations where imminent involvement in hostilities is clearly indicated by the circumstances" pursuant to "a national emergency created by attack upon the United States, its territories or possessions, or its armed forces."

2. The President's constitutional power to defend against an attack upon the United States, its territories or possessions, or its armed forces, includes the power to direct the use of nuclear force in self-defense in extreme circumstances to defend the vital interests of the United States or its allies.

3. Except where the President's response to a national emergency created by attack upon the United States, its territories or possessions, or its armed forces, or where the President acts in the national self-defense in extreme circumstances to defend the vital interests of the United States or its allies,

Congress has the sole power to declare war and authorize the use of nuclear force.

(b) DECLARATION OF POLICY. It is the policy of the United States that whenever the President is in receipt of intelligence indicating that the use of nuclear force may be required in self-defense in extreme circumstances to defend the vital interests of the United States, or its allies, the President shall notify and consult with the Congress as provided in this Resolution prior to directing any such use of force.

SEC. 3.

(a) NOTIFICATION AND CONSULTATION. For purposes of this Resolution, the President shall notify and consult as provided by §2(b) of this Resolution with the Chairs and Ranking members of the congressional intelligence committees and with the congressional leadership. The term "congressional leadership" includes the following:

(1) The majority leader of the Senate.

(2) The minority leader of the Senate.

(3) The speaker of the House of Representatives.

(4) The minority leader of the House of Representatives.

Consultation shall include providing the intelligence committees and congressional leadership with intelligence findings and other material information that support the President's determination that a nuclear response is required and consistent with the requirements of the Constitution and this Resolution.

(b) CONSULTATION PROCEDURES. Upon enactment of this Resolution, the Secretaries of Defense and Homeland Security shall establish in collaboration with the congressional intelligence committees and the congressional leadership procedures for consultation provided for under this Resolution, including but not limited to secure emergency communications protocols and facilities.

SPECIAL COUNSEL REGULATIONS

E. PART 600—PROPOSED REVISIONS TO
THE SPECIAL COUNSEL RULES

§ 600.1 Grounds for appointing a Special Counsel.

The Attorney General, or in cases in which the Attorney General is recused, the Acting Attorney General, will appoint a Special Counsel, **and so notify the Chairman and Ranking Minority Member of the Judiciary Committees of each House of Congress**, when he or she determines that **credible information or allegations** indicate that a criminal investigation of a person or matter is warranted and—

(a) That investigation or prosecution of that person or matter by a United States Attorney's Office or litigating Division of the Department of Justice would present a conflict of interest for the Department or other extraordinary circumstances; and

(b) That under the circumstances, it would be in the public interest to appoint an outside Special Counsel to assume responsibility for **an independent factual inquiry and for prosecution or declination recommendations**.

(c) **If the Attorney General determines after a review of credible information or allegations that a criminal investigation is not warranted or that it would not be in the public interest to make such appointment, the Attorney General shall notify the Chairman and Ranking Minority Member of the Judiciary Committees of each House of Congress in writing to set forth in appropriate detail the legal and factual basis for this conclusion.**

(d) **In any case where the Attorney General determines that a counterintelligence investigation of the President is warranted, he or she shall appoint a Special Counsel.**

> (1) **The Attorney General should make any such determination on the basis with due regard to presidential**

prerogatives to determine the national security interests of the United States.

(2) In making such a determination, the Attorney General shall consider the views of the Director of National Intelligence, the Director of the Federal Bureau of Investigation, and the Assistant Attorney General for National Security.

(3) In the event that, contrary to the advice of either the Director of the Federal Bureau of Investigation or the Director of National Intelligence, the Attorney General declines to open an investigation, he or she shall report this declination, along with the reasons therefore, to the congressional intelligence committees.

(e) Upon receipt of an Inspector General's referral of credible evidence that the President, Vice President or senior officials of a prior administration may have committed federal criminal offenses in the conduct of a counterintelligence or related criminal investigation, the Attorney General shall appoint a Special Counsel.

§ 600.2 Alternatives available to the Attorney General.

When matters are brought to the attention of the Attorney General that might warrant consideration of appointment of a Special Counsel, the Attorney General may:

(a) Appoint a Special Counsel;

(b) Direct that an initial investigation, consisting of such factual inquiry or legal research as the Attorney General deems appropriate, be conducted in order to better inform the decision; or

(c) Conclude that under the circumstances of the matter, the public interest would not be served by removing the investigation from the normal processes of the Department, and that the appropriate component of the

Department should handle the matter. If the Attorney General reaches this conclusion, he or she may direct that appropriate steps be taken to mitigate any conflicts of interest, such as recusal of particular officials, **and the Attorney General shall inform the Chairman and Ranking Minority Member of the Judiciary Committees of each House of Congress of any such conclusion or action. This subparagraph does not apply to investigations of a current President and Vice President of the United States, or investigations of a President or Vice President who are the immediate predecessors of the current President and Vice President, or senior officials of such prior administration.**

*****

§ 600.4 Jurisdiction.

*****

(b) *Additional jurisdiction.* If in the course of his or her investigation the Special Counsel concludes that additional jurisdiction beyond that specified in his or her original jurisdiction is necessary in order to fully investigate and resolve the matters assigned, or to investigate new matters that come to light in the course of his or her investigation, he or she shall consult with the Attorney General, who will determine whether to include the additional matters within the Special Counsel's jurisdiction or assign them elsewhere. **If the Attorney General determines that such additional jurisdiction is not warranted, he or she shall so notify the Chairman and Ranking Minority Member of the Judiciary Committees of each House of Congress, of the Special Counsel's initial conclusion and in appropriate detail the basis for the Attorney General's such determination. The notification requirement set forth in this subsection does not apply where the Attorney General concludes that notification would compromise an ongoing investigation, but the Attorney General shall report this conclusion no later than the date that the Special Counsel's transmits his or her Report to the Congress upon the conclusion of the investigation pursuant to §600.8(b)(3).**

*****

§ 600.7 Conduct and accountability.

(a) A Special Counsel shall comply with the rules, regulations, procedures, practices and policies of the Department of Justice. He or she shall consult with appropriate offices within the Department for guidance with respect to established practices, policies and procedures of the Department, including ethics and security regulations and procedures. Should the Special Counsel conclude that the extraordinary circumstances would render compliance with required review and approval procedures by the designated Departmental component inappropriate **or prejudicial to the performance of his or her duties, he or she shall consult directly with the Attorney General, who shall make the final determination.**

(b) The Special Counsel shall not be subject to the day-to-day supervision of any official of the Department **in the conduct of the investigation.** However, the Attorney General may **direct that the Special Counsel report to him or her periodically on the course of the investigation and that the** Special Counsel provide an explanation for any investigative step. **The Attorney General shall not direct the Special Counsel to omit or abandon pursuit of any investigative step except where any such step is plainly inconsistent with law** or established Departmental practices. If the Attorney General concludes that a proposed **investigative** action by a Special Counsel should not be pursued, the Attorney General shall notify **the Chair and Ranking Minority Member of the Judiciary Committees of each House of Congress.**

(c) **In making recommendations on prosecution or declination, the Special Counsel shall be guided in the legal analysis of the factual record by the best and most clearly established understanding of the law, and the Attorney General may direct that the Special Counsel consult with the Office of Legal Counsel on any legal question. The Special Counsel shall be bound by the Office of Legal Counsel's opinion, but in the event that he or she disagrees with that opinion, the Special Counsel may refer the question to the Attorney General for a final determination.**

*****

(e) The Special Counsel may be disciplined or removed from office only by the personal action of the Attorney General. The Attorney General may only remove a Special Counsel for mis- conduct, dereliction of duty, incapacity, conflict of interest, or for other good cause, including violation of Departmental policies. The Attorney General shall inform the Special Counsel in writing of the specific reason for his or her removal **and shall forward a copy to the Chair and Ranking Minority Member of the Judiciary Committees of each House of Congress.**

(f) **If the Special Counsel is removed from office, he or she shall provide the Attorney General and the Chair and Ranking Minority Member of the Judiciary Committees of each House of Congress with a Report on the status of the investigation through the date of the dismissal and such Report shall include a discussion of the material evidence obtained from investigation. The Report shall detail only such factual findings and a brief statement of their legal relevance or significance, but shall not include any conclusory discussion of whether the evidence tended to support prosecution or declination. Notwithstanding the dismissal of the Special Counsel, he or she shall have access to the investigative record for a period of not less than 30 days following notice of dismissal for purposes of preparing the Report provided for under this subparagraph.**

§600.8 Notification and reports by the Special Counsel **and Attorney General.**

*****

(2) [T]he Special Counsel shall report **to the Attorney General as required for various purposes under this Part. In addition, 90 days before the beginning of the fiscal year, the Special Counsel shall** provide a budget request for the following year. The Attorney General shall determine whether the investigation should continue and, if so, establish the budget for the next year. **In the event that the Attorney General determines that the investigation shall not continue, he or she shall provide a notification to the Chairman and Ranking Minority Member of the**

Judiciary Committees of each House of Congress with an explanation of this decision in appropriate detail.

(b) *Conclusion of Investigation.* (1) At the conclusion of the investigation, the Special Counsel shall provide the Attorney General with a confidential Report setting forth the material facts found in the investigation and the legal basis for the Special Counsel's recommendations about prosecution or declination. The Attorney General shall review the Report and, within 14 days of its receipt, shall make the final determination of whether the matter should be prosecuted or declined and shall promptly notify the Special Counsel of that determination.

(2) The Attorney General shall provide the Chairman and Ranking Minority Member of the Judiciary Committees of each House of Congress with a written notification of the receipt of the Special Counsel's Report and the Attorney General's final determination under subsection (b)(1) of this section, including the factual and legal basis for the such determination. The Attorney General shall provide this notification within seven days of this determination and notice to the Special Counsel and in no event later than three weeks from the date that the Special Counsel submits his or her conclusions to the Attorney General. This notification shall include a statement of any questions of law on which the Attorney General directed the Special Counsel to consult with the Office of Legal Counsel, the opinion rendered by that Office, and any final determination by the Attorney General.

(3) On the date that the Attorney General provides Congress with the notification provided for under subparagraph (2) of this section, the Special Counsel shall separately transmit to the Congress and to the public the fact finding contained in the Report to the Attorney General under subsection (b)(1) of this section. The Special Counsel's Report under this subsection shall detail the Special Counsel's factual findings, but it shall not include any discussion or legal analysis of whether the evidence tended to support prosecution or declination.

(c) In all Reports that the Special Counsel issues pursuant to this Part to the Congress and the public, the Special Counsel shall limit such Report to the matters within the approved scope of the investigation, shall avoid any disclosure that unduly harms privacy interest, and shall redact any and all material protected from disclosure under Section 6(e) of the Federal Rules of Criminal Procedure.

[REPEALED § 600.9 Notification and reports by the Attorney General]

JUSTICE DEPARTMENT RULES AGAINST PARTISAN POLITICAL CONSIDERATIONS

5 C.F.R. Part 3801 (Supplemental Standards of Ethical Conduct for Employees of the Department of Justice)

*****

Section 3801.17 Improper partisan political considerations.

In discharging their official responsibilities, employees should answer at all times to principles of fairness and justice, never to partisan politics. Partisan political considerations must play no role in law enforcement decisions of the Department.

5 C.F.R. Part 2635 (Standards of Ethical Conduct for Employees of the Executive Branch)

*****

Section 2635.702 Use of public office for private gain.

An employee shall not use his public office for his own private gain, for the endorsement of any product, service or enterprise, or for the private gain of friends, relatives, or persons with whom the employee is affiliated in a nongovernmental capacity, including nonprofit organizations of which the employee is an officer or member, and persons with whom the employee has or seeks employment or business relations. The specific prohibitions set forth in paragraphs (a) through (d) of this section apply this general standard, but are not intended to be exclusive or to limit the application of this section.

*****

(f) *Improper partisan political purpose.* An employee shall not use his public office for an improper partisan political purpose of influencing the outcome of a Federal, state, or local election to public office. Employees should be mindful at all times that the Code of Ethics in Government Service requires that they put loyalty to country above loyalty to party and that its prohibitions against unfairly "dispensing of special favors or privileges to anyone" and making of "private promises of any kind binding upon the duties of office" include any official actions, or commitment to take such actions, for an improper election-influencing purpose.

EXAMPLE:

An official of a Department is participating in decisions about economic development grants to states and writes an email to colleagues setting out the partisan political considerations that he believes should affect those decisions. He notes the elected officials in those states who have campaigned, or offered to campaign for the president's reelection, and the campaign fundraising assistance that some have provided. The email also highlights his concern about approving grants to one state whose governor has sharply criticized the president and is the Co-Chair of his opponent's campaign. This employee's reliance on partisan political considerations in the award of federal grant money violated the prohibition on the misuse of office for the improper purpose of influencing an election.

★

ACKNOWLEDGMENTS

Many people helped us to write this book.

We thank the Deans at Harvard and New York University law schools, John Manning and Trevor Morrison, and the Director of the Hoover Institution, Tom Gilligan, for their extraordinary support. We also thank the resourceful librarians at Harvard and NYU law schools for tracking down dozens of hard-to-find documents and other forms of indispensable help.

For research assistance, cite-checking, and other forms of assistance, we thank Jason Altabet, Marty Ascher, Rishabh Bhandari, Connor Burwell, Sam Cohen, Mary K. Cornett, Ben Daus-Haberle, Matthew Gluck, Luke Goveas, Claire Groden, Jacob Harcar, Matthew Kahn, Alexander Khan, Katarina Krasulova, Matthew Morris, Ali Nayfeh, Ariana Newberry, Raymond Ngu, Samuel Patterson, Stephen Petraeus, Brett Raffish, Maddie Reddick, Jacob Richards, and Nathaniel Sobel. Other students, too numerous to mention, helped in other ways, for which we are appreciative.

For great discussions on parts of the book manuscript, we thank workshop participants at the American Enterprise Institute, Harvard Law School, New York University Law School, Stanford Law School, the University of Arizona Law School, the University of Chicago Law School, and the Antonin Scalia Law School. For comments and related help on various parts of the book, we thank Graham Allison, Ben Berwick, Andrew Coan, Dan Epps, Justin Florence, Michael Glennon, Oona Hathaway, Daniel Hemel, Sarah Isgur, Paul Larkin, Nicholas Lehman, Bob Lenhard, Bob Litt, Melanie Marlowe, Greg Miller, Ben Miller-Gootnick, Lisa Monaco, Erica Newland, Jesse Panuccio, Kristy Parker, Rick Pildes, Eric Posner, Jeremy Rabkin, Dana Remus, Kathy Ruemmler, Kori Schake, Gary Schmitt, Ilya Shapiro, Don Simon, Brian Svoboda,

Anne Tindall, Philip A. Wallach, Peter Wallison, Andrew Weissmann, and Adam White. So many others at various times engaged in productive discussions with us about reform issues that we cannot name them all—but we are grateful.

We give enormous thanks to the Lawfare team. Ben Wittes came up with the idea of publishing this book with Lawfare—an option that gave us a great deal of flexibility, including allowing us to work on the book until about a month before publication date. Ben also gave us outstanding comments on every chapter. David Priess gave us excellent comments too. With assistance from Hadley Baker, he also marshaled the book through a very compressed production schedule and helped on a huge array of other matters as well—always with encouragement and good cheer. Amy Marks did an extraordinary job copyediting the manuscript—once again on a very compressed schedule. And we are grateful to Quenby Moone for the great cover design.

Finally, we thank Anita Dunn and Leslie Williams for their support during the hard year of work it took to write this book, and we dedicate the book to them.

★

NOTES

Preface

1. Arthur M. Schlesinger, Jr., The Imperial Presidency ix (First Mariner Books 2004) (1973).

Chapter One – Reconstructing The Presidency

1. Tim O'Donnell, *Trump: 'I Have an Article 2 Where I Have the Right to Do Whatever I Want as President'*, The Week: Speed Reads (July 23, 2019).
2. *See* Susan Hennessey & Benjamin Wittes, Unmaking the Presidency: Donald Trump's War on the World's Most Powerful Office (2020).
3. Eric A. Posner, The Demagogue's Playbook: The Battle for American Democracy from the Founders to Trump 8 (2020).
4. *Id.* at 9.
5. 1 Alexis De Tocqueville, Democracy in America 284 (Vintage Books 1990).
6. *The Lawfare Podcast Bonus Edition: Jim Baker on the Russia Investigation*, Lawfare (May 10, 2019).
7. Arthur M. Schlesinger, Jr., The Imperial Presidency ix (First Mariner Books 2004) (1973).
8. INS v. Chadha, 462 U.S. 919 (1983).
9. The Federalist No. 70 at 423 (Alexander Hamilton) (Clinton Rossiter, ed., 1961).
10. Arthur M. Schlesinger, The Cycles of American History 285 (1999).
11. Morrison v. Olson, 487 U.S. 654, 690 (1988).
12. Arthur M. Schlesinger & Alfred De Grazia, American Enterprise Institute for Public Policy Research, Congress and the Presidency: Their Role in Modern Times 8 (1967).
13. *Nixon's Statement on His Financial Affairs*, N.Y. Times (Dec. 9, 1973).

Chapter Two – Foreign State Influence

1. John Bolton, The Room Where It Happened: A White House Memoir 301 (2020).
2. John Bolton, *The Scandal of Trump's China Policy*, Wall St. J. (June 17, 2020).

3.   1 U.S. Dep't of Justice, Report on the Investigation into Russian Interference in the 2016 Presidential Election 1–2 (2019) [hereinafter Mueller Report].

4.   Michael J. Klarman, The Framers' Coup: The Making of the United States Constitution 227 (2016).

5.   Richard Condon, The Manchurian Candidate (1959).

6.   Anatoly Dobrynin, In Confidence: Moscow's Ambassador to Six Cold War Presidents 176 (2001).

7.   Foreign Agents Registration Act, 22 U.S.C. §§ 611–621 (1938).

8.   U.S. Dep't of Justice, FARA Frequently Asked Questions (Apr. 14, 2020), https://www.justice.gov/nsd-fara/general-fara-frequently-asked-questions#1.

9.   This requirement is now codified at 22 U.S.C. §§ 611 et seq. (2018).

10. S. Rep. No. 89-143 (1965) 4 (Conf. Rep.).

11. Bruce D. Brown, Alien Donors: The Participation of Non-Citizens in the U.S. Campaign Finance System, 15 Yale L. & Pol'y Rev. 503, 509 (1997) (quoting remarks from Sen. William Fulbright in support of the amendment banning U.S. agent political contributions).

12. Buckley v. Valeo, 424 U.S. 1 (1976).

13. 2 U.S.C. § 441e(a) (1976).

14. 11 C.F.R. § 100.52(d)(1) (2002). Congress amended this provision of the law yet again in 2002, in the McCain-Feingold reform legislation (formally the Bipartisan Campaign Reform Act), to clarify that the prohibition on foreign national campaign contributions applied to soft money, a term referring to practices by which prohibited campaign funding seeped into the federal electoral system via state parties and in other ways.

15. Allegations of illicit foreign national funding did not end with the 1996 presidential election controversies. Years later, in 2008, the Republican Party charged that President Obama's 2012 reelection campaign had received prohibited foreign national contributions through its online fundraising portals.

16. Bipartisan Campaign Reform (McCain-Feingold) Act, Pub. L. No. 107-155, 116 Stat. 81 (2002).

17. Citizens United v. Fed. Election Comm'n, 558 U.S. 310 (2010).

18. President Barack Obama, State of the Union Address (Jan. 27, 2010).

19. Bluman v. Fed. Election Comm'n, 800 F.Supp.2d 281, 288 (D.D.C. 2011), aff'd 565 U.S. 1104 (2012).

20. Bluman v. Fed. Election Comm'n, 565 U.S. 1104 (2012).

21. McConnell v. Fed. Election Comm'n, 540 U.S. 93, 153 (2003).

22. 18 U.S.C. § 201(b)(2)(A) (2018).

23. 52 U.S.C. § 30101 et. seq. (2018).

24. FEC Advisory Op. 2014-20 (Mar. 19, 2015).

25. Order No. 3915-2017, Appointment of Special Counsel to Investigate Russian Interference with the 2016 Presidential Election and Related Matters (May 17, 2017).
26. 1 Mueller Report.
27. *Id.* at 110.
28. *Id.* at 5.
29. *Id.* at 2, 66.
30. The White House, Memorandum of Telephone Conversation with President Zelenskyy of Ukraine (2019).
31. Letter to Senator Richard Burr, Chairman, Senate Select Committee on Intelligence, and Representative Adam Schiff, Chairman, House Permanent Select Committee on Intelligence (Aug. 12, 2019) (on file with House Permanent Select Committee on Intelligence).
32. U.S. Gov't Accountability Office, B-331564, Office of Mgmt. & Budget—Withholding of Ukraine Security Assistance (2020).
33. H. Perm. Select Comm. on Intel. in Consultation with H. Comm. on Oversight & Reform, 116th Cong., The Trump-Ukraine Impeachment Inquiry Report 35 (2019) [hereinafter House Intelligence Committee Report].
34. *Id.* at 34–35. The committee also found that the president had obstructed the impeachment inquiry by refusing to produce information in defiance of a lawful subpoena, directing executive branch agencies to defy subpoenas and withhold information, directing executive branch officials not to cooperate in the investigation, and "intimidating, threatening, and tampering with" witnesses. *Id.* at 35–36.
35. H. Comm. on the Judiciary, 116th Cong., Impeachment of Donald J. Trump President of the United States 2 (2019).
36. *Id.*
37. Press Release, U.S. Dep't of Justice, Joint Statement from DOJ, DOD, DHS, DNI, FBI, NSA, and CISA on Ensuring Security of 2020 Elections (Nov. 5, 2019).
38. 1 Mueller Report at 66.
39. Foreign Influence Reporting in Elections (FIRE) Act, S. 1562, 116th Cong. (2019).
40. *See, e.g.*, Memorandum from Vice Chairman Donald F. McGahn to the Federal Election Commission, Background Information Regarding Proposed Enforcement Manual (July 25, 2013); *see also* R. Sam Garrett, Congressional Research Service, R44319, The Federal Election Commission: Enforcement Process and Selected Issues for Congress (2015).
41. Kate Ackley, *Thanks to Mueller, Foreign Agents Come Under Great Scrutiny*, Roll Call (Apr. 8, 2019).

42. Jeremy Herb, *Senate Strips Provision from Intelligence Bill Requiring Campaigns to Report Foreign Election Help*, CNN (June 30, 2020).
43. Donald J. Trump (@realDonaldTrump), Twitter (June 14, 2019, 5:06 pm), https://twitter.com/realdonaldtrump/status/1139640264862162944.
44. 22 U.S.C. § 611 (2018).
45. 22 U.S.C. § 611(o).
46. 22 U.S.C. § 612(a)(8) (2015).
47. 18 U.S.C. § 219(a) (2018) provides that:
Whoever, being a public official, is or acts as an agent of a foreign principal required to register under the Foreign Agents Registration Act of 1938 … shall be fined under this title or imprisoned for not more than two years, or both.
48. Pub. L. No. 89-486, 80 Stat. 249 (1966).
49. Memorandum from Michael A. Carvin, Deputy Assistant Attorney General, to the Department of State Legal Advisor, Applicability of 18 U.S.C. § 219 for Retired Foreign Service Officers (1987).
50. *Id.* note 2 at 86.
51. 11 C.F.R. § 100.52(d)(2) (2014). The established legal allowance for fair market value purchases from commercial firms controlled by foreign nationals was frequently overlooked in the "Steele dossier" controversy. The "dossier" was a package of opposition research purchased by the Clinton presidential campaign and the Democratic National Committee from a private investigative firm in the United States, which had in turn subcontracted the work to a non-U.S. counterintelligence firm.
52. 1 Mueller Report at 187.
53. *Id.*
54. 52 U.S.C. § 30121 (2018).

Chapter Three – Financial Conflicts Of Interest

1. James Poniewozik, *With Trump Water, Wine, and Steak, Is It Primary Night or an Infomercial?* N.Y. Times (Mar. 9, 2016).
2. Anita Kumar, *How Trump Fused His Business Empire to the Presidency*, Politico (Jan. 1, 2020).
3. Donald J. Trump (@realDonaldTrump), Twitter (Mar. 2, 2019, 8:31 am), https://twitter.com/realdonaldtrump/status/1101837499230498816.
4. Ethics Reform Act of 1989, Pub. L. No. 101-194, § 401, 103 Stat. 1724, 1748 (1989).
5. Memorandum from Laurence H. Silberman, Deputy Attorney General, to Richard T. Burress, Office of the President (Aug. 28, 1974).
6. Daphna Renan, *Presidential Norms and Article II*, 131 Harvard L. Rev. 2187, 2216 (2018).

7. Memorandum from Antonin Scalia, Assistant Attorney General, Office of Legal Counsel, to the Honorable Kenneth A. Lazarus, Associate Counsel to the President 3 (Dec. 16, 1974).

8. There is some question in the literature of whether Eisenhower or Lyndon Johnson blazed this trail, but beginning with Johnson, the practice took hold to one degree or the other.

9. Megan J. Ballard, *The Shortsightedness of Blind Trusts*, 56 U. Kansas L. Rev. 43, 54–55 (2007).

10. 5 U.S.C. app. §§ 101–111 (2020).

11. Stop Trading on Congressional Knowledge (STOCK) Act of 2012, Pub. L. No. 112-105, § 11, 126 Stat. 298 (2012).

12. U.S. Const. art. II, § 1, cl. 7.

13. U.S. Const. art. I, § 9, cl. 8.

14. 5 U.S.C. § 7342 (2020).

15. 10 U.S.C. § 1060 (2020).

16. Scott Detrow, *Trump Says He Will Pull Back from Business but Offers No Details Yet*, NPR (Nov. 30, 2016).

17. Sheri Dillon, Remarks at President-Elect Trump's Press Conference (Jan. 11, 2017).

18. Bobby R. Burchfield, *Ethics in the Executive Branch: The Constitutional, Statutory and Ethical Issues Faced by the Ethics Adviser to a President Holding Immense Wealth*, 22 Tex. Rev. L. & Pol. 265, 279–80 (2017–2018).

19. Kelly Phillips Erb, *Trump Says No to Presidential Salary: Could You Decline Your Pay & Cut Your Tax Bill?* Forbes (Nov. 14, 2016).

20. Peter Overby, *Change to President Trump's Trust Lets Him Tap Business Profits*, NPR (Apr. 3, 2017).

21. Restatement (Third) of Tr. § 50(2) cmt. d(2) (Am. Law Inst. 2003).

22. Jennifer Calfas, *Eric Trump Says He'll Give the President Quarterly Updates on Business Empire*, Fortune (Mar. 24, 2017).

23. Betsy Swan, *Trump, Inc. Had A Rough Year, but His D.C. Hotel Is Killing It*, Daily Beast (Dec. 29, 2017).

24. Brian Spegele & Rebecca Ballhaus, *Eric Trump Steers Family Empire Under Father's Close Watch*, Wall St. J. (June 29, 2020).

25. Liz Johnstone, *Tracking President Trump's Visits to Trump Properties*, NBC News (Dec. 29, 2017, updated Oct. 22, 2019); *see also* Trump Golf Count, https://trumpgolfcount.com (last visited July 9, 2020) (259 visits).

26. Chase Peterson-Withorn, *No, Trump Is Not Losing '3 to 5 Billion' Dollars from Presidency*, Forbes (Aug. 14, 2019).

27. David A. Fahrenthold, Joshua Partlow, Jonathan O'Connell, & Carol D. Leonnig, *Newly Obtained Documents Show $157,000 in Additional Payments by the Secret Service to Trump Properties*, Wash. Post (Mar. 5, 2020).

28. Susanne Craig, *Trump Boasts of Rapport with Wall Street, but the Feeling Is Not Quite Mutual*, N.Y. Times (May 23, 2016).

29. Marc Caputo, Meredith McGraw, & Anita Kumar, *Trump Owed Tens of Millions to Bank of China*, Politico (Apr. 24, 2020).

30. Walter M. Shaub, Jr., Director, U.S. Office of Gov't Ethics, Remarks at the Brookings Inst. (Jan. 11, 2017).

31. *Blumenthal v. Trump*, 373 F. Supp. 3d 191, 194 (D.D.C.), *cert. denied*, 382 F. Supp. 3d 77 (D.D.C. 2019), *vacated*, No. CV 17-1154 (EGS), 2019 WL 3948478 (D.D.C. Aug. 21, 2019), and *motion to certify appeal granted*, No. CV 17-1154 (EGS), 2019 WL 3948478 (D.D.C. Aug. 21, 2019), and *vacated as moot*, 949 F.3d 14 (D.C. Cir. 2020).

32. *Blumenthal v. Trump*, 949 F.3d 14, 19 (D.C. Cir. 2020) (quoting *Va. House of Delegates v. Bethune-Hill*, 139 S. Ct. 1945, 1953–54 (2019)). This dismissal also rendered the district-court holding that the members of Congress had stated a cause of action as moot.

33. Anita Kumar, *A Trump Hotel Mystery: Giant Reservations Followed by Empty Rooms*, Politico (Oct. 2, 2018).

34. Donald J. Trump (@realDonaldTrump), Twitter (Oct. 19, 2019, 9:18 pm), https://twitter.com/realDonaldTrump/status/1185726931611852802.

35. Philip Rucker & David A. Fahrenthold, *Trump Says His Doral Golf Resort Will No Longer Host Next Year's G-7 Summit, Bowing to Criticism*, Wash. Post (Oct. 20, 2019).

36. 15 U.S.C. 116 § 9054.

37. Mike Celia, *Trump Businesses Barred from Getting Coronavirus Stimulus Money, Schumer Says*, CNBC (Mar. 25, 2020).

38. Ben Protess, Steve Eder, & David Enrich, *Trump (the Company) Asks Trump (the Administration) for Hotel Relief*, N.Y. Times (Apr. 21, 2020).

39. For the People Act, H.R. 1, 116th Cong. (2019).

40. U.S. Office of Gov't Ethics, Executive Branch Personnel Public Financial Disclosure Report, Form 278, at 4.

41. 5 C.F.R. § 2640.101 (2020).

42. H.R. 1 § 8033.

Chapter Four – Tax Disclosure

1. John A. Farrell, Richard Nixon: The Life (2017); *see also* Stanley I. Kutler, The Wars of Watergate 434 (1990).

2. S. Exec. Rep. No. 93-34 at 178–79 (1974).

3. IRM 4.8.4.2.5.

4. Bill Curry, *Yearly Audits Set for Carter, Mondale*, Wash. Post (June 21, 1977).

5. Prior to the Carter administration, Gerald Ford had released a summary of his tax returns as president.

6. Emily Schultheis, *Hillary Clinton, Bernie Sanders Clash over Releasing Wall Street Transcripts, Taxes*, CBS News (April 14, 2016).

7. Christina Wilkie, *Bloomberg Botches Tax Return Question in Democratic Debate: 'I Can't Go to TurboTax,'* CNBC (Feb. 19, 2020).

8. President Jimmy Carter, Remarks at a State Democratic Party Rally in Miami Beach, Florida *in* 14 Wkly. Compilation Presidential Docs. 43 (Oct. 26, 1978).

9. 424 U.S. 1, 67 (1976).

10. 606 F.2d 654, 673 (5th Cir. 1979).

11. Betsy Klein, Donna Borak, & Lauren Fox, *Trump Repeats Claim He Won't Release His Taxes While He's Under Audit*, CNN (Apr. 10, 2019).

12. Naomi Jagoda, *Trump 'In No Rush' to Release Tax Returns*, The Hill (Feb. 25, 2016).

13. *ABC News Anchor David Muir Interviews Donald Trump and Mike Pence*, ABC News (Sept. 6, 2016).

14. Donald J. Trump (@realDonaldTrump), Twitter (May 8, 2019, 6:56 am), https://twitter.com/realDonaldTrump/status/1126078423816921092.

15. 26 U.S.C. § 6103(f) (2018).

16. Congressional Committee's Request for the President's Tax Returns Under 26 U.S.C. § 6103(f), 43 Op. O.L.C. __ 1, 3 (June 13, 2019).

17. *Id.* at 3 (quoting *Watkins v. United States*, 354 U.S. 178, 200 (1957)).

18. *See* Complaint, *Comm. on Ways & Means v. U. S. Dep't of Treasury*, No. 1:19-CV-1974 (D.D.C.. filed July 2, 2019).

19. Trump v. Vance, ___U.S.___ (2020) at 12, WL 3848062.

20. Trump v. Mazars, LLP,___U.S.___ (2020) at 12, WL 3848061.

21. Patterson v. Padilla, 451 P.3d 1171, 1173 (Cal. 2019) (quoting Cal. Const. art. 2 § 5).

22. Trump v. Comm. on Ways & Means, 415 F. Supp. 3d 98 (D.D.C. 2019).

23. Mazars, *supra* note 20.

24. For the People Act, H.R. 1, 116th Cong. (2019).

25. Nixon v. Adm'r of Gen. Servs. Admin., 433 U.S. 425 (1977).

26. *Id.* at 443, 457.

Chapter Five – The Press

1. N.Y. Times Co. v. United States, 403 U.S. 713, 717 (1971) (Black, J., concurring).

2. Jeffrey K. Tulis, The Rhetorical Presidency 4 (1987).

3. *Id.* at 18.

4. *Id.* at 186.

5. For an analysis of presidents and the press prior to this period, including precursors to current controversies, see Harold Holzer, The Endless Battle Between the White House and the Media—from the Founding Fathers to Fake News 3–118 (2020).

6. Michael Schudson, Why Journalism Still Matters 54 (2018).
7. Arthur M. Schlesinger, Jr., The Imperial Presidency 343 (First Mariner Books 2004) (1973).
8. William E. Porter, Assault on the Media: The Nixon Years 82 (1976).
9. Jack Goldsmith, Power and Constraint: The Accountable Presidency After 9/11, 61 (2012).
10. *See* Bruce A. Williams & Michael X. Delli Carpini, After Broadcast News: Media Regimes, Democracy, and the New Information Environment 25 (2011).
11. George E. Reedy, The Twilight of the Presidency 116 (1970).
12. *See generally* Matthew Pressman, On Press: The Liberal Values That Shaped the News (2018).
13. Daniel P. Moynihan, *The Presidency and the Press*, Commentary (March 1971).
14. David E. McCraw, Truth in Our Times: Inside the Fight for Press Freedom in the Age of Alternative Facts 97 (2019).
15. *Id.*
16. Daniel Okrent, *The Public Editor; Is the New York Times a Liberal Newspaper?* N.Y. Times (July 25, 2004), § 4 at 2.
17. William Safire, Before the Fall: An Inside View of the Pre-Watergate White House 342 (1975).
18. *Id.* at 343.
19. Porter, *supra* note 8 at 59.
20. *Id.* at 256–57.
21. David Greenberg, Republic of Spin: An Inside History of the American Presidency 398 (2016).
22. Porter, *supra* note 8 at 32.
23. *Id.* at 34.
24. Lewis W. Wolfson, The Press Covers Government: The Nixon Years from 1969 to Watergate 3 (1973).
25. Porter, *supra* note 8 at 263.
26. *Id.* at 45.
27. *Id.* at 245.
28. Karl E. Campbell, Senator Sam Ervin, Last of the Founding Fathers 224 (2007).
29. *Id.*
30. Pressman, *supra* note 12 at 242.
31. Ezra Klein, Why We're Polarized 146 (2020).
32. Bernie Sanders (@BernieSanders), Twitter (Oct. 23, 2019, 5:18 pm), https://twitter.com/BernieSanders/status/1187116199873830913.
33. Juliet Eilperin, *Here's How the First President of the Social Media Age Has Chosen to Connect with Americans*, Wash. Post (May 26, 2015).
34. Ian Bogost, *Obama Was Too Good at Social Media*, Atlantic (Jan. 6, 2017).
35. Eilperin, *supra* note 33.

36. Pressman, *supra* note 12 at 249.

37. President Donald Trump, Remarks by President Trump at the Presidential Social Media Summit (July 11, 2019).

38. *See* Knight First Amendment Inst. at Columbia Univ. v. Trump, 928 F.3d 226, 230 (2d. Cir. 2019).

39. Defendants-Appellants' Petition for Rehearing en banc at 14, Knight Inst., 928 F.3d 226 (No. 18-1691).

40. Karen Yourish & Jasmine C. Lee, *The Demise of the White House Press Briefing Under Trump*, N.Y. Times (Jan. 28, 2019).

41. Paul Farhi, *White House Imposes New Rules on Reporters' Credentials, Raising Concerns About Access*, Wash. Post (May 8, 2019).

42. CNN, *Trump Clashes with Jim Acosta in Testy Exchange*, YouTube (Nov. 7, 2018).

43. Brian Stelter, *Sarah Sanders Responds to the CNN suit*, CNN Business (Nov. 13, 2018).

44. Transcript of Motion Hearing at 13, Cable News Network, Inc. v. Trump (D.D.C. Nov. 16, 2018) (No. 18-2610).

45. *Id.* at 8.

46. James Fontanella-Khan, Shannon Bond, & Matthew Garrahan, *US Regulators Demand CNN Sale to Approve AT&T-Time Warner Deal*, Fin. Times (Nov. 8, 2017).

47. Hadas Gold, *AT&T Brings Trump Back into Justice Department's Antitrust Case*, CNN Business (Sept. 20, 2018).

48. Elizabeth Jensen, *Public Editor: Aftermath of an Interview*, NPR (Jan. 28, 2020).

49. Myah Ward, *Trump Praises Pompeo for Confrontation with NPR Reporter: 'You Did a Good Job on Her,'* Politico (Jan. 28, 2020).

50. Letter from A.G. Sulzberger, Publisher, N.Y. Times, to N.Y. Times Staff, A Campaign Targets Our Staff (Aug. 25, 2019).

51. Balt. Sun Co. v. Ehrlich, 437 F.3d 410, 418 (4th Cir. 2006).

52. 13 U.S.C. § 1301 (2018); 18 U.S.C. § 371 (2018).

53. U.S. Dep't of Justice, Report on Review of News Media Policies 1 (July 12, 2013); *see also* 28 C.F.R. 50.10(a)(2) (2019).

54. Inspector General Act of 1978, 5 U.S.C. app. 5a §§ 2, 4 (2018).

55. The discussion of improper motive, which underlies the finding of abuse or fraud in the use of federal resources, appears in the context of personnel actions in an August 2019 State Department inspector general report. *See* State Dep't Inspector General, Review of Allegations of Politicized and Other Improper Personnel Practices in the Bureau of International Organization Affairs (August 2019).

56. 28 C.F.R. § 50.10 (a)(1) (2019).

57. 28 C.F.R.§ 50.10 (a)(2) (2019).

58. 28 C.F.R. § 50.10 (c)(4)(vii) (2019).
59. 18 U.S.C. § 201(a)(3) (2018).
60. Inspector General Act of 1978, 5 U.S.C. app. 5a § 5 (2018).
61. We realize that Trump has engaged in unprecedented action to terminate and intimidate inspectors general—a topic we propose to redress in Chapter 13—but even in the Trump era, many inspectors general have maintained independence and served important functions.
62. Letter from David Ferriero, Archivist of the U.S., to Senators Claire McCaskill and Tom Carper (Mar. 30, 2017).
63. Knight Inst., *supra* note 38 at 233.
64. Presidential Records Act, 44 U.S.C. § 2201 (2018).
65. 44 U.S.C. § 2203 (2018).
66. 44 U.S.C. § 2201(2)(B)-(3).
67. 31 C.F.R § 409 (2019).
68. Sherrill v. Knight, 569 F.2d 124 (D.C. Cir. 1977).
69. 31 C.F.R. § 409.1 (2019).
70. Transcript of Motion Hearing, Cable News Network, Inc. v. Trump, *supra* note 44 at 9.

Chapter Six – The Pardon Power

1. Peter Baker, Maggie Haberman, & Sharon LaFraniere, *Trump Commutes Sentence of Roger Stone in Case He Long Denounced*, N.Y. Times (July 10, 2020).
2. Peter Baker, *Roger Stone Denies Withholding 'the Goods' on Trump in Exchange for Clemency*, N.Y. Times (July 14, 2020).
3. Ex parte Garland, 71 U.S. 333, 380 (1866).
4. Schick v. Reed, 419 U.S. 256, 266 (1974).
5. *See, e.g.,* Michael Stokes Paulsen, *The President's Pardon Power Is Absolute*, Nat'l Rev (July 25, 2017).
6. Garland, 71 U.S. at 373–80.
7. *Id.* at 367.
8. *Id.* at 380.
9. Schick, 419 U.S. at 266.
10. Jeffrey Crouch, The Presidential Pardon Power 19 (2009).
11. Letter from A. Mitchell Palmer, Attorney General, to Representative George W. Edmonds, Chairman, House Committee on Claims (Sept. 25, 1919).
12. Compare Brown v. Walker, 161 U.S. 591, 601 (1896) (pardon power of the president "has never been held to take from congress the power to pass acts of general amnesty") with Legislative Proposal to Nullify Criminal Convictions Obtained Under the Ethics in Government Act, 10 Op. O.L.C. 93, 94 (1986)

("the Constitution gives Congress no authority to legislate a pardon for any particular individual or class of individuals").

13. The Laura, 114 U.S. 411, 415 (1885).

14. Garland, 71 U.S. at 333, 381; Knote v. United States, 95 U.S. 149, 154 (1877).

15. Burdick v. United States, 236 U.S. 79, 93–94 (1915).

16. Hoffa v. Saxbe, 378 F. Supp. 1221, 1236 (D.D.C. 1974).

17. Ohio Adult Parole Auth. v. Woodard, 523 U.S. 272, 289 (1998) (O'Connor, J., concurring).

18. The Federalist No. 74 at 447–49 (Alexander Hamilton) (Clinton Rossiter, ed., 1961).

19. Margaret Colgate Love, *The Twilight of the Pardon Power*, 100 J. Crim. L. & Criminology 1169 (2010).

20. *Id.* at 1175.

21. John Gramlich & Kristen Bialik, *Obama Used Clemency Power More Often Than Any President Since Truman*, Pew Research Center (Jan. 20, 2017).

22. Love, *supra* note 19 at 1179.

23. *Id.*

24. *Id.* at 1192.

25. Proclamation 6518 by President George H.W. Bush, Grant of Executive Clemency (Dec. 24, 1992).

26. Letter from President William Jefferson Clinton to Representative Henry Waxman (Sept. 22, 1999).

27. Louis Fisher, 'The Law': When Presidential Power Backfires: Clinton's Use of Clemency, 32 Presidential Stud. Q. 586, 593 (2002).

28. William Jefferson Clinton, *My Reasons for the Pardons*, N.Y. Times (Feb. 18, 2001), § 4 at 13.

29. James Comey, A Higher Loyalty: Truth, Lies, and Leadership 160–61 (2018).

30. Statement by the President on Executive Clemency for Lewis Libby, President George W. Bush (July 2, 2007).

31. Massimo Calabresi & Michael Weisskopf, *George W. Bush Never Pardoned Scooter Libby and It Broke His Relationship with Dick Cheney*, Time (Apr. 13, 2018).

32. Robert Costa, et. al., *Trump Fixates on Pardons, Could Soon Give Reprieve to 63-Year-Old Woman After Meeting with Kim Kardashian*, Wash. Post (June 5, 2018).

33. Donald J. Trump (@realDonaldTrump), Twitter (June 4, 2018, 8:35 am), https://twitter.com/realDonaldTrump/status/1003616210922147841.

34. This paragraph is based on the analysis in Jack Goldsmith & Matthew Gluck, *Trump's Aberrant Pardons and Commutation*, Lawfare (July 11, 2020).

35. Donald J. Trump (@realDonaldTrump), Twitter (Aug. 25, 2017, 10:00 pm), https://twitter.com/realDonaldTrump/status/901263061511794688.

36. Press Release, the White House, Statement from the Press Secretary Regarding the Pardon of I. "Scooter" Lewis Libby (Apr. 13, 2018).

37. Donald J. Trump (@realDonaldTrump), Twitter (May 31, 2018, 9:18 am), https://twitter.com/realDonaldTrump/status/1002177521599860736.

38. Press Release, the White House, Statement from the Press Secretary Regarding the Pardon of Dinesh D'Souza (May 31, 2018).

39. Philip Rucker, et al., *Trump Pardons Conservative Pundit Dinesh D'Souza, Suggests Others Also Could Receive Clemency,* Wash. Post (May 31, 2018).

40. Ted Cruz (@tedcruz), Twitter (May 31, 2018, 9:32 am), https://twitter.com/tedcruz/status/1002181080349380608.

41. David A. Graham, *Trump Is Weaponizing Pardons,* Atlantic (May 31, 2018).

42. Press Release, the White House, Statement from the Press Secretary Regarding Executive Clemency for Patrick Nolan (May 15, 2019).

43. Arnold Steinberg, *It's Time for President Donald Trump to Pardon Pat Nolan,* American Spectator (Aug. 14, 2018).

44. Michael D. Shear & Maggie Haberman, *Trump Grants Clemency to Blagojevich, Milken and Kerik,* N.Y. Times (Feb. 18, 2020).

45. *Id.*

46. U.S. Dep't of Justice, Report on the Investigation into Russian Interference in the 2016 Presidential Election 129–30 (unredacted ed. 2020).

47. *Id.* at 133.

48. Caitlin Oprysko, *Trump: Roger Stone Has 'Very Good Chance of Exoneration' but Will 'Let the Process Play Out,'* Politico (Feb. 20, 2020).

49. Chris Sommerfeldt, *Rudy Giuliani Says Mueller Probe 'Might Get Cleaned Up' with 'Presidential Pardons' in Light of Paul Manafort Going to Jail,* N.Y. Daily News (June 15, 2018).

50. Kevin Breuninger & Brian Schwartz, *Trump Will Decide 'When He's Ready' Whether to Pardon Ex-campaign Boss Paul Manafort, White House Says,* CNBC (Mar. 11, 2019).

51. *See, e.g.,* Application of 28 U.S.C. § 458 to Presidential Appointments of Federal Judges, 19 Op. O.L.C. 350, 357 (1995); Memorandum for Laurence H. Silberman, Deputy Attorney General, from Robert G. Dixon, Jr., Assistant Attorney General, Office of Legal Counsel, *Re: Whether Governor Rockefeller, If Appointed as Vice President, Is Required to Execute a Blind Trust in Order to Avoid Possible Violation of 18 U.S.C. § 208* at 2 (Aug. 20, 1974).

52. Application of 28 U.S.C. § 458 to Presidential Appointments of Federal Judges, 19 Op. O.L.C. 350, 357 (1995).

53. 18 U.S.C. § 201 (1994).

54. On July 23, 2020, Representative Schiff offered a bill to accomplish something like what we propose here. *See* Abuse of the Pardon Prevention Act, H.R.__, 116th Cong.

55. *Confirmation Hearing on the Nomination of the Honorable William Pelham Barr to Be Attorney General of the United States: Hearing Before the Senate Committee on the Judiciary,* 116th Cong. 112 (2019) (statement of William P. Barr).

56. Memorandum for Rod Rosenstein, Deputy Attorney General, from William P. Barr, *Re: Mueller's "Obstruction" Theory* at 1 (June 8, 2018).

57. Donald J. Trump (@realDonaldTrump), Twitter (June 4, 2020, 6:48 am), https://twitter.com/realDonaldTrump/status/1268494718394085376.

58. Jack Goldsmith, *A Smorgasbord of Views on Self-Pardoning,* Lawfare (June 5, 2018).

59. Andrew McCarthy, *Yes, a President May Be Indicted … and May Pardon Himself,* PJ Media (July 24, 2017).

60. Presidential or Legislative Pardon of the President, 1 Op. O.L.C. Supp. 370, 370 (1974).

61. On July 23, 2020, Representative Jamie Raskin introduced a bill that would "declare presidential self-pardons invalid." *See* Kyle Cheney, *House Dems Push Legislation to Criminalize Quid-Pro-Quo Pardons,* Politico (July 23, 2020).

Chapter Seven – Justice Department Independence

1. U.S. Const. art. II, § 3.

2. Free Enter. Fund v. Pub. Co. Accounting Oversight Bd., 561 U.S. 477, 499 (2010).

3. Robert H. Jackson, Attorney General, Address at the Second Annual Conference of United States Attorneys: The Federal Prosecutor 1, 4 (Apr. 1, 1940).

4. *Removing Politics from the Administration of Justice: Hearings on S. 2803 and S. 2978 Before the Senate Committee on the Judiciary,* 93rd Cong. 202 (1974) (statement of Archibald Cox).

5. *See* Dahlia Lithwick & Jack Goldsmith, *Politics as Usual: Why The Justice Department Will Never Be Apolitical,* Slate (Mar. 14, 2007).

6. *Id.* at 16–17 (statement of Ted Sorenson).

7. *See* Eric Holder, Attorney General, Statement Regarding a Preliminary Review into the Interrogation of Certain Detainees (Aug. 24, 2009).

8. *See* Jeffrey H. Smith, *U.S. Interest Might Not Be Served by CIA Prosecutions,* Wash. Post (Aug. 24, 2009).

9. Federal Bureau of Investigation, Domestic Investigations and Operations Guide § 10 (2011).

10. Standards of Conduct for the White House Staff, ¶ 11 (Oct. 28, 1974) [hereafter Ford White House Standards].

11. These norms are supported by constitutional law, *see* United States v. Armstrong, 517 U.S. 456, 464–65 (1996), and federal prosecution guidelines, *see* U.S. Dep't of Justice, Principles of Federal Prosecution § 9-27.260.

12. *See* Andrew Kent, *Congress and the Independence of Federal Law Enforcement,* 52 U.C. Davis L. Rev. 1927, 1934 (2019).

13. *Excerpts from Senate Hearing on Attorney General Gonzales,* Wall St. J. (Apr. 20, 2007). In addition, Deputy Attorney General Paul McNulty testified originally that all but one of the firings were done for "performance-related reasons." *See* U.S. Dep't. of Justice Office of the Inspector General and Office of Professional Responsibility Report, *An Investigation into the Removal of Nine U.S. Attorneys in 2006* 67–68 (2008) [hereinafter IG Report].

14. *Excerpts from Senate Hearing on Attorney General Gonzales, supra* note 12.

15. IG Report at 325.

16. *Id.* at 187, 199, 331; *see also* 18 U.S.C. § 1503(a) (2018), 18 U.S.C. § 1346 (2018).

17. Letter from Ronald Welch, Assistant Attorney General, to the Honorable John Conyers, Jr., Chairman of the Committee on the Judiciary (Dannehy conclusions) (July 21, 2010), https://legaltimes.typepad.com/files/conyers.dannehy.ola.resp.pdf [hereinafter Dannehy Letter].

18. 18 U.S.C. § 1503.

19. Dannehy Letter at 3.

20. United States v. Howard, 569 F.2d 1331, 1336 note 9 (5th Cir. 1978); *see generally* Daniel J. Hemel & Eric A. Posner, *Presidential Obstruction of Justice*, 106 Cal. L. Rev. 1277, 1319–20 (2018).

21. The U.S. attorney firings are not the only evidence of the perception of a mounting threat to depoliticized law enforcement. In 2007, the House Judiciary Committee held hearings on the topic of "Allegations of Selective Prosecution: The Erosion of Public Confidence in Our Federal Justice System." The hearing chair, Representative Bobby Scott, spoke of "a growing list of cases in which U.S. attorneys have allegedly attacked political rivals, while allowing similar activity by its allies to go unchallenged." The committee heard testimony about a study that found patterns of disproportionate federal prosecutions of local officials affiliated with the opposing party. Hearings, Allegations of Selective Prosecution (Serial No. 110-61).

22. United States v. Skilling, 561 U.S. 358 (2010).

23. *President Obama: Steve Kroft Questions President Obama on Topics Including Russia's Incursion in Syria, ISIS, and the 2016 Presidential Race,* CBS News: 60 Minutes (Oct. 11, 2015), https://www.cbsnews.com/news/president-obama-60-minutes-syria-isis-2016-presidential-race/.

24. Kyle Feldscher, *James Comey Book: President Obama and Loretta Lynch 'Jeopardized' the Hillary Clinton Email Investigation*, Wash. Examiner (Apr. 15, 2018).

25. Foreign Intelligence Surveillance Act of 1978, Pub. L. No. 95-511, 92 Stat. 1783, codified at 50 U.S.C. § 1801, et seq.; Omnibus Crime Control and Safe Streets

Act of 1968, Pub. L. 90-351, 82 Stat. 197 (1968), codified at 34 U.S.C. § 10101 *et. seq.*

26. 26 U.S.C. § 7217 (2018).

27. Privacy Act of 1974, Pub. L. No. 93-579, 88 Stat. 1896, codified as amended at 5 U.S.C. § 552a (2018); *see also* Right to Financial Privacy Act of 1978, Pub. L. No. 95-630, 92 Stat. 3697.

28. Freedom of Information Act and Amendments of 1974, Pub. L. No. 93-502, 88 Stat. 1561, amending Freedom of Information Act of 1966, Pub. L. No. 88-554, 80 Stat. 383.

29. Inspector General Act of 1978, Pub. L. No. 95-452, 92 Stat. 1101, codified as amended at 5 U.S.C. app. §§ 1–13 (2018). On these and other reforms, see Kent, *supra* note 11.

30. Section 203 of the Crime Control Act of 1976, Pub. L. No. 94-503, 90 Stat. 2407, 2427, codified at 28 U.S.C. § 532; *see generally* Andrew Kent et al., *Why Did Congress Set a Ten-Year Term for the FBI Director?* Lawfare (May 17, 2017).

31. *See Removing Politics from the Administration of Justice: Hearings on S. 2803 and S. 2978 Before the Subcommittee on Separation of Powers of the Senate Committee on the Judiciary,* 93d Cong. 84 (1974) at 3 (statement of Sam Ervin).

32. Sharon LaFraniere et al., *Trump's Unparalleled War on a Pillar of Society: Law Enforcement,* N.Y. Times (Feb. 3, 2018).

33. Michael S. Schmidt & Michael D. Shear, *Trump Says Russia Inquiry Makes U.S. 'Look Very Bad',* N.Y. Times (Dec. 29, 2017) at A1.

34. Peter Baker, *'Very Frustrated' Trump Becomes Top Critic of Law Enforcement,* N.Y. Times (Nov. 3, 2017) (quoting President Trump's statements on the Larry O'Connor Show).

35. *Id.*

36. Ashley Parker et al., *Trump Sought Release of Classified Russia Memo, Putting Him at Odds with Justice Department,* Wash. Post (Jan. 27, 2018).

37. *See, e.g.,* Donald J. Trump (@realDonaldTrump), Twitter (May 18, 2017, 8:07 am), https://twitter.com/realdonaldtrump/status/865207118785372160; Donald J. Trump (@realDonaldTrump), Twitter (Dec. 2, 2017, 7:06 pm), https://twitter.com/realdonaldtrump/status/937141061343956992.

38. Press Release, House Judiciary Committee, Goodlatte and Judiciary Republicans Renew Call for Second Special Counsel to Address Issues Outside the Scope of Mueller's Investigation (July 27, 2017).

39. *See* Matt Zapotosky, *Sessions Considering Second Special Counsel to Investigate Republican Concerns, Letter Shows,* Wash. Post (Nov. 13, 2017).

40. *William Barr Interview: Read the Full Transcript,* CBS News (May 31, 2019) (transcript of interview with Jan Crawford). Before he became attorney general, Barr stated that the Justice Department was "abdicating its responsibility" by not looking at the Uranium One matter. *See* Peter Baker, *'Lock Her Up' Becomes*

More Than a Slogan, N.Y. Times (Nov. 14, 2017). But in his confirmation hearings, Barr noted that he had no specific information about Uranium One that would say that it had not been handled appropriately and insisted that he did not intend to suggest that the Clinton Foundation merited a criminal investigation. *See* Aaron Blake, *William Barr Tries to Clean Up His Clinton Comments—But Stumbles into a New Mueller Problem*, Wash. Post (Jan. 15, 2019).

41. Donald J. Trump (@realDonaldTrump), Twitter (Feb. 12, 2020, 6:53 am), https://twitter.com/realdonaldtrump/status/1227561237782855680.

42. Anne Flaherty, *Barr Blasts Trump's Tweets on Stone Case: 'Impossible for Me to Do My Job': ABC News Exclusive*, ABC News (Feb. 13, 2020).

43. Katie Benner & Charlie Savage, *Targeting Bolton, Justice Dept. Again in Alignment with Trump's Desires*, N.Y. Times (June 18, 2020).

44. Press Release, U.S. Attorney's Office for the Southern District of New York, Statement of Geoffrey S. Berman (June 20, 2020), https://www.justice.gov/usao-sdny/pr/statement-geoffrey-s-berman.

45. Letter from Attorney General William Barr to United States Attorney Geoffrey Berman (June 20, 2020).

46. *See* Jack Goldsmith & Nathaniel Sobel, *The Durham Investigation: What We Know and What It Means*, Lawfare (July 9, 2020); Jack Goldsmith, *The Good, the Bad and the Ugly in the Attorney General's CBS Interview*, Lawfare (June 2, 2019).

47. *See* Alyza Sebenius & Ben Brody, *Trump Says U.S. Should Sue Facebook, Google*, Bloomberg (June 26, 2019).

48. Kyle Daly, *Trump: Tech Companies, Not Russia, Trying to 'Rig the Election,'* Politico (June 26, 2019).

49. *See* 5 C.F.R. Part 3801; 5 C.F.R. Part 2635.

50. U.S. Dep't. of Justice, Justice Manual, §9-27.260.

51. U.S. Dep't. of Justice, Federal Prosecution of Election Offenses 8 (8th ed. 2017).

52. 5 C.F.R. § 2635.702(a).

53. 5 C.F.R. § 2635.702(d).

54. *Id.*

55. *Accord* Hemel & Posner, *supra* note 19 at 1320.

56. The Judiciary Act of 1789, 1 Stat. 73, § 35.

57. 10 U.S.C. § 113 (2018).

58. Judges—Appointment—Age Factor, 3 Op. O.L.C. 388, 389 (1979).

59. *See* most notably, *Myers v. United States*, 272 U.S. 52, 128 (1926); 20 Op. O.L.C. 279, 280 (1996). The Office of Legal Counsel has issued a number of hard-to-reconcile opinions on the issue, some of which are in application fairly restrictive toward Congress's qualifications power. *See, e.g.*, Inspector Gen. Legislation,

1 Op. O.L.C. 16, 18 note 3 (1977); Common Legislative Encroachments on Exec. Branch Authority, 13 Op. O.L.C. 248, 250 (1989).

60. *See* Seth P. Waxman, Solicitor General, Address to the Supreme Court Historical Society: Presenting the Case of the United States as It Should Be (June 1, 1998).

61. Constitutionality of Statute Governing Appointment of United States Trade Representative, 20 Op. O.L.C. 279, 280 (1996).

Chapter Eight – The Special Counsel

1. Donald C. Smaltz, *The Independent Counsel: A View from Inside*, 86 Geo. L.J. 2307, 2378 (1998).

2. Andrew Coan, Prosecuting the President: How Special Prosecutors Hold Presidents Accountable and Protect the Rule of Law, 28 (2019).

3. Ron Chernow, Grant, 808 (2017).

4. Title VI of the original Ethics in Government Act called the special counsel a "special prosecutor." Title VI of the Ethics in Government Act of 1978, Pub. L. 95-521, 92 Stat. 1824. The title "special prosecutor" was changed to "independent counsel" in the 1982 revisions to the act. Ethics in Government Act Amendments of 1982, Pub. L. 97-409, 96 Stat. 2039 (1983).

5. 28 U.S.C. § 591(a) (2018).

6. 28 U.S.C. § 594(a) (2018).

7. 28 U.S.C. § 596(a)(1) (2018).

8. 28 U.S.C. § 595(c) (2018).

9. *See The Future of the Independent Counsel Act: Hearings Before the Senate Committee on Governmental Affairs*, 106th Cong. (1999); *Reauthorization of the Independent Counsel Statute, Part I: Hearing Before the Subcommittee on Commercial and Administrative Law of the House Committee on the Judiciary*, 106th Cong. (1999).

10. *Future of the Independent Counsel Act, supra* note 9 at 370.

11. *Id.* at 245–46.

12. George J. Mitchell & Robert Dole, The Independent Counsel Statute: Report and Recommendations vi (American Enterprise Institute and the Brookings Institution, May 1999).

13. Office of Special Counsel, 64 Fed. Reg. 37,038 (July 9, 1999), codified at 28 C.F.R. Part 600.

14. *Id.*

15. 28 C.F.R. § 600.1(a).

16. 28 C.F.R. §§ 600.4(a), 600.7(b), 600.8.

17. 64 Fed. Reg. 37,040–41.

18. *Id.*

19. 28 C.F.R. § 600.9.

20. 28 C.F.R. § 600.9(c).

21. *See* Exhibit A, Letter from Deputy Attorney General James B. Comey to Patrick J. Fitzgerald (Dec. 30, 2003); Exhibit B, Letter from Deputy Attorney General James B. Comey to Patrick J. Fitzgerald (Feb. 6, 2004).

22. This is apparent in the regulations themselves, which contemplate that a special counsel need be appointed only when the "investigation or prosecution ... by a United States Attorney's Office or litigating Division of the Department of Justice would present a conflict of interest for the Department ...; and ... it would be in the public interest to appoint an outside special counsel to assume responsibility for the matter." 28 C.F.R. § 600.1. *See also id.* 600.2 (noting "Alternatives Available to the Attorney General").

23. Press Conference, U.S. Dep't of Justice, Appointment of Special Prosecutor to Oversee Investigation into Alleged Leak of CIA Agent Identity and Recusal of Attorney General Ashcroft from the Investigation (Dec. 30, 2003) (Appendix D) [hereinafter Fitzgerald Appointment Press Conference].

24. Order 3915-2017, Appointment of Special Counsel to Investigate Russian Interference with the 2016 Presidential Election and Related Matters (May 17, 2017).

25. *Id.*

26. U.S. Dep't of Justice, Report on the Investigation into Russian Interference in the 2016 Presidential Election 1–2 (2019) [hereinafter Mueller Report].

27. Mueller Report at 2.

28. As noted in the text, Rosenstein appointed Mueller not pursuant to the special counsel regulations but pursuant to his general appointment and related authorities under 28 U.S.C. §§ 509, 510, and 515, and then stated at the end of his appointment that the special counsel regulations "are applicable *to the Special Counsel*" (emphasis added). *See* Order 3915-2017, Appointment of Special Counsel to Investigate Russian Interference with the 2016 Presidential Election and Related Matters. Nonetheless, Mueller, Rosenstein, and Barr treated the regulations as fully governing their actions; thus, the Mueller investigation provides a rich set of experiences under the regulations.

29. Office of Special Counsel, 64 Fed. Reg. 37,038 (July 9, 1999), codified at 28 C.F.R. Part 600.

30. Office of Special Counsel, 64 Fed. Reg. 37,038 (July 9, 1999), codified at 28 C.F.R. Part 600; *see also* 28 C.F.R. § 600.7.

31. This can also be seen in the last sentence of Section 600.7(a) ("Should the Special Counsel conclude that the extraordinary circumstances of any particular decision would render compliance with required review and approval procedures by the designated Departmental component inappropriate, he or she may consult directly with the Attorney General") and 600.7(d) ("The Attorney General may remove a Special Counsel for misconduct, dereliction

of duty, incapacity, conflict of interest, or for other good cause, including violation of Departmental policies").

32. *William Barr Interview: Read the Full Transcript*, CBS News (May 31, 2019) (transcript of interview with Jan Crawford).

33. 2 Mueller Report at 1–2.

34. *William Barr Interview.*

35. *Id.*

36. *Id.*

37. *See* Hannah Gilberstadt, *For the First Time, Majority of Republicans Express Confidence in Fairness of Mueller's Investigation*, Pew Research Center (July 23, 2019). Other polls after Mueller released his report reached similar conclusions. *See, e.g.*, Emily Guskin, *How Americans View Mueller and Impeachment, in Five Charts*, Wash. Post (July 23, 2019).

38. Seila Law LLC v. Consumer Fin. Prot. Bureau, 591 U.S. ___ (2020); Free Enter. Fund v. Pub. Co. Accounting Oversight Bd., 561 U.S. 477 (2010).

39. Seila Law LLC, *supra* note 38, slip. Op. at 12.

40. Mike Rappaport, *Reforming the Special Counsel*, Law & Liberty (June 7, 2019). The distinction was first suggested in this context in Benjamin Wittes, Starr: A Reassessment (2002).

41. 28 C.F.R. § 600.9(c).

42. 28 C.F.R. § 600.1.

43. 28 C.F.R. § 600.4(b).

44. Office of Special Counsel Final Rule: *Supplementary Information*, 64 Fed. Reg. 37,038 (July 9, 1999).

45. 28 C.F.R. § 600.7(b).

46. 28 C.F.R. § 600.6.

47. 28 C.F.R. § 600.7(a).

48. Office of Legal Counsel, A Sitting President's Amenability to Indictment and Criminal Prosecution 256 (Oct. 16, 2000).

49. *Id.*

50. H.R. 2678, 116th Cong. (2019).

51. Office of Legal Counsel *supra* note 48 at 255.

52. 28 C.F.R. § 600.7(d).

53. *Id.*

54. Morrison v. Olson, 487 U.S. 654, 691–92 (1988).

55. *See* Office of Legal Counsel, Application of 28 U.S.C. § 458 to Presidential Appointments of Federal Judges 351 (Dec. 18, 1995), https://www.justice.gov/file/20126/download.

56. *Id.* note 11 at 357.

57. 2 Mueller Report at 171.

58. Daniel J. Hemel & Eric A. Posner, *Presidential Obstruction of Justice*, 106 Cal. L. Rev. 1277, 1320 (2018).

59. 2 Mueller Report at 177–78.

Chapter Nine – *The Bureaucracy Against The President*

1.   Jack Nelson, *Removal of Wiretap Files at FBI Linked to Hoover's Sanity*, L.A. Times (May 15, 1973), § I at 7.

2.   Final Report of the S. Select Comm. to Study Governmental Ops. with Respect to Intel. Activities, Book II: Intelligence Activities and the Rights of Americans, S. Rep. No. 94-755 at 225 (1976).

3.   *Id.* at 226.

4.   Jack Goldsmith & Benjamin Wittes, *The "Grand Bargain" at Risk: What's at Stake When the President Alleges Politics in Intelligence*, Lawfare (Apr. 4, 2017).

5.   Office of the Inspector General, U.S. Dep't of Justice, A Review of Various Actions by the Federal Bureau of Investigation and Department of Justice in Advance of the 2016 Election at 40–41 (2018) [hereinafter OIG Midyear Report].

6.   Federal Bureau of Investigation, Domestic Investigations and Operations Guide § 10.1.2.1 (2016) [hereinafter DIOG].

7.   *Id.* at §§ 7.7, 7.10, DIOG Appendix G § G.9.1 (classified); Federal Bureau of Investigation, Counterintelligence Division Policy Implementation Guide § 3.1.2 (2010) [hereinafter CDPG].

8.   Press Release, Federal Bureau of Investigation, Statement by FBI Director James B. Comey on the Investigation of Secretary Hillary Clinton's Use of a Personal E-Mail System (July 5, 2016).

9.   OIG Midyear Report at 244.

10. The most important such norm was the separation of investigative and pros-ecutive functions as a check on the government's power to bring criminal charges. Horowitz maintained that Comey's announcement of his nonprosecu-tion recommendation violated this norm by making it "virtually impossible for any prosecutor to make any other recommendation," which meant that Comey "thereby effectively operated as not only the FBI Director, but also as the Attorney General." Horowitz also suggested that Comey's unilateral announcement may have violated department regulations regarding the public release of information, as well as its media policy. *See* Release of Information by Personnel of the Department of Justice Relating to Criminal and Civil Proceedings, 28 C.F.R. § 50.2(b)(9) (2019); U.S. Dep't of Justice, United States Attorneys' Manual § 1-7.400 (2018) [hereinafter USAM].

11. Formal policies that undergird this norm include (but are not limited to): Release of Information by Personnel of the Department of Justice Relating to Criminal and Civil Proceedings, 28 C.F.R. § 50.2(b)(3)(iv) (2019); USAM § 1-8.030

(presently embodied in § 1-8.210 and expanded to include all "Department employees"); Memorandum From Eric Holder, Attorney General, to Heads of Department Components and All United States Attorneys, Communications with the White House and Congress 2 (May 11, 2009).

12. OIG Midyear Report at 372.

13. Laura Ingraham, *Prosecutors, Politics and Personal Ambition*, FOX News (June 14, 2018) (interview with Rep. Devin Nunes).

14. Office of the Inspector General, U.S. Dep't of Justice, Review of Four FISA Applications and Other Aspects of the FBI's Crossfire Hurricane Investigation 347 (2019) [hereinafter OIG Crossfire Hurricane Report].

15. Matt Apuzzo, Maggie Haberman, & Matthew Rosenberg, *Trump Told Russians That Firing 'Nut Job' Comey Eased Pressure from Investigation*, N.Y. Times (May 19, 2017).

16. Andrew G. McCabe, *The Threat* 239 (2019).

17. Adam Goldman, Michael S. Schmidt, & Nicholas Fandos, *F.B.I. Opened Inquiry into Whether Trump Was Secretly Working on Behalf of Russia*, N.Y. Times (Jan. 11, 2019).

18. *Joint Executive Session Before the House Committee on the Judiciary and the Committee on Government Reform and Oversight*, 115th Cong. 40, 42 (2018) (interview of James A. Baker (Day 2)) [hereinafter Baker Testimony].

19. *Id.* at 41.

20. CDPG § 1.1; Office of the Attorney General, The Attorney General's Guidelines for Domestic FBI Operations 43 (2016).

21. Baker Testimony at 65.

22. One report focused on Crossfire Hurricane itself, *see* OIG Crossfire Hurricane Report at iii. The other two evaluated issues that intersected with that investigation: Comey's handling of classified information related to the investigation of Trump, *see* OIG Comey Report, *infra* note 27, and the FBI's investigation into Hillary Clinton's use of a classified email server, *see* OIG Midyear Report at 45.

23. In previous writing, we also proposed reforms to redress Horowitz's significant criticisms of the many material errors in the FISA-authorized electronic surveillance of Carter Page, a businessman who advised the Trump campaign. *See* Bob Bauer & Jack Goldsmith, *The FBI Needs to Be Reformed*, Atlantic (Dec. 16, 2019) (arguing that "Congress needs to consider adding criminal or civil penalties for gross factual misrepresentations before the FISA court, akin to the penalties in FISA for electronic surveillance without court approval[,]" and "should also consider ways to introduce some sort of adversarial process, at least in the most sensitive contexts"). We stand by these suggestions but do not pursue them further here since there has already been congressional

engagement and FBI reform on the issue, and this issue is outside our core concerns in this book.

24. OIG Crossfire Hurricane Report at iii.

25. *Id.* at 294.

26. Government's Motion to Dismiss the Criminal Information Against the Defendant Michael T. Flynn at 7, United States v. Flynn, No. 17-232 (D.D.C. May 7, 2020).

27. Office of the Inspector General, U.S. Dep't of Justice, Report of Investigation of Former Federal Bureau of Investigation Director James Comey's Disclosure of Sensitive Investigative Information and Handling of Certain Memoranda 40 (2019) [hereinafter OIG Comey Report].

28. The facts in this passage first appeared in Jack Goldsmith, *Will Donald Trump Destroy the Presidency?*, Atlantic (Oct. 2017).

29. This section draws from our analysis in Bob Bauer & Jack Goldsmith, *The FBI Needs to Be Reformed*, Atlantic (Dec. 16, 2019).

30. As the inspector general noted, "the Midyear investigation was opened with an 'Unknown Subject(s) (UNSUB),' and at no time during the investigation was any individual identified by the FBI as a subject or target of the investigation, including former Secretary Clinton." OIG Midyear Report at 40. But "a primary focus of the Midyear investigation was on former Secretary Clinton's intent in setting up and using her private email server." *Id.* at 41.

31. David Kris, National Security Investigations and Prosecutions (3d ed. 2019).

32. U.S. Dep't of Justice, Federal Prosecution of Election Offenses 8 (8th ed. 2017).

33. *Id.*

34. Logan Act, 18 U.S.C. § 953 (2018).

35. Government's Motion to Dismiss the Criminal Information Against the Defendant Michael T. Flynn at 15 note 4, United States v. Flynn, No. 17-232 (D.D.C. May 7, 2020).

36. *Id.* at 5.

37. 50 U.S.C. § 3091 (2018).

38. OIG Crossfire Hurricane Report 55.

39. 28 C.F.R. § 600.1 (2010).

40. Jack Goldsmith, *Will Donald Trump Destroy the Presidency?* Atlantic (Oct. 2017).

41. Anonymous, *I Am Part of the Resistance Inside the Trump Administration*, N.Y. Times (Sept. 25, 2018).

42. Goldsmith, *supra* note 38.

43. 34 C.F.R. Appendix to Part 73.

44. Pub. L. No. 96-303, 94 Stat. 855 (July 3, 1980).

Chapter Ten – Investigating Past Administrations

1. John Bolton, The Room Where It Happened: A White House Memoir 458 (2020).

2. Tucker Higgins, *Elizabeth Warren Wants to Create a Justice Department Task Force to Investigate Trump Administration Corruption*, CNBC (Jan. 21, 2020).

3. *See* Benjamin Wittes, *Memo to Democrats: Stop Talking About Prosecuting Trump*, Lawfare (June 12, 2019).

4. Rishika Dugyala, *Pardon Trump? Yang Says He Might*, Politico (Feb. 2, 2020).

5. Bill Barrow, *Biden Says He Would Not Pardon Trump or Block Investigations*, ABC News (May 15, 2020).

6. Proclamation No. 4311, 39. Fed. Reg. 32,601 (Sept. 10, 1974).

7. Evan Thomas, Being Nixon: A Man Divided 840 note 1 (2015).

8. John Robert Greene, The Presidency of Gerald Ford 53 (1995).

9. Barry Werth, 31 Days: The Crisis That Gave Us the Government We Have Today 243 (2006).

10. Thomas, *supra* note 7 at 844.

11. *Transcript of Ford's First News Conference Since He Assumed the Presidency*, N.Y. Times (Aug. 29, 1974).

12. President Gerald R. Ford, Remarks on Signing a Proclamation Granting Pardon to Richard Nixon (Sept. 8, 1974).

13. Adam Clymer, *Ford Wins Kennedy Award for 'Courage' of Nixon Pardon*, N.Y. Times (May 22, 2001).

14. *See, e.g.*, Greene, *supra* note 8 at 193.

15. Bolton, *supra* note 1 at 458.

16. David Johnston & Charlie Savage, *Obama Reluctant to Look into Bush Programs*, N.Y. Times (Jan. 11, 2009).

17. Dan Balz & Perry Bacon Jr., *Congress Debates Fresh Investigation of Interrogations*, Wash. Post (Apr. 23, 2009).

18. All the facts conveyed in the next few paragraphs, and more details, are collected in Jack Goldsmith & Nathaniel Sobel, *The Durham Investigation: What We Know and What It Means*, Lawfare (July 9, 2020).

19. *William Barr Interview: Read the Full Transcript*, CBS News (May 31, 2019) (transcript of interview with Jan Crawford).

20. Tim Hains, *Full Interview: AG Bill Barr Criticizes Inspector General Report on the Russia Investigation*, Real Clear Politics (Dec. 11, 2019) (transcript of interview with NBC's Pete Williams).

21. Ian Schwartz, *Barr: 'Unexplained Misconduct' That May Involve Bad Motive Cannot Be Squared with Innocent Mistakes*, Real Clear Politics (Dec. 20, 2019) (transcript of interview with Fox's Martha MacCallum).

22. Ian Schwartz, *Barr: Russian Collusion Probe into Trump 'One of the Greatest Travesties in American History,'* Real Clear Politics (Apr. 10, 2020) (transcript of interview with Fox's Laura Ingraham).

23. Mattathias Schwartz, *William Barr's State of Emergency*, N.Y. Times Magazine (June 10, 2020).

24. The facts, arguments, and analysis over the next few pages originally appeared in a *Lawfare* post by Jack Goldsmith and Nathaniel Sobel in July 2020. *See* Jack Goldsmith & Nathaniel Sobel, *The Durham Investigation: What We Know and What It Means*, Lawfare (July 9, 2020).

25. U.S. Dep't of Justice, Justice Manual §§ 1-7.001, 1-7.400(B) (2018).

26. *Id.* § 1-7.400(C).

27. *Id.* § 9-27.760.

28. 28 C.F.R. § 50.2(b).

29. See *generally* Offices of the Inspectors General, Unclassified Report on the President's Surveillance Program (2009).

Chapter Eleven – The White House Counsel

1. Darby A. Morrisroe, First Lawyer: The Institutionalization of the Office of White House Counsel, 1943–1989, 142 (August 2007) (unpublished Ph.D. dissertation, University of Virginia).

2. Vicki Quade, *The President Is His Only Client*, Barrister, Spring 1988 at 34.

3. Jeremy Rabkin, *At the President's Side: The Role of the White House Counsel in Constitutional Policy*, 56 Law & Contemp. Probs. 63, 94 (1993).

4. Daniel J. Meador, The President, the Attorney General, and the Department of Justice 40 (1980).

5. Interview of Peter Wallison, former White House Counsel, by Jeff Chidester, Stephen F. Knott, Darby Morrisroe, and Christine Nemacheck, Miller Center of Public Affairs, University of Virginia (Oct. 28–29, 2003).

6. Miller Center, University of Virginia, *Bernard Nussbaum Oral History* (2002).

7. Wallison, *supra* note 5 at 100.

8. Jack Goldsmith, *President Obama Rejected DOJ and DOD Advice, and Sided with Harold Koh, on War Powers Resolution*, Lawfare (June 17, 2011).

9. Memorandum from Acting Assistant Attorney General David J. Barron, Office of Legal Counsel, to Attorneys of the Office (July 16, 2010).

10. Jack Goldsmith, *The Decline of OLC*, Lawfare (Oct. 28, 2015).

11. Jack Goldsmith, The Terror Presidency: Law and Judgment Inside the Bush Administration 144 (2007).

12. Barton Gellman, Angler: The Cheney Vice Presidency 320 (2008).

13. Michael Kruse, *Can Trump Still Sue His Way Out of Trouble?* Politico (June 3, 2019).

14. *Id.*

15. Jonathan Mahler & Matt Flegenheimer, *What Donald Trump Learned from Joseph McCarthy's Right-Hand Man*, N.Y. Times (June 20, 2016).
16. Michael Kruse, *'He Brutalized for You,'* Politico (Apr. 8, 2016).
17. *Id.*
18. Emily Jane Fox, *Michael Cohen Would Take a Bullet for Donald Trump*, Vanity Fair (Sept. 6, 2017) (interview with Michael Cohen).
19. *Id.*
20. Michael Rothfeld & Joe Palazzolo, *Trump Lawyer Arranged $130,000 Payment for Adult-Film Star's Silence*, Wall St. J. (Jan. 12, 2018).
21. Paula Reid, Pat Milton, & Kathryn Watson, *Ex-Trump Attorney Michael Cohen Pleads Guilty to Campaign Finance Violations*, CBS News (Aug. 21, 2018).
22. *Read Michael Cohen's Full Sentencing Statement and Why 'Blind Loyalty' to Trump Was the Biggest Mistake of His Life*, NBC News (Dec. 12, 2018).
23. 1 U.S. Dep't of Justice, Report on the Investigation into Russian Interference in the 2016 Presidential Election 34 (2019) [hereinafter Mueller Report].
24. Michael S. Schmidt, *Obstruction Inquiry Shows Trump's Struggle to Keep Grip on Russia Investigation*, N.Y. Times (Jan. 4, 2018).
25. Michael S. Schmidt & Maggie Haberman, *White House Counsel, Don McGahn, Has Cooperated Extensively in Mueller Inquiry*, N.Y. Times (Aug. 18, 2018).
26. Donald J. Trump (@realDonaldTrump), Twitter (May 11, 2019, 6:39 pm), https://twitter.com/realDonaldTrump/status/1127342552745762816.
27. Washington v. Trump, 847 F. 3d 1151, 1166 (9th Cir. 2017).
28. *See* Jack Goldsmith, *The Man Who Should Have Stopped the Flynn Mess*, Daily Beast (Apr. 10, 2017); Jack Goldsmith, *The Spotlight Will Now Shift to the White House Counsel*, Lawfare (Feb. 14, 2017).
29. Donald J. Trump (@realDonaldTrump), Twitter (Oct. 1, 2019 at 7:41 pm), https://twitter.com/realDonaldTrump/status/1179179573541511176.
30. Donald J. Trump (@realDonaldTrump), Twitter (Jan. 23, 2020 at 7:52 am), https://twitter.com/realDonaldTrump/status/1220328518288052225.
31. Letter from President Trump to Speaker of the House Pelosi (Dec. 17, 2019).
32. Letter from White House Counsel Pat A. Cipollone to the Speaker of the House and Committee Chairs (Oct. 8, 2019) (on file with Lawfare Blog) (emphasis in the original).
33. Peter Baker, *Trump Team, Opening Defense, Accuses Democrats of Plot to Subvert Election*, N.Y. Times (Jan. 25 2020).
34. Bruce Ackerman, *Abolish the White House Counsel and the Office of Legal Counsel, Too, While You're at It*, Slate (Apr. 22, 2009).
35. The White House, Remarks by President Trump to the Nation at the White House (Feb. 6, 2020).

36. Letter from House Impeachment Managers to White House Counsel Pat A. Cipollone (Jan. 21, 2020) (on file with the U.S. House Permanent Select Committee on Intelligence).

37. Maggie Haberman & Michael S. Schmidt, *Trump Told Bolton to Help His Ukraine Pressure Campaign, Book Says*, N.Y. Times (Jan. 31, 2020).

38. U.S. Dep't of Justice, Office of Legal Counsel, *About the Office*, https://www.justice.gov/olc (last visited July 25, 2020).

39. Barron, *supra* note 8.

40. George Reedy, Twilight of the Presidency 18, 26 (1970).

Chapter Twelve – War Powers And Nuclear Weapons

1. The Federalist No. 51 at 418 (Alexander Hamilton) (Clinton Rossiter, ed., 1961).

2. *See* 3 The Records of the Federal Convention of 1787 318–19 (Max Farrand, ed., 1911) (Statement of James Madison of Virginia, Aug. 17, 1787); The Prize Cases, 67 U.S. (2 Black) 635 (1863).

3. *See* The President's Constitutional Authority to Conduct Military Operations Against Terrorists and Nations Supporting Them, 25 Op. O.L.C. 188 (2001).

4. *See* Authority of the President Under Domestic and International Law to Use Military Force Against Iraq, 26 Op. O.L.C. 143, 152 (2002).

5. *See* Curtis A. Bradley & Jack L. Goldsmith, *Obama's AUMF Legacy*, 110 Am. J. Int'l L. 628 (2016); Jack Goldsmith & Matthew Waxman, *The Legal Legacy of Light-Footprint Warfare*, 39:2 Washington Quarterly 7 (Summer 2016); Jack Goldsmith, *The Contributions of the Obama Administration to the Practice and Theory of International Law*, 57 Harv. Int'l L.J. (2016).

6. Authority to Use Military Force in Libya, 35 Op. O.L.C. 1 (2011); Authority to Order Targeted Airstrikes Against the Islamic State of Iraq and the Levant, 38 Op. O.L.C. 1 (2014).

7. Little v. Bareme, 6 U.S. 170 (2 Cranch) (1804).

8. U.S. Dep't of Defense, Report on Nuclear Employment Strategy of the United States Specified in Section 491 of 10 U.S.C. 4 (2013) (emphasis added).

9. An Act for the Development and Control of Atomic Energy, Pub. L. No. 79-585, § 6, 60 Stat. 755, 763 (1946); An Act to Amend the Atomic Energy Act of 1946, as Amended, and for other Purposes, Pub. L. No. 83-703, 68 Stat. 919, 936 (1954) (emphasis added).

10. *See* S. Rep. No. 79-1211 pt. 2 at 19 (1946); *see also* Richard G. Hewlett & Oscar E. Anderson, Jr., 1 The New World: A History of the United States Atomic Energy Commission 1939/1946 499–530 (1962).

11. *See, e.g.,* Draft Report by the National Security Council on United States Policy on Atomic Warfare, *in* 1 U.S. Dep't of State, Foreign Relations of the United States, 1948, General: The United Nations pt. 2 625, 628 (Neal H. Peterson,

Ralph R. Goodwin, Marvin W. Kranz, & William Z. Slany, eds., 1976). ("The decision as to the employment of atomic weapons in the event of war is to be made by the Chief Executive when he considers such decision to be required.")

12. Constitutionality of Nuclear Regulatory Commission's Imposition of Civil Penalties on the Air Force, 13 Op. O.L.C. 131, 132 note 2 (1989).

13. U.S. Dep't of Defense, JP 3-72, Nuclear Operations III-4 (2019).

14. U.S. Dep't of Defense, Nuclear Posture Review Report ix (2010).

15. *Id.* at 21.

16. For elaboration of this paragraph, with an explanation of the legal infrastructure, see Sarah Grant & Jack Goldsmith, *What If President Trump Orders Secretary of Defense Mattis to Do Something Deeply Unwise?* Lawfare (Aug. 22, 2017).

17. For the first version, *see* Gil Troy, *The Most Patriotic Act of Treason in American History?* Daily Beast (Apr. 11, 2017). For the second version, *see* Garrett M. Graff, *The Madman and the Bomb*, Politico Magazine (Aug. 11, 2017). Some historians have denied that this event ever happened. *See* Stanley Kutler, *The Imaginings of James R. Schlesinger*, Huffington Post (June 1, 2014). Others who were there at the time insisted that something like it did. *See* Jeffrey H. Smith, *Of Laws, Not Men*, Just Security (June 9, 2017). In a 2007 interview, Schlesinger denied that he told the chairman, General George Brown, not to take an unverified order from Nixon. Schlesinger instead says that he told Brown to check with Schlesinger if Brown received an order from the "White House staff," not Nixon himself. When asked about ordering Brown to disobey an order from Nixon, Schlesinger emphasized that "you can't do it" because "the president is the commander-in-chief." He added that his instructions to Brown were designed to preserve, rather than undermine, the "integrity of the chain of command." Interview by Timothy Naftali with James Schlesinger, Nixon Library (Dec. 10, 2007).

18. Press Conference with President Truman, Nov. 30, 1950, *in* VII Foreign Relations of the United States, Korea 1261, 1261–62 (John P. Glennon, ed., 1976).

19. The President's News Conference of Mar. 17, 1954, *in* Public Papers of the Presidents of the United States: Dwight D. Eisenhower 1954, January 1 to December 31, 1954 320, 325 (David C. Eberhart, ed., 1960).

20. Fred Kaplan, The Bomb: Presidents, Generals, and the Secret History of Nuclear War 10 (2020).

21. For this and other statements, *see JFK on Nuclear Weapons and Non-Proliferation*, Carnegie Endowment for International Peace (Nov. 17, 2003).

22. President John F. Kennedy, Radio and Television Report to the American People on the Soviet Arms Buildup in Cuba (Oct. 22, 1962).

23. Graff, *supra* note 17.

24. Robert Norris & Hans Kristensen, *U.S. Nuclear Threats: Then and Now*, Bulletin of the Atomic Scientists (Sept./Oct. 2006) at 69. In 1991, President George H.W. Bush had privately decided against using nuclear force but nonetheless communicated via diplomatic intermediaries to "convey an explicit nuclear threat to Saddam Hussein." *Id.* at 71.

25. Philip Rucker & Carol Leonnig, A Very Stable Genius: Donald J. Trump's Testing of America (2020).

26. On Jan. 2, 2017, President Trump tweeted, "North Korea just stated that it is in the final stages of developing a nuclear weapon capable of reaching parts of the U.S. It won't happen!" Donald J. Trump (@realDonaldTrump), Twitter (Jan. 2, 2017, 6:05 pm), https://twitter.com/realDonaldTrump/status/816057920223846400.

27. Meghan Keneally, *From 'Fire and Fury' to 'Rocket Man,' the Various Barbs Traded Between Trump and Kim Jong Un*, ABC News (June 12, 2018).

28. Philip Rucker & Karen DeYoung, *Trump Reiterates Warning to N. Korea: 'Fire and Fury' May Not Have Been 'Tough Enough,'* Wash. Post (Aug. 10, 2017).

29. The White House, Remarks by President Trump to the 72nd Session of the United Nations General Assembly (Sept. 19, 2017).

30. Keneally, *supra* note 27.

31. Eli Watkins, *Trump Taunts North Korea: My Nuclear Button Is 'Much Bigger,' 'More Powerful'*, CNN Politics (Jan. 3, 2018).

32. *Authority to Order the Use of Nuclear Weapons: Hearing Before the Senate Committee on Foreign Relations*, 115th Cong. 2 (2017) (statement of Senator Benjamin L. Cardin, Ranking Member, Senate Committee on Foreign Relations).

33. Kaplan, *supra* note 20 at 282.

34. *Id.* at 285.

35. H.R. 669, 115th Cong. § 2(b) (2017).

36. Authorization for Use of Military Force Against Iraq Resolution of 2002, Pub. L. 107-243, § 3(a), 116 Stat. 1498, 1501 (2002).

37. Authorization for Use of Military Force, Pub. L. 107-40, § 2(a), 115 Stat. 224, 224 (2001).

38. Jeh Johnson, General Counsel, U.S. Dep't of Defense, Dean's Lecture at Yale Law School: National Security Law, Lawyers, and Lawyering in the Obama Administration (Feb. 22, 2012).

39. Authorization for Use of Military Force of 2018, S.J. Res. 59, 115th Cong. (2018).

40. For a good introduction to the approach in the Biden bills, and a great overview of the problem of constraining presidential war powers, see Michael Glennon, Constitutional Diplomacy (1991).

41. *See Authority to Order the Use of Nuclear Weapons, supra* note 32 at 4–5 (testimony of General Robert Kehler (ret.), former commander, U.S. Strategic Command).
42. *Id.* at 27 (statement of Senator Marco Rubio, Member, Senate Committee on Foreign Relations).
43. Richard K. Betts & Matthew Waxman, *Safeguarding Nuclear Launch Procedures: A Proposal*, Lawfare (Nov. 19, 2017).
44. War Powers Resolution, 50 U.S.C. § 1541(c) (2018).

Chapter Thirteen – Vacancies Reform

1. U.S. Const. art II, § 2, cl. 2.
2. U.S. Const. art II, § 2, cl. 3.
3. Act of May 8, 1792, ch. 37, § 8, 1 Stat. 279, 281.
4. Act of Feb. 13, 1795, ch. 21, 1 Stat. 415.
5. Act of July 23, 1868, ch. 227, § 3, 15 Stat. 168.
6. *See* Keith E. Whittington, *The Confirmation Process We Deserve*, Pol'y Rev. (June 1, 2001).
7. Michael J. Gerhardt, The Federal Appointments Process: A Constitutional and Historical Analysis 61 (2003).
8. Todd Garvey & Daniel J. Sheffner, Congressional Research Service, R45442, Congress' Authority to Influence and Control Executive Branch Agencies 27 (2018).
9. Staff of S. Comm. on Governmental Affairs, 105th Cong., Report on Federal Vacancies Reform Act (1998).
10. *See* Morton Rosenberg, Congressional Research Service, 98-892, The New Vacancies Act: Congress Acts to Protect the Senate's Confirmation Prerogative 3 (1998).
11. *See* Morton Rosenberg, Congressional Research Service on Validity of Designation of Bill Lann Lee as Acting Assistant Attorney General for Civil Rights (Jan. 14, 1998) (appended to *Oversight of the Implementation of the Vacancies Act: Hearing on S. 1764 Before the Senate Committee on Governmental Affairs*, 105th Cong., 62-115 (1998)).
12. 5 U.S.C. §§ 3345–3349 (2018).
13. 5 U.S.C. § 3345(a) (2018).
14. Anne Joseph O'Connell, Actings, 120 Colum. L. Rev. 613, 631 (2020).
15. NLRB v. Noel Canning, 573 U.S. 513 (2014).
16. Nina A. Mendelson, *The Permissibility of Acting Officials: May the President Work Around Senate Confirmation,* 72 Admin L. Rev. (forthcoming 2020) (manuscript at 26).

17. See *Federal Vacancies Reform Act of 1998 — Assistant Attorney General for the Office of Legal Counsel, U.S. Department of Justice,* U.S. Government Accountability Office Opinion B-310780.

18. Sarah Wheaton, *White House to Demote ATF Chief — To Keep Him on the Job,* Politico (Oct. 8, 2016).

19. Darren Samuelsohn, *Obama's Vanishing Administration,* Politico (Jan. 5, 2016).

20. Philip Shenon, *Interim Heads Increasingly Run Federal Agencies,* N.Y. Times (Oct. 15, 2007).

21. Id.

22. Burgess Everett & Marianne Levine, *The Senate's Record-Breaking Gridlock Under Trump,* Politico (June 8, 2020.

23. Amanda Becker, *Trump Says Acting Cabinet Members Give Him 'More Flexibility,'* Reuters (Jan. 6, 2019).

24. Brian Naylor, *An Acting Government for the Trump Administration,* NPR (Apr. 9, 2019).

25. Chiqui Esteban, *Who's in Charge? Many Months of Acting Secretaries,* Wash. Post: The Fix (July 24, 2019).

26. Alan Fram, *GOP Mutters, Gently, As Trump Sidesteps Senate for Top Aides,* Associated Press (June 17, 2019).

27. Anne Joseph O'Connell, *Acting Leaders: Recent Practices, Consequences, and Reforms,* Brookings (July 22, 2019).

28. See O'Connell, supra note 14 at 652–55; Aaron Blake, *Trump's Government Full of Temps,* Wash. Post (Feb. 21, 2020).

29. 12 U.S.C. § 5491(b)(5)(B) (2018).

30. Philip Rucker, Dan Lamothe, & Josh Dawsey, *Trump Forces Mattis Out Two Months Early, Names Shanahan Acting Defense Secretary,* Wash. Post (Dec. 23, 2018).

31. Garrett M. Graff (@vermontgmg), Twitter (Jan. 7, 2020), https://twitter.com/vermontgmg/status/1214702040817061888.

32. Mendelson, supra note 16 (manuscript at 26).

33. Memorandum from Steven A. Engel, Assistant Attorney General, Office of Legal Counsel, to Emmet T. Flood, Counsel to the President (Nov. 14, 2018); see also Authority of the President to Name an Acting Attorney General, 31 Op. O.L.C. 208 (2007).

34. Steve Vladeck, *Ken Cuccinelli and the Federal Vacancies Reform Act of 1998,* Lawfare (June 10, 2019).

35. L.M.-M. v. Cuccinelli, No. CV 19-2676 (RDM), 2020 WL 985376 at *3 (D.D.C. Mar. 1, 2020).

36. See 5 U.S.C. app. § 3 (2018).

37. See Mendelson, supra note 16 (manuscript at 27) (quoting Secretary of the Interior, Order No. 3345, Amendment No. 32, May 5, 2020); Dep't of the Interior, Temporary Redelegation of Authority for Certain Vacant Non-Career Senate Confirmed Positions 1 (May 5, 2020)).
38. The offices were assistant secretary, Land and Minerals Management; director, Bureau of Land Management; special trustee for American Indians; director, National Park Service; and director, Office of Surface Mining Reclamation and Enforcement. See Id.
39. O'Connell, supra note 14 at 655.
40. Washington Post & Partnership for Public Service, *Tracking How Many Key Positions Trump Has Filled So Far,* Wash. Post: PowerPost (last visited July 13, 2020).
41. For the best efforts, from which we have learned much and drawn heavily, even when we do not always agree, see O'Connell *supra* note 14; Ben Miller-Gootnick, Note, *Boundaries of the Federal Vacancies Reform Act,* 56 Harv. J. on Legis. 459 (2019); Mendelson *supra* note 16; Steve Vladeck, *Trump Is Abusing His Authority to Name 'Acting Secretaries.' Here's How Congress Can Stop Him,* Slate (Apr. 9, 2019).
42. The Constitutional Separation of Powers Between the President and Congress, 20 Op. O.L.C. 124, 164 (1996) (quoting Memorandum for Neil Eggleston, Associate Counsel to the President, from Walter Dellinger, Assistant Attorney General, Office of Legal Counsel, Re: Appointment of an Acting Staff Director of the United States Commission on Civil Rights 3 (Jan. 13, 1994)).
43. See Authority of the President to Remove the Staff Director of the Civil Rights Commission and Appoint an Acting Staff Director, 25 Op. O.L.C. 103 (2001); The Constitutional Separation of Powers Between the President and Congress, 20 Op. O.L.C. 124 (1996).
44. See, e.g., 31 U.S.C. § 703 (2018) (specifying the procedures that occur when a vacancy arises in the office of comptroller general or deputy comptroller general); 6 U.S.C. §113 (2018) (specifying that in the event that both the secretary and deputy secretary of homeland security positions are vacant, the under secretary of homeland security for management shall serve as acting secretary).
45. See Memorandum from Steven A. Engel to Emmet T. Flood, supra note 33; Designation of Acting Director of the Office of Management and Budget, 27 Op. O.L.C. 121 (2003); see also United States v. Eaton, 169 U.S. 331 (1898); Mendelson, supra note 16. Supreme Court Justice Clarence Thomas has argued that nonconfirmed officials can never serve as an acting official in a principal office. See NLRB v. SW Gen., Inc., 137 S. Ct. 929, 945–49 (2017) (Thomas, J., concurring).
46. O'Connell, supra note 14 at 710.

47. All of these options are discussed in O'Connell, id. at 722.
48. 5 U.S.C. § 3347 (2018).
49. 5 U.S.C. § 3345 (2018). See also Miller-Gootnick, supra note 41.

Chapter Fourteen – Other Reforms

1. Congressional Research Service, R42659, The Posse Comitatus Act and Related Matters: The Use of the Military to Execute Civilian Law 1 (2018).
2. U.S. Const., art. IV, § 4.
3. 18 U.S.C. § 1385 (2018).
4. 10 U.S.C. §§ 251–253 (2018).
5. Thaddeus Hoffmeister, *An Insurrection Act for the Twenty-First Century,* 39 Stetson L. Rev. 861, 905 (2010).
6. Sterling v. Constantin, 287 U.S. 378, 400 (1932).
7. Hoffmeister, supra note 5 at 863.
8. John Warner National Defense Authorization Act for Fiscal Year 2007, Pub. L. No. 109-364, §1076, 120 Stat. 2083, 2404 (2006) (repealed 2008).
9. President Donald J. Trump, Statement on George Floyd Protests (June 1, 2020).
10. Helene Cooper et al., *Milley, America's Top General, Walks into a Political Battle,* N.Y. Times (June 5, 2020).
11. See Letter from William P. Barr, Attorney General, to Muriel Bowser, Mayor, District of Columbia, and Karl A. Racine, Attorney General for the District of Columbia 2 (June 9, 2020) (setting out legal authorities for actions to quell disorder in the District).
12. See Ian Shapira, *For 200 years, the Insurrection Act Has Given Presidents the Power to Deploy the Military to Quell Unrest,* Wash. Post (June 3, 2020).
13. *Defense Secretary Esper Briefing on Protests Across the U.S.,* C-SPAN (June 3, 2020).
14. Lolita C. Baldor, *Army: Esper Reverses Plan to Send Active-Duty Troops Home,* Associated Press News (June 3, 2020).
15. Interview by Sean Spicer with President Donald J. Trump (June 3, 2020).
16. Aubree Eliza Weaver, *Barr Says Trump Never Demanded 10,000 Active-Duty Troops,* Politico (June 7, 2020).
17. Letter from Adam Smith, Chairman, House Armed Services Committee, to the Honorable Mark T. Esper, Secretary, U.S. Department of Defense 1 (June 10, 2020).
18. Missy Ryan, *In Letter, Pentagon Leaders Outline Military Role in Recent Unrest,* Wash. Post (June 11, 2020).
19. Helene Cooper, *Milley Apologizes for Role in Trump Photo Op: 'I Should Not Have Been There,'* N.Y. Times (June 11, 2020).
20. Jeffrey Goldberg, *James Mattis Denounces President Trump, Describes Him as a Threat to the Constitution,* Atlantic (June 3, 2020).

21. 32 U.S.C. § 502(f) (2018).

22. See Letter from Attorney General Barr, *supra* note 11 at 2. See also Steve Vladeck, *Why Were Out-of-State National Guard Units in Washington, D.C.? The Justice Department's Troubling Explanation,* Lawfare (June 9, 2020).

23. See A Guide to Emergency Powers and Their Use, Brennan Center for Justice (last visited July 24, 2020).

24. 50 U.S.C. §§ 1601–1651 (2018).

25. See Declared National Emergencies Under the National Emergencies Act, Brennan Center for Justice (last visited July 20, 2020); Executive Order No. 13936, 85 Fed. Reg. 43,413 (July 14, 2020).

26. Presidential Proclamation No. 9,844, 84 Fed. Reg. 4949–50 (Feb. 15, 2019).

27. Harold Hongju Koh & John Choon Yoo, *Dollar Diplomacy/Dollar Defense: The Fabric of Economics and National Security Law,* 26 Int'l Law. 715, 744 (1992).

28. See Gerhard Casper, *An Essay in Separation of Powers: Some Early Versions and Practices,* 30 Wm. & Mary L. Rev. 211, 228–29 (1989).

29. Marshall v. Gordon, 243 U.S. 521, 541 (1917).

30. Josh Chafetz, Executive Branch Contempt of Congress, 76 U. Chi. L. Rev. 1083, 1131 (2009).

31. In re Chapman, 166 U.S. 661, 671 (1897).

32. 2 U.S.C. § 194 (2020).

33. The foundational opinion is Prosecution for Contempt of Congress of an Executive Branch Official Who Has Asserted a Claim of Executive Privilege, 8 Op. O.L.C. 101, 102 (1984) ("[A] United States Attorney is not required to refer a contempt citation ... to a grand jury or otherwise to prosecute an Executive Branch official who is carrying out the President's instruction[.]"). See also Application of 28 U.S.C. § 458 to Presidential Appointments of Federal Judges, 19 Op. O.L.C. 350, 355–56 (1995).

34. See Letter from Ronald C. Machen Jr., U.S. Attorney, to the Honorable John A. Boehner, Speaker, U.S. House of Representatives (Mar. 31, 2015).

35. Response to Congressional Requests for Information Made Under the Independent Counsel Act, 10 Op. O.L.C. 68, 87 (1986).

36. 28 U.S.C. § 1365(a) (2020).

37. See Chafetz, supra note 30 at 1150.

38. Congressional Research Service, R45653, Congressional Subpoenas: Enforcing Executive Branch Compliance 12 (2019).

39. United States v. House of Representatives, 556 F. Supp. 150, 152 (D.D.C. 1983).

40. Comm. on the Judiciary v. Miers, 558 F. Supp. 2d 53, 56 (D.D.C. 2008).

41. Todd Ruger, *How Congress Can Break Through Trump's Stonewalling,* Roll Call (May 14, 2019).

42. Michael W. McConnell, *The Way Trump Is Asserting the Rights of His Office Is Not Impeachable,* Wash. Post (May 1, 2019).

43. Jonathan H. Adler, *McConnell and Chafetz on Trump's Resistance to Congressional Oversight,* Reason: The Volokh Conspiracy (May 3, 2019).

44. Letter from Pat A. Cipollone, White House Counsel, to the Honorable Nancy Pelosi, Speaker, U.S. House of Representatives, at 2 (Oct. 8, 2019).

45. H.R. Rep. No. 116-346, at 136 (2019) (Conf. Rep.).

46. See H.R. Res. 755, 116th Cong. (2019) (enacted).

47. H.R. Rep. No. 116-346, at 142 at 154.

48. Jonathan Shaub, *Should the House Have Gone to the Courts on Obstruction Before Impeaching?* Lawfare (Jan. 10, 2020).

49. Comm. on the Judiciary v. McGahn, 951 F.3d 510, 514 (D.C. Cir. 2020), rehearing en banc granted, opinion vacated sub nom. United States House of Representatives v. Mnuchin, No. 19-5176, 2020 WL 1228477 (D.C. Cir. Mar. 13, 2020).

50. H.R. 4010, 115th Cong. § 2 (2017).

Conclusion

1. Gene Healy, The Cult of the Presidency: America's Dangerous Devotion to Executive Power 268 (2008).

2. Saikrishna Prakash, The Living Presidency: An Originalist Argument Against Its Ever-Expanding Powers 2 (2020).

3. The White House, Remarks by President Trump Before Marine One Departure (July 12, 2019).

4. Arthur Schlesinger, Jr., The Imperial Presidency 491 (2004).